Capital Punishment in America
Race and the Death Penalty over Time

Capital Punishment in America
Race and the Death Penalty over Time

Martin Guevara Urbina

LFB Scholarly Publishing LLC
El Paso 2012

Library of Congress Cataloging-in-Publication Data

Urbina, Martin G. (Martin Guevara), 1972-
  Capital punishment in America : race and the death penalty over time
/ Martin Guevara Urbina.
      p. cm.
  Includes bibliographical references and index.
  ISBN 978-1-59332-445-2 (pbk. : alk. paper)
1. Capital punishment--United States. 2. Discrimination in capital
punishment--United States. I. Title.
  HV8699.U5U734 2012
  364.660973--dc23
                                    2012001977

ISBN 978-1-59332-445-2

Printed on acid-free 250-year-life paper.

Manufactured in the United States of America.

Dedication

Ilse Aglaé Peña

My most sincere gratitude to Ilse Aglaé Peña for giving me support, encouragement, and strength to write this book. In effect, Ilse taught me not to be afraid to write and freely write as if I do not care, in the world of academic writing. To my good fortune, Ilse has given me a glorious treasure that has changed my life forever, as she has taught me a lesson in the very essence of life, the meaning of life in our struggles to find our destiny. Her words of wisdom, compassion, and care during uncertain and tearful moments have enabled me to continue with my academic research and publication.

Beyond academic writing, her sublime personality and magical playfulness has inspired me to finalize a book of poems, *Cincuenta Poemas de Amor Para el Alma y el Corazon: Fifty Love Poems for the Soul and the Heart*, and thus capture the beauty of expression as it comes to heart and mind, which sometimes evolves into everlasting treasures. I will forever be indebted with Ilse for her intellectual support, good humor, soft-toned laughter, sweetness, playfulness, loyalty, and infinite care.

Intriguingly, always with an unforgettable and refreshing laughter, a polite smile, and warm words of comfort, Ilse has noted that we should welcome each day with courage, a smile, and great faith! Indeed, during moments in which I have tried to weave something out of the shreds of nothing, Ilse has been a stimulus, a pillar of strength. Her magical spirit has in fact guided me through some of the darkest moments of my life. In truth, it has been my good fortune that our lifelines crossed, a divine encounter, as I struggled with the uncertainties of life. *De todo corazón y con un amor infinito, gracias Ilse, tú has sido mi bendición*!

Con un amor eterno,
--Martin

Table of Contents

List of Tables

Preface

"Until lions have their own historians, histories of the hunt will glorify the hunter."

--African proverb

A close analysis of the existing literature on capital punishment, specifically, executions and commutations, shows strong evidence of differential treatment in favor of Caucasians, vis-à-vis minority defendants, particularly African Americans. However, until recently, the focus of academic discussions and academic investigations has been almost exclusively African American and Caucasians, with limited or no attention given to the Latino experience in the context of capital punishment (Urbina, 2007). In effect, the majority of prior studies have followed an African American/Caucasian approach, to the exclusion of Latinos, now the largest minority group in the United States, and applying a commutation /execution approach to the exclusion of the various other possible death sentence outcomes, besides executions and commutations (Urbina, 2002a, 2002b).

Even when Latino defendants are included in the analysis, they receive minimal attention or they are treated as a monolithic group, without delineating the ethnic differences between specific ethnic groups, like Cubans, Mexicans, and Puerto Ricans, as documented by Urbina in a forthcoming book, *Hispanics in the US Criminal Justice System: The New American Demography*. As such, little is known about capital punishment, and, in a sense, punishment in general, for Latinos and Latinas, whose experiences with the criminal justice system differ from those of Caucasians and other minority groups, like African Americans. In effect, similar to the "white/black" dichotomy approach of research and publication, capital punishment research and publication has normally taken a binary approach, executions and/or commutations, excluding other possible death sentence outcomes: sentence declared unconstitutional, sentence overturned, and conviction overturned (Urbina, 2003a, 2004a). Beyond the historical dynamics and nature of crime and punishment, little is known about the historical treatment of the various ethnic communities; that is, in their everyday life experience in society as a whole.

Therefore, the central objective of this book is to provide a sound examination that goes beyond traditional approaches to analyzing death penalty information, with the ultimate objective of addressing theoretical and methodological shortcomings empirically, quantitatively analyzing death sentence outcome data for California, Florida, and Texas between 1975 and 1995, as an illustration. Seeking to bring out the Latina and Latino experience from the shadows of the past, a qualitative analysis of Latinos executed in the United States between 1975 and 2010 will be provided.

While the disproportionate representation of minorities, particularly African Americans and Mexicans (the largest ethnic group within the Latina/o community), in the criminal justice system, including capital punishment, is well documented, much less analyzed and discussed are the historical and contemporary mechanisms and beliefs that govern the minority experience. In an attempt to better understand why, how, and when racial and ethnic minorities are more likely to experience prejudice or discrimination, a review of historical relationships between America's three largest groups will be detailed, African Americans, Caucasians, and Mexicans. In our investigation of race and ethnic differences in death sentencing, Urbina's (2003a) theoretical typology, *the four-threat theory of death sentence outcomes*, will be utilized to test a series of research hypotheses. In effect, logistic regression, controlling for time under the sentence of death, prior felony convictions, age of defendant at the time of the offense, marital status, and education, shows that discrimination in death sentence outcomes is not a phenomenon of the past in the US, but still prevalent. The findings reveal that race, ethnicity, and several legal variables continue to play a significant role in the legal decision-making process, a practice that extends into the 21st Century. Focusing primarily (but not exclusively) on race and ethnicity, the results are discussed in relation to the four-threat theory, which attempts to explain race and ethnic difference in capital punishment over time, and within historical forces of the past, like conquest, colonialism, slavery, immigration, and criminal law. In short, the author reports sound evidence that testifies to a historical legacy of brutality, manipulation, oppression, marginalization, prejudice, discrimination, and to white America's continued fear about racial and ethnic minorities, a movement extending into 2011.[1]

---

[1] Parts of Chapter 5 appear in *Journal of Ethnicity in Criminal Justice* (v. 1, no. 1), and parts of Chapter 6 appear in *Social Justice* (v. 31, no. 95).

Acknowledgments

Truly, it would have been impossible to conduct the research and write this book without the everlasting patience, advice, and unconditional support of several energetic, passionate, dedicated, and loyal individuals.

To begin, my most profound gratitude goes to Professors Marilyn McShane and Frank P. Williams III, series editors, for their divine kindness, wisdom, and support. I am confident that their valuable recommendations have enriched the final product.

My deep appreciation and many thanks also go to Leo Balk, my publisher, for being so helpful, understanding, and patient throughout the entire publishing process. This book would of never have come to fruition without his approval, assistance, perseverance, and sagacious advice during the early stages of the project.

I also like to thank my colleagues at Sul Ross State University—Rio Grande College for their emotional and analytical support during the process of this project. I am pleased and honored with the high level of professionalism, understanding, and compassion that I have received from them.

Con mucho carino, respecto y solidaridad, I would like to thank Isabel Perez for assisting with the editorial process. With great excitement and motivation, Isabel devoted long hours to the tedious and laborious task of editing the numerous tables in the book. Her sublime personality and extraordinary humanity have been a real blessing.

I'd like to say a special thanks to Ilse Aglaé Peña for assisting, advising, and supporting me from the time the book contract was signed to the time we submitted the finalized book to the publisher. With great pride and honor, I must say that, in truth, not only did Ilse assisted in every stage of the project, but she did the great majority of research for Chapter 6: Race, Ethnicity, and Gender from 1608 to 2010:

A qualitative analysis. In effect, adding more work to her extremely tight schedule, Isle insisted throughout the entire process on getting things done to perfection, always with a refreshing laugh and a captivating smile. More profoundly, for days before submitting both the first and final drafts, Ilse cheerfully worked late hours assisting with final details (even though she was extremely sick while finalizing both drafts); yet, still making sure that everything was being done, ensuring that I was doing my part, and checking on my wellbeing, as reflected in the following lines: "Como va el libero? . . . Ya terminaste Martin?" Though, with a warm and lovely smile, she did say, "me obligo a ir enfermisima!"

Lastly, I would like acknowledge the heroic and magical efforts of all the people who contributed to the making of this book. I am well aware that seldom we have the privilege to work with talented, sincere, and loyal people. In essence, faithful and courageous crusaders who are active in the cause for equality, justice, and, in effect, participate in the betterment of society and universal peace.

Martin Guevara Urbina, Ph.D.

## CHAPTER 1

Introduction: The Contours of Capital Punishment

"Man is born free, and everywhere he is in chains."

--Jean-Jacques Rousseau

Even though capital punishment has deep roots in American history and culture, death penalty commentators and researchers have concentrated on the historical experience of two of the three largest groups in the US, African Americans and Caucasians, focusing almost exclusively on the unequal death sentencing of African American and Caucasian defendants and on issues like deterrence, capital punishment states and crime rates vs. non-capital punishment states, and capital punishment and crime rates over time, especially during the pre-*Furman*/post-*Furman* period. As a result, data on Mexicans, the third largest minority group in the US, (and Latinos and Latinas in general) is either non-existent or extremely difficult to locate. Worse, some of the existing information on Latinos contains various reliability and validity shortcomings, leading to consequential implications and ramifications (Aguirre and Baker, 1988; Urbina, 2007).[2] In effect, only a few studies have examined unequal death sentence outcomes, executions and commutations, by race and ethnicity (Urbina, 2003b,

---

[2] At the practical level, until recently, it was difficult to identify a population of criminal defendants that included sufficient numbers of Latinas or Latinos. At the ideological level, Hawkins (1994:105) attributes the inattention to ethnic group differences in legal sanctions to "biases and themes inherent in extant theories of social control in the United States."

2004a). In particular, it is difficult to find studies that have examined: (1) a capital sentence of the individual when declared unconstitutional by State or US Supreme Court, (2) a conviction affirmed, but sentence overturned by appellate court, or (3) a conviction and sentence overturned by appellate court, as three possible death sentence outcomes by race and ethnicity. Similarly, it is difficult to locate studies that have analyzed the experiences of death row inmates who still remain under the sentence of death, which, by default, means life imprisonment. That is, since no formal action has taken place by the correctional system, this in and of itself constitutes a possible death sentence outcome.

A close examination of the existing literature, as detailed in Chapters 3 and 4, reveal two major limitations of earlier approaches utilized in the study of capital punishment. Researchers have opted to either omit people of Latina/o heritage, or treat them as a monolithic group, usually under the broad popular labels of "Hispanic," or "Latino." Consequently, various fundamental issues, as they pertain to the historical dynamics of capital punishment, are yet to receive adequate investigation, publication, and dialogue (Perea, 1997, Urbina, 2007). For instance, people of Latina and Latino heritage combined not only constitute the largest minority group in the United States, but they are a very diverse and multi-ethnic population, whose experiences in the United States, and, by extension, treatment by the criminal justice system, differs from those of African Americans, as documented by Urbina in a forthcoming book, *Latinas y Latinos in the United States: 21st Century Dynamics of Multiculturalism*. Equally important, the fact that the diverse experiences of the various ethnic groups (e.g., Mexicans/Mejicanos, Mexican Americans, Cubans, Puerto Ricans, and people from South and Central America) that make up the Latino population lack delineated investigations to better understand the reality of Latinas and Latinos in its totality. Essentially, how the various ethnic groups view themselves and each other, how they are perceived by the Caucasian majority, and how they are treated by the criminal justice system, including law enforcement, the judicial system, and the penal system, varies in numerous fundamental ways.

Methodology, exclusive focus on executions or commutations yields a limited and, possibly, skewed, picture of death sentence outcomes and capital punishment as a whole. The conditions and process, for instance, under which death sentence outcomes take place, vary widely. While racial and ethnic differences might be nonexistent or relatively small at any particular stage of the legal decision-making process, cumulative effects of these differences on the overall judicial and penal patterns of outcomes could be significant (Urbina, 2007).

Therefore, the primary goals of the current study are to: (1) analyze prior death sentence and death sentence outcomes studies that test for race and/or ethnicity effects to determine the degree to which race/ethnicity influence crime and punishment; (2) include a Latino category, Mexican and Cuban, in the quantitative analysis; (3) disaggregate the Latino category in the qualitative analysis; (4) provide a discussion of the Latinos who were executed from 1975 to 2010; (5) explore powerful historical forces, like conquest, colonialism, slavery, and immigration, that have defined and re-defined the scope and nature of law, crime, and punishment; (6) provide an examination of the history of US race and ethnic relations, focusing on the countries three largest groups, African Americans, Caucasians, and Mexicans; (7) analyze and provide a sound theoretical framework that will account for the differential treatment of the various racial and ethnic groups who are sentenced to death; (8) utilize Urbina's (2003a) typology of death sentences and death sentence outcomes in the examination of capital punishment; (9) analyze the legal decision-making process across multiple decision points, executions, commutations, and sentence and/or conviction overturns by the courts as well as cases for individuals who still remain under the sentence of death; and (10) provide a discussion of death sentence outcomes and capital punishment in America as a whole.

By using multiple methods of theoretical and empirical analysis and various sources of information, the results of this study should further our knowledge of race and ethnic differences in death sentence outcomes of not only African Americans and Caucasians, but also of the Mexican community and the Latino population as a whole; that is, the various ethnic groups that make up the Latino community. By analyzing the latest "punitive movement" against criminal offenders, we are able to go beyond the traditional dichotomous approach of theorizing and conducting research, revealing which convictions and/or sentences were overturned by an appellate court, which capital sentences were declared unconstitutional by a state or the US Supreme Court, who was granted a commutation, who was executed, who still remained under the sentence of death as of 1995, and the frequency of these events.

In effect, by focusing on what is often considered the most severe form of criminal punishment, critical questions, especially concerning the magnitude of race and ethnic differences in death sentence outcomes, may be raised about the various issues, like offender characteristics and legal variables, surrounding the capital punishment debate, historically. Evidently, these are essential issues in terms of their social, political, legal, ethnical, moral, and economic implications, especially in the 21st Century, with advocates of law-and-order arguing that the criminal justice system is being too soft on violent crime and that the way to reduce criminal behavior is by becoming more punitive, and, more globally, witnessing crime and punishment that transcend borders and criminal justice systems (Ruddell and Urbina, 2004, 2007).

Methodologically, in order to determine whether certain disparities exist in death sentence outcomes, this study will include both tabular analysis and logistic regression analysis (selected based on the nature of the data and the level of measurement of the variables), to determine the influence and significance of crucial factors such as the state where the criminal sentencing occurred, race, ethnicity, sex, education, marital status, age when the capital offense was committed, and prior felony convictions in death sentence outcomes. Empirically, this approach should clarify whether African Americans, Mexicans, and, possibly, Cubans have received more punitive sentence outcomes, vis-à-vis their white counterparts. Specifically, race and ethnicity would be expected to have independent effects on unequal death sentence outcomes after statistically controlling for legal and socio-demographic factors. Given the long and turbulent history of race and ethnic relations in the US, and the complex and mysterious environment in which the legal decision-making process operates, it is predicted that African Americans and Mexicans are likely to receive more severe death sentence outcomes.

From an historical standpoint, it must be emphasized that understanding death sentence outcomes and their implications and ramifications requires a refined understanding of historical forces, situations, circumstances, and events in the context of criminal behavior, law, order, and justice, as well as the relationships between Caucasians (Caucasian, "white," Anglo, or Euro-American categorical designations used interchangeably herein to signify the non-minority, dominant race in America) and non-Caucasians (African Americans, people of Mexican heritage, and other racial and ethnic minorities). While conflict in relations between Caucasians (whites) and African Americans (blacks) has been traced by a number of scholars, documentation regarding the relationships between Mexicans, or people of Latin heritage in general (Hispanic or Latino–categorical designations used interchangeably herein to signify the minority ethnic group in the United States who is neither African American nor Caucasian), and Anglo-Americans remains minimal and difficult to locate. In effect, not too long ago, Sampson and Lauritsen (1997:364) observed, "despite the volume of previous research on race and ethnic comparisons, we know very little about criminal justice processing other than for blacks and whites. Quite simply, there is little empirical basis from which to draw firm conclusions for Hispanic [and Asian, and Native] Americans." Moving into the 21st Century, Steffensmeier and Demuth (2001) concluded that the most obvious *shortfall* is the limited attention to the treatment of Latinos in the judicial system. In a recent study, the author reports that in comparison to hundreds of studies that have been conducted on race (blacks versus whites), only 53 studies have analyzed the effects of ethnicity on the lengthy criminal or juvenile justice *process*, which covers a wide and complex range of legal decision-points. Of the 53 ethnic studies reported by Urbina (2007), 34 treat Latinas/os as a monolithic group, 15 analyzed the Mexican experience, and four included Puerto Ricans in the analyses, with one of the four Puerto Rican studies also analyzing the Colombian, Dominican, and Cuban experience, clearly revealing the limited focus on Mexicans, and more so within the various other ethnic subgroups composing the Latina/o population.

Indicating the wide diversity of Latinas and Latinos within their ethnic community, people of Latin heritage can be of any "color" (including "white") and not necessarily speak Spanish, and thus the terms of primary use in this book will be Caucasian or Euro-American when referring to the non-minority population. Similarly, since people of Latin heritage may also be "black," the term of primary use will be African American when referring to the black population who is not of Latina/o heritage or Caucasian in the following chapters of this book. As noted by Acuna (2010), the term Latino carries less political baggage than the term Hispanic, and thus the term of primary use in this book will be Latino/a when referring to people of Latin heritage who are not Caucasians or African Americans. As for specific ethnic groups, the terms Mejicano/a, Mexican, Mexican American, Chicano/a, Tejano/a, and Californio will be used interchangeably when referring to people who have roots in the Republic of Mexico, independent of their status, US citizen, permanent resident, or undocumented worker, in the United States. As for the second and third largest Latina/o subgroups, the terms Cuban and Cuban-American will be used interchangeably when referring to people who have roots in Cuba, independent of their immigration status, a moot classification for Puerto Ricans since they are US citizens whether they reside on the Island or on the mainland.[3]

In short, while keeping death sentences and death sentence outcomes in mind, various other social issues must be carefully consider to obtain a more holistic view of capital punishment and, ultimately, punishment in general. First, as mentioned above, the few studies that have empirically explored the historical relationship between Mexicans and Euro-Americans have followed a dichotomous approach. The relationships have been treated as Caucasians versus Latinos giving limited attention, if any, to Mexicans and the various ethnic groups that constitute the largest and one of the fastest-growing minority groups in the United States. Crucially, most studies have not equated the fact that the relationships between Latino groups and Euro-Americans have not only varied widely, but the experiences of these various ethnic minority groups in the United States have been at times polar opposites.

While some scholars, such as William Wilbanks and William Pridemore, argue that race and ethnicity does not matter in the processing of criminal defendants in the American judicial system, a close and objective analysis of historical trends reveals a very different picture, as detailed in the following chapters of this book. In truth, from the so-called discovery of America in 1492 to 2011, and in spite of official documents, like the Declaration of Independence and the Constitution, far from being color-blind, the United States has been extremely "color-conscious." As a consequence, the administration of justice by the criminal justice system, to include the police, the judicial system, and the correctional system, has been grossly informal, irregular, subjective, biased, and discriminatory. As vividly

---

[3] For a discussion of the origin as well as the social, economic, and political significance of language (terms) identification, see Acuna (2010).

documented by various scholars, historically, the criminal justice system has demonstrated a clear tendency to take more punitive actions against minorities, particularly African Americans and Mexicans, than Euro-Americans (Acuna, 2010; Almaguer, 2008; Bender, 2005). Similarly, for Mexicans and Latinas and Latinos in general, racially prejudiced and discriminatory actions have also been witnessed at most, if not all, stages of the criminal justice system (Cobas, Duany, and Feagin, 2009; Mirande, 1987, 1989; Urbina, 2007). Not only paralleling Shorris' (1992:157) observation that "in every Latino neighborhood in the United States, with the possible exception of some parts of Miami, police treat all children, especially adolescent boys, as if they are criminals," but several recent studies reveal a more devastating trend in some geographical areas (Duran, 2009a; 2009b; Rios, 2006; Romero, 2006).

In thinking about death sentences, death sentence outcomes, and the global nature of punishment, consider the following. Together, although the relationship between race, ethnicity, and punishment varies geographically (Ruddell and Urbina, 2007), the widespread over-representation of minorities in penal institutions, including death row, suggests that ideas of ethnicity, race, and difference have shifted from a *driving force to a necessary element* for the criminal justice system, now a multi-billion dollar enterprise, to appear functional and progressive. In effect, nowhere is this draconian movement more apparent and repressive than in the US where the penal population moved beyond 2 million in 1999, for the first time in history, with detrimental race and ethnic variation in the distribution of punishment. In fact, by the end of 2005, African Americans (39.5%) and Latina/o (20.2%) accounted for 59.7%, while Caucasians represented 34.6% of inmates sentenced to more than one year in prison (Harrison and Beck, 2006), a major population disproportion, where Latinas ad Latinos constituted approximately 15.1% (45.4 million) and African Americans constituted about 13.5% (40.7 million) of the total general population in 2007. More globally, in a February 28, 2008, report, the US was ranked as the number 1 incarcerator in the world, with more than one of every 100 adults (2, 319,258) in jail or prison. According to the report, "For some groups, the incarceration numbers are especially startling," particularly for "black and brown" people, including minority women, mostly African American women and Latinas (Urbina, 2008), a punitive and aggressive movement that does not necessarily correspond with the actual realities of crime, punishment, safety, equality, or justice, as detailed in the following chapters.

As for the polemic issue of race and ethnic effects in the criminal justice system, the work of Gilroy (1993) and Urbina (2008) provide an expedient point of academic departure. According to Gilroy, ideas and ideologies of race and modernity are historically linked, and race, as we perceive it today, is a social construct dating to the late 18th and early 19th Centuries, an era when the prison was invented and thus moving punishment, including executions, from out of the public domain to secrecy behind bars, setting the stage for penal power, control, and expansion, vividly illustrated by Foucault (1995) and Lynch (2007). Acuna (2010), Aguirre and Baker (2007), and Almaguer (2008) report that historical ideas of ethnicity and modernity are indeed linked, though, actually dating back to the early days in the Americas, a strategy set in placed by movements like conquest, colonialism, slavery, criminal law, and US capitalism and imperialism. In the context of the criminal justice system, Urbina (2003a, 2008) reports that variation in punishment is largely governed by threat differentials; that is, the level of financial, political, or social threat that minority populations pose to white America, especially the *voting class*.

These propositions have consequential implications not only for punishment and the death penalty, but for the entire American criminal justice system. For instance, what if ideas of race and ethnicity which, as social scientists document, are historically contingent and constructed, are necessary for the criminal justice system, to include law enforcement, the judicial system, and the correctional system, to *survive and expand*, a crucial observation in the context of the recent globalization of crime and punishment? Likewise, consider the implications if indeed variation in punishment is governed by threat differentials, also a critical observation in the context of the current *international war on terror*. More globally, could the United States sustain its multi-billion dollar criminal justice system, if one out of four African American men of a certain age were not under some form of incarceration or surveillance (Irwin and Austin, 2000; Tonry, 2006)? Worse, if current incarceration trends continue, an African American male born in 2001 has a 1 in 3 chance of going to prison during his lifetime (Bonczar, 2003). Similarly, could the criminal justice system survive and grow without the "new minority," Latinas/os, most of whom are Mexican, who overtook the African American population in

2000? Similarly to African Americans, a Latino born in 2001 has a 1 in 6 chance of going to prison during his lifetime, while a Caucasian male has a 1 in 17 chance of going to prison (Bonczar, 2003), even though, as illustrated in a forthcoming book by Urbina, *Hispanics in the US Criminal Justice System: The New American Demography*, these figures do not necessarily correspond to crime variation in the context of race and ethnicity, clearly indicating that race and ethnicity matters in crime and punishment. Beyond male-race variation, could the criminal justice system *survive and continue* to grow without the newly "targeted" population, female offenders, especially African American women and Latinas, mostly Mexicans? The lifetime probability of going to prison among African American women (5.6%) is almost as high as for Caucasian men (5.9%), but a lower probability for Latinas (2.2%), with Caucasian females (0.9%) having a much lower lifetime chance of going to prison (Bonczar, 2003). Ultimately, would the criminal justice system *survive, grow, and prosper* without the "intergenerational connection," minority offenders and their children, especially poor minority children? With thousands of people joining the American criminal justice system primarily because of employment and job security, would the system, with an annual budget of 228 billion dollars as of 2007 (a budget bigger than the GDP of some countries), survive economically? Or, quite simply, what if young white women and men were being detected, arrested, indicted, prosecuted, convicted, placed on probation, sentenced to jail or prison, placed on death row, or executed at the same rate? Would the American society support such practices by the police, the courts, or the penal system, if the pool of people were coming from white communities and not from the ghettos and barrios of America, or communities of poor white people? Would white America be asking for the development of more laws, the implementation of existing criminal laws, the creation of more jails and prisons, asking government and law enforcement officials to be more punitive on criminal defendants, and seeking the death penalty at a higher rate? Evidently, in analyzing the realities of crime and punishment, the connections between modern punishment trends and historical practices of conquest, colonialism, slavery, imperialism, immigration, group identity, and, most recently, globalization must be brought to light? In short, just as it has been documented that punishment is an expression of historically contingent sensibilities (Garland, 1990), *ideas of race, of ethnicity, of gender, of class, of difference, and of "other,"* play into the type of behavior that Americans define as crime and strategies of when and how Americans respond to criminal behavior. Together, the noted figures of arrests, prosecutions, convictions, sentencing, incarceration, and executions indicate that race and ethnicity matter in the US, and, possibly, in no other area is it more pressing than in the area of crime and punishment.

To obtain an in-depth perspective of the prejudice and discrimination, deeply rooted in American history and culture, and the differential treatment of racial and ethnic minorities by the criminal justice system and, by extension, the general public, the American historical experience must be examined in its totality. To begin, as detailed in the following chapter, "History of US Race and Ethnic Relations," the simultaneous interaction of both structural and ideological forces that ultimately shape and re-shape the experiences of minorities in the United States must be equated to obtain a sound and holistic picture of the American reality; otherwise, people are being educated with one-sided information, skewed data, and sometimes outright lies. Chapter 2 also details powerful historical forces that were originally set in place, strategically, to control the population; that is, blacks who were defined as slaves by law, and, later, Mexicans who were conquered in war with the United States. By providing an historical analysis of race and ethnic relations in the United States, we are able to better understand the significance of race and ethnicity in the US society, and, by extension, crime and punishment. In addition, the chapter sets forth specific hypotheses for the empirical examinations detailed in this book. Chapter 3, "Death Sentencing and Death Sentence Outcomes: Review of Prior Empirical Studies," analyzes prior death sentence and death sentence outcomes studies to gain insight into the influence of race and ethnicity in the various stages of the judicial process, like prosecution, conviction, and sentencing. The chapter then explains the limitations of prior research as well as various remedies to deal with both theoretical and methodological shortcomings, especially when seeking to equate Mexicans, or Latinos in general, in the analysis. Chapter 4, "A Case Study of Three American States," explains the methods for the quantitative study included in this book, in addition to looking into why the various possible death sentence outcomes constitute a complex situation, academically and legally. More importantly, a central objective of this chapter is to explore methodological problems that research encounter in the process of conducting ethnic research. Chapter 5, "Research Findings for California, Florida, and Texas: A Quantitative Analysis," outlines and describes the results of the logistic regression analysis, with data presented in 14 tables. Chapter 6, "Race, Ethnicity, and Gender from 1608 to 2010: A Qualitative Analysis," explores the historical legacy of executions in America within the context of ethnicity, race, and gender, focusing on post-*Furman* executions of Latino inmates, 1975 to 2010. Further, the problem of not having accurate statistics on Mexicans and Latinos in general is examined. More globally, dating back to 1608, the chapter also details executions during slavery, female executions, juvenile executions, the execution of foreign nationals in the United States, and, providing qualitative findings of the executed Latinos from 1975 to 2010, report that race and ethnic discrimination in the distribution of punishment extends into the 21st Century. The concluding chapter, "Transforming an Historical Culture of Executions," discusses the conclusions of the quantitative and qualitative methods detailed in this book and their implications for prisoners, policymakers, and society, ending with a examination as to how America could possibly develop a more humane, safe, just, and equitable model of law-and-order. Finally, in the Afterword, "The Future of Capital Punishment," the death penalty is examined within the context of broader American society and the international community.

## CHAPTER 2

History of U.S. Race and Ethnic Relations

"What to do with those whom society cannot accommodate? Criminalize them. Outlaw their actions and creations. Declare them the enemy, then wage war. Emphasize the differences–the shade of skin, the accent in the speech or manner of clothes. Like the scapegoat of the Bible, place society's ills on them, then "stone them" in absolution. It's convenient. It's logical. It doesn't work."

--Luis Rodriguez

Given the various historical forces governing the nature of law-and-order, the dynamics of the death penalty provide a lens for studying race and ethnic relations in the United States, which in turn influence the nature of crime, law, and punishment, including the death penalty. As such, when interpreting the conditions of brutality, prejudice, manipulation, oppression, discrimination, marginalization, and inequality faced by minority groups, one needs to look beyond culture-based explanations, which tend to minimize the role of ideological, political, educational, and economic structures. In effect, to break down barriers to historical understanding among the various racial and ethnic groups that comprise the United States, one needs to analyze the relationships between minority groups and Caucasians, as cited by Shorris (1992:xv), ". . . tell them who we are and that we are not all alike." Clearly, racial and ethnic relationships continue to be complex and elusive in 2011, playing a major role in crime and punishment, as reported by Urbina in *Latinas y Latinos in the United States: 21st Century Dynamics of Multiculturalism.*

13

This chapter begins by exploring the historical relationships between America's three largest groups, African Americans, Caucasians, and Mexicans and their historical interactions with the American criminal justice system, to include policing, the judicial system, and the correctional system. This historical background will compliment research findings reported in the following chapter and further enhance our understanding of *when, why, and how* African Americans and Mexicans (and Latinos in general), are more likely to be executed or less likely to have their sentences and/or convictions overturned by the courts, as proposed by Urbina's (2003a) theoretical typology, *the four-threat theory of death sentence outcomes*. Then, after the examination of specific race and ethnic histories, with a careful examination of prior empirical and theoretical research (see Chapter 3), revealing the influence of race and ethnicity in crime and punishment, a typology of death sentence outcomes will be detailed and specific hypotheses for each group within each state will be presented.

AFRICAN AMERICANS IN THE LAND OF EQUALITY

The Early Days in the Americas

A study of race and ethnicity in America clearly reveals that Europeans held extremely negative views of black people long before the founding of the English colonies, although these negative ideas did not develop into full-blown racist ideologies until the 1700s. Levin (2002) documents that negative images of African Americans were accepted and even welcomed by the framers of the Declaration of Independence and the US Constitution. As Gordon (1964:89) explains, "the founding fathers of the American nation were by no means men of unthinking prejudices," and, worse, "blacks formed no part in the imagined community of Jefferson's republic" (Foner, 1998:86). In fact, despite Jefferson's indictment of slavery, he himself was a slave owner with racist ideas. Setting the ideological foundation, which would govern the American experience for centuries to come, "Jefferson argued that what he saw as the ugly color, offensive odor, and ugly hair of African American slaves indicated their physical inferiority and that their alleged inability to create was a sign of mental inferiority" (Feagin and Vera, 1995:68). Of course, Jefferson was not the only one, others like Lincoln and Andrew Jackson committed more than their share of vicious and vindictive crimes against humanity, that is, women, non-whites, and even poor whites (Acuna, 1998, 2010; Levin, 2002).

Considering the long and controversial history of immigration and citizenship, for 80 years, only Euro American immigrants could become naturalized citizens, not allowing African Americans to become citizens until 1870, creating serious implications for the African American community, which, in reality, extend into 2011. In fact, the 1849 California State Constitutional Convention initially relegated African Americans to second-class legal status, while the first draft of the "Right to Suffrage" stated that only white men who were citizens of the United States would be entitled to vote, establishing a mechanism that would marginalize and silence African Americans for years to come (Almaguer, 2008). African Americans were not only denied the right to vote, but also to hold public office, to testify in court against Caucasian individuals, to serve on juries, to attend public schools, or to homestead public land, essentially, keeping the African American population *bankrupt* (Urbina, 2008). It was not until the ratification of the 14th Amendment in 1870 that African Americans were granted the "same" legal rights as Caucasian people. Realistically, though, the granting of rights was far more symbolic than pragmatic, as the subordinate status of African Americans created tremendous and devastating consequences in their everyday lives, primarily on the basis of race.

Invariably, on one level, ". . . the world of white and black are distinct" (Ezekiel, 1995:310), *white and black world* that has actually become more distant (Hacker, 2003). On another level, the history of African Americans in the United States has been very different from that of other minority groups, like Mexicans, as detailed in the following section of this chapter. Unlike white people who migrated to this land in search of riches, or, arguably, religious freedom, African Americans were ". . . brought into this country by force and compelled under the lash to lend his brawn and sturdy sinews to promote its material growth and prosperity . . ." (Cooper, 1988:194). Strategically, brought to this country as forced labor and in servitude, kept in servitude until a century and a quarter ago, and in political, economic, and social subjugation since, African Americans have been treated by the ruling elite as a social burden, unwilling to assimilate, and threatening to white America. As a result, the cultural and social gap between African Americans and Caucasians has remained deep and wide, revealing the historical influence of race (Gates and West, 1997; Hacker, 2003).

In the early days, as Almaguer (2008) documents, slavery economically subordinated the nation's African American population to Caucasians, and their second-class social/political status structurally ensured that African Americans could not compete effectively with Caucasians at any level of the social, political, educational, or economic structure. In fact, history reveals that in the case of African Americans, the law silently but definitely separated people into various groups based on race and ethnicity, with intended objectives to silence the African American community. Among these groups, precisely because of their internal histories as well as their external treatment, significant cultural and social differences existed, creating divisions, hostility, violence, and brutality (Gates and West, 1997; Levin, 2002).

Defining a Black Race

Even though, African Americans were used to make white people rich, they have been seen through racist eyes as people who do not want to work, who would rather be on welfare, or simply unemployed, who gain money through bullying, cheating or selling drugs, who rob and kill and who are violent by nature. African Americans, racists believe, want to hurt Caucasians, to assault verbally and physically, to rob Caucasian people, and to rape Caucasian women (Bosworth and Flavin, 2007; Gans, 1995). As we were about to enter the 21st Century, Ezekiel (1995:311) reported, "Pressed for detail, white racists will estimate that eighty percent of black people are this sort."

Of course, highly governed by the powerful historical forces of race and ethnicity, "the white tendency to view people of African descent as deviant or criminal is centuries old. Since the 1400s, rather than seeing a common humanity uniting Europeans and Africans, Europeans and their American descendants have mostly seen difference" (Feagin and Vera, 1995:68; Urbina, 2008). These anti-African images were imported by the colonies, where images born in European vengeance, ignorance, and hypocrisy were used to justify and legitimize the manipulation, subjugation, and exploitation of Africans brought and sold as slaves, for the profit of white people (Feagin and

Vera, 1995).[4] Similarly, the negative stereotype of African American men as uncivilized and fear-inspiring "savages" who are a sure threat to Caucasian women is not new in that it dates back several centuries, again, revealing the historical influence of race in the US (Bosworth and Flavin, 2007).

Views That Never Die

While some individuals, among them social scientists, claim that prejudice and racism are demons of the past; that is, that race no longer plays a role in the US, such attitudes are still alive and active at every level of the American society, as vividly documented by Bonilla-Silva (2006). Even at the highest levels of government, for example, presidents and presidential candidates continue to make (or make use of) remarks or images reflecting racial and ethnic stereotypes, propagating the image that black people are a real threat to society. Reflecting the racist views of the founding fathers, it is well known that while in office, President Richard M. Nixon had negative views of African Americans, while Nancy Reagan reminded Caucasian Americans of the color and race line during her husband's presidential campaign, four and a half centuries after the so-called discovery of America in 1492. Speaking to Ronald Reagan in a telephone call being carried by a loudspeaker during the campaign, Ms. Reagan said that she would like for him to be with her in Illinois with "all these beautiful white people," an indication of how "white" that Republican campaign was. In the 2008 presidential election, President Barack Obama was accused by culture warriors of not being American, stirring up the race debate across the country.

The history of the African American race in the US, including slavery since 1619, raises many critical questions about the construction of *difference*, or, as noted by Urbina (2008), *indifference*. How can one group of individuals treat another as if they were not human? Hess, Markson, and Stein (1998:258) observe that it can be accomplished, "only by defining 'the other' as so very different as to be 'non-human,'" a conclusion also reached by Almaguer (2008),

---

[4] According to Rex (1983), the first blacks to be introduced into the United States in 1619 were not legally defined as slaves in the complete sense in which the status of slavery eventually came to be defined.

resonating the old proverb that "The devil is always painted black (or brown, or red, or yellow) by white painters." It is also evident that this process is easiest when the "other," the "stranger," or the "outsider" has little resemblance to us, as in the case of black African tribal peoples compared to the European Christians on this continent who bought and sold them.[5]

In modern times, race and ethnicity continue to play a significant role, as racists have found new mechanisms of manipulation, suppression, marginalization, and control, along with a wave of influential supporters, ranging from academics in elite universities to high ranking government officials. For instance, in plain 20th Century (1974) at Oxford University, John R. Baker concluded his study by rating human races on their innate capacity for originating civilization and ethical standards, and finds African blacks in last place (King, 1981). In effect, to no surprise, in addition to giving inferior positions on biological and cultural scales to living in "primitive" communities, Westerners have also rated minorities very low in morality, thus allowing the Western Caucasians to define and re-define themselves as "the better person," the one who conquered, not the one who was conquered. *Feeding* the historical American psychic, these images are further rationalized and legitimized by bestselling and award winning books claiming to have "proved anew that blacks and poor people are more stupid than everyone else . . . Or, 'generally inferior' to the rest of humanity . . ." (Acuna, 1998; Urbina, 2003c; Williams, 1997:47).

Among the long list of books by intellectual racists are *The Bell Curve* by Herrnstein and Murray (1994), *Why Race Matters* by Levin (1997), *The g Factor* by Jensen (1998), and *Race, Evolution, and Behavior* by Rushton (1999), showing that stereotypes persist and even offer the intellectual rationalization and legitimization for modern racists in society, indicating the significance of race in modern times. To Herrnstein and Murray (1994), for example, the source of inferior test scores, higher unemployment, and other inequalities among African Americans is genetic; it's as simple as that, to the authors of a

---

[5] It should be noted that this kind of belief and treatment is also true with respect to women. Not only do many individuals believe that God has blond hair and blue eyes, but that God is also male.

highly popular book.[6] As such, as vividly reported by Gans (1995:60), the influence of race extends to crime and punishment, including executions:

> an underclass of young people becomes considerably more threatening when it is called 'feral,' and even worse is the idea of a biological underclass, which implies a genetic and thus permanent inferiority of a group whom public policy can render harmless only by sterilizing, imprisoning, or killing them.

Ideologically and politically satisfactory "answers" are frequently easier and cheaper to find in already available statistics from which "undeserving" behavior and "undesirable" motives can be inferred (Cobas, Duany, Feagin, 2009; Gans, 1995; Urbina, 2008). In the context of crime and punishment, it is even cheaper, more convenient, and more satisfying for some to argue that personal beliefs are more accurate and convincing than empirical data, or, as Representative William McCollum of Florida once said in a discussion of the death penalty, "While statistics might not indicate that it deters crime, it's common sense that it does" (Gans, 1995:128). More globally, racial images and myths, like "welfare queen," "Willie" Horton, or "ghetto pathology," have served as convenient weapons, especially during election time. Expressing the historical significance of race, crime, and vengeance of the US, a Republican gubernatorial candidate in Massachusetts, for example, once demanded the reinstatement of the death penalty, and the Democratic candidate went so far as to say that he would like to pull the electric switch (Feagin and Vera, 1995), again, truly consequential statements by high profile individuals.

Controlling a Black Population

Analyzing the significance of race in everyday life, Cooper (1988:92) reports that from the beginning of time, humanity has had its

---

[6] According to Acuna (1998), the ultraconservative, racist Pioneer Fund underwrote much of the research for the *Bell Curve* and *Race, Evolution, and Behavior*.

vultures and sharks . . . That this virulence breaks out most readily
and commonly against colored persons in this country, is due of
course to the fact that they are, generally speaking, weak and can
be imposed upon with impunity.

Reflecting the hegemonic ideology dating back to the founding fathers,
Cooper (1988:163) documents an historical trend in her analysis of
America's race problem: "America for Americans! . . . Lynch,
suppress, drive out, kill out! America for Americans!" Statements that
were widely cited in newspapers throughout the country, and, more
fundamentally, resonating the very essence of the Declaration of
Independence and the Constitution.

Beyond law-and-order, race plays a significant role in various
social situations. For instance, dismissals from jobs, denials of loans,
and foreclosures of mortgages were among the several manipulating
and suppressing tactics used to decimate the ranks of active and vocal
African Americans (Franklin and Moss, 1988:436). As if this was not
enough, Anglos most threatened were normally ready to use other
means necessary (Levin, 2002). In analyzing the life of African
Americans, for instance, Gates and West (1997:56) characterize the end
of the 20th century as "a ghastly century whose levels of barbarity,
bestiality, and brutality are unparalleled in human history," a situation
that extends into the 21st Century (Bosworth and Flavin, 2007; Hacker,
2003).

As a means of gaining and maintaining absolute control of the
black population, African Americans were not only viewed as an
inferior caste, widely disfranchised, and usually segregated in areas
ranging from public restrooms to universities, but were frequently
lynched and mobbed (Almaguer, 2008; Gates and West, 1997). In fact,
Caucasian racial violence in the South after Reconstruction was a
means of social control of what latter would be viewed as a threatening
surplus population. Caucasians in positions of power preserved white
domination, through intimidation, the threat of violence, and brutal
violence, like lynching and hanging. Case in point: In the century after
Reconstruction, it has been estimated that somewhere between 3,000
and 5,000 African Americans were lynched by Caucasians. In effect,
documenting the influence of race in crime, Aguirre and Baker (1999)
report that executions and lynching of African Americans were a major
force of brutality, suppression, and social control as late as the early
20th Century. It has been estimated that from 1882 to 1899 there were

1,043 lynchings for homicide, from 1900 to 1929 there were 750 lynchings, and 44 lynchings took place between 1930 and 1977. Over this 85-year time frame, 73% of these illegal murders were of African Americans. Many of the victims were burned alive, chained to iron stakes that had been driven into the ground, and others were hanged. The "lucky" ones were shot soon after the burning or the hanging began. There are many horrendous accounts of desperate individuals crawling from the flames and being pushed back in. Bodies were slashed, and fingers were cut off. Often the victim's genitals were cut off (Carrigan and Webb, 2003; Dike, 1982; Ezekiel, 1995; Johnson, 1990; McGehee and Hildebrand, 1964; Reggio, 1997; Sellin, 1980).[7] One case that will forever be remembered, I would hope, is the case of legendary US Supreme Court Justice Thurgood Marshall. In 1946, while in Columbia, Tennessee, on NAACP business, Marshall was stopped on a lonely road by sheriff's deputies and highway patrol officers while clansmen waited nearby at the Duck River. The future Justice of the US Supreme Court was rescued from the lynch mob by an armed escort of local African Americans who grabbed him from police custody. The following day they returned to the scene and found a lynch rope and noose still hanging from a tree by the river. They cut it down and gave it to young Marshall for a souvenir (Marshall joined the US Supreme Court in 1967). An investigation was requested, but no officers were ever prosecuted and, even more strangely, no charges were ever brought against Marshall's African American rescuers, who were well known to the local law enforcement officials (Rowan, 1993). Again, this historical situation shows the continued influence of race, an embarrassing situation in the mid-20th Century, especially for a country that prides itself for peace, equality, and justice.

Of course this was not an isolated situation; rather, it's more of a reflection of historical trends. Another vivid illustration of modern brutality, prejudice, and discrimination is the well documented attacks on the Philadelphia-based MOVE organization by law enforcement

---

[7] These acts are an indication of vigilante law, a prominent part of US "legal" history. These cruelties may be viewed as "death sentences" by popular demand. However, since these were not considered legal executions, they do not count as a form of death sentencing. Thus, the fact that numerous studies have found no statistically significant relationship between the number of African Americans and Caucasians executed is due, in part, to incomplete data.

officials. In fact, some observers document that members of the organization were subjected to some of the worst forms of injustices seen in 20th Century America, where race played a major role in crime and punishment. More specifically, founded in 1972 by Vincent Leaphart, MOVE spoke out vehemently against all forms of government, and on August 8, 1978 MOVE members and law enforcement officers were engaged in a deadly confrontation. Since, one officer was killed, allegedly by MOVE members, nine MOVE members were convicted on third degree murder charges and received 30 to 100 year sentences. Then, on May 13, 1985, there was a second major controversial confrontation. The police, including snipers, destroyed the compound using M-16 assault rifles, M-60 machine guns, 50-caliber machine guns, and a bomb. By the time the tragedy was over, the fire had destroyed the MOVE compound as well as 61 other houses, leaving 260 people homeless. The bodies of six adults and five children were pulled from the burned house. There were only two survivors, and one of the two was convicted on riot and conspiracy charges. Criticism for the aftermath of 10,000 rounds of ammunition, tear gas, and explosives was not delayed, but it took a long time before the city had to take responsibility for what had happened. After a long struggle, a jury found the city guilty of using excessive force and of violating MOVE's constitutional right to protection against unreasonable search and seizure (Anderson and Hevenor, 1987; Goldberg, 1996; Nelson and Maddox, 1996; Wagner-Pacifici, 1994).

There are numerous reasons, deeply rooted in American history and culture as to why Caucasians have always turned against African Americans. Two of these reasons, though, have become pressing for white people; that is, "One is personal and present, the fear of Negro political domination. The other is for his posterity—the future horror of being lost as a race in this virile and vigorous black race" (Cooper, 1988:219). Ezekiel (1995) adds that such viciousness and cruelties can be seen simply as the furthest extent of the cry of superiority, power, and control, the mob's ultimate proclamation of the degradation of the African American community, especially the young. Such cruelty may also be fueled by the aggressors' fear of their own sexuality. To Urbina (2003a, 2008), contrary to essentialist ideologies of scientific racist thinkers, cultural history, *indifference*, not phenotype or biology, continues to be a driving force in defining identity. In other words, race, ethnicity, and culture play a major role in determining how society judges its members and how individuals react to one another.

In combination with intertwining historical forces, culture, not biology, leads one segment of society to attempt, often with great success, to cripple or kill off another that it considers racially different, or threatening (Ruddell and Urbina, 2004). This in part is affirmation of the charge of genocide against "white" America, invariably reflecting the historical influence of race and ethnicity in the US.

Modern Times

While much progress has been made, race continues to play a major role in society in modern times. For instance, contrary to conventional wisdom that the change in law, the "formal end of slavery," resulted in justice, equality, and glory for African Americans, the end of slavery in 1865 brought one kind of freedom but left former slaves under the control of a range of "Jim Crow" laws designed to limit their choices of jobs, residential location, right to vote, education, and various other restrictions. These limitations, once again written into law, created the system of de jure segregation that was not dismantled until the civil rights acts of the 1960s (Feagin and Vera, 1995). In truth, many Anglos continue to view African Americans in very negative ways. Writing about the "American dilemma" in the mid-20th Century, Myrdal (1944) noted that a tension existed in the United States between the widely proclaimed ethic of equality and the reality of everyday prejudice, racism, and inequality. A few years later, the Kerner Commission not only cited America as racist, but noted that "Our nation is moving toward two societies, one black, one white–separate and unequal" (Tabb, 1970:134). The current situation nicely illustrated in the words of Hacker in his book, *Two Nations: Black & White, Separate, Hostile, Unequal* (2003), truly illustrating the significance of race in the US in the 21st Century.

Currently, based on Census 2010 data, African Americans, the second largest minority group comprised about 12.6% (38.9 million) of the total US population, but remain disadvantaged along many dimensions of social stratification. African Americans are over-represented at the lower end of the income and occupation hierarchies, but under-represented in positions of political, educational, and economic power. Considering that employment and income govern other facets of life, the employment and income gaps that had been narrowing between 1965 and 1980 began to widen once again, as the

Reagan and Bush administrations opted to cut programs that assisted racial minorities and failed to enforce regulations designed to reduce discrimination in housing and jobs. The result has been labeled American apartheid, in reference to the systematic residential segregation of African Americans in areas where employment opportunities are almost nonexistent, a situation that has been worsened by the economic crises that began 2007, the worst crises since the Great Depression of 1929.

In the area of crime and punishment, prior to 9/11, one of the most debated historical ruptures was the LA riots. Contrary to the negative portrayal of the situation, Brigham's (1996) analysis of the 1992 Los Angeles riots reveal that over two-thirds of the African Americans arrested were unemployed; of all looters, 60% were high school drop outs, and 87% reported income of less than $1,000 per month. Evidently, if one is seeking a realistic snap shot of the "underclass" in the United States, one need only explore for a moment the profile of those involved in the looting and burning of Los Angeles, a profile that is virtually unaltered since the Watts riot of 1965.

To place the current situation of African Americans into perspective and the continued influence of race, consider the following figures. The proportion of African Americans living in poverty is no lower now than in the early 1970s, with 24.7% of African Americans living in poverty in 2008, compared to 8.6% of Caucasians. In 2008, the median household income for African Americans was $34,218, compared to $65,637 for Asians, $55,530 for Caucasians, and $37,913 for Latinas and Latinos. As a whole, during one of the worst economic crises in the history of the country, the poverty level was $21,954 for a family of four in 2009. In 2009, the unemployment rate for African Americans was 15.7% overall, 17.1% for men age 20 and over, 12.4% for women, and 41.3% for both sexes for those 16 to 19 years of age. The comparable data for Caucasians are 9.5% overall, 9.9% 7.4% for Caucasian men and women age 20 and over respectively, and 25.3% for both sexes for those 16 to 19 years of age. In 2008, a report released by Trust for America's Health showed that African American babies were dying at a more than twice the rate of their Caucasian counterparts. In 2009, the National Coalition for the Homeless reported that the homeless population in 2007 was 47% African American and 35% Caucasian. At the turn of the 21th Century, African Americans made up only 4% of all college professors, 3% of physicians, 2% of lawyers, and only slightly more than 1% of teachers in elementary grades were African American males. In 2009, educational attainment data show that African Americans held only 869,000 of all professional and doctoral degrees (17,538,000).

During the last four decades, some observers have argued that the situation is getting better, and that the effects of race are now minimal or non-existent. However, in terms of education, crime and punishment, the situation remains relatively the same, if not worse, and race is being redefined to categorize people. At the turn of the 21th Century, a study by the Justice Policy Institute found that after 20 years of punitive criminal justice penalties, there were more African American men in jail or prison than in college, with 791,600 African American men behind bars, and 603,032 enrolled in colleges or universities at the end of 2000. In effect, based on the latest statistics, like the disproportionate minority confinement data, the situation is not significantly better. In fact, giving warriors of law-and-order the ideal excuse that they were waiting for, the September 11, 2001 terrorists attacks on the US resulted in yet another more potent war on presumed criminal offenders, with the government now using a combination of existing criminal laws, anti-drug laws, and anti-terrorists laws to detect, arrest, indict, prosecute, convict, and warehouse African Americans, especially young men who are defined as "dangerous" or "gangsters," in jails and prisons (Bosworth and Flavin, 2007). According to the Bureau of Justice Statistics, by 2008, there were 847,000 African American inmates (more than the 838,100 African American men who enrolled in college in the fall of 2007), compared to 712,500 Caucasian men and 427,000 Latino inmates. As such, the rate of incarceration for African American men was 6.6 times that of Caucasian men, with one in 21 African American men incarcerated, compared to one in 138 Caucasian men. Further, while traditionally the majority of people under the control of the criminal justice system have been men, the rates of women, especially African American women, under the control of the penal system have increased drastically during the last few years (Urbina, 2008). Case in point: Highly attributed to the introduction of crack cocaine into the ghetto and the war on drugs, the government has implemented very punitive measures against "crack mothers." Unfortunately, little effort was made to access the special needs of troubled women before the criminalization of crack mothers became a media spectacle.[8] Realistically, these statistics are more a reflection of the influence of race and ethnicity than the actual danger of presumed criminals.

Finally, in 2004, for men ages 15 to 19 years, the homicide rate was 3 per 100,000 among Caucasians, 6.9 per 100,000 among Asian/Pacific Islanders, 17.2 per 100,000 among American Indian/Alaskan Natives, 25.9 per 100,000 Among Latinas/os, and 56.9 per 100,000 among African Americans.[9] While people tend not to mention or even acknowledge the everyday significance of race in society, in this case the experience of African Americans, the current situation is largely attributed to US historical racism, much of which has been created and maintained by law. In September 1974, for example, Bostonians rioted when authorities attempted to integrate the school system. An Anglo demonstrator summed up the mood of the "Archie Bunkers," a term now synonymous with bigot, when he yelled: "The real issue is nigger" (Acuna, 1988:365)! Not surprisingly, in the 21st Century, Americans remain separate and unequal (Levine, 2003). In effect, in 2011, 57 years after the 1954 Brown case, many schools remain separate and unequal, highly governed by the influence of race, and, of course, factors like economics.

In Case You Are Not Dead

Beyond law-and-order, as reported by Peña and Urbina in a forthcoming publication, "The Dynamics of Education and Globalization in the New Millennium: The Unspoken Realities," one of the more recent assaults on the African American community is the termination of affirmative action in some universities. Clearly, this is a new controlling strategy and propaganda advocating that race no longer

---

[8] Although there is no official date as to when the "war on drugs" started, it appears that the Anti-Drug Abuse Act of 1986 set the tone for the prosecution of drug related offenses. Some scholars, however, claim that the law was not designed to be applied evenly (Currie, 1993; Irwin and Austin, 2000; Tonry, 2006; Walker, 2010). Currie (1993:31) claims that "the drug war has been overwhelmingly targeted at the communities of the poor and near-poor, especially the minority poor." Furthermore, classifying the war on drugs as the "American Nightmare," Currie (1993:10) argues that "twenty years after the drug war began in earnest, we are far worse off than when we started."

[9] Given the current American social arrangements, it is evident that the dominant Caucasian race is not sufficiently motivated to stop intra-racial homicides.

plays a role and thus prejudice and discrimination in the US no longer exist, with some people, including renowned intellectual racists, going as far as saying that Caucasians are now the victims of discrimination. For instance, after centuries of not allowing blacks into universities, whites are now claiming that unqualified African Americans are entering the privileged world of universities because of affirmative action. The truth is, though, that far more Caucasians have entered the gates of the ten most elite institutions through 'alumni preference' than the combined numbers of all African Americans and Latinas/os entering through affirmative action (Acuna, 1998; Stein, 1995), a trend that probably extends into the 21st Century, as in 2010, just 4.5% of students on the University of Texas at Austin campus were African Americans. Yet, it is more convenient to say what people rather hear: that race no longer plays a role in society.

Even worse, some politicians and law enforcement officials apparently see nothing strange in the fact that just in the last few years the US government has spent billions of dollars fighting or preparing for wars, not to mention the millions of dollars spent on space exploration. Yet, many of these same politicians and government officials throw up their hands before they will consider overhauling our schools, cleaning the slums, creating jobs, and making a serious and honest attempt to abolish poverty, especially among women and children (Urbina, 2008).

During the time when the government was supposedly targeting poverty, Congress allocated only $1.6 billion annually to eliminate the so-called "discovery of poverty," truly, an embarrassing amount compared with the multi-billion dollar annual budgets on things like the military. In fact, considering that there were 30 to 40 million in poverty in the United States, this amount did not go very far (Acuna, 1988). Actually, from its beginning the war on poverty was in trouble; it lacked resources, motivation, and honesty, beyond the political and academic rhetoric of good intentions. To this day, money that could be allocated to improving lives is being siphoned off for space, missile, and armament programs, taking precedence over people (Urbina, 2008). Nicely put by Harrington (1971:5), "clothes make the poor invisible too: America has the best-dressed poverty the world has ever known."

Lastly, as illustrated by the following cases, this pattern has been active since the Republicans began dismantling social services. President Nixon's advisor, Arthur Burns, defined poverty as an "intellectual concept" in 1969.   Soon afterward, President Nixon appointed Burns to the Federal Reserve Board. At the highest level of the judicial system, the new Burger Court was less interested in improving access for minorities.   Then, President Reagan's second Attorney General Edwin Meese III proclaimed that there was no authoritative evidence that hunger existed in America. To top it off, President Reagan himself firmly believed that hunger and poverty did not exist and blamed hunger, if it existed, on a "lack of knowledge."[10] In short, taken together, it seems difficult to conclude that race now plays a minimal or no role in the US, particularly in the areas of crime and punishment.

As the Road Comes to an End

Some critics claim that although the long and turbulent fight against racial manipulation, violence, prejudice, and discrimination cannot be said to have been won, and sometimes has actually driven anti-African American and anti-Caucasian attitudes underground, its net effect has been mostly positive. Gans (1995), for instance, claims that the country is better off for that long and difficult fight. Others, however, report that institutionalized prejudice and racism remains an extremely powerful determinant of the life chances of African Americans (Aguirre and Baker, 2007; Aguirre and Turner, 2006; Bosworth and Flavin, 2007).

The frustration of African Americans is perhaps best illustrated in the case of W.E.B. Du Bois. As Gates and West (1997:111) point out, after 95 years of the most courageous and unflagging devotion to African American freedom and progress witnessed in the 20th Century, Du Bois not only left America for Africa but concluded, "I just cannot take any more of this country's treatment. We leave for Ghana October 5th and I set no date for return. . . . Chin up, and fight on, but realize that American Negroes can't win."   Nation of Islam leader Don Muhammad remarked: "Blacks have been in America 437 years, and

---

[10] In fact, as time progressed, Reagan seemed unable to distinguish fact from fiction. Once, after watching *Rambo*, Reagan declared that he knew what to do about the terrorists.

people who have been here 437 days have walked past us" (Levin and McDevitt, 1993:148).

As a whole, race continues to play a significance role and prejudice and racism continue to pervade every institution in the United States from churches to universities, with African Americans continuing to experience and suffer the many cruelties of discrimination (Aguirre and Turner, 2006; Hacker, 2003; Moore, 2007). Frequently, Caucasians support the cause of equality and "equal" justice for African Americans, only when it is in their interest to do so (Bell, 1980). Bell (1992) has argued that racism is so fundamental to this nation that African Americans will probably never gain equality with Caucasian Americans. To African American nationalists, American "democracy" is a modern form of tyranny and manipulation on the part of the ruling Caucasian majority over the African American minority (Gates and West, 1997). In effect, Bonilla-Silva (2006) documents that racism has been reinvented, like an elusive and evasive historical *demon* that refuses to die. Of course, today, racism tends to be more subtle, in that many racists wear suits, not sheets, with some of them sitting in high ranking positions of prestige or power. In the contexts of the crime and punishment, Urbina (2008) reports that the current state of the criminal justice system is merely a rectification of the original slavery system, designed, by law, to keep African Americans in their place. Beyond the cages of steel, which have become a savage warehouse for African Americans, the latest movement, globalization, is transforming itself into yet another form of slavery, details Urbina in a forthcoming book, revealing the significance of race and ethnicity in the globalization movement.

What Are the Choices?

The significance of race in American society, in fact, seems to be much more profound than people like to admit. As in the early days in America, whites need African Americans to maintain its "equilibrium." To Cooper (1988:173), the United States needs African Americans for "ballast if for nothing else." Following Hacker, Gans (1995:92-93) cites:

> whites need the 'nigger,' because it is the 'nigger' within themselves that they cannot tolerate. . . . Whatever it is that whites

feel 'nigger' signifies about blacks–lust and laziness, stupidity or squalor–in fact exists within themselves. . . By creating such a creature, whites are able to say that because only members of the black race can carry that taint, it follows that none of its attributes will be found in white people.

At the end of the Tunnel

Under the ideology of *Manifest Destiny*, two sets of relations existed side by side: pre-capitalism and slavery. Racial prejudice and ideologies still rationalize and legitimize widespread Caucasian prejudice and discrimination against African Americans. All in all, modern racial discrimination is, as the late US Supreme Court Justice William O. Douglas put it in the late 1960s, a "spectacle of slavery unwilling to die" (Feagin and Vera, 1995:168). Delgado (1995) articulates a Law of Racial Thermodynamics: racism is never eliminated but always comes back in new forms in more appropriate times. In effect, slavery-era arguments are very much alive, though normally translated into modern political and media jargon (Aguirre and Turner, 2006; Bonilla-Silva, 2006). It is also evident that the character of racial action is highly influenced by the social, economic, educational, and political resources at the discriminator's command, with race and ethnicity intertwined in complex but significant ways.

While legislation has made several forms of discriminatory acts illegal, it has not been able to end the broad array of blatant, subtle, and covert racism in the area of crime and punishment, the criminal justice system as a whole, or society in general, to include areas like jobs, housing, politics, and education. Not surprisingly, rationalized and legitimized prejudice and racism has become the soup of the day, with race and ethnicity, arguably, determining IQ, and IQ is supposed to determine economic status. African American men are still considered more likely to be criminals, in need of strict penal control, as eloquently documented by Lynch (2007). In fact, today the obsessive fear of the mythical African American rapist monster continues unabated (Bosworth and Flavin, 2007). As such, as in the early days, the fear of the African American rapist is used to rationalize and legitimize Caucasians' continued bad faith toward African Americans in the United States.

Finally, even though Caucasians and Africa Americans have lived and worked together in the US for almost five centuries (485 years), the two races are still in a certain sense strangers to one another, a phenomenon that continues in 2011. As detailed herein, at best, little has changed for the better in relations between African Americans and Caucasians, but, more realistically, blacks and whites generally remain apart, hostile, and equal, highly governed by the historical dynamics of race. A few decades ago, Adrian Dick Gregory remarked, "In the South, whites don't care how close Negroes get, just as long as they don't get too big. In the North, whites don't care how big Negroes get, just as long as they don't get to close," a mentality that has not changed significantly, if at all. In essence, more than ever before in American history, African Americans are succumbing to and internalizing the racial assumptions that there can be no meaningful bonds of intimacy between African Americans and Caucasians (hooks, 1995). Though, as Shorris (1992:159) points out, "the truth of racism is that the power to define belongs to the racist," again, illustrating the powerful influence of race in everyday life.

In the next section, the experiences of the second largest minority group, Mexicans, in the US will be explored. As will discussed, in many ways the experiences of Mexicans, and ethnic minorities in general, are similar to those of African Americans, but in many ways the experiences of African Americans and Mexicans, who are part of the largest minority group, Latinos, in the US, are very different. Historically, as the two largest minority groups, with the longest history in the US, African Americans and Mexicans share many similarities and many differences. As such, having detailed the significance of race (African Americans), the role of ethnicity (Mexicans) in society and criminality is now examined.

MEXICANS IN THE LAND OF OPPORTUNITY

Even though the Latina and Latino population is composed of various ethnic subgroups, like Cubans, Central Americans, Puerto Ricans, and South Americans, normally categorized under the broad labels of "Hispanic" or "Latinos," the majority of Latinas and Latinos in the US are of Mexican heritage.[11] In effect, not only do Mexicans constitute

---

[11] The final count for the 2010 census has not yet been released, but at the turn of the 20th Century, African Americans (34.7 million or 12.3%) and Latinos/as (35.3 million or 12.5%) constituted approximately 70 million residents–

the second largest minority group in the US, but they, like African Americans, have the longest history in the country. As such, given that Mexicans (29,189, 334 or 64.3%) constitute the largest ethnic group within the Latina and Latino population, the significance and influence of ethnicity in the American society, to include crime and punishment, is now detailed.[12]

From the Shadows of the Past

In the United States, it rarely occurs to scholars to ask how the experiences and perceptions of Mexicans differ from those of the

---

approximately 1/4 (or 25%) of the total US population (281,421,906). This did not include the 3.8 million Latino/a residents of Puerto Rico. As for ethnicity, Mexicans constituted the largest (20,640,711 or 7.3%) Latino/a group in the United States, Puerto Ricans constituted the second largest (3,406,178 or 1.2%), and Cubans constituted the third largest (1,241,685 or 0.4%) Latino/a group. Other Latinos/as, Central and South Americans, combined constituted 10,017,244 (3.6%) of the population. More specific, the figures for these Latinos/as in 2000 were: 1.7 million of Central American descent, 1.4 million of South American origin, 765,000 of Dominican heritage, 100,000 of Spanish background, and 6.1 million of other Latino/a origins. As such, people of Mexican heritage constituted 58% of the total Latino/a population, an increase of 7.1 million since 1990. Together, Mexican Americans and Puerto Ricans, who are concentrated in New York and New Jersey, accounted for 68% of the nation's Latinos/as and an even a greater percentage of the nation's Latino/a citizens. Further, according to the March 2000 Current Population Survey, more than one-quarter of the foreign-born population was from Mexico, which had the largest share of any country. However, along with Mexico, Cuba, and Puerto Rico, the Dominican Republic and El Salvador also ranked among the ten leading countries of foreign birth in the United States. Also, about three in four Latinos/as lived in seven states with one million or more each: California, Texas, New York, Florida, Illinois, Arizona, and New Jersey.

[12] Keep in mind that based on 2000 census figures, in Texas and California (two of the three states included in the analysis), Mexicans constitute the largest Latino minority group, and in Florida (the third state included in the analysis) Cubans constitute the largest Latino minority group. It is important to emphasize that since Puerto Ricans are concentrated in states that have few individuals under the sentence of death (in comparison to California, Florida, and Texas, the three states with the most people under the sentence of death), this Latino group will not be included in the analysis. Additionally, Puerto Ricans are concentrated in states that are less likely to execute, in comparison to California, Florida, and Texas, especially the latter two.

dominant group. As Acuna (2010), points out, scholars tend to isolate people of Mexican heritage from the social relationships that created them. In the words of Acuna (1998:60):

> it is logical to conclude that the experiences of Third World nations is not like the experiences of colonizers. Similarly, the experience of workers is not that of their patron (boss), and the experience of Mexicans in the U.S. is not those of other ethnic and mainstream groups.

In effect, Mejicanos (Mexican nationals) and Mexican Americans differ from other ethnic groups by duration in the mainland, number, and by character. As such, the challenge of the serious ethnic scholar is to reclaim these historical experiences and views that have been manipulated, skewed, or omitted from the pages of history (Chomsky, 2007; Noboa, 2005; Urbina, 2003c), especially as we seek to better understand the role of ethnicity in society.

As the largest Latina/o subgroup (approximately 29,189, 334 or 64.3% in 2007), some people of Mexican origin are descendants of people who settled in the Southwest territories before that area was annexed by the United States in 1848 under the Treaty of Guadalupe Hidalgo. Others have lived in the United States for several generations, and still others have entered more recently in response to employment "opportunities" in US factories and in agriculture.[13] Thus, unlike racial and ethnic groups, many of whom arrived in the second half of the 20th Century, Mexicans live in the light of their own history in the United States; that is, like African Americans, Mexicans have a long history in this country.

The Conquest: Quick, Swift, and Certain

As in the case of African Americans, understanding the influence of ethnicity in the United States requires a detailed examination of historical events. To begin, Chicano playwright and film-maker Luis

---

[13] It has been argued that the first Latinos settled in the continental United States in 1598, when Juan de Onate established a small colony at Santa Fe in what is now the state capital of New Mexico. Interestingly, 42% of New Mexico's population was Latino/a in 2000, highest of any state.

Valdez has succinctly summarized the disastrous outcome of the 1848 Treaty of Guadalupe Hidalgo, which transformed Northern Mexico into the US Southwest, in his now famous philosophical phrase: "We did not come to the United States at all. The United States came to us." Or, "we never crossed a border. The border crossed us." At a practical level, the treaty ended the war, and the United States grabbed over half (this includes California, Texas, Nevada, Utah, and parts of Arizona, Colorado, Kansas, New Mexico, Oklahoma, and Wyoming) of Mexico's soil, a US expansionist war which turned out to be extremely costly to Mexico and to Mejicanos left behind.

The treaty did not stop the bitterness or the brutal and vicious violence between these two communities; instead, "it gave birth to a legacy of hate" where race/ethnicity was a driving force (Acuna, 1988:9), extending into 2011. The conquest, for example, set a pattern for ethnic and racial antagonism, viciousness, and violence, justified by the now popular slogans like "Remember the Alamo!" and myths about the Mejicanos' or Chicanos' treachery and legitimized by high ranking government officials and intellectual racists. In effect, to this day, the Alamo has been a shrine to anti-Mexican sentiment, the ultimate symbol of the supposed glorious victory of the superior moral character of "white" over "brown." In truth, the only Texans who died defending the Alamo were eight Mexican nationals who opposed Santa Anna's highhanded politics. Ideologically, though, as with Native Americans and later with African Americans, the government had a justification to institutionalize prejudice, racism, discrimination, and vicious brutality toward people of Mexican heritage. More globally, in addition of the influence of race and ethnicity, the Anglo conquest was also a well calibrated capitalist conquest, as vividly documented by Gomez (2007).

Mexicans as "Half Civilized"

The significance of ethnicity was evident before and after conquest, as in the minds of some Americans, the Spanish conquest clearly demonstrated the inferiority of the Mexican Indian, as a stronger race would not have been defeated. The Manifest Destiny (US policy of expansionism) and the "free labor ideology," then, further fused the general sense among Caucasians that Mexicans represented a degenerate "race" and culture and, by extension, that the region's rich natural resources were theirs to grab and exploit exclusively (Acuna, 2010; Urbina and Smith, 2007). In the words of Almaguer (1994:33), "the notion of manifest destiny implied the domination of civilization over nature, Christianity over heathenism, progress over backwardness, and, most importantly, of white Americans over the Mexican and Indian populations that stood in their path."

According to Fredrickson (1981:5),

> Land hunger and territorial ambition gave whites a practical incentive to differentiate between the basic rights and privileges they claimed for themselves and what they considered to be just treatment for the 'savages' [Indians and Mexicans] who stood in their path, and in the end they mustered the power to impose their will.

Acuna (2010) asserts that the United States forged its present borders through expansionist wars, and, except in Hollywood movies, no such thing as the "Winning of the West" ever took place. Over and over, though, even as Mexico celebrated its 200 years of independence from Spain, the myth of the "bloodless conquest of Mexico" has been repeated by the majority of historians and is still believed by most people (Carrigan and Webb, 2003; Gomez, 2000, Mirande, 1987).

After the conquest, though, the influence of ethnicity became even more pressing, as Anglos believed that "'there never was a more docile animal in the world than the Mexican,'" proceeding to treat Mexicans as such to further maximize their exploitation (Reisler, 1997: 25). Then, to reassure themselves of their "new victory" and, above all, to maintain and further their will, whites made wide use of old and new forms of manipulation, suppression, marginalization, and control. For instance, Caucasian antipathy toward Mexicans is illustrated by the bag of stereotypes which include labels and phrases like *birth of laziness, backward, indolent, submissive, unproductive, prodigal, illiterate, nomadic, unable to rise in occupational status and contribute to community stability, lazy peon, and irrigation labor equals Mexicans.* In short, "The Mexican . . . was ambiguously deemed 'half civilized' and ambivalently integrated into an intermediate status within the new society" (Almaguer, 1994:4).

As mentioned above, "the concept that people of color are less than equal has been ingrained since the outset of U.S. constitutional experience" (Acuna, 1998:23). In later years, such labels have not only been rationalized, legitimized, and accepted, but given new life by a number of individuals. Even Jean-Baptiste Lamy, a conservative French priest, was ambitious and openly racist. In 1851, he argued that Mexicans were poor, childlike creatures, given to gluttony, thievery, and wild sexuality (Shorris, 1992). These stereotypes have been supported by scholars such as Dr. Roy L. Garis of Vanderbilt University who claimed, sometime during the depression, that "their [the Mexicans'] minds run to nothing higher than animal functions . . . Yet there are Americans clamoring for more of this human swine to be brought over from Mexico" (Shorris, 1992:153). Now, in plain 21st Century, Huntington (2004:32) charges that "the single and most immediate and most serious challenge to America's traditional identity comes" from Mexicans, truly revealing the role of race and ethnicity in modern times as well as hypocrisy and profound oceans of ignorance that exist even among the most learned scholars (Urbina, 2003d).

Oppression and Suppression

Critically, the influence of race and ethnicity takes various forms. Along with stereotypes, for example, Anglos were able to use the law very effectively to intimidate, suppress, control, and silence Mexicans. As vividly documented by Acuna (2010) and Gomez (2000), Anglos gained control of the land by making use of the law or manipulating the law. In fact, even when legislation has been passed, purportedly to help Mexicans, the end result has often been devastating. For instance, while the California State Constitutional Convention of 1849 formally granted Mexicans the same citizenship rights as "free white persons" in the state of California, Mexicans in California have never been seriously defined or viewed as "white" (Acuna, 2010; Almaguer, 2008).

In other instances, law has served as a "cover-up" as well as a convenient and useful weapon against Mexicans, as noted by Lopez (2004). For instance, while it has been noted by a number of individuals that unlike African Americans, Native Americans, or Asian Americans, Mexicans were the only ethnic population in California during the 19th Century that Anglos deemed worthy to formally marry, few are willing to acknowledge that the marriages, especially those between the old Mexican ruling elite and prominent Anglos, made the

Yankee conquest of Mexicans smoother than it might otherwise have been (Acuna, 2010; Gomez, 2000).[14]

Another convenient and powerful weapon has been the American media, a trend that extends into the 21st Century (Urbina, 2008). As Almaguer (1994:34) points out, on March 15, 1848, The Californian effectively summarized the negative feelings toward non-Caucasians by saying, "We desire only a White population in California," truly showing the significance of race and ethnicity in the US. Such view is well illustrated by some of the California delegates who argued against the "introduction into this country of negroes, peons of Mexico, or any class of that kind" (Almaguer, 1994:37).

Together, with ideological justifications, a racist media, and, above all, access to the law, Anglo settlers were in a powerful position to treat the Chicano population as people without rights who were merely obstacles to the acquisition and exploitation of natural resources and land. According to Camarillo (1984:25):

> once the subdivision of rancho and public lands had begun, the dominance of the emerging economic system of American capitalism in the once-Mexican region was a foregone conclusion. The process of land loss and displacement of the Mexican pastoral economy was fairly complete throughout the Southwest by the 1880s.

At this point in time, perhaps more than ever, along with the influence of race and ethnicity, the significance of economics becomes extremely obvious. As Mexicans lost more and more of their resources, they became weaker and weaker, creating divisions, chaos, and uncertainty. The exploitation was absolute, for Mexicans had no allies, neither in the unions, nor in the churches, nor in educational institutions, nor in the government. To the Anglos, the Mejicanos were

---

[14] While little is known about the various class and skin color divisions among the Mexican population, especially those of Euro-Spanish decent and Indian decent, there is an indication that the experiences of Euro-Spanish decedents and Indian decedents have been different in Mexico and in the United States, including name labels, stereotypes, and actual discrimination. Some scholars have stated that there has been an almost caste-like distinction between the two groups historically (Acuna, 1988; Meyer and Sherman, 1995).

the surplus labor that kept wages low; yet, a necessary evil (Castaneda, 2009; Chomsky, 2007). Embarrassingly, in South Texas, the now famous King Ranch was pieced together out of the bad luck and lack of capital of many Mexicans.

Anglo victory on Mexican lands was quick, vicious, vindictive, and brutal. In fact, Anglo domination was so ruthless and so thorough that any response would have been futile. In essence, the Mexicans not only lost in war, and, by extension, their land, but their language, and their culture, as eloquently illustrated by Bender (2005), McWilliams (1990), and Mirande (1987). In effect, Mexicans were socially, politically, educationally, and economically disenfranchised and forced to turn on each other, under the divide and further conquer mentality. Their income per capita fell, and their infant mortality rate rose (Shorris, 1992), again, vividly illustrating the powerful influence of race and ethnicity in the US.

The role of race and ethnicity can be seen in various early writings. For instance, based on the writings of authors like Jovita Idar (1885-1946), the life of the Mexican became a nightmare under Anglo control, and continued to be so for Mexicans in places like Texas during the late 1800s and early 1900s, as documented by Carrigan and Webb (2003). The famous Texas Rangers, or "Los Rinches," were routinely lynching Mexican men, women, and children. In effect, reports show that "For a Mexican living in America from 1882 to 1930, the chance of being a victim of mob violence was equal to those of an African American living in the South" (Dunbar and Kravitz, 1976; McWilliams, 1990). Writing for La Cronica, Idar documented the lynching and hanging of a Mexican child in Thorndale, Texas, by the Texas Rangers and the brutal and vicious burning at the stake of 20-year old Antonio Rodriguez in Rocksprings, Texas. Of Rodriguez, Idar wrote:

> The crowd cheered when the flames engulfed his contorted body. They did not even turn away at the smell of his burning flesh and I wondered if they even know his name. There are so many dead that sometimes I can't remember all their names.

The prejudice, racism, and brutality against Mexicans in the Southwest made Idar take more radical actions. In 1913, she started writing articles in favor of the famous revolutionary forces of General Francisco Villa, and she went to Mexico to serve as a nurse in la Cruz

Blanca on the side of General Villa. As one would expect, this attracted the attention of the US federal government and the Texas Rangers, who were having a difficult time apprehending Pancho Villa.

When Idar returned to Laredo in 1914 and wrote an article critical of President Woodrow Wilson's deployment of troops to the border, the infamous Texas Rangers went to Laredo to destroy her printing press. Texas Rangers Hicks, Ramsey, Chamberlain, and another, whose name is not known, went up to the door and found Jovita blocking the entrance with her hands firmly grasping the frame and feet planted on the threshold. The Rangers asked her to move out of the way, but Jovita stood her ground. A crowd gathered to witness the spectacle. In one of the greatest historical acts of bravery by a young Mexican woman, the Rangers backed down and left town. The newspaper, the voice of La Raza, was safe for a while, but, as expected, only for a short time because the Texas Rangers came back in the stealth of the night and completely destroyed the newspaper. The vicious Texas Rangers, viewed as respectable and honorable police officers in the *popular imagination* and normally glorified by white historians, had silenced a strong, effective, and vital voice for political and social justice for Mexicans in Texas (La Voz de Aztlan, 2000).

The significance of ethnicity can also be seen in the labor force. That is, another strategic mechanism of oppression was the peonage system, which, according to Gonzalez and Fernandez (1998), amounted to a new form of slavery. Like African Americans under the slavery system, Mexican peons who ran away were hunted down, prosecuted, and punished. For example, N.B. Appel owned a mercantile store in Tubac. His servant, indebted to him for $82.68, ran away and allegedly stole a rifle and other materials. Authorities prosecuted the Mexican peon and returned him to Appel. Found guilty, he publicly received 15 lashes (*Weekly Arizonian*, 1859). In Riverton Ranch, seven peons escaped but were returned and charged with debt and theft. The overseer, George Mercer, whipped them and cut off their hair as punishment. Mercer's shears got out of control and he took some skin with the hair. Stories of the "scalping" spread as far as San Francisco (*Weekly Alta Californian*, 1859).

The cruelties of the peonage system were not only long lasting, but have also served as a symbol of insult to all Mexicans, an exploitive system extending into the 21st Century. To this end, American employers have been able to manipulate existing myths and stereotypes about Mexicans to rationalize their use in the labor market (Chacon and Davis, 2006; Chomsky, 2007; Fox and Rivera-Salgado, 2004). As a consequence, Mexicans, assigned the dirtiest, back-breaking jobs, often labeled as "Mexican work," have received lower wages for the same jobs and normally the first fired during difficult times (Castaneda, 2009). In effect, while language and culture set the Chicano community apart from the world of European Americans, appearance also has a major impact on their employment and earnings. Mexican American people with dark skin or Native American features find it difficult to obtain employment, and if employed, receive significantly lower earnings than their more Anglo-looking peers, all other characteristics being equal (Urbina, 2007), again, another manifestation of race and ethnicity.

Lastly, Mexicans, sometimes referred to as "greasers," were normally viewed as *gente sin razon* (people without reason) by the *gente de razon* (people with reason). They were viewed with utter disdain, as people who could be tolerated only as long as they kept to themselves. "Whites Only" or "No Mexicans Allowed" signs served as bitter reminders of their second-class citizenship and, of course, the role of race and ethnicity. Embarrassingly, in a country that has prided itself around the world as a nation that values respect, diversity, freedom, and democracy, all through the 1940s, signs that said, "No Mexicans Allowed," "We don't serve dogs or Mexicans," or "We do not serve dogs, Niggers, or Mexicans" were common in the United States. Yet, today, like back then, some people claim that race and ethnicity play no role in everyday life.

Immigration: Wetbacks or Exiles?

In modern times, there is probably no other area in which ethnicity plays a bigger role than in the area of immigration. In 2011, immigration issues have once again dominated political and media arenas, which have been highlighted by scandals, name calling, and various kinds of accusations, more a reflection of prejudice, discrimination, hypocrisy, fear, and ignorance than reality. Although immigrants enter the United States from virtually every country, Mexico has long been identified as one of the primary sources of the economic, social, and political problems associated with mass migration, especially "illegal" immigrants, a powerful term used to negatively describe undocumented workers in the United States, as eloquently documented by Castaneda (2009).

In the context of crime and punishment, while arguing that it's not a matter of race or ethnicity, but national stability and security, politicians, law enforcement officials, and the media talk about "illegal aliens" to dehumanize and demonize undocumented people, routinely targeting people of Mexican descent (De Genova, 2004; Romero, 2008). As an historical reminder of the dynamics of American criminal law and America's supposed objective government and law enforcement officials, legendary former FBI director J. Edgar Hoover once remarked: "You never have to bother about a President being shot by Puerto Ricans or Mexicans. They don't shoot very straight. But if they come at you with a knife, beware" (*Time*, 1970:16). A few years later, former CIA director William Colby stated in 1978 that Mexican migration represented a greater threat to the United States than does the Soviet Union. Then, in 1985, Dallas Mayor Pro Tem Jim Hart warned voters that "aliens" had "no moral values" and were destroying the city's neighborhoods and threatening the security of Dallas. According Hart, Dallas women could be "robbed, raped or killed" (Cockcroft, 1982:58), views that are further legitimized by racist thinkers teaching in some of most renowned universities in the world, like Samuel Huntington of Harvard University.

In truth, at one level, "immigration" is a political euphemism that refers to people of color, especially people of Mexican heritage. Case in point: The then Immigration and Naturalization Service's (INS) infamous witch hunt of 1954, known as "Operation Wetback," was a product of a racist tradition of blaming the victim for the rough cycles of economics and inequality. This all-out assault was directed by retired generals (in some ways similar to the witch hunt of the 1930s), and resulted in the apprehension and repatriation of approximately 1,075,168 Mexicans (Chomsky, 2007; Gutierrez, 1997). Ruiz (1997:138) documents that Mexicans, many of whom were native US citizens, "were the only immigrants targeted for removal." Resonating historical white hegemony, like those who favored the return of African Americans to Africa, nativists wished to preserve both their ideological and racial purity. Not surprisingly, as if the influence of ethnicity and economic basis of racism needed additional proof, blatant and explicitly racist statements about Mexicans have once again surfaced in

2010, paralleling the anti-Mexican rhetoric of the 1930's Depression years.

Over the years, arguments have been made that constitutional guarantees do not apply to undocumented workers in the United States (Kong, 2010; Motomura, 2010). In effect, racially discriminatory legislation, like the Alien Land Laws of 1913 and 1920, declared it unlawful for "aliens ineligible for citizenship" to own private property in the state and further stipulated that immigrants were not allowed to lease land for terms longer than three years. Toward the end of the 20th Century, during the 1994 earthquake in California, immigration hawks and cheerleaders of the 1978 *Regents of the University of California v. Bakke* case angrily protested and demanded that undocumented Mexicans be denied disaster relief.

In the 1980s, some Anglos believed that an "immigration crisis" existed and had to be controlled using whatever means necessary. Further inflaming immigration debates, the conservative Reagan administration blamed undocumented workers for high unemployment, especially in the Southwest. As such, legislation such as the Simpson-Rodino law was the politicians' solution to this manufactured panic that carried a political, moral, prejudiced twist based more on the role of ethnicity than the actual economic threat. Apparently, in an election year and conservative era, it was extremely important for Americans to feel safe and secure. In the 1990s, immigrants became once again the scapegoat and target for many US social ills, evidenced by the anti-immigrant movement that resurfaced in 2010, spearheaded by Arizona Governor, Jan Brewer.

On another level, the dynamics of ethnicity are manifested in more subtle, but significant and consequential ways. Anglos have used the rationale that Mexican workers are both culturally and biologically suited to perform the back-breaking jobs that are "beneath" American workers. While the majority of Chicanos now live in urban areas where the men typically find work as laborers and machine operators and the women as domestic servants, like *cocinera, costurera*, or office cleaners, a segment still work in the dangerous agriculture industry, affirming the stereotype of the Mexican farmhand, with the danger issue seldom mentioned or at least discussed in a meaningful manner. Estimates show that with the exception of mining, the agricultural industry has the highest death rate of any industry. In this regard, at the turn of the 21th Century, according to statistics released on June 26, 2002 at the League of United Latin American Citizens (LULAC) national convention, workplace fatalities among Latinos rose by 53% between 1992 and 2000, with at least 815 Latinos dying on the job in 2000. Paradoxically, according to the US Census Bureau, only 7.3% of Latina and Latino workers, most of whom are Mexican, were employed in managerial or professional occupations in 2009.

The problems of workplace fatalities and injuries are magnified by the probabilities that workers and their families are uninsured. The US Census Bureau released data in 2009 confirming that Latinos are the most likely of all people to lack access to health insurance, with 32.4% of Latinos not having health insurance, compared with just 12.0% of Caucasians and 17.2% of African Americans. Latino children continue to have the highest un-insurance rates among US children.

Among the issues not covered in the media or by racially motivated right-wing individuals is the fact that the largest populations of undocumented people in the United States today are probably not Mexicans (or Haitians) but Canadians, Irish, Poles, Russians, and other white immigrants, individuals who are seldom hunted by immigration officials. After living for several years just south of the Canadian border, for example, I realized that while entire communities of undocumented whites exist throughout the Midwest, the border patrol is not out looking for "illegal" whites, like Canadians, as it is along the 2000-mile border with Mexico. As a powerful symbol of insult to the Mexican community, the social construction of "illegal alien" is often applied to all Chicanos (Mexicans), despite the fact that the majority of Mexicans are legal US residents (Chacon and Davis, 2006; De Genova, 2004; Ngai, 2005). Actually, the label often applies to anyone who looks brown or speaks Spanish, again, with race and ethnicity being the defining elements (Oboler, 2006; Urbina, 2007).[15]

To this day, people normally do not accept statistics that point to the fact that undocumented workers are not the burden that some individual want us to believe, nor are they willing to recognize the contribution of these individuals. Contrary to *conventional wisdom*, even during the supposed war on poverty in the 1960s, less than five percent of all Mexican immigrants received any form of public

---

[15] I have always been astonished by the responses I get when I have asked the questions: "What does a Mexican look like?" "Do I look Latino?" "Do I look Mexican?"

assistance (Becklund, 1985). Close to the same timeframe, as reported by Sanchez (1998:104):

> those decrying the social costs of undocumented immigration fail, of course, to recognize the $29 billion paid by Latinos in taxes in 1990 . . . as well as the contributions of this labor force in the face of extreme exploitation and oppression.[16]

In the 21st Century, immigrants are still being demonized; yet, they are more likely to pay taxes than they are to use public services. As of 2005, Social Security was receiving about $7 billion a year through false social security numbers, allowing the government to break even, because that's about the same amount as the difference between what the agency paid out in benefits and what it received in payroll taxes; yet, these immigrants will never be able to receive Social Security benefits (Chomsky, 2007).

Another historical fact that is seldom mentioned is that few are willing to accept and confront the brutal reality that before this last aggressive anti-immigrant movement over 300 Mexicans were dying annually in the process of trying to cross El Rio Bravo or the barbed-wire fences into the hostile "paradise" of "el norte." Then, starting in 2000 one person dies daily (on average) trying to enter the US along the 2000-mile border. The Mexican authorities and news agencies like Notimex, however, claim that US figures are grossly under-estimated because US statistics only include people who die in the US to the exclusion of those who die in the Mexican side of the border, not to mention that probably hundreds of dead bodies are never found. The US police and "La Migra" (the Border Patrol), the failed police arm of the US Department of Homeland Security, kill some of them; others die

---

[16] Talking about figures that are seldom mentioned, consider the following statistics. According to the U.S. Census Bureau, Latinos owned 1.2 million businesses in the United States in 1997. These firms employed almost 1.4 million people and generated $186.3 billion in revenues. Latino-owned firms made up 6% of the nation's 20.8 million non-farm business. Among the minority-owned business in 1997, Latinos/as owned 39% of the firms, more than any other minority group. Among the Latino/a groups, Mexicans owned by far the highest number of Latino/a-owned firms. In 1997, 472,000 firms were owned by Mexicans. Among the Latino-owned firms in 1997, Latinas owned 28% of the business.

trying to cross the freeways and the dangerous Rio Grande under the protection of the night; others are killed by bandits or "cholos."

Even before the latest anti-immigrant assault, in a matter of a few weeks, between July 31 and August 14, 1989, seven murders, shootings, and stabbings of migrant workers were reported to police in the tiny cluster of farm towns in San Diego County. A report released by the Mexican consul in El Paso, Texas, stated that over 2,000 abuses of human rights occurred in Texas in 1988 alone. Interestingly enough, all of the victims were Mejicanos or Mexican Americans. The majority of the abuses took place along the border. In San Ysidro, California, a 23-year old Mexican man was shot by a Border Patrol agent, who claimed that the man had thrown a rock at him. However, a jury in US District Court found the wounded Mexican not guilty of throwing rocks. In another incident, Border Patrol agents shot a boy who they claimed was throwing rocks at them. Like many of the individuals shot by the border police, the bullet entered his body from the back. In effect, everywhere along the California border the response to brutal violence has been to create more vicious violence. Case in point: A Border Crime Prevention Unit organized jointly by the San Diego police and the Border Patrol shot 31 individuals (19 died), all Mexican citizens, in five years. One witness described how Border Patrol agents sat him in a chair, handcuffed him from behind and pushed his face down toward some dog feces on the floor, saying, "That's what you are" (Shorris, 1992:273). From whatever angle the situation is analyzed, it is evident that ". . . serious violations of the rights of Mexican nationals were found to be the norm rather than the exception" (Garcia y Griego, 1997:69; Romero and Serag, 2005), again, illustrating the role of race and ethnicity in recent years. More globally, the Border Patrol has become a universal nightmare for many Mexicans, some of whom are US citizens (Chacon and Davis, 2006; Chavez, 2008; Gutierrez, 1997; Romero, 2001, 2008). In fact, due to the terrorist attacks of September 11, 2001, the situation got much worse as more and more barriers are being implemented under the rationale of "national security" (Bacon, 2009; Bosworth and Flavin, 2007; Corcoran, 2006). Ultimately, 9/11 gave immigration warriors what they were waiting for, an ideal excuse to justify and legitimize their vicious attack on immigrants, as reported by Welch (2006). In essence, while national security should be a primary concern, the government is trying to save lives on one end, while increasing the danger for innocent people on the other end, governed more by the influence of race and ethnicity than the actual realities of crime.

As a last resort, undocumented workers have relied on appellate courts. In September 2002, though, the US Department of Justice decided to reduce the power and number of immigration appellate judges. Reducing the authority and number from 23 to 11, Secretary John Ashcroft argued that such drastic changes were necessary. Obviously, these changes worsen the existing situation for undocumented people (Kong, 2010; Motomura, 2010).

In sum, no one really knows how many Mexican immigrants are killed.[17] The unknown dead lie somewhere in the hot desert and the rough mountains. No one counts the useless cruelties, the physical, emotional, and psychological beatings of the 1,933-mile border that has ended the dreams of many Mejicanos and people from Central and South America. Those who manage to cross into the "land of opportunity," quickly begin to feel the "after-shock" of their conquest and the continued influence of race in ethnicity in the US. They immediately learn that in order to survive, they often need to alter their way of life, a situation that also has long-lasting "side-effects." Shortly after, they encounter a world of prejudice, exploitation, and discrimination (Cobas, Duany, and Feagin, 2009; Chavez, 2008; Urbina, 2007). For instance, notice that when undocumented Mexican nationals enter the United States, they are branded with the now famous label "wetback," and often treated like a war criminal. As in the past, Mexicans often look to Mexico City, not Washington or the state capitol, for protection and redress of grievances.

At a more profound level, the life of "el mojado" (the wetback) resembles the life of the "pocho," which now means a Mexican American who has traded his language and culture for the illusory blandishments of life in the United States. As illustrated by Shorris (1992:170), the pocho lives on the cultural, social, racial, and ethnic fault line. The pocho is a profoundly homeless individual, utterly unprotected, despised on every side at all times. The pocho is viewed

---

[17] In a way, this is a form of "death sentence" and "executions." This contributes to an actual undercount of Mexicans sentenced to death (and executions) without due process (similar to police beatings in the Barrio and the ghetto).

as too Mexican for the Anglos and too "agringado" [white] for the Mexicans. In Mexico, the pocho is the butt of a million jokes:

> "My name is John Sanchez," the pocho tells the border guard on his way in to Mexico.
> "And what is your occupation?" the border guard asks.
> "I am a Latin Lover."
> The border guard laughs, "A Latin Lover?"
> "Yes, when I walk down the street in my patria chica [my adopted country], Phoenix, Arizona, the gringos all say, 'Here comes that fucking Mexican.'"

Of course, the purpose of the joke is to reassure the Mejicanos who remain in Mexico that perhaps they have made the right choice.

Despite numerous studies that show otherwise, the propaganda promoted is that immigrants from Mexico are stealing jobs, undermining wage rates, committing crimes, threatening public health, and straining the already overburdened social welfare and public education system. The historical record, however, clearly indicates that the experience of Mexicans during the 19th and 20th Centuries was the history of adaptation to US labor market needs. Most Mexicans migrated to perform pick and shovel work, generally living in savage conditions, where often only the weeds grew. History also reveals Mexicans struggling to obtain not only equality and justice but basic human rights as well. As such, it is heartbreaking to see resolutions being passed across the country proclaiming that English be the sole official language. During the summer of 2002, for instance, Brown County (Green Bay), Wisconsin's all white board of supervisors passed a proposal for "English only." By late 2006, 28 states had, through legislation or through the initiative process, declared English as their official language. Ironically, many area immigrants are picking up the fruits and vegetables that the local citizens are eating for dinner. Yet, with this type of legislation, we might as well have a display at all points of entry to the country stating, "We do not want you, if you cannot speak English."[18] While the United States is "tearing down

---

[18] Based on 2000 census figures, 28 million of US residents age five and over speak Spanish at home. Spanish-speakers constitute a ratio of more than 1-in-

walls" in other countries, it continues to build sophisticated walls along the 1,933-mile US-Mexican border. More realistically, how much of this action is attributed to national security? How much of this action is a result of Anglo disdain toward Mejicanos? Yet, as some people read this, they rather hear that race and ethnicity play no role in society, and certainly not in the areas of crime and punishment.

Access to Opportunities

Although some people are unwilling to acknowledge it, the effects of race and ethnicity govern the Mexican experience from birth to death. Interestingly, the argument has been made that time is often the best "healer." In the case of Mexicans, however, this has been more of an illusion than a reality. Contrary to the expectation of some Mexicans, World War II did little for Chicanos (Ortego, 2007). Even during the War, Mexicans continued to be viewed as second and third class citizens (Morin, 1966). The fact that 25% of the US military personnel on the infamous Bataan "Death March" were Mexicans, and the fact that Mexicans earned more medals of honor during World War II than any other ethnic or racial group, did little to improve the tensions back home (Morin, 1966). As of 2002, according to the Veterans Affairs, Latinos have been awarded the Medal of Honor 40 times, with most of them awarded to Mexicans. Yet, Sergeant Macario Garcia, from Sugarland, Texas, a recipient of the Congressional Medal of Honor, could not buy a cup of coffee in a restaurant in Richmond, California. In the mid-20th Century, "An Anglo-American chased him out with a baseball bat" (Perales, 1974:79). While some observers like to think the Garcia incident was not an isolated event, in Three Rivers, Texas, a funeral parlor refused to bury Felix Longoria, a Mexican soldier who had been decorated for heroism in World War II.

   Tom Brokaw's widely acclaimed book, *The Greatest Generation* (1998), particularly irritated Mario T. Garcia, a University of California–Santa Barbara Chicano Studies Professor. The book, which told the vivid stories of Americans who weathered the Great Depression and World War II, did not include a single Latino. "It's unconscionable," said Garcia, "for Brokaw, plus his publisher, to have marginalized the Latino experiences in World War II" (Cardenas,

---

10 residents. Among all those who speak Spanish, slightly more than half also reported speaking fluent English.

2002:2; see also Barrios, 2001). Garcia's (and many others) discontent is not new in that Hollywood has failed to portray Latina and Latino heroes. Instead, Hollywood has done an excellent job propagating the image that Mexicans and Latinos in general are violent, unfaithful, and criminal.

In the world of education, the significance of race and ethnicity is also pressing. In the mid-1940s few Mexican children were enrolled in school, and few adults were going to college. The GI bill of 1944 helped millions of people to higher education, but most colleges and universities in the US still excluded Latinas, Latinos, and blacks, or made it almost impossible for Latinas and Latinos to attend. This was, in part, a deliberate policy to bar the sons and daughters of a conquered people, especially migrant workers, from enrolling in school. For instance, one school board stated that "to admit the Mexicans into white schools would be to demoralize the entire system and they will not under any pressure consider such a thing" (Acuna, 1988:157). One school superintendent testified that he considered Mexicans inferior in hygiene, economic abilities, and intelligence and that he would never allow Mexicans in all-white schools, even if the Mexican children met all the required qualifications (Aguirre, 2005). To top it off, Stanford psychologist, Lewis Madison Terman (1906), who is responsible for instituting the IQ test in America, placed the academic imprimatur on prejudice and racism in the early 1930s, giving life to the stereotype that Mexicans could not compete intellectually with Caucasians.

The negativity and ramifications of ethnicity, race, culture, class, geography, and capability is more subtle now, but there are still psychologists and other social scientists offering racist views on intelligence. Not too long ago, Lloyd Dunn cited in 1987 that "While many people are willing to blame the low scores of . . . Mexican-Americans on their poor environmental conditions, few are prepared to face the probability that inherited genetic material is a contributing factor" (Shorris, 1992:156). Crucially, like Terman, this scientific racist thinker is the author of psychological tests used to determine how children should be educated in the US.

Racism also impacts the experiences of Mexican students, limiting educational opportunities and ultimately, chances to succeed. Years after the 1954 *Brown* case, in 1968, "there was no city or town in the United States in which Latino students were educated according to constitutional guarantees of equality of treatment under the law" (Shorris, 1992:104). For poor Latino children, with the majority being Mexican, the situation is even worse, in that to finish high school they need to overcome additional barriers, like history, culture, poverty, psychology, prophecy, language, stereotypes, and the wall.

Even in the 21st Century, with the globalization of knowledge in full swing, Latinos have the lowest ratios of completed education, as noted by Peña and Urbina in "The Dynamics of Education and Globalization in the New Millennium: The Unspoken Realities." Toward the end of the 20th Century, critics observed, "today's entering Latino kindergartner is as likely to go to jail as meet the admission standards of the state universities" (Acuna, 1990:B7). Worse, according to the law of probability in El Barrio, "twelve years after the class picture was taken, more of the children will have died or been killed than graduated from a four-year college" (Shorris, 1992:212). Then, at the turn of the century, statistics released in June 2002 at the League of United Latin American Citizens (LULAC) national convention revealed that the high school dropout rate for Latino children was estimated to be about 33.5%. For migrant children, the situation is even worse, with high school dropout rates estimated as high as 80%. In effect, according to a national study released by the University of Washington in 2002, Mexican immigrant teenagers have the highest school dropout rates among all immigrant groups. In 2005, among youth aged 16 to 24, Latinas and Latinos accounted for 41% of all high school dropouts. In 2005, it was also estimated that 6% of Caucasians aged 16 to 24 were not enrolled in school nor had completed high school, compared with 11% of African Americans and 23% of Latinas and Latinos. Ten years ago, based on 2000 census data, of the nation's 35.3 million Latinas and Latinos, only 11% had received a post-secondary education. For those who do succeed, the educational attainment rates differ substantially by ethnic group, as only 6.2% of those of Mexican origin completed four years of college or more, compared with 18.5% of those of Cuban origin. Educational attainment data for 2009 show that Latinas or Latinos hold only 838,000 of all professional and doctoral degrees (17,538,000), truly a demoralizing and disheartening situation in plain 21st Century. Yet, some people rather argue that race and ethnicity are not contributing factors.

In fact, contrary to *conventional wisdom*, the Mexican community actually benefitted little from the civil rights movement of the 1950s and 1960s. For the Mexican community, even the United Civil Rights Committee, formed in Los Angeles in 1963, refused to admit Mexicans. As such, not until the Cisneros case in 1970 did "a Federal district court . . . [rule] that Mexican Americans constitute an identifiable ethnic minority with a past pattern of discrimination in Corpus Christi, Texas." In effect, it was not until the 1970s that the courts ruled: "we see no reason to believe that ethnic segregation is no less detrimental than racial segregation." Three years later, the US Supreme Court cited that "Negros and Hispanos" suffered identical patterns of prejudice and discrimination, finally officially acknowledging the significance and influence of ethnicity.

Still, little has changed since then, as a series of historical events continue to manipulate, suppress, marginalize, and silence the Mexican community. Cases such as the infamous 1978 *Regents of the University of California v. Bakke* decision have had a far-reaching impact on the relationship between Caucasians and people of color in the United States. In fact, with the passage of Proposition 209, the product of the gradual promotion of a racist intent on the part of the right-wing white elite marks the termination of affirmative action in various places. Consequently, a remedy for discrimination is buried. Further, in addition to Proposition 209, Proposition 187, prohibiting school enrollment to undocumented students and eliminating the provision of all health services to immigrants who are not in the country "legally," has had a dramatic impact not only on Chicanos, but on Latinos in general as well as African Americans. Then, to top it off, in July 2002, under the rationalization of "national security," the government opted to implement additional restrictions on commuter students who study at American universities, hurting thousands of Mexican students.

With statistics already embarrassingly low, the federal court-imposed ban on affirmative action at the University of Texas Law School quickly resulted in a 92% decline in African American admissions and a 74% decline in Latino admissions. Similarly, as a result of the University of California Regents' 1995 decision to do away with racial preferences, African American admissions at Berkeley's Law School dropped from 75 in 1996 to 14 in 1997, while at UCLA's Law School, African American admissions fell from 104 to

21 (Acuna, 1998).[19] In 2010, just 4.5% of students on the UT-Austin campus were African Americans.

As if there was not enough support for the claims of race and ethnic effects, including prejudice, neglect, hardship, and discrimination, a book recently came out in defense of those who claim that discrimination is a thing of the past. In *Increasing Faculty Diversity: The Occupational Choices of High-Achieving Minority Students* (2003), Cole and Barber claim to have discovered that discrimination plays a small, if any, role in limiting the number of minority professors in academe. To them, the crux of the problem is simple: (1) affirmative action; (2) minority students' poor grades, and (3) short supply of minority professors. Such conclusions sound wonderful and exciting to opponents of affirmative action and those, including academic racists, who wish to maintain the status quo, taking the book as confirmation of what they've passionately argued all along. Reality, though, differs. In plain 21st Century, 2001, according to the National Science Foundation, Latinas and Latinos earned only 4.4% of the 40,744 doctorates nationwide. Within the ranks of full-time faculty members, the minority proportion is even lower, as Latinas and Latinos represent less than 3% of all full-time professors. Embarrassingly, the conclusions directly contradict those in *The Shape of the River: Long-Term Consequences of Considering Race in College and University Admissions* (1998) by former Harvard president, Derek Bok, and William Bowen, who strongly endorse affirmative action. In truth, in many ways, one of the biggest battles for Latinos is penetrating the fortress of higher education (Mirande, 2005; Moore, 2007; Noboa, 2005; Pizarro, 2005), a battle that for Mexican women is even more complicated, as vividly illustrated by Romero (1997) and Romero and Margolis (1998, 2000).

In short, the 19th Century was characterized by vicious violence, brutality, lynching, rapes, murders, and hangings of Mexicans, extending into the 20th Century. The 20th Century was plagued with cyclical media blitzkriegs against Mexicans, especially undocumented workers, beginning with reports promoting violence against the "zoot-suiters" of the 1940s; the deportation of "wetbacks" in the 1930s and 1950s; and the constant raids and border violence against Mexicans,

---

[19] Contrary to popular belief, the major beneficiaries of affirmative action were not African Americans and certainly not Latinos, but Caucasian women.

especially undocumented workers, during the 1970s, 1980s, and 1990s. Then, as an extra layer of oppression, cases like Bakke, as Acuna (1998), signaled a return to the fiction of separate but equal doctrine. Political and government forces, assisted by scientific racist thinkers, were trying furiously to turn back the clock of racial history; once again resonating ideological views pronounced by the founding fathers, highly governed by the forces of race and ethnicity. Of course, 21st Century assaults on issues like affirmative action, immigration, and educational attainment have more to do with the political and hegemonic ideology of warriors of culture, immigration, power, and control than with pure scholarship, eloquently explored by Mirande (2005), Moore (2007), and Zuberi and Bonilla-Silva (2008). Lastly, such cases point to the fact that the often hostile reaction and consternation of whites to the entry of Mexicans into the privileged world of the academy is but a modern-day expression of the same historical patterns of social closures. As renowned constitutional scholar Richard Delgado would say, some issues just keep coming back in one form or another.

Social Change: How Far Have We Come?

An historical analysis clearly indicates that the role of race and ethnicity interacts with multiple facets of social life. As such, the history of Chicano-Anglo relations goes beyond the story of cultural conflict, prejudice, and racism. Influential factors, such as economics, are crucial in shaping and re-shaping the social, cultural, political, educational experience, and the distribution of justice. There is in fact evidence of a complex interplay between factors like class, race, and ethnicity, which continues to shape contemporary racial and ethnic politics. For example, as a consequence of economic discrimination and social isolation, upward mobility has been severely limited (Bacon, 2009; Chomsky, 2007). As detailed by Urbina in a forthcoming book, *Latinas y Latinos in the United States: 21st Century Dynamics of Multiculturalism*, although this capitalist country claims that people in the US are all equal under the law, Mexicans are actually in inferior positions.

Acuna (1998:10) points out that while

injustice and inequalities are rationalized as mutations, as anomalies, which will disappear in time because American society provides opportunity for those who want to better themselves . . . a study of history shows quite a different reality, one of exploitation, racism, and in recent years, a closing of opportunity.

Given America's racial history, today we are faced with continuing political repression, and the repression of human rights is ongoing, not only against African Americans and Mexicans, but certainly against Latinas and Latinos in general and other racial minorities.

The Eurocentric cultural arrogance continues to racialize, categorize, stigmatize, intimidate, subordinate, and marginalize the nation's diverse ethnic populations on the basis of race, ethnicity, language, accent, religion, or other cultural identifiers. In effect, while few observers are willing to acknowledge it, dominance over Mexicans continues to be partially based on physical characteristics and ancestry, in combination with various powerful historical forces. By extension, inequalities in the hiring, promotion, and retention of racialized groups in employment, including the private sector, government, and educational institutions, continue. As a whole, the Southwest remains a contested racial and ethnic frontier and the site of continued social, cultural, educational, political, and economic struggle over the extension of the most cherished civil rights, equal opportunities, and justice to all groups, not just white men. In a few words, America continues to be a social world fundamentally structured along class, ethnic, and racial lines, determining where one lives, works, social status, and, above all, the distribution of justice. Unfortunately, national leaders like former President Bill Clinton and President Barack Obama have only recently acknowledged that white prejudice and racism continues to be the nation's chief destructive sword.

As the 20th Century was coming to an end, there were notions that we were finally reaching equality, after 500 years, and as we entered the 21st Century, there were notions that the *playing field* was now even, with race and ethnicity no longer playing a role in everyday life. Reality, though, reveals a much different picture. For instance, isn't it ironic that Los Angeles, the city with the highest population of Mexicans outside Mexico City, is considered to be the most permanently and brutally segregated city in the country. In fact, in some ways, cities like Los Angeles are now more segregated than in

1954 when Brown was decided by the US Supreme Court. At the end of the 20th Century, the rich-poor gap in Los Angeles ranked third behind that of Calcutta and Rio de Janeiro (Acuna, 1998).[20] This, of course, is not limited to L.A., or economics, as Latinos in public schools across the United States were more segregated than they were in the 1950s, a trend extending into 2011. Family income and educational attainment for Latinos remain below the US average, while family size is higher. Mexicans Americans earn far less than Caucasians even after three generations because they receive less schooling than almost all other racial and ethnic groups in the United States, according to a report issued May 22, 2002, by the Public Policy Institute of California, a situation that was worsened by the latest economic crises. Grogger and Trejo (2002), authors of the study, noted that this is especially true in California, where more than 20% of the population is Mexican. The Bureau of Census reported that the 2000 rate (21.2%) of Latinos living in poverty matched the record lows reached in the 1970, even though the median income of Latino/a "households" in 2000 was $33,455, the highest ever recorded up until then. In effect, a total of 7.2 million Latinas and Latinos were poor in 2000, not statistically different from 1999. In particular, Latino males in 1997 earned just 66% as much as Caucasian men, down from 74% in 1980. Similarly, according to a list released on June 26, 2002 at the League of United Latin American Citizens (LULAC) national convention, between 1990 and 1996, Latino women saw their median wage decline by 3%, from $330 to $320 per week. In 1996, Latinas earned 72% as much as Caucasian women and 89% as much as African American women. Of the Latino elderly, 66% earn less than $16,700, and 30% earn less than $8,350 annually. LULAC also announced that since 1994, Latino homeownership has lagged Caucasian by 29%. African American homeownership lagged Caucasian by 27.5% during the same period. In short, contrary to the popular imagination, the percentage of young Latinos living in poverty in the United States has actually increased drastically during the last 40 years. Braun (1991:x) notes that "despite the false appearance of economic growth, the pillars

---

[20] During the 1980s and 1990s, the average Latino taxpayer in Los Angeles was earning approximately $10,000 a year, and African Americans were making about $12,000.

of the American economy have become rotten with neglect," a trend that clearly extends into the 21st Century. Evidently, "segregation creates the structural niche within which a self-perpetuating cycle of minority poverty and deprivation can survive and flourish" (Massey, 1990:350), a widening wage gap that has been driven by prejudice and discrimination against people of color, where still in 2011, Mexicans normally do not get paid what they are worth compared to Anglos. But, to some people, *race and ethnicity play no role!*

In sum, the evidence does not support the old adage that "they all look alike," or the belief that one can "pull oneself up by one's own bootstraps," or the argument that race and ethnicity now plays a minimal role, if any. The status of Mexicans has not changed significantly over the past several decades. In fact, there is clear evidence that the marginal gains made during the 1960s and 1970s are not only evaporating, but in some areas the situation is actually worse. For instance, in the area of crime and punishment, in the 1970s, people of Mexican descent again became bandits, blamed for stealing jobs from Americans. Once again, Mexicans were made outlaws, stereotyped, criminalized, and paid lower wages, all in an effort to demonstrate the pseudo-necessity for greater funding to criminal justice agencies, with an annual budget of 228 billion dollars as of 2007. For the poor, as well as for the industrial working community, the first half of the 1980s became a nightmare. Then, when things appeared to be getting a little better, a series of events, attacks on affirmative action, attacks on bilingual education, attacks on undocumented workers, especially after the September 11, 2001 terrorist attacks on the US, and attacks on the welfare states, started to take place, leading to what appears as the first universal nightmare of the 21st Century for Mexicans and Latinos in general. Of course, for some Mexicans and other Latinos, the nightmare has gotten worse and worse during the last 40-odd years, further escalating with the anti-terrorist and ant-immigrant movements (Bosworth and Flavin, 2007; Corcoran, 2006; Kong, 2010; Morin, 2008; Romero, 2008; Tonry, 2006). As with African Americans, the criminal justice system, to include policing, the judicial system, and the penal system, has relied on strict social control to incapacitate what it sees as a threatening surplus population: at times, for good reason; at times, for bad reason; and at times, for no reason. As an example, I will mention two events that I utilized earlier to illustrate the treatment of African Americans: the incapacitation of gangsters and the criminalization of crack mothers. First, more than ever the government is now making use of whatever social control legislation is in existence to warehouse African Americans and Mexicans, especially those who are defined as "drug dealers," "gangsters" or "terrorists" in jails and prisons (Duran, 2009a, 2009b, 2009c; Urbina, 2008). Second, as noted earlier, traditionally the majority of people under the control of the criminal justice system have been men. However, as with African American women, the rate of Latinas, especially Mexican, under the control of the criminal justice system has increased drastically during the last few years, as documented by Urbina (2008). Like African American women, Latinas are not immune from the evils of crack cocaine in the barrio or the punitive measures of the war on drugs or the war on terror (Diaz-Cotto, 2006; Oboler, 2009; Urbina, 2008). Though, these punitive criminal sanctions are more a reflection of the historical forces of race and ethnicity than the actual danger of crime.

Lastly, for Latino youth, the situation is getting worse (Urbina, 2005, 2007; Urbina and Kreitzer, 2004; Urbina and White, 2009). At the turn of the century, Congressman Ciro D. Rodriguez expressed his disappointment about the treatment of young Latinos in light of a report released on July 18, 2002. The report, *Donde Esta la Justica? A Call to Action on Behalf of Latino and Latina Youth in the U.S. Justice System*, revealed growing disparities in the treatment of Latino youth in the American juvenile and criminal justice systems, disparities later confirmed in various studies (Duran, 2009a, 2009b, 2009c; Rios, 2006). Finally, after experiencing the initial consequences of the Anglo-American conquest involving the loss of lands, racial and ethnic oppression, labor exploitation, and second-class citizenship, people of Mexican extraction continue to face historical barriers in plain 21st Century. In effect, in 2011, Mexicans continue to be strangers in their own land. The Mejicanos, once among the great cultures of the world, now find themselves among the poorest, least educated, politically powerless, and the most despised in a *gabacho* world, where the unspoken mentality is that Mexicans should still be bowing to the *gringos!*

Other Voices

As noted herein, the Latina and Latino population is composed of various ethnic subgroups, constituting a diverse community, multinational in origin, multiethnic, and, by extension, hold diffuse ideologies. In the words of Shorris (1992:444):

> Latinos are the first immigrants and the last, indivisible families of individuals, brown when they are white, poor when they are rich, racist victims of racism, always on the rise while dying in a fall; they are required to forget even as they learn.

Together, Latinos' ethnic differences and Mejicanos' *conquered* legacy distinguishes them from other minorities and parallels the involuntary origins of African Americans, who were subjected to racial slavery for entire centuries. In effect, just as African American ghettos reflect a history of slavery, Jim Crow legislation, and a struggle for civil and economic equality, so the nation's Latino barrios reflect a history of conquest, colonialism, immigration, and a continuous struggle to maintain cultural identity. Today, the various ethnic groups, while they make a smaller percentage of the Latina and Latino population, constitute a significant part of the US population at large and they continue to grow (Urbina, 2007). As of 2007, Puerto Ricans accounted for 9.1% (4,114,701) and Cubans 3.5% (1,608,835) of the Latina/o community, making up the second and third largest ethnic groups within the Latina/o population. As such, as the various Latina/o subgroups as well as other racial groups, like Asian Americans, grow in number, the experiences of these ethnic groups need to be analyzed in order to obtain a more holistic and realistic picture of their experiences in the United States.

Finally, the literature clearly indicates that race (African Americans) and ethnicity (Mexicans) continue to play a significance role in the American society, and, probably, in no other area of social life is it more pressing than in crime and punishment. In effect, as detailed herein, in plain 21st Century incidents between agents of the criminal justice system and the Mexican and African American communities indicate that prejudice and discrimination against Mexicans and African Americans continue, a situation that is not restricted to a given time or place. As various scholars make clear, racialized relations in states like California, Florida, and Texas reverberated along a number of racial and ethnic fault lines and not a simple binary form or along one principal fault, with the allocation of group position in the social hierarchy often being the outcome of both cultural and material considerations (Acuna, 2010; Almaguer, 2008;

Chavez, 2008; De Genova and Ramos-Zayas, 2003; Meeks, 2007). More crucially, prejudice and discrimination against Mexicans and African Americans is not restricted to a particular stage of the criminal justice system, as reported in the following chapters.

DEATH SENTENCE OUTCOMES: A NEW TYPOLOGY

To begin, as noted in Chapter 1, many studies have empirically examined the effects of race and, on a few occasions, ethnicity in capital punishment processing; yet, the focus has been almost exclusively on executions or commutations, to the exclusion of other possible death sentence outcomes. Therefore, a central objective of this book is to provide a quantitative analysis of the various possible capital punishment outcomes in three death penalty states: California, Florida, and Texas. Working from Urbina's (2003a) four-threat perspective and the historical analyses of race and ethnic relations discussed in this chapter, one can in fact gain insight into how the distribution of punishment, death sentence outcomes, in the United States are influenced by race and ethnicity in combination with a number of intertwining historical factors, such as class, country of origin, ideologies, power, economic production (both ideologically and economically), among others, at different points in time and space. In fact, given the various historical facts, events, figures, and illustrations discussed in this book, it is evident that these and other factors led to expected disparities in death sentence outcomes. What follows, then, is the development of specific hypotheses for each racial (African American and Caucasian) and ethnic (Mexican and Cuban) group (using Cuban as a proxy for the purpose of comparison and exploratory analysis) within each state following Urbina's (2003a) four-threat theory, while taking the numerous historical factors into consideration.

The Four-Threat Theory of Death Sentence Outcomes and its
Applicability to Three American States: California, Florida, and Texas

According to Urbina (2003a), each threat (racial/ethnic, political, economic, or social) in and of itself has its own merits, but the final outcome is the product of various historical and intertwining factors operating in a complex fashion, depending on time and space. As the historical record clearly indicates, threatening conditions need to be explored from various angles. Together, after taking the various historical factors, the complex multitude of threatening conditions, and the specific histories of relations between Caucasians, Mexicans, and African Americans into consideration, the four-threat theory of death sentence outcomes suggests two perspectives, for California, Florida, and Texas (in ascending order):

1. African Americans are slightly more likely to be executed than Mexicans, definitely more likely than Cubans, and, certainly more likely than their Caucasian counterparts.
2. African Americans are slightly less likely to be granted a commutation than Mexicans, definitely less likely than Cubans, and certainly less likely than their Caucasian counterparts.

Before stating three additional hypotheses, it is important to emphasize that the four-threat theory of death sentence outcomes leads to competing hypotheses. One could reasonably predict that in California, Florida, and Texas (in ascending order):

1. African Americans are slightly less likely to have their sentence declared unconstitutional by State or US Supreme Court than Mexicans, definitely less likely than Cubans, and certainly less likely than their Caucasian counterparts.
2. African Americans are slightly less likely to have their sentence overturned by an appellate court than Mexicans, definitely less likely than Cubans, and certainly less likely than their Caucasian counterparts.
3. African Americans are slightly less likely to have their conviction and sentence overturned by an appellate court than Mexicans, definitely less likely than Cubans, and certainly less likely than their Caucasian counterparts.

However, given the nature of the decision-making process, the opposite may also be possible. That is, African Americans, Cubans, and Mexicans may be more likely to receive these death sentence outcomes than their Caucasian counterparts due to the high possibility of "errors" during the various stages of the judicial process or lack of resources, which set grounds for overturning the sentence or conviction by the courts, in capital trials involving minority defendants. Given this, it is reasonable to make the following three predictions, that in California, Florida, and Texas (in ascending order):

1. African Americans are slightly more likely to have their sentence declared unconstitutional by State or US Supreme Court than Mexicans, definitely more likely than Cubans, and certainly more likely than their Caucasian counterparts.

2. African Americans are slightly more likely to have their sentence overturned by an appellate court than Mexicans, definitely more likely than Cubans, and certainly more likely than their Caucasian counterparts.

3. African Americans are slightly more likely to have their conviction and sentence overturned by an appellate court than Mexicans, definitely more likely than Cubans, and certainly more likely than their Caucasian counterparts.

As far as legal and extralegal variables, the type of relationships described above are more likely if the offender is an unmarried male, with prior felony convictions. Further, the type of relationships described above will increase as the offender's education decreases, and the number of years under the death sentence increases, as the age of the offender when the offense was committed increases.

Notice that the type of relationships described above are most likely in Texas, an extremely punitive state with a high concentration of Mexicans and a fair number of African Americans but where few Cubans live; less likely in Florida (but only slightly), a punitive state where the majority of Cubans are concentrated and with a high concentration of African Americans but where fewer Mexicans live; and least likely in California, a less punitive state (in terms of executions) with a high concentration of Mexicans and a fair number of African Americans but where fewer Cubans live.

From a racial and ethnic standpoint, notice that the theory suggests that on the punitive sanction scale, African Americans are followed by Mexicans, Cubans, and Caucasians in descending order in each relationship. As such, African Americans stand on the far end of the "harsh side" of the scale, and Caucasians stand on the far end of the "lenient" side of the scale. Actually, African Americans and Mexicans are close by and stand on the harsh side of the punitive sanction scale, while Cubans and Caucasians are close by and stand on the lenient side of the scale. Since Cubans, especially light-skinned elites, do not seem to pose a substantial "threat" to the Anglo majority, it would be expected that their death sentence outcomes to be very close to their Caucasian counterparts.

In sum, in the constant struggle to determine which race and ethnic groups are to survive and prosper, Mexicans and African Americans have been labeled by multitude sources, like the media, politicians, academicians, and authorities, as pathological, uncontrollable brutes, incapable or unwilling to comprehend social limits. In fact, since African Americans and Mexicans are often viewed as pariahs and treated as scapegoats for society's ills and failures, one could reasonably predict that Mexicans and African Americans, often viewed as criminals by nature, will be controlled at whatever cost. As such, one could logically predict that African Americans and Mexicans, the two largest minority groups in the United States, are the two groups most likely to be executed, least likely to be granted a commutation, least likely to have their sentence declared unconstitutional, and least likely to have their sentence or conviction overturned by the courts.

From a transnational standpoint, since African Americans seem to be emerging as a kind of a great global surplus, and viewed as a threat, one could logically predict a disproportionate number of African American males receiving extremely harsh sanctions, as reported in two recent studies by Ruddell and Urbina (2004a, 2007). Similarly, according to Urbina and Smith (2007), since Mexicans have not been considered fully human or fully civilized, rather perceived as a threat, allowing US political leaders and control agents to use punitive sanctions as a "safety valve" when times are tough, one could reasonably state that the Mexican community has suffered and will continue to suffer the most punitive sanctions within the Latino community, placing them next to the African American community.

Finally, one needs to emphasize that by applying such methods of formal social control to threatening individuals, governed more by the influence of race and ethnicity than actual threats, not only segregates them from society but identifies and reinforces the parameters of actions that social control agents find socially rational, legitimate, and thus acceptable. The legal system provides the structural opportunity for control agents, like legislators, governors, judges, and parole boards, to operate interdependently to control individuals defined as threatening by the dominant Caucasian majority, including social control agents and some segments of society at large, again, more of a reflection of the historical influence of race and ethnicity than the realities of crime and safety.

CONCLUSION

The inevitable conclusion is that while the four-threat theory of death sentence outcomes contains competing hypotheses, the rate of harsh sentences in the US has increased drastically in recent years. While some people argue that race and ethnicity no longer play a role crime and punishment, most of those receiving such sanctions have been African American and Mexican males, most of whom are disadvantaged, poor, illiterate, or powerless. In short, based on the proposed "death sentence outcomes typology," death sentence outcomes in the United States will largely depend on the defendant's race, ethnicity, resources, social status, threatening conditions of the day, a multitude of historical factors, the economic and political current of the day, the social control ideology of the day, and the winds of luck. Several years ago, as the war on drugs was gaining momentum, Newman (1985:6) summed up the situation when he noted, "society is not divided into groups of "equals."" More recently, Walker (2010) reports that there is *no one system* of justice, Kappeler and Potter (2004) characterize the criminal justice system as a *dual* system of justice, and Urbina (2004a:256) documents that the "criminal justice system is actually divided into four very distinct systems: one for the poor and defenseless, one for the rich and powerful, one for Euro-Americans, and one for African Americans and Latinos, particularly Mexicans." These are 21st Century observations resonating with 16th Century philosopher Anacharsis that "Laws are just like spider's webs, they will hold the weak and delicate who might be caught in their meshes, but will be torn to pieces by the rich and powerful." In the next chapter, the non-equals thesis will be closely examined by providing a review and examination of prior capital punishment studies which have tested for race/ethnicity effects. That is, a detailed evaluation of the influence of race/ethnicity in various stages of the judicial process is provided to better understand the role of race and ethnicity in the context of crime and capital punishment.

## CHAPTER 3

Death Sentencing and Death Sentence Outcomes: Review of Prior Empirical Studies

"From my earliest years, I have accepted many false opinions as true."

--Rene Descartes

As detailed in the previous chapter, the role of race and ethnicity has historically been significant, influential, and consequential in everyday life and the area of crime and punishment is no exception. In effect, the significance of the dynamics of the relationship between racial-ethnic minorities and the criminal justice system is perhaps no more obvious than in capital punishment, especially death sentence outcomes. This is because, in part, through racial and ethnic policies (whether explicit or implicit), state institutions organize and enforce the racial and ethnic politics of crime and punishment, clearly showing that racial and ethnic discrimination in both death sentencing and death sentence outcomes has deep historical roots. In fact, as detailed in Chapter 2, extra-judicial prejudice and discrimination take place before a defendant even enters a courtroom, as police officers more often aggressively pursue crime in African American and Mexican communities, or prosecutors who, aware of juror's prejudices, are frequently more likely to prosecute minorities for homicide, which, in many states, could possibly carry the death penalty. In this chapter, then, the central objective is to detail prior research studies that have analyzed the role of race-ethnicity in various stages of the death sentencing process, to better understand the influence of race and ethnicity in crime and punishment in its totality.

RACE AND ETHNICITY AND DEATH SENTENCING: PRIOR
RESEARCH

While some critics argue that race and ethnicity no longer play a
significant role in crime and punishment, others argue that race and
ethnicity continue to be influential factors in crime and punishment;
that is, minorities, particularly African Americans and Mexicans, are
still being discriminated by legal decision-makers.   To further
empirically answer this question, then, the primary objective of this
chapter would be to review and analyze the existing academic literature
in its totality. As such, I opted to present the following table, detailing
the effects of race (American American) and ethnicity (Mexican, or
Latino) found in prior death penalty studies, followed by a review and
examination of the cited studies, allowing us to see the role of race and
ethnicity in various stages of the legal process.

Based on these studies, the information is conflicting regarding the
influence of race and ethnicity in crime and punishment. A number of
early studies found race and ethnicity to be influential factors in the
death sentencing judicial process, some studies found no race
differences, and a few found mixed results.

Some early studies found that race was a significant factor in death
sentencing (e.g., Florida Civil Liberties Union, 1964; Partington, 1965;
Wolfgang and Reidel, 1973, 1975).   Wolfgang and Reidel (1973,
1975), for instance, discovered that race was found to be a significant
factor in death sentencing in six Southern states between 1945 and
1965.

Some more recent studies have found similar findings (e.g.,
Baldus, Woodworth, Zuckerman, Weiner, and Broffitt, 1998; Keil and
Vito, 1995; Radelet and Pierce, 1991). Radelet and Pierce's (1991)
multivariate Florida study, for example, showed that for Caucasian
victims, the defendant was six times more likely to get the death
penalty than in cases with African American victims. African American
defendants who killed Euro-Americans were more than twice as likely
to receive the death penalty than Caucasian defendants who killed
Caucasians. Further, African American defendants who killed
Caucasians were 15 times more likely to be sentenced to death than
were African American defendants who killed African Americans.

Table 1: Empirical Studies of Race, Ethnicity, and Death Sentence*

Author (s) & (Year)	Jurisdiction [Time Period Covered]	Race/ Ethnicity [Gender]	Capital Offense	Dependent Variables	Independent Variables	Primary Sample	Main Type of Analysis	Race/ Ethnic Effect?
Brearley (1930)	South Carolina [1920-1926]	African American, Caucasian [male & female]	homicide	convicted	race and sex of victim and offender ...	407 capital cases	percentages	yes
Johnson (1941)	North Carolina, Virginia, Georgia [1930-1934]	African American, Caucasian [?]**	homicide	death sentence	race of offender & victim...	122 death sentences	tabular analysis (no sig. test or measure of association)	mix
Garfinkel (1949)	North Carolina (10 counties) [1930-1940)	African American, Caucasian [male & female]	homicide	charge/conviction/ death sentence/	degree of homicide, race of offender & victim...	821 capital cases	percentages (no sig. tests or measure of association)	mix
Ehrmann (1952)	Mass. (6 counties) [1925-1941]	African American, Caucasian, Chinese [?]	homicide	indictments, convicted	Race, offense, county...	113 capital cases	observation, descriptive statistics	N/A
Bensing & Schroeder (1960)	Cleveland, Ohio [1947-1953]	African American, Caucasian [male & female]	homicide	death sentence/ other	degree of homicide	662 capital cases	tabular analysis (no sig. test or measure of association)	no

Table 1 (Continued): Empirical Studies of Race, Ethnicity, and Death Sentence*

Author (s) & (Year)	Jurisdiction [Time Period Covered]	Race/ Ethnicity [Gender]	Capital Offense	Dependent Variables	Independent Variables	Primary Sample	Main Type of Analysis	Race/ Ethnic Effect?
Bridge & Mosure (1961)	Ohio [1949-1959]	African American, Caucasian [male & female]	homicide	death sentence	race, age, marital status, weapon, education, prior record, birth place, occupation, type of crime, alcohol and narcotics, victim/ offender relationship, mental capacity…	67 death sentences	tabular analysis (no sig. test or measure of association)	no
Wolf (1964)	New Jersey [1937-1961]	African American, Caucasian [male]	homicide	death sentence/life in prison	Felony/non felony, race, age	159 capital cases	test of significance	no
Florida Civil Liberties Union (1964)	Florida [1940-1964]	African American, Caucasian Native American [male & female]	rape	death sentence/ other	race, sex…	285 rape cases	tabular analysis (no sig. test or measure of association)	yes

Table 1 (Continued): Empirical Studies of Race, Ethnicity, and Death Sentence*

Author (s) & (Year)	Jurisdiction [Time Period Covered]	Race/ Ethnicity [Gender]	Capital Offense	Dependent Variables	Independent Variables	Primary Sample	Main Type of Analysis	Race/ Ethnic Effect?
Partington (1965)	Virginia [1908-1963]	African American, Caucasian [male]	rape	death sentence/ other	type of rape, race	2,798 rape cases	frequencies (no sig. test or measure of association)	yes
Judson, Pandell, Owens, McIntosh & Matschull (1969)	California [1958-1966]	Mexican African American, Caucasian Native American, Oriental, other [male & female]	homicide	death sentence/ life sentence	race, age, sex, SES, prior record, occupation, characteristics of offense	238 first degree murder cases. (Mexican N=25)	test of sig., measure of association	no
Kalven (1969)	California (1958-1966)	? [?]	homicide	death penalty	?	238 death-eligible cases	?	N/A
Koeninger (1969)	Texas [1924-1968]	Latin, African American, Caucasian [male & female][a]	Homicide, rape, armed robbery	life in prison/prison term with possible parole	age, birth place, education, occupation, employment, prior record, weapon, drugs…	460 death sentences (Latino/a:N=45)	percentages	yes

Table 1 (Continued): Empirical Studies of Race, Ethnicity, and Death Sentence*

Author (s) & (Year)	Jurisdiction [Time Period Covered]	Race/ Ethnicity [Gender]	Capital Offense	Dependent Variables	Independent Variables	Primary Sample	Main Type of Analysis	Race/ Ethnic Effect?
Wolfgang & Reidel (1973;1975)[b] Note: These results also appeared in Wolfgang (1974) and Wolfgang Riedel (1976)	Alabama, Arkansas, Florida, Georgia, Louisiana, Mississippi, North Carolina, South Carolina, Tennessee, Texas, Virginia [1945-1965]	African American, Caucasian [male]	rape	death sentence/ other	race of defendant & victim, nature of offense, character of defendant & victim, relationship between victim and offender…	3,000 rape cases; various sub-samples	null hypothesis & chi-square statistical test	yes
Kelly (1976)	Oklahoma [March 31, 1974]	Mexican, African American, Caucasian, Native American [?]	homicide	life-death sentence (combined)	age, marital status, education, prior record, type of crime, plea entered, type of attorney…	356 capital cases (Mexican N=?)	multiple regression	no Mexican: slight (-) effect

Table 1 (Continued): Empirical Studies of Race, Ethnicity, and Death Sentence*

Author (s) & (Year)	Jurisdiction [Time Period Covered]	Race/ Ethnicity [Gender]	Capital Offense	Dependent Variables	Independent Variables	Primary Sample	Main Type of Analysis	Race/ Ethnic Effect?
Riedel (1976)	United States (28 states); region; Florida, Georgia, Texas, Louisiana, North Carolina, Oklahoma, [December 31, 1971; June 29, 1972 to January 2, 1976; June 29, 1972 to August 1975]	Caucasian/ non-Caucasian [?]	homicide	death sentence	race, age, employment, marital status, mental illness, prior record, victim characteristics, circumstances of offense & trial…	493 pre-*Furman* cases & 376 post-*Furman* cases; 142 post-*Furman* capital cases	chi-square	yes
Zimring, Eigen, & O'Malley (1976)	Philadelphia [1970]	African American, Caucasian [?]	homicide	life in prison/death sentence	race of offender & victim…	204 capital cases	Fisher's Exact Test	yes
Lewis & Peoples (1978)	Florida [February to June 1977]	African American, Caucasian, other [male]	homicide	death row	multiple demographic, legal & extra legal variables	83 death row inmates	interviews	N/A

Table 1 (Continued): Empirical Studies of Race, Ethnicity, and Death Sentence*

Author (s) & (Year)	Jurisdiction [Time Period Covered]	Race/ Ethnicity [Gender]	Capital Offense	Dependent Variables	Independent Variables	Primary Sample	Main Type of Analysis	Race/ Ethnic Effect?
Boris (1979)	large northeastern industrial city [1972]	African America, Caucasian [?]	homicide	dismissed or prosecuted at preliminary hearing	race of offender & victim, occupation, education, age & # of arrests and convictions of offender & victim…	383 capital cases	multiple regression	no
Arkin (1980)	Dade County, Florida [1973-1976]	African American, Caucasian [probably male & female]	homicide	conviction, sentence length, death sentence	race of offender & victim, type of felony…	350 capital cases	percentages	mix
Baldus, Pulaski, Woodworth & Kyle (1980)	California [pre-*Furman* period]	Mexican, African American, Caucasian, Native American [?]	homicide	life sentence, death sentence (violation of state law and/or 8th Amendment)	# of victims, criminal record, motive, mitigating factors, persons wounded, alcohol & drug use, weapon, employment…	239 death penalty cases (Mexican N=26)	multiple regression analysis	no (Mexican: no effect)

Table 1 (Continued): Empirical Studies of Race, Ethnicity, and Death Sentence*

Author (s) & (Year)	Jurisdiction [Time Period Covered]	Race/ Ethnicity [Gender]	Capital Offense	Dependent Variables	Independent Variables	Primary Sample	Main Type of Analysis	Race/ Ethnic Effect?
Bowers & Pierce (1980)	Florida, Texas, Ohio, Georgia [1972-1977]	African American, Caucasian [male & female]	homicide	death sentence	race of offender & victim, jurisdiction, 7 aggravating & mitigating factors…	various sub-samples of capital cases	percentages, probabilities	yes
Radelet (1981)	Florida (20 counties) [1976-1977]	African American, Caucasian [?]	homicide	death sentence	victim/defendant relationship, race of victim & defendant	637 capital cases	chi-square, log-linear analysis	no
Thompson & Zimgraff (1981)	one southeastern state [1969,1973,1977]	Caucasian, non-Caucasian [male]	robbery	sentence length	race, class, education, occupation, previous incarcerations, total # of sentence received…	1,194 cases	multivariate analysis	yes

Table 1 (Continued): Empirical Studies of Race, Ethnicity, and Death Sentence*

Author (s) & (Year)	Jurisdiction [Time Period Covered]	Race/ Ethnicity [Gender]	Capital Offense	Dependent Variables	Independent Variables	Primary Sample	Main Type of Analysis	Race/ Ethnic Effect?
Zeisel (1981)	Florida [1973-1980]	African American, Caucasian [probably male & female]	homicide	death sentence	race of offender & victim	228 capital cases	percentages	yes
Foley & Powell (1982)	Florida (21 counties) [1972-1978]	African American, Caucasian, other [male & female]	homicide	trial, jury recommendation, judge's decision	age, sex, education, occupation, prior convictions…	829 capital cases	linear analysis of covariance	yes
Jacoby & Paternoster (1982)	South Carolina [June 8, 1977 to November 30,1979]	African American, Caucasian [?]	homicide	death sentence requests by prosecutor	race of victim…	205 capital cases	proportions, ratios	yes
Baldus, Pulaski & Woodworth (1983)	Georgia [January 1,1970 to September 29, 1972; March 28, 1973 to June 30,1978]	African American, Caucasian [male & female]	homicide	assessment of degree of comparative excessiveness in Georgia's death-sentencing system	aggravating & mitigating factors	130 pre-*Furman* capital cases; 594 post-*Furman* capital cases; focused on 68 death sentences	multiple regression analysis; logistic regression	yes

Table 1 (Continued): Empirical Studies of Race, Ethnicity, and Death Sentence*

Author (s) & (Year)	Jurisdiction [Time Period Covered]	Race/ Ethnicity [Gender]	Capital Offense	Dependent Variables	Independent Variables	Primary Sample	Main Type of Analysis	Race/ Ethnic Effect?
Bowers (1983)	Florida [1976-1977]	African American, Caucasian [?]	homicide	homicide indictment	race, region, type of attorney, aggravating factors...	508 capital case	multiple regression	yes
Paternoster (1983)	South Carolina [June 8, 1977 to December 31, 1981]	African American, Caucasian [?]	homicide	death sentence requests by prosecutor	race of offender & victim, # of offenders & victims, victim/offender relationship, sex & age of victim, weapon...	321 capital cases	ratios, logit analysis..	yes
Radelet & Vandiver (1983)	Florida [January 1, 1973 to December 31,1981]	African American, Caucasian [male]	homicide, rape	upholding death sentence by state Supreme Court (affirmed or non-affirmed)	race of defendant & victim, victim's sex, # of victims, type of attorney...	145 direct appeal decision	multiple regression	yes

Table 1 (Continued): Empirical Studies of Race, Ethnicity, and Death Sentence*

Author (s) & (Year)	Jurisdiction [Time Period Covered]	Race/ Ethnicity [Gender]	Capital Offense	Dependent Variables	Independent Variables	Primary Sample	Main Type of Analysis	Race/ Ethnic Effect?
Gross & Mauro (1984; 1989) Note: These results are part of the same study.	Arkansas, Florida, Georgia, Illinois, Mississippi, North Carolina, Oklahoma, Virginia [January 1, 1976 to December 31, 1980]	African American, Caucasian [male & female]	homicide	death sentence	race of offender & victim, nature of felony, relationship to victim, # of victims, weapon, location, aggravation…	379 death sentences (various sub-samples)	tabulations, multiple logistic regression analysis	yes (race effect in all eight states)
Paternoster (1984)	South Carolina [June 8, 1977to December 31, 1981]	African American, Caucasian [?]	homicide	death sentence requests by prosecutor	7 statutory aggravating circumstances…	300 capital cases	descriptive statistics, probit analysis	yes
Barnett (1985)	Georgia [between March 28, 1973 & June 30, 1978	African American, Caucasian [probably male & female]	homicide	death sentence	region, prior record, nature of crime, race of victim & defendant…	606 capital cases	descriptive statistics, s-values (using Barnett's scale)	no

Table 1 (Continued): Empirical Studies of Race, Ethnicity, and Death Sentence*

Author (s) & (Year)	Jurisdiction [Time Period Covered]	Race/ Ethnicity [Gender]	Capital Offense	Dependent Variables	Independent Variables	Primary Sample	Main Type of Analysis	Race/ Ethnic Effect?
Baldus, Woodworth, & Pulaski (1985)	Georgia[between March 28, 1973& June 30, 1987]	African American, Caucasian [male & female]	homicide	death sentence requests by prosecutor, death sentence	race of defendant & victim, mitigating an aggravating factors, status of defendant …	606 capital cases	regression analysis (using Barnett's scale)	no
Liebman (1985)	Georgia [1973-1985]	? [?]	homicide	death sentence: disproportionate or excessive	aggravating & mitigating factors…	133 capital cases	case comparison	N/A/
Radelet & Pierce (1985)	Florida [32 counties] [1973-1977]	African American, Caucasian [male & female]	homicide	upgraded/down graded: felony charges/ non-felony charges	race, sex, & age of victim, relationship to victim, age, # of victims, weapon…	1,017 capital cases	chi-square, logistic regression	yes

Table 1 (Continued): Empirical Studies of Race, Ethnicity, and Death Sentence*

Author (s) & (Year)	Jurisdiction [Time Period Covered]	Race/ Ethnicity [Gender]	Capital Offense	Dependent Variables	Independent Variables	Primary Sample	Main Type of Analysis	Race/ Ethnic Effect?
Foley (1987)	Florida (21 counties) [1972-1978]	African American, Caucasian [male & female]	homicide	death sentence	race & sex of victim & defendant, age, education, prior record, relationship to victim, # of victims, accomplices, county, attorney, weapon, additional offenses…	829 capital cases	chi-square, multiple analysis of covariance	yes
Klein & colleagues (1987)	Los Angeles County [August 1977-January 1986]	? [?]	homicide	death sentence/ life without possibility of parole	sex factors related to circumstances of crime & victim	874 death eligible cases	logistic regression	mix

Table 1 (Continued): Empirical Studies of Race, Ethnicity, and Death Sentence*

Author (s) & (Year)	Jurisdiction [Time Period Covered]	Race/ Ethnicity [Gender]	Capital Offense	Dependent Variables	Independent Variables	Primary Sample	Main Type of Analysis	Race/ Ethnic Effect?
Smith (1987)	Louisiana [October 1, 1976 to December 31, 1982]	African American, Caucasian [male]	homicide	death sentence	race & sex of victim, # of victims, weapon, victim/ offender relationship, location of offense	504 death eligible cases	logistic regression	yes
Ekland-Olson (1988)	Texas [February 1974 to December , 1983]	Latino/a, African American, Caucasian [male & female]	homicide	death sentence	race of victim & offender, sex of offender & victim, age, relationship to victim….	1,148 capital cases (Latino/a:N=~280)	multivariate analysis	mix

Table 1 (Continued): Empirical Studies of Race, Ethnicity, and Death Sentence*

Author (s) & (Year)	Jurisdiction [Time Period Covered]	Race/ Ethnicity [Gender]	Capital Offense	Dependent Variables	Independent Variables	Primary Sample	Main Type of Analysis	Race/ Ethnic Effect?
Paternoster & Kazyaka (1988)	South Carolina [June 8, 1977 to December 31, 1981]	African American, Caucasian [?]	homicide	death sentence requests by prosecutor/death sentence imposed (convictions)	race of offender and victim, prior record, # of victims, # of offenders, victim-offender relationship, # of mitigating & aggravating factors, weapon...	302 death-eligible cases	logistic regression	yes
Vito & Keil (1988)	Kentucky [December 22, 1976 to October 1, 1986]	African American, Caucasian [?]	homicide	death sentence requests by prosecutor	race of victim, 8 aggravating factors	458 capital cases	multivariate analysis	yes

Table 1 (Continued): Empirical Studies of Race, Ethnicity, and Death Sentence*

Author (s) & (Year)	Jurisdiction [Time Period Covered]	Race/ Ethnicity [Gender]	Capital Offense	Dependent Variables	Independent Variables	Primary Sample	Main Type of Analysis	Race/ Ethnic Effect?
Heilburn, Foster & Golden (1989)	Georgia [1974-1987]	African American, Caucasian [male]	homicide	life sentence/death sentence	age, education, school problems, running away from home, problems with police, employment, marital difficulties, fighting, vagrancy, lying…	243 capital cases	ANOVA	no
Keil & Vito (1989)	Kentucky [December 22, 1976 to October 1, 1986]	African American, Caucasian [?]	homicide	death sentence requests by prosecutor/death sentence	prior convictions, multiple victims, sex of victims, race of offender & victim…	466 capital cases	logit regression	yes
Balus, Woodworth & Pulaski (1990) Study 1: PRS[c]	Georgia [between 1973 & 1978]	African American, Caucasian [male & female]	homicide	death sentence requests by prosecutor/ Life sentence/death sentence	over 150 aggravating & mitigating factors	156 pre-*Furman* cases & 594 post-*Furman* capital cases	multivariate analysis	yes

Table 1 (Continued): Empirical Studies of Race, Ethnicity, and Death Sentence*

Author (s) & (Year)	Jurisdiction [Time Period Covered]	Race/ Ethnicity [Gender]	Capital Offense	Dependent Variables	Independent Variables	Primary Sample	Main Type of Analysis	Race/ Ethnic Effect?
Balus, Woodworth & Pulaski (1990) Study 2:CSS	Georgia [between 1973 & 1978]	African American, Caucasian [male & female]	homicide	grand-jury indictment, plea barging by prosecutor, jury guilt trial decisions, prosecutorial decision to seek death sentence after guilty trial, jury penalty-trial sentencing decisions	Over 230 variables	1,066 capital cases	multivariate analysis	yes
Keil & Vito (1990)	Kentucky [December 22, 1976 to October 1, 1986]	African American, Caucasian [probably male & female]	homicide	death sentence requests by prosecutor/death sentence	nature of crime, prior records, relationship to victim….	401 capital cases	cross-tabulation analysis, logit analysis	yes

Table 1 (Continued): Empirical Studies of Race, Ethnicity, and Death Sentence*

Author (s) & (Year)	Jurisdiction [Time Period Covered]	Race/ Ethnicity [Gender]	Capital Offense	Dependent Variables	Independent Variables	Primary Sample	Main Type of Analysis	Race/ Ethnic Effect?
Karns & Weinberg (1991)	Penn. [1978-1990]	Latino/a, African American, Caucasian, Asian, other [male & female]	homicide	death sentence requests by prosecutor, life imprisonment, death sentence	race of victim & offender, gender of offender & victim, aggravating factors…	1,174 capital cases (Latino/a:N= 64)	Cramer's V	mix
Klein & Rolph (1991)	California [1977-1984]	Latino, African American, Caucasian [?]	homicide	death sentence	15 variables related to defendant, victim & circumstances of offense	496 jury penalty cases (Latino: N=?)	cluster and CART analysis	no
Radelet & Pierce (1991)	Florida [1976-1987]	African American, Caucasian [probably male & female][d]	homicide	death sentence	race, age, sex, county and date of crime, weapon	10,142 homicide cases & 368 death sentences	logistic regression	yes

Table 1 (Continued): Empirical Studies of Race, Ethnicity, and Death Sentence*

Author (s) & (Year)	Jurisdiction [Time Period Covered]	Race/ Ethnicity [Gender]	Capital Offense	Dependent Variables	Independent Variables	Primary Sample	Main Type of Analysis	Race/ Ethnic Effect?
Marquart, Ekland-Olson & Sorensen (1994)	Texas [various time frames between 1923-1988]	Latino/a, African American, Caucasian, other [male & female]	rape, homicide, arm robbery	death sentence/life imprisonment	race, age, sex of victim & offender, education, occupation…	various subsamples of 900-plus death sentence (Latino/a N= various subsamples)	uncertainly coefficient, Somer's D^2, likelihood ratio chi-square	mix
Sorensen & Wallace (1995)	Missouri [1977-1991]	African American, Caucasian [male & female]	homicide	death sentence	offender & victim racial characteristics, aggravation…	194 capital cases	logistic regression	no
Keil & Vito (1995)	Kentucky [1976-1991]	African American, Caucasian [?]	homicide	death sentence	6 characteristics of defendant & circumstances of offense	577 death eligible cases	logistic regression	yes

Table 1 (Continued): Empirical Studies of Race, Ethnicity, and Death Sentence*

Author (s) & (Year)	Jurisdiction [Time Period Covered]	Race/ Ethnicity [Gender]	Capital Offense	Dependent Variables	Independent Variables	Primary Sample	Main Type of Analysis	Race/ Ethnic Effect?
Rohrlich & Tulsky (1996)	Los Angeles [1990-1994]	Latino, African American, Caucasian, other [probably male & female]	homicide	death sentence	race of defendant & victim... (no controls for the death-eligibility of cases or through relative criminal culpability)	9,442 capital cases processed through L.A. courts (Latino/a: N=?)	logistic regression (not specifically stated, it appears that logistic regression was used)	no
Thomson (1997)	Arizona [1982-1991]	Latino, African American, Caucasian, Asian, Native American [?]	homicide	death sentence	race/ethnicity of victim & offender	2,028 capital cases (Latino: N=417)	tabular analysis (no. sig tests or measure of association)	mix

Table 1 (Continued): Empirical Studies of Race, Ethnicity, and Death Sentence*

Author (s) & (Year)	Jurisdiction [Time Period Covered]	Race/ Ethnicity [Gender]	Capital Offense	Dependent Variables	Independent Variables	Primary Sample	Main Type of Analysis	Race/ Ethnic Effect?
Baldus, Woodworth, Zucherman, Weiner & Broffitt (1998)	Philadelphia [1983-1993]	Latino, African American, Caucasian, Asian [?]	homicide	death sentence/life sentence	race & socio economic status of defendant & victim, statutory aggravating & mitigating circumstances, level of culpability	various subsamples: 118 death sentence, 230 lifesentence,176 non-penalty trial cases[e]	logistic regression	yes
Aguirre, Davin, Baker & Lee (1999)	California [1989-1994]	Latino, African American, Caucasian [probably only male]	homicide	life in prison with no parole/death sentence	race/ethnicity, age, sex, victim impact evidence, jury was "death qualified", murder in combination with various felonies & race of defendant & victim	151 capital cases (Latino: N=~22)	cross-tabulation analysis	yes (Latino: moderate positive effect)

Table 1 (Continued): Empirical Studies of Race, Ethnicity, and Death Sentence*

Author (s) & (Year)	Jurisdiction [Time Period Covered]	Race/ Ethnicity [Gender]	Capital Offense	Dependent Variables	Independent Variables	Primary Sample	Main Type of Analysis	Race/ Ethnic Effect?
Brock, Cohen & Sorensen (2000)	Texas: Dallas County (Dallas), Tarrant County (Fort Worth), Harris County (Houston), & Bexas County (San Antonio) [1980-1996]	Latino, African American, Caucasian [male & female]	homicide	death sentence	race/ethnicity, victim race, offender/victim race, seriousness . . .	28,286 homicide arrests; 583 death sentences	multivariate analysis, z-tests	yes
Baldus, Woodworth, Grosso & Christ (2002)	Nebraska [1973-1999]	Caucasian, minority (African American & Latino combined) [male & female]	homicide	charging & sentencing: death sentence waived by plea, death-eligible cases advancing to penalty trial with state seeking a death sentence, death sentences are imposed in a penalty trial . . .	race, socioeconomic status, jurisdiction, statutory aggravating & mitigating circumstances . . .	185 prosecutions in 175 death-eligible capital cases	logistic regression	No

Table 1 (Continued): Empirical Studies of Race, Ethnicity, and Death Sentence*

Author (s) & (Year)	Jurisdiction [Time Period Covered]	Race/ Ethnicity [Gender]	Capital Offense	Dependent Variables	Independent Variables	Primary Sample	Main Type of Analysis	Race/ Ethnic Effect?
Berk, Li & Hickman (2005)	Maryland [July 1, 1978-Decmber 31, 1999]	Caucasian, African American [probably male & female]	homicide	initial decision to seek death penalty, death penalty	race, race of victim, jurisdiction, prior record . . .	1,061 capital cases	classification and regression trees (CARTs), random forests	mix, no
Paternoster & Brame (2008)	Maryland [July 1, 1978-Decmber 31, 1999]	African American, Caucasian [probably male & female]	homicide	death sentence	race, victim race (93 background characteristics	1,130 death-eligible cases	TWANG (Toolkit for Analysis for Nonequivalent Groups), propensity score models	Yes

Table 1 (Continued): Empirical Studies of Race, Ethnicity, and Death Sentence*

Author (s) & (Year)	Jurisdiction [Time Period Covered]	Race/ Ethnicity [Gender]	Capital Offense	Dependent Variables	Independent Variables	Primary Sample	Main Type of Analysis	Race/ Ethnic Effect?
Patemoster & Brame (2008)	Maryland [July 1, 1978-December 31, 1999]	African American, Caucasian [probably male & female]	homicide	death sentence	race, victim race (93 background characteristics	1,130 death-eligible cases	TWANG (Toolkit for Analysis for Nonequivalent Groups), propensity score models	Yes
Phillips (2008)	Texas: Harris County [1992-1999]	Latino, African American, Caucasian, Asian [male & female]	homicide	DA decision to pursue a death trial, jury's decision to impose a death sentence	race, ethnicity, victim race, legal dimensions of case, defendant social characteristics	504 capital cases	multivariate analysis, logistic regression	Latinos: no African American: yes

Overall Summary: Yes: 34   No: 15   Mixed: 9   NA: 4

* Some studies were included even though the data were not analyzed for processing points or outcomes but were relevant to ethnicity/race effects; each of these studies analyzed variables important to understanding potential sources of differential treatment, but they did not analyze data directly regarding decision-making outcomes.

** ? = unable to determine from text.

a According to Koeninger (1969:135), "most persons here classified as 'Latin' are white Texas of Mexican extraction."

b The 1975 study is an analysis of a subset of the data in the 1973 study. The two are treated as a single study.

c The authors present findings two studies: Procedural Reform Study (PRS) and Charging and Sentencing Study (CSS).

d Latinos were coded with Caucasians.

e Latinos: 70 (47%) of all death-eligible offenders; 34 (49%) of white offenders who advanced to jury penalty trial.

Baldus et al. (1998:1676) found that the race and ethnic differences in death sentencing in Philadelphia were substantial, consistent, and statistically significant, or nearly so; African American defendants were "treated more punitively than other defendants" on average, especially in cases involving Caucasian victims, in death sentencing decisions.[21]

At the turn of the century, Brock, Cohen, and Sorensen (2000:68) found that in Texas:

> Killers of whites are always over-represented among death sentences, but the extent of over-representation depended on the race of the offender. While the ratio was one and a half to one for Whites who killed Whites, the ratio for Hispanic who killed Whites was nearly two and a half to one and exceeding four to one for Blacks who killed Whites. In contrast, killers of minorities were under-presented, especially if the killer was White. Killers of Hispanics were over-represented among Blacks, but severely under-represented when the offenders were also Hispanic.

The authors then conclude that in Texas, sometimes referred to as the "capitol of capital punishment," "prospective candidates for execution are screened and selected to a large extent on the basis of race" (Brock,

---

[21] Baldus et al.'s (1998:1717-1718) analysis of outcomes of prosecutorial and jury decision making show that

> in both the analysis of all jury penalty trials and the analysis of the jury weighting decisions, the contrast in the treatment of these two groups [Caucasians and Latinos] versus the black defendants was more substantial for the Hispanic white defendants than it was for the non-Hispanic white defendants.

Baldus at el. (1998:1718), however, also found that

> the race-of-victim effect estimated in an analysis of jury death sentencing for failure to find mitigation after finding statutory aggregation suggest comparable levels of treatment of defendants whose victims are non-Hispanic whites and defendants whose victims are Hispanic whites.

Cohen, and Sorensen, 2000:70). More recently, Paternoster and Brame, two of the most renowned experts in capital punishment research, found that African Americans who kill Caucasians face a greater risk being sentenced to death than other defendants. According to Paternoster and Brame (2008:991), "our analysis of the Maryland death penalty data leads us to the conclusion that black defendants who kill white victims (BD-WV) are more likely to receive adverse treatment than similarly situated non-BD-WV defendants." In another recent study, Phillips (2008) analyzes whether race of offender influence the District Attorney's decision to seek a death penalty trial, or the jury's decision to impose a death sentence on defendants indicted for homicide in Harris County (Houston), Texas between 1992 and 1999. Crucially, while Texas has earned an international reputation for executions, Harris County is arguably the capitol of capital punishment in Texas. Phillips (2008:834, 837) reports that "the odds of a death trial are 1.75 times higher against black defendants than white defendants, but drop to 1.49 times higher for a death sentence," concluding that "the bottom line is clear: race continues to shape case outcomes decades after the Supreme Court declared in *Gregg v. Georgia* (1976) that guided discretion would eliminate arbitrariness in the administration of capital punishment."

A number of other studies, though, have not found race and ethnicity to be influential in death sentencing. Among the studies that did not find race or ethnic differences in death sentencing are a number of early studies (e.g., Bensing and Schroeder, 1960; Bridge and Mosure, 1961; Judson, Pandell, Owens, McIntosh, and Matschull, 1969; Wolf, 1964). Judson et al. (1969), for instance, found that the race variable was statistically non-significant in death sentencing in California for the years 1958 to 1966.

Studies by Klein and Rolph (1991) and Rohrlich and Tulsky (1996) did not find race effects to be statistically significant. According to Sorensen and Wallace (1995), when one takes into consideration offender and victim racial characteristics, no overall statistically significant racial effects were found in the final stage of the capital process: death sentencing. For cases involving race of offender and victim and level of aggravation, cases were not significantly more likely to result in death sentences. Caucasian defendants were not significantly more likely to receive a death sentence than African

American defendants. In cases involving Caucasian victims, cases were not significantly more likely to result in death sentencing.

A number of studies have reported mixed results regarding the role of race and ethnicity in death sentencing. Among these studies are a number of early studies (e.g., Garfinkel, 1949; Johnson, 1941). Garfinkel (1949), for instance, found no race difference between African American killers as a group and Caucasian killers as a group, but when the defendant was African American and his victim was Caucasian, the defendant was sentenced to death in 43% of the cases. If the defendant was Caucasian and the victim was African American, the defendant ran no such risk of being sentenced to death.

Klein et al. (1987) did not find a statistically significant relationship for the race of the defendant, but the variable for the race of the victim did enter at the .01 level of significance. Thomson (1997) found that Caucasian offenders are about one and one-half times as likely to receive death sentences as minority offenders (4.7% versus 3.3%). Death sentencing rates were similar for African American and Latino offenders (3.7% and 3.6%). Overall, "white homicide offenders in Arizona are more likely to receive death sentences than minority homicide offenders" (Thomson, 1997:71-72), but Caucasian-victim homicides, especially involving minority offenders, were much more likely to result in death sentences than minority-victim homicides.

Marquart et al. (1994) did not find a statistically significant race difference between death sentences and life sentences between 1923 and 1971 in Texas, but found a statistically significant race of offender and race of victim difference between death sentences and life sentences between 1942 and 1971 for convicted murderers. In rape cases, the most powerful predictor of a death sentence was the combination of the racial or ethnic characteristics of the victim and the offender. "The probability that black offenders would be sentenced to death for rape remain between five and ten times the probability for white offenders" from 1925 to 1965, according to Marquart et al. (1994:54). When an African American male raped a Caucasian female, the case was approximately 35 times more likely to result in a death sentence than a prison sentence. As for ethnic effects, if a Latino male raped a Caucasian female, the comparative chances were about two to one.

Finally, Marquart et al. (1994) found that between 1974 and 1988, 80% of the convicted Anglo defendants and 79% of the convicted African American defendants were sentenced to die. Latino offenders were sentenced to death at lower rates, 63%. Cases involving African

American offenders and Caucasian victims were also associated with a higher likelihood of a death sentence, but the initially statistically significant effect disappeared once type of offense, presence of co-defendants, number of victims, and age and sex of the victim were controlled, the next topic of discussion.

First, while few researchers have included sex as a control variable in their analysis, in part due to the small number of females under the sentence of death in comparison to males, prior findings show that death sentencing is gendered. For instance, data for 1955 to 1958 show that there was a "greater reluctance to apply the death sentence to women than to men" (Bridge and Mosure, 1961:61). Marquart et al. (1994) found that while nearly 15% of the individuals charged with first-degree murder were women, no females were admitted under the sentence of death in Texas during the period under study. Further, Marquart et al. (1994) found that between 1974 and 1988, males were more likely to be sentenced to death than females, 77% compared with 55%, but the difference was not statistically significant.

Another variable of controversy is the age of the offender when the act was committed. An early study by Bridge and Mosure (1961) found that the highest percentage (22.4%) of those sentenced to death were the 25 to 29 year-old cohort. The average age of the 67 admitted under death sentences was 33 years. Marquart et al. (1994) found a statistically significant age difference between death sentences and life sentences between 1923 and 1971 for convicted murderers, but not between 1942 and 1971. Marquart et al. (1994) also claim that, between 1974 and 1988, older offenders were sentenced to death in 80% of the cases, compared to 73% in the younger category, and the difference was statistically significant.

Marital status is also a variable in question. Bridge and Mosure (1961) found that 70% of the individuals under study were not married. Marquart et al. (1994) found that between 1923 and 1972 in approximately two-thirds of the cases, the defendant was single or divorced at the time of the offense.

Another variable that has been questioned and continues to create controversy in the criminal justice system is the level of education of the offender. Bridge and Mosure (1961) found that the average duration of formal education completed was seven and a half years. In fact, while all were declared legally sane at the time of their crimes, intelligence scores ranged from 49 to 120. Marquart et al.'s (1994) findings showed that between 1923 and 1972, most of the offenders were uneducated, and found a statistically significant education difference between death sentences and life sentences between 1941 and 1971 for convicted murderers. However, between 1974 and 1988, Marquart et al. (1994) found that the level of education made no statistically significant difference in the probability of a death sentence.[22]

Lastly, another factor of debate, especially between liberal and conservative legal scholars and policy-makers, is whether the defendant had a criminal history when the crime was committed and its future implications, like stability and recidivism. Marquart et al.'s (1994) Texas study found that between 1923 and 1972, most of the offenders did not have a prior prison record. Specifically, Marquart et al. (1994) found a statistically significant criminal history (property convictions and prison) difference between death sentences and life sentences between 1941 and 1971 for convicted murderers. Though, between 1974 and 1988 the number of prior arrests alone made little difference. Overall, when there was some evidence of past criminal activity, the probability of a death sentence increased. In effect, the authors claim that the variable most likely to increase this probability was offender's prior prison record, followed by cases involving multiple victims. In both cases, the effect was statistically significant.

In sum, while the death sentencing results are conflicting, there is an indication that early discrimination is not remedied at the death sentencing stage, as shown by recent studies, using highly advanced statistical models.[23] As shown in Table 1, young African American and

---

[22] In a related issue, Marquart et al. (1994) found a statistically significant occupational difference between death sentences and life sentences between 1941 and 1971 for convicted murderers. In addition, Marquart et al. (1994:172) claims that data from 1974 to 1988 show that "contrary to the idea that only the poor are sentenced to die, 'professionals' were more likely to received the death sentence, once convicted, than were offenders whose occupation was categorized as 'other'"–82% compared with 76% (likelihood ratio chi-square=.4655).

[23] Bentele (1985:591), who conducted a qualitative comparison of 85 homicide cases of defendants who were sentenced to life in prison and defendants who were sentenced to death by the Georgia Supreme Court in 1981, concluded that "Georgia's death row population is no more

Latino men remain heavily over-represented among those receiving death sentences, clearly showing that race and ethnicity continue to play a major role in crime and punishment. Together, empirical studies dating back to the 1930s indicate that, all things being equal, racial minorities, especially African Americans and Latinos, are disproportionately more likely to receive the death sentence for homicide than their Caucasian counterparts; again, all things considered, race and ethnicity continue to be influential factors in the legal process. As the threat theory suggests, the implication could be that the results are due, in part, to the support of the rich and powerful, combined with powerful historical forces and the complicated history of race and ethnic relations. As such, one could reasonably predict that the "get tough" movement has given some individuals the worst of both worlds: punishment (death sentencing) without due process. To better understand the influence of race and ethnicity in capital punishment in American over time, an analysis of prior death sentencing outcomes studies follows.

DEATH SENTENCE OUTCOMES: PRIOR RESEARCH

While there is extensive literature testing the influence of race/ethnicity in death sentencing, there are only a few empirical studies that have given close attention to the influence of race and ethnicity in death sentence outcomes. The studies that have been conducted have focused exclusively on commutations and/or executions. As in the previous section, the following table contains information from prior empirical studies that have tested for the role of race/ethnicity in final outcomes, followed by a review and examination of the referenced studies, allow us to see the effects of race/ethnicity in various stages of the legal process. However, given the fact that early studies rarely use statistical significance tests and contain various theoretical or statistical limitations, they will not be discussed in detail.

---

fairly selected now than the one 'freakishly' chosen in *Furman*." That is,

> the new law has failed to bring about fair and evenhanded imposition of sentences. The safeguards that the *Gregg* plurality relied on to avoid discriminatory and freakish application of the penalty have not performed that function (Bentele, 1985:638).

Table 2: Empirical Studies of Race, Ethnicity, and Death Sentence Outcomes

Author(s) & (year)	Jurisdiction [Time Period Covered]	Race/Ethnicity [Gender]	Capital Offense	Dependent Variable	Independent Variables	Primary Sample	Main Type of Analysis	Race/ Ethnic effect?
Mangum (1940)	Florida, Kentucky, Missouri, N. & S. Carolina, Oklahoma, Tennessee, Texas, Virginia [1909-1938]	African American, Caucasian [?].*	homicide	executed/ commuted	race and sex of victim & offender	1,272 death sentences	Percentages, ratios (no sig. tests or measure of association)	yes
Johnson (1941)	North Carolina [1933-1939]	African American, Caucasian [?]	homicide	executed/ commuted	race of offender & victim.…	123 death sentences	(no sig. tests or measure of association)	mix
Ehrmann (1952)	Mass. (6 counties) [1925-1941]	African American, Caucasian, Chinese [?]	homicide	executed		113 capital cases	Observation, descriptive statistics	N/A

Table 2 (Continued): Empirical Studies of Race, Ethnicity, and Death Sentence Outcomes

Author(s) & (year)	Jurisdiction [Time Period Covered]	Race/Ethnicity [Gender]	Capital Offense	Dependent Variable	Independent Variables	Primary Sample	Main Type of Analysis	Race/ Ethnic effect?
Giardini & Farrow (1952)	22 states [1924-1952]	Mexican, African American, Caucasian, Native American [probably male & female]	homicide, rape, robbery, other	executed/ commuted	type of offense, state, time lapses between dispositions	749 death sentences (Mexican: N=38)	Percentages (no sig. tests or measure of association)	N/A (race/ethnicity were not included in the analysis)
Johnson (1957)	22 states [1924-1952]	Mexican, African American, Caucasian, Native American [probably male & female]	homicide, rape, burglary	% executed/ admissions to death row	race, education, occupation....	650 death row admission	Percentages, test of significance	yes

Table 2 (Continued): Empirical Studies of Race, Ethnicity, and Death Sentence Outcomes

Author(s) & (year)	Jurisdiction [Time Period Covered]	Race/Ethnicity [Gender]	Capital Offense	Dependent Variable	Independent Variables	Primary Sample	Main Type of Analysis	Race/Ethnic effect?
Sellin (1959)	Various states[various time frames(e.g., 1926-1937]	African American, Caucasian, Native American, Chinese, Filipino, Japanese [male & female]	various felonies	executed/ commuted	offense, race, and sex of offender…	Various samples(e.eg., 1473; 1872)	Tabular analysis (no sig. tests or measure of association)	yes
Bridge & Mosure (1961)	Ohio [various time frames between 1910-1959]	African American, Caucasian [male & female]	homicide	executed/ commuted	race and sex of offender, region, motive, drugs, weapon, age, place of birth marital status, occupation, education, mental health, family background, prior record…	67 death sentences	Percentages, ratios (no sig. tests or measure of association)	yes

Table 2 (Continued): Empirical Studies of Race, Ethnicity, and Death Sentence Outcomes

Author(s) & (year)	Jurisdiction [Time Period Covered]	Race/Ethnicity [Gender]	Capital Offense	Dependent Variable	Independent Variables	Primary Sample	Main Type of Analysis	Race/Ethnic effect?
McCafferty (1962)	Maryland [1936-1961]	African American, Caucasian [male & female]	homicide, rape	executed/ commuted	race, age, education, marital status, prior record, elapsed time, victim/defendant relationship, place of birth, occupation, motive, weapon, county of conviction…	102 death sentences	Percentages, ratios (no sig. tests or measure of association)	yes
Wolfgang, Kelly, & Nolde (1962)	Penn. [1914-1958]	African American, Caucasian [male & female]	homicide	executed/ commuted	felony/non-felony, type of counsel, race, age, marital status, nativity, occupation	439 death sentences	Test of significance, chi-square	mixed (felony, yes; non-felony, no)

Table 2 (Continued): Empirical Studies of Race, Ethnicity, and Death Sentence Outcomes

Author(s) & (year)	Jurisdiction [Time Period Covered]	Race/Ethnicity [Gender]	Capital Offense	Dependent Variable	Independent Variables	Primary Sample	Main Type of Analysis	Race/ Ethnic effect?
Bedau (1964)	New Jersey [1907-1960]	Caucasian/ non-Caucasian [male & female]	homicide	executed/ commuted	felony/non-felony, race, age, sex, prior record, time under death sentence, nativity, SES, occupation, appeals taken, stays, and reprieves & retrials granted…	235 capital; cases	Test of significance, chi-square, Yates' correction for continuity	no
Bedau (1965)	Oregon [1903-1964]	Caucasian/ non-Caucasian [male & female]	homicide	executed/ commuted	race, age, sex, nativity, occupation, type of murder, victim/ defendant relationship, type of counsel, sentencing power of the trial jury, facility of appellate review, use of clemency power…	92 capital cases	Percentages, ratios (no sig. tests or measure of association)	no

Table 2 (Continued): Empirical Studies of Race, Ethnicity, and Death Sentence Outcomes

Author(s) & (year)	Jurisdiction [Time Period Covered]	Race/Ethnicity [Gender]	Capital Offense	Dependent Variable	Independent Variables	Primary Sample	Main Type of Analysis	Race/ Ethnic effect?
Carter & Smith (1969)	California [December 2, 1938 to January 23,1963]	Mexican African American, Caucasian, Native American, Chinese, Filipino, Japanese [male]	homicide, kidnapping & assault by life termer	executed	race, offense, victim-offender relationship, weapon, prior record, age, place of birth, education, intelligence, family & occupational background, marital status, psychiatric data	187 executions (Mexican: N=12)	Percentages	yes
Koeninger (1969)	Texas [1924-1968]	Latin, African American, Caucasian [male & female]	homicide, rape, armed robbery	executed/ commuted	age, birth place, education, occupation, employment, prior record, weapon, drugs…	460 death sentences (Latino/a: N=45)	Percentages	yes

Table 2 (Continued): Empirical Studies of Race, Ethnicity, and Death Sentence Outcomes

Author(s) & (year)	Jurisdiction [Time Period Covered]	Race/Ethnicity [Gender]	Capital Offense	Dependent Variable	Independent Variables	Primary Sample	Main Type of Analysis	Race/ Ethnic effect?
Johnson (1970)	Louisiana [1900-1950]	African American, Caucasian [male]	rape	executed/ commuted	race, type of execution...	49 death sentences	Percentages, ratios (no sig. tests or measure of association)	yes
Bowers (1984)	United States (Ohio, Virginia, New Jersey, New York, Penn., North Carolina) [various time frames-e.g., 1920-1962]	Caucasian/ non-Caucasian "unclassified" [probably male & female]	homicide, rape...	executed	age, appeal, region	5,743 capital cases	Descriptive statistics	yes
Ekland-Olson (1988)	Texas [February 1974 to July 1987]	Latino, African American, Caucasian [male & female]	homicide	executed/ commuted	year of conviction, race of offender & victim...	247 capital cases (Latino: N=~31)	It appears that multivariate analysis was sued	mix

Table 2 (Continued): Empirical Studies of Race, Ethnicity, and Death Sentence Outcomes

Author(s) & (year)	Jurisdiction [Time Period Covered]	Race/Ethnicity [Gender]	Capital Offense	Dependent Variable	Independent Variables	Primary Sample	Main Type of Analysis	Race/ Ethnic effect?
Aguirre & Baker (1989)	Arizona, California, Colorado, New Mexico, Texas [1977-1986];Arizona [1910-1936]; California [1893-1967]; Colorado [1890-1901]; New Mexico [1933-1960]; Texas [1924-1986]	Mexican African American, Caucasian, Native American, Chinese [probably male & female]	homicide	executed (compared with granted appeals)	appeal (yes/no)	Southwest: 5,708 (105 Mexicans); Arizona: 63 (21 Mexicans); California: 267 (52 Mexicans) ; Texas:358: (23 Mexicans)	tabular analysis	N/A
Vandiver (1993)	Florida [1924-1972]	African American, Caucasian [male & female]	homicide, rape	executed/ commuted	race of defendant & victim, age, type of crime…	255 death sentences	chi-square, phi-square, corrected contingency coefficient	mix

Table 2 (Continued): Empirical Studies of Race, Ethnicity, and Death Sentence Outcomes

Author(s) & (year)	Jurisdiction [Time Period Covered]	Race/Ethnicity [Gender]	Capital Offense	Dependent Variable	Independent Variables	Primary Sample	Main Type of Analysis	Race/ Ethnic effect?
Marquart, Ekland-Olson & Sorensen (1994)	Texas [1923-1972]	Latino/a African American, Caucasian, other [male & female]	homicide , rape, arm robbery, burglary	executed/ commuted	offender, victim, & offense variables	510 death sentences Latino/a: N=48)	percentages, ratios, & significance tests	yes
Aguirre & Baker (1997)	Arizona, California, Colorado, New Mexico, Texas [1975-1987]	Mexican [male & female]	homicide, rape, robbery-murder, rape-murder, murder-burglary, rape-robbery, sodomy, buggery-bestiality, theft-steal...	executed	offense, age, occupation, (also includes method of execution)	14,570 (301 Latinos/as; 244 Mexicans) (These include state, federal, territorial & military executions)	tabular analysis	N/A

Table 2 (Continued): Empirical Studies of Race, Ethnicity, and Death Sentence Outcomes

Author(s) & (year)	Jurisdiction [Time Period Covered]	Race/Ethnicity [Gender]	Capital Offense	Dependent Variable	Independent Variables	Primary Sample	Main Type of Analysis	Race/ Ethnic effect?
Pridemore (2000)	South states/ non-south states [1974-1995]	African American/ non African American [male & female]	not specified (but it appears that the sample contains various felonies)	executed/ commuted	offense, age, occupation, (also includes methods of execution)	414 death sentences	logistic regression	no
Baldus, Woodworth, Grosso & Christ (2002)	Nebraska [1973-1999]	Caucasian, minority (African American & Latino combined) [male & female]	homicide	executed	race, socioeconomic status, jurisdiction, statutory aggravating & mitigating circumstances . . .	29 death sentences	logistic regression	yes

Overall Summary: Yes: 11   No: 3   Mixed: 4   NA: 4

* ? = unable to determine from text.

a To Koeninger (1969:135), "most persons here classified as 'Latin' are white Texas of Mexican extraction."

Race and Ethnicity

Beginning with the effects of race and ethnicity, the two variables of primary interest, a number of early studies have found racial and ethnic differences in death sentence outcomes (e.g., Bridge and Mosure, 1961; Johnson, 1957; Johnson, 1970; Mangum, 1940; McCafferty, 1962; Sellin, 1959). For instance, Mangum (1940) found that the ratio of executions was higher for African Africans (73.5%) than Caucasians (55.5%) in Florida between August 1928 and December 1938. In Texas, the percentage was 83.2% for African Americans and 79.4% for Caucasians between February 8, 1924 and December 1, 1938.

Johnson (1957) found that first degree murderers and rapists had the highest execution rates, especially if the victim was a Caucasian female. Specifically, for homicide, 43.8% of Caucasians were executed compared with 62% of African Americans; for rape, 42.9% of Caucasians were executed compared with 56.4% of African Americans; and for burglary, 26.3% of African Americans, but no Caucasians, were executed for burglary in North Carolina from 1909 to 1954.[24] Sellin (1959) found that the likelihood of commutation in Ohio, given only race of offender, likewise penalized African Americans. Less than half as many African Americans as Caucasians sentenced to death benefitted from commutation.

Similarly, Bridge and Mosure (1961) found that a greater percentage of Caucasians than African Americans sentenced to death received commutations in Ohio from 1949 to 1959. Forty-nine percent of Caucasians had their sentences commuted versus 22% of African Americans. Conversely, 51% of Caucasians were executed compared with 78% of African Americans. McCafferty's (1962) Maryland study showed that of the 20 Caucasian inmates who were disposed of

---

[24] Johnson (1957) also found that among killers, the highest execution rate (72%) was exhibited when a crime for economic gain was involved. The most frequent themes found in commutation statements by governors for murderers and rapists included the failure of the case to meet legal requirements, mental abnormality, lack of premeditation, evidence was deemed doubtful or otherwise inappropriate, bad reputation of the victim, the victim's contribution to the crime, the defendant's socially underprivileged status, requests for commutations by court and other officials or by the jurors. Also, occupational data showed that capital offenders were more heavily representative of the labor class.

between 1936 and 1961, ten were executed and eight were commuted. For the 72 African American inmates, 47 (65.3%) were executed and 26 (36.1%) had their sentences commuted.[25] Johnson's (1970) Louisiana study showed that of the 39 executions, all but two were African American. Of the convicted rapists sentenced to death, whose death sentence was commuted to life imprisonment, two Caucasian men, one-half of all the Caucasian rapists sentenced to death, had their death sentences commuted. According to Johnson (1970:217), "it is very difficult to secure commutation for a Negro convicted of rape."[26]

Some early studies, however, did not find race to be an influential factor in death sentence outcomes. Bedau (1964) found that after controlling for felony/non-felony cases, race was not a significant factor in executions or commutations in New Jersey between 1907 and 1960.[27] A year later, Bedau (1965) discovered no race differences in Oregon between 1903 and 1964. Of the 83 Caucasians sentenced to death, 52 were executed and 21 had their sentences commuted; of the

---

[25] McCafferty (1962) also found that of the 27 rape cases, six were Caucasian and 21 were African American. Of the 52 homicide cases, 11 were Caucasian and 41 were African American. Additionally, the extent to which commutation was used was proportionately lower for murderers, 31.1%, as contrasted to those convicted of rape, 36.6%. Individuals born in Maryland appeared to have a better chance to escape execution than those born in other states, whether the offense was murder or rape.

[26] Johnson (1970) further found that in addition to the number of African Americans put to death by the state of Louisiana, there were three others put to death in Louisiana by the US government. This made a total of 40 African Americans executed for rape, compared to two Caucasian men. In short, of the Caucasians convicted of rape and sentenced to death, two were executed and two were commuted. Of the African Americans convicted of rape and sentenced to death, 37 were executed and 3 were commuted. Thus, the total number of African Americans executed in Louisiana from 1900 to 1950 for rape totaled 40.

[27] Bedau (1964) found that among Caucasian killers sentenced to death, felony murder was significantly correlated with execution; among non-felony killers, previous criminal record was significantly related with execution. No statistically significant relation was found between execution and foreign born, or occupation.

nine non-Caucasians sentenced to death, six were executed and two had their sentences commuted.[28]

In studies that have shown mixed evidence regarding the role of race and ethnicity in crime and punishment, Johnson (1941) found that for African American killers of Caucasian victims, the chance of commutation of the death sentence (19.5% of sentences commuted) was considerably lower than for any other capital offenders sentenced to death (35.6% for African American killers of African Americans, and 31.7% for Caucasians who killed Caucasians) during the period under study in North Carolina. In intra-racial homicides, the percentages of death sentences commuted were about the same for African Americans and Caucasians, but when the offender was African American and the victim was Euro-American, the chance of receiving a commutation was one in five, instead of one in three. Wolfgang, Kelly, and Nolde (1962) found a statistically significant association between race and type of disposition, but only in felony cases. Specifically, compared to Caucasians, a significantly higher proportion of African Americans were executed instead of having their sentences commuted. However, controlling for felony/non-felony cases, Wolfgang et al. (1962) found race to be a significant factor in executions and commutations that pertain to felony cases, but not non-felony cases in Pennsylvania between 1914 and 1958.[29]

---

[28] Bedau (1965) also found that of the 65 death sentences that were issued to native-born, 39 were executed and 18 were commuted; of the nine foreign-born whites, eight were executed and one was commuted. And, by far the largest number–43% of all executions–were given to the group labeled "laborer." Of the 25 felony cases, 18 were executed and five were commuted; and of the 66 non-felony cases, 40 were executed and 17 were commuted. Of the 46 cases involving court-appointed counsel, 33 were executed and ten were commuted; and of the 22 private counsel cases, 11 were executed and six were commuted. In a related vein, of the 40 in which the jury had mandatory sentencing power, 24 were executed and 12 were commuted; and of the 52 involving discretionary power, 34 were executed and 11 were commuted.

[29] Wolfgang, Kelly, and Nolde (1962) further found that proportionately more felony murderers than non-felony murderers actually suffered the death penalty, and more non-felony cases had their sentences commuted.

Criminal History

In addition to the influence of race and ethnicity, the offender's prior criminal history is an influential factor in death sentence outcomes.[30] Bridge and Mosure (1961) found that of the 37 who were executed in Ohio during the period under study, five had no previous criminal record, 13 had minor offenses, and 19 had felony convictions. Of the 23 who had their sentences commuted, six had no previous criminal record, 11 had minor offenses, and six had felony convictions.[31] McCafferty's (1962) Maryland study found that for those executed, seven out of ten had prior convictions; for those whose sentences were commuted, 59.4% had prior convictions. For those disposed of during the time under analysis, one-half of those with no prior conviction record were executed. For those with records who were disposed of, 60.3% were executed. Bedau's (1964) New Jersey study found a statistically significant relationship between carrying out the death sentence and previous criminal record, and between commutation and no previous criminal record. Lastly, Bedau's (1965) data showed that of the 39 with a prior conviction, 27 were executed and eight had their sentences commuted; and of the 16 death sentences with no prior conviction, three were executed and nine were commuted.

Other Demographic Variables

As with death sentencing, although few studies examine gender due to the small number of women under the death sentence, available studies suggest that death sentence outcomes are gendered. Fewer females have been executed in the United States compared to males (Bowers, 1974; Johnson, 1957). Homicide statistics show that of the 3,464 legal executions carried out in 16 different states between 1830 and 1967, 35

---

[30] Johnson (1957) observed that his data do not support the common assumption that death row population is composed of the most hardened criminals (i.e., those with previous prison sentences).

[31] Bridge and Mosure (1961:54) further found that "the most important single determinant of which murderers shall be executed in Ohio is discretionary sentencing by juries or three-judge courts." Of those commuted, 30.6% had court-appointed counsel and 44.4% had private counsel. Of those executed, 57.2% had court-appointed counsel and 50% had private counsel.

(1%) were females (Bowers, 1974; Sellin, 1980; see also Gillespie, 2000). Of the 35 females executed, seven of the 33 whose race was known were African American (Sellin, 1980). Finally, Bedau (1964) found a statistically significant association between death sentence commutation and females, and between the carrying out of death sentences and males.

For the next variable, age, prior research findings are quite mixed, but there is an indication that this variable has been an influential factor in death sentence outcomes.[32] Wolfgang, Kelly, and Nolde (1962) found that the polar ends of the age groups (15-19 years, and those 55 years and older) had the lowest frequency of execution and consequently, the highest frequency of sentence commutation. The highest frequency (92%) of executions occurred in the age group 20 to 24 years. Bedau (1964) found no statistically significant relation between execution and age, but did find a statistically significant association between sentence commutation and extreme youth. Bedau's (1965) data showed that youth, especially those under 20 years of age, increased the likelihood of sentence commutation. For the next-youngest age group (20-24), only two of the 15 death sentences were commuted, making it one of the lowest percentages of commutations among all age groups. His data also showed that young males guilty of felony murder are, if sentenced to death, not likely to receive commutation, and thus end up being executed.

As far as educational level of capital offenders, prior research findings also show that this variable has been an influential factor in death sentence outcomes. McCafferty (1962) found that the median school grade completed for those executed was seventh grade. Murderers who were executed had a median grade completed of 7.5, whereas for those executed for rape, the median was 5.3.[33]

As far as marital status of the criminal offender, a symbol of stability, prior research findings are inconclusive. McCafferty (1962)

---

[32] Johnson (1957) found that one of the most frequent themes found in commutation statements by governors for murderers and rapists was extreme youth or elderliness of the offender.

[33] McCafferty (1962) also found that among inmates executed, laborers accounted for about six out of ten, and for those commuted, the ratio of laborers was five out of ten. When an inmate was sentenced to death for killing during a robbery or burglary, there was a greater chance that the defendant would be executed than for murders committed for other reasons.

found that six out of ten inmates executed were single. For those executed for homicide, seven out of ten were single; for those executed for rape, five out of ten were single. Single inmates had a somewhat greater probability of being executed than married offenders. Wolfgang et al. (1962:308), however, found "no important differences appear between the executed and commuted when examined in terms of marital status." In all, the data show that in combination with race and ethnicity, these various factors have a significant influence in crime and punishment.

Death Sentence Outcomes

In addition to these noted factors, a third set of factors include the time spent under the death sentence, and the state where the death sentence outcome decision was made, which is crucial to better understand capital punishment in its totality. For the first factor, little empirical work has been done, but prior findings suggest that the length of time between the death sentence and final disposition could be a critical factor. Bedau (1965) found that, overall, the mean time served from imposition of the death sentence to final disposition was 16 months. McCafferty (1962) found that the average days of elapsed time between the death sentence and disposition was lowest for prisoners executed. For the 57 executed, the average number of days was 220; for the 36 executed for murder, the average number of days was 257; for those executed for rape, the average number of days was 158. Inmates who had their death sentences commuted averaged 388 days between sentence and commutation. Murderers whose sentences were commuted averaged 448 days and rapists 312 days. Giardini and Farrow (1952) found that the time between the sentence of death and commutation was, on average, 9.6 months in Pennsylvania and 15.2 months in Kentucky. Marquart et al. (1994) found that the time from admission to death row to execution lengthened from something close to a month and a half in the 1930s to a period closer to five months in the late 1950s. The mean time for the 58 who were executed was 14 months.

Statistics for state and death sentence outcomes show that executions and sentence commutations vary by state (Sellin, 1980). Giardini and Farrow (1952), for instance, found that Pennsylvania executed an average of 8.6 offenders per year compared to Texas' average of 10.1 cases. In effect, when considering only homicide cases for Texas, the average drops to 7.6 cases per year. Further, if one considers only homicide, Texas commuted 20% of the cases, compared to Pennsylvania's 18%. The difference, according to the authors, was not significant.[34]

The next two scholars, who have conducted evaluations of early studies testing for the effects of various factors, including the role of race and ethnicity, have made some critical observations of not only the findings but also of methods used to arrive at such conclusions. Hagan's (1974) reevaluation of the data shows some racial bias in sentencing for capital offenses, but only in the context of southern jurisdictions. Kleck (1981) reported some racial bias in death sentencing for capital offenses in the context of capital offenses. According to Kleck (1981), reevaluation of data on execution rates by race from 1930 to 1967, and on death sentencing rates from 1967 to 1978 show, except in the South, African American homicide offenders have been less likely than Caucasians to receive a death sentence or be executed. For the 11% of executions applied for rape, discrimination

---

[34] Giardini and Farrow (1952) also found that of the 399 inmates under the sentence of death in Pennsylvania, 64.2% were Caucasian, 35.6% were African American, and one was Mongolian. Of the 350 inmates under the sentence of death in Texas, regardless of the offense, 30% were Caucasian, 58.9% African American, and 10.8% included 38 Mexicans and one Indian. When considering the 269 Texas cases convicted of homicide, 32.7% were Caucasian, 54.6% were African American, and 12.3% included 33 Mexicans and one Indian. When considering the 73 Texas cases convicted of rape, 16.4% were Caucasian, 76.7% were African American, and 6.9% were Mexican. When considering the eight Texas cases convicted of robbery, 62.5% were Caucasian and 36.5% were African American. It should be emphasized that when analyzing studies, especially early studies, the numbers for African Americans and Latinos could be skewed. Since only "legal death sentences" and "legal executions" are considered, the figures for African Americans and Latinos, especially Mexicans, are underestimated. Lynchings, for example, are seldom mentioned in research. Further, the disposition of the cases whose death sentence was commuted to life imprisonment varies by state. Of the two cases discharged in Texas, one was by court order and the other by the governor. The 41 cases conditionally released in Pennsylvania included five that were released for deportation. Only one case was released for deportation in Texas. Of the 41 Pennsylvania cases that were conditionally released, 31 were Caucasian and ten were African American. Of the 22 Texas cases, eight were Caucasian, 11 African American, and three Mexican.

against African American defendants who had raped Caucasian victims was substantial, but only in the South.

However, when considering early studies, as Hagan (1974) and Kleck (1981) point out, one needs to consider the various methodological limitations that might impact statistical difference regarding the effects of race and ethnicity. As Kleck (1981) observes, a major shortcoming of early studies is that they nearly all fail to control for factors that might be influential, like prior criminal record. Most studies that included controls did not control all relevant factors simultaneously. Several early studies rarely used significance tests or measures of association. When significance tests were used, the authors relied primarily on them, but a problem with conclusions developed "solely on the basis of significance tests is the tendency to confuse substantive and causal significance with statistical significance" (Hagan, 1974:379). As a consequence, "we can only conclude that . . . the 'racial hypothesis' remains open to some doubt" (Hagan, 1974:368; see also Aguirre and Baker, 1990; Urbina, 2007). One, however, cannot neglect the fact that these early studies, while not employing advanced analytical techniques or relying on sophisticated theoretical frameworks, clearly indicate that race/ethnicity is an important factor that needs to be analyzed critically, using a sound theoretical framework, and more advanced analytical techniques, especially since prior results show mixed results regarding the influence of race/ethnicity (Urbina, 2007).

As the next three studies, especially the last one, are central to this inquiry, I will discuss them in some detail. The first study is important not only because it is a more recent death sentence outcomes study, but also because it analyzes the impact of race in crime and punishment. The Florida (one of the three states included in the statistical analysis presented in this book) data analysis employs various analytical techniques including chi-square, phi-square, and the corrected contingency coefficient. Using State Pardon Board files, opinions of the Florida Supreme Court and newspaper accounts, Vandiver (1993) examined all commutations and all executions (N=255) in Florida death sentences between 1924 and 1966, focusing particularly on whether the race ("white"/"black") of the defendants and victims influenced the decision to commute the sentence.

First, based on her analysis, of the total 255 (including two females) death sentences, 89 (34.9%) were Caucasian and 166 (65.1%) were African American. Forty-nine men (19.2%) were given the death sentence for rape, and 206 (80.8%) for murder. Furthermore, 92.9% of the death sentences were imposed for a crime against only one victim. In 74.5% of the cases the victims were Caucasian, while in 25.5% they were African American. Sixteen defendants were 18 years old or younger at the time of their convictions, and 14 of those young defendants were African Americans.

According to Vandiver (1993:324), commutations were granted in 59 (23.1%) of the death sentences, while 196 (76.9%) were executed, but the data "shows no evidence that a defendant's race influenced commutation decisions." However, the victim's race had a strong influence upon the decision to commute the sentence; 44.3% of the defendants whose victims were African American received commutations, while only 15.2% of defendants whose victims were Caucasian received commutations.

African American defendants had a 41.1% chance of receiving a commutation if their victims were African American, but only a 5.3% chance if their victims were Caucasian. Commutations were granted to three African American defendants out of 55 condemned for the murder of Caucasian victims. The author tested whether the relationship of defendants and victims can account for racial differences. Among the category of "primary crimes" (homicides in which the victim and offender knew each other), a significant relationship between offender and non-stranger is observed, but such a relationship does not hold for the category of "non-primary" (homicides which occur between strangers) crimes.

After introducing "contemporary felony" (a crime, homicide, accompanied by additional felonies) as a control variable, the results showed that for non-felony cases, there was a statistically significant relationship between race and death sentence outcome. However, for felony cases, the relationship did not attain significance at the .05 level, although the relationship is in the predicted direction. African Americans were less likely to have their sentences commuted and more likely to be executed. A homicide committed in the course of an armed robbery might receive a harsher sanction than a murder arising from an argument. Further, a contemporary robbery could aggravate the punishment imposed for a rape charge. The results "support the hypothesis that defendants with contemporary felonies were less likely to receive commutations than those defendants whose crimes were not accompanied by additional felonies" (Vandiver, 1993:327).

Vandiver (1993) found that defendants whose death sentences had been imposed for committing rape had a lower chance of receiving commutation than those condemned for murder. After exploring this relationship by examining the influence of racial combinations of defendants and victims, while controlling for crime of conviction, "race continues to significantly influence outcome" (Vandiver, 1993:330). Of the 40 African American men sentenced to die for rape, only two (5%) received a commutation.

In short, race of both defendants and victims influenced the decision to execute or commute condemned prisoners in Florida between 1924 and 1966. In the words of Vandiver (1993:343), "the statistical analysis used in this study supports the hypothesis that the race of both defendants and victims influenced decisions to grant clemency [commutation]," revealing that race was influential in crime and punishment.

Vandiver's (1993) study provides insight into executions and commutations, but the findings need to be interpreted with extreme caution. As the author acknowledges, there are a number of shortcomings. First, given the fact that the commutation and execution process operates in a very complex and subtle manner, the study lacks a more holistic theoretical base. Second, because of the small sample size, the missing data, and very small numbers in some of the tables, confident "interpretation of these results is difficult . . ." (Vandiver, 1993:327). Third, because of the lack of additional and critical control variables, like ethnicity and prior criminal record, it is difficult to draw solid conclusions. Fourth, "the statistical analysis . . . was limited to very simple cross-classifications" (Vandiver, 1993:324). As such, based on these limitations, the results regarding the role of race in crime and punishment must be viewed as tentative in this particular study.

The next study by Marquart et al. (1994) is central to the current study because it analyzes the effects of race and ethnicity in capital punishment in Texas (one of the three states included in the study presented in this book), employing various analytical techniques, like percentages or ratios. Specifically, Marquart et al. (1994) analyzed 510 capital offense offenders (507 males and 3 females) sentenced to die in

Texas between 1923 and 1972. They analyzed the distribution of commuted and executed capital offenders by offender variables (race, ethnicity, mean age in years, gender, prior criminal record), offense variables (murder, rape, robbery by firearms), and victim variables (relationship to offender, race of victim, gender of victim, number of victims).

The results showed that of the 510 individuals sentenced to die, 92 had their sentences commuted (75 for murder, ten for rape, and seven for armed robbery) and 361 were eventually executed (71% for murder, 27% for rape, and one percent for armed robbery). All three of the women sentenced to die for capital murder had their death sentences commuted.[35]

Of the 361 who were executed, 107 (30%) were Caucasian, 229 (63%) were African American, and 24 (7%) were Latino. According to Marquart et al. (1994:23),

> once sentenced to die, blacks were more likely to be executed, 61 percent of the condemned whites having been eventually executed, compared with 82 percent of the blacks. Among Hispanics, the comparable figure was 50 percent, whereas only 20 percent of the black offenders received clemency. Interestingly, 46 percent of the Hispanic inmates received a commutation.

Their analysis of the percentage of African Americans versus Caucasians convicted of homicide who were eventually executed between 1924 and 1971 shows that the average yearly proportion of African Americans sentenced to die who were eventually executed was 84%, while 68% of the Caucasians sentenced to death were eventually executed over the same period. In effect, in cases of homicide, while the ratio of death sentences of Caucasians was following a downward trend, the rate of execution for African Americans remained almost 20 percentage points higher than for Caucasians. Similarly, death

---

[35] Marquart et al. (1994) also note that in eight cases, the death sentence was reversed or dismissed, two died while under death sentence awaiting execution, and the death sentences of 47 inmates were vacated by the Supreme Court's *Furman* decision in 1972. (It is important to keep in mind that the *Furman* releases were card-blanche and the others had specific release or execution dates.)

sentences involving the additional charge of rape were more likely to result in an eventual execution than were death sentences involving any other type of additional felony charge, like robbery or burglary.

Of the 92 who had their death sentences commuted, 38 were Caucasian, 37 African American, and 17 were Latino. Among capital cases in which Caucasian victims were killed, 73% resulted in executions. By contrast, 62% of the capital cases involving African American victims and 46% of those involving Latino victims eventually resulted in the execution of the offender.

Lastly, based on their distribution of commuted (100) and executed (361) capital offenders by offender, offense, and victim variables, "race in combination with the type of offense charged, was a dominating influence on the commutation process" (Marquart et al., 1994:116). The authors found that offense variables and race and ethnicity were statistically significant at the .01 level, clearly revealing the role of race and ethnicity in capital punishment.

All in all, 29% of all those who arrived on death row between 1923 and 1972 were granted clemency. However, according to Marquart et al. (1994:119), Caucasian and Latino offenders benefitted more than African American offenders, "whose ancestors could be traced to the shores of Africa." Among the three major ethnic and racial groups (African Americans, Latinos, and Caucasians), Latinos, who were the least likely to receive a death sentence for murder, were the most likely to have their death sentences commuted, partly due to the higher proportion of "acquaintance" killings.[36]

An extensive criminal history (three or more offenses) also influenced the chances of being granted a commutation; that is, those with an extensive criminal history were less likely to have their death sentences commuted. Further, cases that involved single victims were more than twice as likely to result in a commutation (23%), compared to crimes in which two or more persons were victimized (11%). Moreover, Latino-victim cases were the most likely to be commuted; 50% (11 of the 22 cases) resulted in commutation. African American victim cases were the second most likely to result in commutation, 33% of such cases being commuted, compared with 19% of cases involving

---

[36] Marquart et al. (1994) also remind us that there is some indication that Latino offenders may have been less likely to be convicted of capital rape.

Caucasian victims. When the victim and offender were acquaintances or family members, just over one-third of the death sentences were eventually commuted. However, about one in ten of the death sentences for crimes involving strangers (especially women in rape cases) resulted in commutation. In short, commutation was more likely to have been bestowed on Caucasians who killed other Caucasians. Those who crossed racial lines to kill, especially African Americans, were more likely to be dispatched to the electric chair. In rape cases, again African American defendants were the least likely to be granted a commutation. Again, these findings indicate that race and ethnicity are influential factors in crime and punishment.

However, while Marquart et al.'s (1994) study provides insight into execution and commutation, the findings need to be interpreted with caution, given the fact that the study contains a number of shortcomings. First, given the fact that the commutation and execution process operates in a very complex, subtle, and manipulative manner, especially in recent years, the study needs a more holistic theoretical base. Second, since the authors combined (with no rationale for doing so) commutations, death sentences that were "reversed or dismissed" and/or death sentences that were vacated by the US Supreme Court's *Furman* decision, confident interpretation of these results is difficult. Though, it appears that the authors' main concern was that the inmates were released and not why they are released. The authors were analyzing post-incarceration behavior, i.e., amount of post-release crime like homicide. Third, since the authors used the terms "commutation" and "clemency" interchangeably without making reference as to what was being discussed, it is difficult to draw conclusions. Fourth, because of the lack of additional and critical control variables, like education, it is difficult to draw solid conclusions regarding the role of race and ethnicity. Fifth, the statistical analysis was limited to very simple techniques. As such, based on these limitations, the findings regarding the impact of race and ethnicity in capital punishment must be viewed as tentative.

A study by Pridemore (2000) is one of the more recent death sentence outcomes study which analyzes the influence of race in various states, including California, Florida, and Texas (our three states of interest in the research presented in this book), in post-*Furman* capital cases, employing a highly advanced analytical technique (logistic regression analysis). Pridemore (2000) sought to determine which extralegal factors were significant in the commutation and execution decision-making process, which has been "highly discretionary," (and with no oversight) in capital cases from 1974 to 1995 (Pridemore, 2000:601). "Rather than directly testing a fully specified theory," the author seeks to answer the following questions:

> Do factors found to influence the final disposition of capital cases before the *Furman* decision still play a role in final dispositions today? Second, do distinctly political elements influence a governor's decision? Finally, what other possible characteristics might affect this process (Pridemore, 2000:607)?

His first hypothesis was that factors such as offender's race, age, sex, and prior felony, which were significant factors in the past, will still be significant today. According to Pridemore (2000), the young and the old are more likely to be granted a commutation in lieu of death than are offenders age 25 to 55. Since a prior felony is likely to mark the offender as a continuing danger, inmates with at least one prior felony conviction are more likely to be executed than those without them. Females, as in the past, are more likely than males to have their death sentences commuted. Further, as in the past, African Americans are less likely than Caucasians to be granted a commutation.

His second set of hypotheses deals with a governor's possible political motives, reelection, and thus a perceived need to appear tough on crime. While Pridemore (2000:602) notes that "the decision to commute may be political, exercised by the governor . . . with an eye to groups in the community who may be able to leverage power in their favor," he predicts no significant differences between Democrat and Republican governors in office at the time of the execution or commutation, due to the current punitive trend. Though, he predicts that, since "opinion polls continue to show strong public support for the death penalty," a significant relationship between the date of final disposition (execution) and election year will prevail as a symbol of their "get tough" approach. As such, in the words of Pridemore (2000:608), "I expect that offenders whose execution date falls in an election year are less likely to receive a commutation than those who are scheduled for execution at another time."

Thirdly, he predicted that offenders with higher levels of education are more likely to receive a commutation than those with lower levels of education, due to the offender's possible future productivity. Similarly, he predicted that married offenders are more likely than unmarried offenders to have their sentences commuted, due to the offender's possible future stability, and thus, are less likely to recidivate. Further, since "both southern society and southern justice are thought to be more punitive [a large proportion of the executions taking place there] and more violent than elsewhere in the country," Pridemore (2000:609) predicted that "such a tradition still exists and that offenders in the south are more likely than those in other regions to be executed."

After weeding out 40 "irrelevant" commutations, the author sought to measure the significance of race ("nonblack/black"), sex, age at disposition (continuous), education (less than high school/high school diploma/GED), marital status (not married/married), region (non-south/south), party (Republican/Democrat), election (no/yes), and the presence of a prior felony (no/yes), on the dichotomous dependent variable (commuted/executed) using the Bureau of Justice Statistics (BJS) data set (1997), which originally contained 454 death sentences (141 commutations and 313 executions) between 1974 and 1995.

Based on his selected sample of 414 death sentences (313 executions and 101 commutations), an adequate sample for the analytic technique being used and appropriate for testing the hypotheses under study, there were 405 men, nine women; 166 Caucasians, 215 African Americans; 272 had prior felony convictions, 99 did not; the average age at the final disposition was 36 and one-half years; 96 executions and commutations took place during a gubernatorial election year, 318 did not; 136 of the final dispositions were decided by Republican governors, 278 by Democratic governors; 298 executions and commutations occurred in southern states, 116 occurred in non-southern states; 149 received a high school diploma, 226 never finished high school; and 261 were not married, but 141 were. Based on Pridemore's (2000) logistic regression analyses, the offender's race (p=.754) and the presence of a prior felony (p=.754) were not significant factors in the execution decision-making process. However, the offender's age at disposition was significant (p<.001). In the post-*Furman* era, older inmates were not likely to be granted a commutation, but inmates 15 to 24 at the time of the final disposition are much more likely than older inmates to be granted a commutation.[37] Females are more likely to have their death sentences commuted, according to the author.

The study concludes that "neither Democratic nor Republican governors are significantly more likely than their counterparts to choose an execution over commutation (p=.361)," but governors are significantly more likely to select execution in an election year than in a non-election year (p=.009) (Pridemore, 2000:614). In addition, neither education (p=.998) nor marital status (p=.221) were influential factors in the decision-making process, but region appeared to be a strong factor in the execution/commutation process. Southern governors are much more likely than non-southern governors to choose execution over commutation (p<.001).

In a separate model, Pridemore (2000:615) limited the analysis to cases (374) that occurred between 1978 and 1995 to control for the "*Furman* impact." While the findings for race, sex, age, prior felony convictions, and education remain relatively unaltered, the governor's political party was now significant (p=.02): Democratic governors were more likely to execute than their Republican counterparts. Further, the significance level of election year changed to .106 and married offenders appeared to be granted a commutation more so than the unmarried. Among individuals with an original 50% chance of execution, the probability of execution decreased by 15% if they were married. Pridemore (2000:616) also found a significant interaction effect between race and region which indicated that "race does not seem to be a factor in the overall model, but perhaps nonblacks are treated differently depending on the region of the country." In testing for interaction between race and region as well as race and prior felony conviction, two different models employing interaction terms for race and region and for race and prior felony conviction were used, but there were "no significant differences" (Pridemore, 2000:616). Lastly, according to the author, between 1978 and 1995, offenders with a 50% chance of being executed faced a 20% increase in the likelihood of execution if they were a southern death row inmate.

---

[37] It should be underscored that variation could be due in part to the fact that the age of legality varies from state to state (e.g., in some states the legal age at which an individual may be executed is 18, by statute).

According to Pridemore (2000:613), "several factors are correlated" with the decision to commute or execute, and "some degree of support is shown for each of the three sets of hypotheses." Finally and perhaps most significant, is a concluding statement by Pridemore (2000:617): "it is a relief to find that race is not a factor in the decision to execute or commute." As with the earlier works, this study provides a sophisticated execution and commutation analysis, but "the findings presented here must be interpreted cautiously," because the study contains a number of critical limitations (Pridemore, 2000:617:621). First, there is a probability that the aggregation of race led to no effects; that is, that race plays no role in capital punishment. For instance, a "black/nonblack" dichotomy indicates that Pridemore (2000) categorized a very distinct population, Latinos, with Caucasians and African Americans without providing a rationale for doing so. In effect, no reference was made as to how the Latino population (probably the majority being Mexican) was handled in his analysis. There is also the probability that race was not significant because of multicollinearity among the independent variables. As such, confident interpretation of these results suggesting that race plays no role in capital punishment is difficult.

Second, since the data clearly indicate that the impact of race and ethnicity varies from place to place (e.g., state to state), the "South/non-South" dichotomy approach utilized by the author, with little rationale for doing so, runs into similar problems. Pridemore (2000:608) acknowledges that

> it is true that certain segments of the population, via their power in society, may be able to influence a governor's decision to execute or commute. Because most states contain much higher proportions of white than black vote . . . a governor may be less inclined to commute a black offender's sentence.

While the number of death sentences, executions, and commutations vary widely across states, "the models estimated . . . operate on the assumption that the decision-making process is uniform across the country and that each governor in each state from 1974 to 1995 faced similar circumstances in making his or her decisions"

(Pridemore, 2000:620).[38] In effect, Texas and Florida, two of our three states of interest, accounted for more than two-fifths of the cases (118 and 55, respectively, or 42%). Also, California, Florida, and Texas, our three states of interest for the analysis presented in this book, in combination commuted 48 death sentences, representing more than 48% of all the granted commutations. This, though, is not to imply that these three states should be lumped together for the purpose of analysis, as will be discussed in Chapter 4.

As a third point, it is probable that age at the time of the offense would be a more appropriate measure than age at disposition to determine the impact of the death sentence on final disposition. Historically, age at the time of the offense, which carries a moral and passionate connotation, has often been controversial in terms of policy.

Fourth, the author assumes that everyone executed applied for clemency. He does, however, acknowledges that "it is likely that a handful of condemned did not seek a commutation" (Pridemore, 2000:622). Interestingly enough, while I agree with Pridemore (2000:622) that "it seems reasonable that nearly everyone facing death (or attorneys or family members working on their behalf) would apply for clemency," it also seems reasonable that the majority of those who did not seek a commutation were probably foreign nationals, given the fact that often the respective consulate, who is supposed to notify the defendant's relatives, is not notified by authorities (see Chapter 6). This information, however, is not available in the data set.

Finally, the rationale for the exclusion of "commutations for judicial expediency" (five in Virginia and 29 in Texas) and commutations granted by former New Mexico Governor Toney Anaya (five) is not, in my view, convincing. An additional case was "deleted because the jurisdiction of the disposition was the District of Columbia," not involving "state executives" (Pridemore, 2000:610). Actually, the mayor of the District of Columbia has commutation powers similar to state governors. For instance, while Pridemore

---

[38] It should be emphasized that death penalty discrimination is not restricted to the South (Baldus et al., 1998). This indicates that race differences in death sentence outcomes will vary by state and region. Thus, African Americans may be more likely to be executed in the South, but only if they are the dominant majority. In California, Florida, and Texas, it will be ethnic discrimination; that is, Latinos will be the group being discriminated against.

(2000:610) excluded Anaya's commutations because the "circumstances surrounding the crime and the characteristics of the offender were not relevant to the decision to commute," he decided to keep Ohio Governor Richard Celeste's commutations (eight) because of the Governor's claim that the death sentences "had been imposed unfairly." However, in the "Statement by Toney Anaya on Capital Punishment" (1993), Anaya made a similar (and more appealing) argument.

Therefore, because of these shortcomings, it is difficult to draw valid and reliable conclusions from Pridemore's (2000) analyses, especially regarding the role of race and ethnicity in crime and punishment. One needs not only to be cautious when examining the results, but also with the author's interpretations of the findings. Overall, it is obvious that the wide discretion that led to the *Furman* (1972) decision, which supposedly was reduced by *Gregg* (1976), has not been eliminated. Additionally, such decisions attempted to remedy the capricious element in processing capital cases at the sentencing stage, but not for later stages: death sentence outcomes, executions and commutations. In the next section, after providing a brief summary of the strengths and weaknesses as well as the gaps in prior studies, I will address what I see as the most critical concerns, which are crucial as we seek to better understand the role of race and ethnicity in capital punishment.

SUMMARY OF PRIOR DEATH SENTENCE AND DEATH SENTENCE OUTCOMES RESEARCH

Strengths of Prior Studies

As we explore the influence of race and ethnicity in capital punishment, we must examine the logistics of existing studies. Prior studies have provided insight into the death-sentencing decision-making process, as well as the death sentence outcomes phenomena. Researchers have not only gone to great lengths to identify influential factors in the decision-making processes, but have paved the way for additional studies, using more advanced quantitative and qualitative techniques, and more sound theoretical perspectives. While there is considerable debate over the various issues surrounding the death sentence and death sentence outcomes, there are some conclusions that can be made based on prior studies testing for the role of race/ethnicity in crime and punishment.

First, a review of the literature, which includes various time frames, jurisdictions, and, at times, large samples, on capital punishment clearly indicates that in the past death sentences were imposed capriciously in the United States. Second, on most issues relative to executions and commutations in capital cases prior research is inconclusive. Though, as the two tables above indicate, the influence of race and ethnicity on death sentence outcomes seems to be in favor of Caucasians. As such, based on the findings, one cannot rule out the possibility that race plays a much more significant and substantial role in determining who should receive a death sentence and who should not, who should be executed and who should not, and who should receive a commutation and who should not. On all three levels, there is an indication that African Americans have received the least justice.

Weaknesses of Prior Studies

It should be emphasized that while prior studies have become more sophisticated over the years, they still contain a few shortcomings (see Klepper, Nagin and Tierney, 1983). First, most death sentences as well as death sentence outcomes (executions/commutations) analyses have been based on bivariate analytical techniques, like cross tabular analysis, ratios, chi-square, or trends over time. Second, most studies have included a number of relevant independent variables, but the included variables were not controlled for simultaneously. Third, few attempts have been made to make a clear distinction between the various possible death sentence outcomes. For instance, on a number of occasions, various possible death sentence outcomes were combined for the purpose of analysis without making reference to what was being analyzed or providing a rationale for a given combination. As will be discussed in Chapter 4, the process leading to commutations, which are mostly granted by state governors, is extremely political and not necessarily focused on possible trial errors. The decisions to overturn sentences or convictions, which are issued by appellate courts, rely on processes that are more concerned with trial errors and less political, since federal judges are appointed and not elected. This is not to say that federal judges are not political. Additionally, at times, the various terms, like "commutation," "executive clemency," "clemency," have been used interchangeably without making clear distinctions about what was being analyzed or discussed, making it difficult to capture the effects of race and ethnicity in their totality.

Fourth, a number of previous studies examined whether racial differences occur at a single point in the legal process (death sentencing stage), and often focus solely on whether death sentencing decisions favor African Americans or Caucasians. However, while racial differences in legal processing might be relatively small at any particular stage of the lengthy legal process, cumulative effects on the overall patterns could be significant and substantial (Urbina, 2007). As such, the legal decision-making process needs to be analyzed by the totality of outcomes; that is, across multiple decision points. Fifth, death sentencing or death sentence outcomes jurisdiction has usually been operationalized as "South/non-South," and thus neglects the fact that disparities in death sentence outcomes vary depending on time and space, state to state. Again, these limitations make it difficult to fully capture the impact of race and ethnicity in capital punishment.

Finally, as Ruddell and Urbina (2004) points out, the exact perceived threats, to include racial and ethnic, operating have remained largely unmeasured in prior studies. The "threats" typically have not been included in a sophisticated fashion in empirical tests of the threat perspectives. Inferences of the type of threat operating generally have been based solely on Blalock's (1967) expectations of certain types of nonlinearities in the relationship between non-Caucasian, usually African American "concentration" and "discrimination" without reference to other minority groups (Urbina, 2007). In addition, since discrimination has usually meant sentencing of non-capital cases, the analyses of executions or commutations, as two possible death sentence outcomes, have not only been limited, but little has taken place beyond these two decisions-making points.

Gaps in Prior Studies

While prior research has definitely enhanced our understanding of the role of race and ethnicity in the decision-making process, a number of significant issues need further examination. First of all, as Pridemore (2000:601) points out, "in the voluminous literature surrounding capital punishment . . . relatively little contemporary empirical work focuses directly on the characteristics of the final clemency decision to commute or execute, especially post-*Furman*." Not only have few empirical death sentence outcomes (executions or commutations) studies been conducted, but it is difficult to locate studies that have empirically explored the following three additional death sentence outcomes, which constitute a significant number of final outcomes in the post-*Furman* era: (1) "capital sentence declared unconstitutional by State or US Supreme Court," (2) "conviction affirmed, sentence overturned by appellate court," and (3) "conviction and sentence overturned by appellate court" (Pridemore, 2000:601). Little emphasis has been given to inmates remaining on death row (under the sentence of death), which constitutes an "outcome." Since no action has taken place for those remaining under the sentence of death, this is an indication, by default, of life imprisonment. As such, there is certainly not only a need to go beyond executions and commutations, but also to include those remaining on death row.

Second, due in large part to the un-availability of information, capital punishment research has traditionally taken a dichotomous African American/Caucasian approach and thus, little attention has been given to other minority groups.[39] Traditionally, studies have totally left out other racial and ethnic groups, or combined them with the Caucasian and African American groups, though one cannot be certain as often no reference has been made as to how populations were handled in the analysis. For instance, two studies of death penalty discrimination in Texas (Ekland-Olson, 1988 and Marquart et al., 1994) included the Latino group in their analysis, but no attempt was made to disaggregate the Latino population. Thomson's (1997:69) study of racial and ethnic discrimination in death sentencing in Arizona, which begins at the earliest stage of the capital punishment process, acknowledges the diversity of "three distinct minority groups: Mexican-Americans, African Americans, and Native Americans," yet makes no attempt to disaggregate the Latino group. As noted in Tables 1 and 2, few studies have included Mexicans (or other minority groups) in the analysis, and little attempt has been made to disaggregate the Latino population in capital punishment studies (Urbina, 2007).[40]

---

[39] For a detailed discussion on the rationales and ramifications of using a dichotomous approach of theorizing and conducting research, see Perea (1997).

[40] Trujillo (1974) found that only 18 studies focused on Mexicans between 1900 and 1940; yet, Savitz (1973) found over 500 studies that focused on African Americans and the criminal justice system during the same time period (see also Holmes and Daudistel, 1984; Romero and Stelzner, 1985).

Addressing the Weakness and Gaps of Prior Studies

Given the various limitations of prior death sentence outcomes research, there are a number of questions that remain unexplored, as we seek to test the influence of race and ethnicity in crime and punishment in its totality. For instance, do similar disparate trends exist in the three additional possible death sentence outcomes? Do similar disparities exist for Mexicans and Latinos in general (vis-a-vis African Americans and Caucasians)? How severe is the death sentence outcomes disparity among these US populations once the Latino group is included in the equation? How severe is the death sentence outcomes disparity among these segments of society once the Latino category is disaggregated and included in the equation? Which ethnic Latino members are on death row? Lastly, which ethnic Latino members have been executed in the United States? Given the nature of the data, it will not be possible to address each and every one of these concerns, but great efforts will be made to address most of them.

First, prior theoretical and empirical work has focused primarily on the experiences of African Americans (vis-a-vis Caucasians), giving the Latino history little emphasis, especially the history of US race and ethnic relations, particularly between African Americans, Caucasians, and Mexicans. As noted herein, not only do Mexicans have a distinct history, but so do the various ethnic groups that make up the Latino population.

Second, not only will the "Latino" group be included in the current tabular and logistic regression analyses, but an effort will be made to disaggregate the Latino category for descriptive purposes. Specifically, the ultimate goal is to disaggregate the entire Latino category. However, in this particular examination, only "Latinos" who were executed from 1975 to 2010 in the US (including the three states of primary interest and three death penalty states with a significant Latino population), will be disaggregated for the information presented in this book (see Chapter 6). While this will provide insight into only one of the five selected dichotomous dependent variables, executed (versus those still on death row) Latinos, it will allow speculations to be made about the other four dependent variables in the analysis, allowing us to gain further insight into the role of ethnicity in capital punishment.

Third, given the complexity and confusion, especially with the terminology and rationale for categorization, of death sentence outcomes, I extend the examination of executions and commutations to include three additional death sentence outcomes (dependent variables), as well as those who still remain under the sentence of death, in the following chapter.

Fourth, in addition to race and ethnicity, every relevant factor in the data set will be included in the analysis, which will consist of tabular analysis and logistic regression analysis (considered to be the most advanced and adequate analytic technique for this type of quantitative research). Further, in addition to making certain adjustments, like more appropriate coding, to the independent variables, careful attention will be given to missing data, which, in the past, usually has been discarded. Lastly, a central objective for detailing the logistics of the research methodology is that we are able to uncover and access various problems and questions that arise when utilizing limited data, like the exclusion of Mexicans or treating Latinos as a homogenous group.

Finally, these steps will allow for more inclusive testing of the role of race and ethnicity in capital punishment, moving beyond the two traditional approaches: (1) the Caucasian and African American dichotomist approach, and (2) the sole execution or commutation approach, which has been mostly qualitative, or limited to tabular techniques. In the following chapter, a detailed discussion of the analyses undertaken for this book will be provided, followed by the research findings in Chapter 5.

## CHAPTER 4

A Case Study of Three American States

"Knowledge of everyday life has the quality of an instrument that cuts a path through a forest and, as it does do, projects a narrow cone of light on what lies just ahead and immediately around; on all sides of the path there continues to be darkness."

--Berger and Luckmann

This study will utilize a data set from the Inter-university Consortium for Political and Social Research (ICPSR #6956), *Capital Punishment in the United States, 1973-1995*, by U.S. Department of Justice, Bureau of Justice Statistics (1997). *Capital Punishment in the United States, 1973-1995* provides annual data on inmates under the sentence of death, as well as those who had their sentence commuted or vacated and prisoners who were executed. The data set includes several basic socio-demographic variables, like race, ethnicity, state, sex, age, marital status at the time of imprisonment, level of education, and region of incarceration. Criminal history data includes prior felony convictions and prior convictions for criminal homicide and the legal status at the time of the capital offense. The data set contains a total of 6,228 cases, and provides information on prisoners whose death sentences were removed, in addition to data on those inmates who were executed. The data set also provides information about inmates who received a second death sentence by year end 1995 as well as prisoners who were already on death row.

As mentioned earlier (see Tables 1 and 2), it is difficult to locate studies that include Mexicans or Latinos as a whole, along with African

Americans and Caucasians, in their analysis. On the few occasions that Mexicans (or other Latino groups), have been included, researchers have treated this diverse population as a whole, usually under the broad label of "Hispanic," or "Latino." In effect, as one of the largest and most widely used data sets, this particular data set, for example, hinders the ability to analyze the role of race and ethnicity in capital punishment in its totality in that it excludes various relevant factors, creating a methodological problem for researchers from the onset.

As such, one of the primary goals of this research project will be to disaggregate the Latino (Hispanic) categories. Of course, the ultimate objective would be to disaggregate the data for each category, recode the data, and compute the analyses. This task, though, is beyond the scope of this particular study, but a crucial mission for future research, as we continue to examine the role of race and ethnicity in crime and punishment. Given the fact that most published material usually includes only the race of the offender and not the ethnicity, one would need to search not only each individual case but also various non-conventional sources of information that require a number of resources. Thus, in the current study, the focus will be on disaggregating the Latino category for those who were executed during the last 35 years, starting with the year before *Gregg* (1976) was decided to capture the capital punishment movement after the landmark decision that was supposed to reduce race discrimination, but giving little attention to the role of ethnicity. Therefore, one objective will be to find out the exact ethnicity of all the Latinos who were executed in the United States from 1975 to 2010 (see Chapter 6).

In keeping with federal regulations, though, the data (disaggregated Latino category) will not be recoded with the exact ethnicity of individuals, another methodological problem not only for the current study but for future studies as well. Therefore, the results will be utilized for descriptive purposes. Based on the obtained results, however, we should be able to make a few tentative conclusions as to role of race and ethnicity in capital punishment: executions, commutations (usually granted by the state governor), and overturned sentences or convictions by the US Supreme Court or state appellate court.

The central objective will be to assess whether the effects of race and ethnicity in death sentences and death sentence outcomes are amplified in "threatening" contexts (Ruddell and Urbina, 2004; Urbina, 2003a, 2004a), testing for the three general hypotheses in Chapter 2. First, the odds of being executed are highest for African Americans, followed by Latinos (both "black" and "white" Latinos) and Caucasians. Second, the odds of receiving a commutation are highest for Caucasians, followed by Latinos and African Americans. Third, the odds of having a death sentence or conviction overturned by the US Supreme Court or state appellate court is highest for Caucasians, followed by Latinos and African Americans. Lastly, among the Latino population, Mexicans have received the most severe punishment in each category. Again, a consequential problem is that the data coding does not allow for the testing of specific ethnic groups, forcing us to rely on ethnicity as a homogenous group, which could result in serious validity concerns.

In essence, by extending the analysis of executions, commutations, and overturned death sentences or convictions by the US Supreme Court or state appellate court, and by exploring the role of race and ethnicity in distinctive contexts specified by socio-demographic variables and criminal history records, we are able to see the problems of existing data sets, the corresponding complexity of research methodology, the problems and questions that arise in the application of statistical techniques, and, by extension, possible implications and ramifications. To begin, of the 37 variables in the data set, only eight independent variables, the most relevant in the data set for this particular study, were selected to operationalize our hypotheses. Logically, based on prior research, these are legitimate case characteristics that need to be controlled for. However, to simplify and facilitate the analysis, some of these variables had to be re-coded, and a few moderate modifications had to be made, adding another layer of complexity, as detailed below.

STATES UNDER STUDY: CALIFORNIA, FLORIDA, AND TEXAS

As detailed below, the complexity of the process carries consequential implications and ramifications. To begin, following the data set coding, for variable 7 (Q1: State), only the three selected states (California, Florida, and Texas) were analyzed. The variable was named STATE, and dummy variables were created for California (0/1) and Florida (0/1). Texas was selected as the reference category since Texas has the most state executions, the leading executing state in America.

These three states were selected for three reasons: (1) each has the death penalty, a large population under the sentence of death, and often implements the death penalty; (2) California, Florida, and Texas are important because these states set a national trend; and (3) since the exact ethnicity of inmates is not known, these states will be used as a proxy for studying Mexicans and Cubans, for comparative and exploratory purpose. According to census figures, Cubans constitute the largest Latino minority group in Florida, and Mexicans constitute the largest Latino minority group in California and in Texas.[41] In addition, the high courts in California, Florida, and Texas spend a substantial amount of time on capital appeals, and have a highly developed capital jurisprudence. Further, because state correctional policies and agencies, such as paroling authorities, determine length of stay in correctional facilities, states are the appropriate unit for examining death sentence outcome disparities as operationalized herein. Still, a central question becomes pressing and, possibly, consequential: Are the noted proxies fully capturing ethnicity in each given state?

Lastly, other issues that tend to complicate research methodology are court decisions impacting the application of capital punishment Therefore, before spelling out the operationalization of other variables in the study, especially the dependent variables, it would be wise to provide a discussion of two historical landmark decisions and the various possible death sentence outcomes in the United States. It should be emphasized that such an examination is not only critical in the operationalization of the dependent variables, but also in selecting the time frame for the present study, to avoid possible questions of reliability and validity in research findings.

GETTING OUT FROM UNDER THE SENTENCE OF DEATH IN THE UNITED STATES

Before analyzing the possible death sentence outcomes, we must make note of extremely important US historical events which are relevant to

---

[41] As noted earlier, based on 2000 census figures, Mexicans constitute the largest Latina/o group in California (followed by Puerto Ricans and Cubans, respectively) and Texas (followed by Puerto Ricans and Cubans, respectively), and Cubans constitute largest Latina/o group in Florida (followed by Puerto Ricans and Mexicans, respectively). Additionally, California, Florida, and Texas are three of the top states of preference for residence for Latinos.

the study of capital punishment in America, to ensure that the role of race and ethnicity is properly captured in each stage of the death penalty process, and, ultimately, avoid having inconclusive results.

Two Landmark Decisions: *Furman* and *Gregg*

As an illustration of the complexity and thus possible problems that could arise in death penalty research, consider the dynamics of two major death penalty cases. On June 29, 1972, the US Supreme Court set aside death sentences for the first time in its history. In its decision in *Furman v. Georgia*, *Jackson v. Georgia*, and *Branch v. Texas* (hereafter referred to as the *Furman* decision), the Court held that the capital punishment statutes in those three cases were unconstitutional because they gave the jury complete discretion to decide whether to impose the death penalty or a lesser punishment in capital cases. Notably, the US Supreme Court did not rule that the death penalty itself was unconstitutional, only the way in which it was being administered. Specifically, *Furman* declared the Georgia statute unconstitutional because of its lack of precision and not because of the method of execution. All other existing state statutes were very similar. As such, one by one those state supreme courts declared their own statutes unconstitutional under the *Furman* reasoning, a process that took a year or two (Streib, 1999). Given these factors, there has been some confusion and some critical questions arise:

First, as a result of the *Furman* decision in 1972, a challenge was launched by a 26-year-old African American male with a sixth-grade education, who was diagnosed as having some degree of mental defect. What exactly, then, happened to all of the inmates who were on death row at that particular time? The judicial response to the *Furman* decision was that the sentences of 631 defendants awaiting execution under pre-*Furman* discretionary statutes were vacated (Wolfgang, 1978). In other words, the practical effect of the *Furman* decision was that the Supreme Court voided nearly all death penalty laws then in effect (in some 35 states), and all death row inmates (over 600 men and women) had their death sentences overturned to life imprisonment with opportunity of parole. Some of those inmates were eventually paroled, but many of them were not (Bohm, 1999; Bohm and Haley, 1997).

Further, the US Supreme Court did not directly order that all death sentences be vacated. Rather, challenges were filed in the different states under the authority of *Furman*, and state courts and the lower federal courts granted relief to the prisoners. As such, this action occurred through measures taken by the various state courts for the most part (Acker, 1999). *Furman* did not set a "fixed" date for the states to carry out the order. It simply said that these defendants could not be executed (Streib, 1999). Therefore, different states used different approaches.   Some just converted the death sentences to life imprisonment, while others set new sentencing hearings for each offender. But, again, the bottom line is that they all received either life without parole or some form of life with a parole option (Streib, 1999).

Second, was anyone allowed to be placed on death row between the *Furman* (1972) and *Gregg* (1976) decisions? Yes. The legislative response was reinstatement of the death penalty along the lines suggested by Chief Justice Burger. In fact, by the fall of 1974, 30 states had enacted new death penalty statutes that were designed to meet the Court's objections. Following the enactment of the new death penalty statutes, the number of individuals sentenced to death soared. Death sentences began to be imposed under these new laws as early as 1973, resulting in confusion for those vested in capital punishment.

According to Bohm (1999), by early 1973, just a couple of months after *Furman*, the Florida legislature met in special session to enact a new death penalty statute, Florida being the first state to do so. Though, according to Acker (1999), it was not only Florida that reinstated the death penalty through new legislation (as early as late 1972), but many more did so during 1973. As Acker (1999) points out, the year-end total of death row inmates for 1972 would reflect the prisoners sentenced to death before *Furman*, and the year-end total for 1973 could reflect those sentenced to death under the post-*Furman* legislation. So there probably was very little time during which no one was sentenced to death. In fact, in 1975 alone, 285 defendants were condemned to death, more than double the number sentenced (mostly for murder, but some were sentenced for rape and kidnapping) in any previously reported year (Bohm and Haley, 1997). Wolfgang (1978) reports that by Spring 1976, 34 states had passed new death penalty statutes and, as of January 2, 1976, there were 407 individuals sentenced to death under the new statutes. Although the number under the sentence of death declined (42 in 1973) as a result of *Furman*, the national death row census never dropped to zero. This is because each state implemented and responded to *Furman* at a different pace between 1972 and 1973. By December 31, 1972, most states had no one under a "valid" sentence of death (Streib, 1999).[42] However, many states, Florida included, immediately passed a new death penalty statute and began sentencing offenders under it as soon as they could; again, resulting in more confusion for investigators and legal scholars.

The constitutionality of those death sentences and of the new death penalty statutes was quickly challenged, and on July 2, 1976, the US Supreme Court announced its rulings in five cases. In *Woodson v. North Carolina* and *Roberts v. Louisiana*, the Court rejected "mandatory" statutes that automatically imposed death sentences for defined capital offenses. But, in *Gregg v. Georgia, Jurek v. Texas*, and *Proffitt v. Florida* (hereinafter referred to as the *Gregg* decision), the Court approved several different forms of "guided-discretion" statutes.

Those statutes, the Court noted, struck a reasonable balance between giving the trial jury some guidance and allowing it to consider the background and character of the defendant and the circumstances of the crime. In short, state legislatures then began passing new death penalty statutes between 1972 and 1974. And, trial courts began sentencing offenders to death under these new statutes. A few of these 1972 to 1973 sentences finally worked their way up to the US Supreme Court in 1976 in *Gregg*. The most dramatic effect of the *Gregg* decision was the resumption of executions under the "new guidelines" on January 17, 1977, when Utah executed Gary Gilmore by firing squad.

Third, no one was executed during the four-year period between the *Furman* decision in 1972 and *Gregg* in 1976. In fact, Gary Gilmore's January 17, 1977 execution was the first in the United States since 1967 (Acker, 1999), and while people were being placed on death row as a result of new state statutes, no one was executed due to their

---

[42] One problem with the commonly reported data is that prisons report individuals actually imprisoned on their death rows, not those who are actually under a death sentence. Several prisons probably still had many people on their death rows, even though the courts either had reversed their death sentences or were in the process of doing so. This problem continues until today, with the population of people imprisoned on death row not being the same as those under sentence of death (Streib, 1999). Thus, at times, the data that is being analyzed contains individuals whose sentence has been overturned, but still remain on death row. When this is the case, the sample of sentences overturned is actually larger than the one reported in official documents.

laws' unconstitutionality. One important caveat to all of this is the fact that some offenders were sentenced to death under federal law, and thus were not eligible for a commutation by the state Pardon Board or the governor (Vandiver, 1993). To this end, between 1973 and 1975 nine individuals were sentenced to death under federal law, but none were executed during this time frame. Also, military authorities carried out additional executions during the period under study: 160 between 1930 and 1995. Practically, then, (and contrary to popular belief), not all death sentences were commuted to life imprisonment, nor were all executions ended as a result of *Furman* (Urbina, 2002b).

As such, based on what happened in the aftermath of *Furman*, the present quantitative analysis covers the years 1975 to 1995, with the qualitative analysis for executed Latinos covering from 1975 to 2010. Specifically, given all the variability in what occurred (e.g., the timing when states enacted new statutes and when death sentencing resumed in death penalty states), and the fact that only 11 individuals were sentenced to death in 1973 (including cases for California, Florida, and Texas only) and 48 in 1974, it is best to exclude sentencing years 1973 and 1974. As a result of *Gregg*, however, there was no consistent pattern (death sentences or death sentence outcomes) across states. It is important to point out that all death sentences before 1972 were vacated as a result of *Furman*. In 1975, 83 individuals were sentenced to death in the three states under study. After 1975, every year has 80 or more individuals sentenced to death except 1977 (49) and 1979 (62). Further, after 1979, most years are 100 or more. Thus, to avoid the "*Furman* effect" on the dependent variables in the analysis, the current study will cover the years 1975 to 1995. Since the focal point of the proposed research is to analyze the role of race and ethnicity in capital punishment: executions, commutations, sentences declared unconstitutional, and sentences or convictions overturned in Texas, California, and Florida between 1975 and 1995, the sub-sample will only consist of death penalty cases (2001), the unit of analysis, covering these three states from 1975 to 1995.[43] Evidently, without taking these issues into consideration, the research methodology could be flawed, resulting in skewed results.

---

[43] By limiting the analysis to 1975-1995, 152 cases were lost: 86 in California, 44 in Florida, and 22 in Texas.

Getting off Death Row: Who Decides? Why?

Seeking to capture the influence of race and ethnicity in crime and punishment also requires an examination of the various stages of the death penalty process. There are several official "ways" (besides execution), for example, that an inmate may be removed from under the sentence of death in the United States. The most common are clemency, commutation, and appellate actions, with only a selected few "actors" having the power/authority to make such decisions, as noted below.

Clemency

Clemency is a discretionary executive power (Ammons, 1994). The clemency power is not inherent in any particular branch of government, although it is usually associated with the executive branch.[44] Radelet and Zsembik (1993) report that rationales underlying clemency include unrestricted mercy, a "free gift" of the executive, needing no defined justification or pretense of fairness; a quasi-judicial rationale indicating that governors and clemency officials may consider factors that were not presented or considered by trial judges, prosecutors, juries, or appellate courts; and a retributive notion of clemency, which is intended to ensure that only the most deserving among those sentenced to death are actually executed.[45]

The reasons for granting clemency include doubts of guilt, changes in the political climate, and laws that reflect societal enlightenment concerning the nature and scope of certain behavior. In other words, clemency is an instrument of equity in criminal law, designed to promote the general welfare by preventing injustice. Clemency is considered an appropriate means of reducing wrongful convictions or sentences that are too severe for a given offense. Radelet and Pierce (1991) note that historically, the most frequent reasons for extending clemency in capital cases were issues such as the fairness of the trial, the disparities in sentencing, and the geographic equalization of

---

[44] The word clemency is derived from two Latin words: clemens, meaning merciful and clementia, meaning mildness.

[45] Please see Radelet and Zsembik (1993) and Vandiver (1999) for two qualitative analyses of commutations.

sentences, all of which may relate to racial and ethnic disparities; that is, the influence of race and ethnicity. In short, reasons for clemency vary widely, but often fall into the following three categories: (1) to promote justice where the reliability of the conviction is in question; (2) to promote justice where the reliability of the sentence is in question; and (3) to promote justice where neither the reliability of the conviction nor the sentence is implicated (Palacios, 1996).

Clemency decisions are made personally by elected officials, the President of the US or a state governor. The most common, though, is a state governor granting clemency in the form of a sentence reduction, usually to life imprisonment, or pardon (invalidating both guilt and sentence). In fact, in most states today the governor has primary authority to grant clemency. The clemency power gives a governor the final word as to whether a convicted individual will remain in prison, for how long the inmate is to remain in prison, or whether the death sentence will be carried out by the state. In other words, governors have the choice of reducing the sentence, delaying an execution, or totally forgiving the convicted individual.

In most states, the governor may either make clemency decisions directly or exercise this power in conjunction with an advisory board. A few states have parole or pardon boards that make clemency decisions, and in several states this power is shared between the governor and a parole or pardon board. The mayor of the District of Columbia also has clemency powers. Clemency, however, does not indicate that an inmate will automatically be released from prison. In effect, while some have received clemency in the past, few have actually received a pardon (Ammons, 1994).

Commutation

Executive clemency is extended to inmates serving death sentences usually in the form of a commutation, often because of errors that occur during the bifurcated (two-stage) trial. In Texas, for instance, a death sentence can be imposed only by unanimous vote of the trial jury; that is, every jury member has to agree. If an error occurs at the sentencing phase of a trial, the case cannot be remanded for a new sentencing proceeding. In the capitol of capital punishment, Texas Court of Criminal Appeals has indicated that it may not reduce the punishment assessed by the trial jury. Instead, if the jury fails to agree, a mistrial shall be declared. If the sanction was erroneously imposed, the case stands in the same position as if the jury had failed to reach a verdict and the entire case must be retried from the beginning.

According to Palacios (1996), errors occur at every point in the conviction and sentencing process. A commutation could be a result of plea bargaining, to avoid the time and expense of a retrial. A commutation, usually by a governor, reduces the original sentence, if considered to be inappropriate, to a lesser degree of punishment, usually life imprisonment. At any stage in the appeals process, the governor could step in and issue a commutation. In Florida, for instance, the governor, who is not required to specify precise reasons for clemency, must have the approval of three cabinet members to commute a sentence. The governor could overturn the death sentence to one of life imprisonment either with an extended mandatory term or without possibility of parole. Most governors, though, have not welcomed commutation petitions. According to Radelet, Lofquist, and Bedau (1996), the rate of commutations in American capital cases has fallen to a fraction of the rate seen in earlier years in the United States, mostly due to the conservative political climate and fear of voter reprisal, a trend extending into the 21st Century, fused by the September 11, 2001 terrorist attacks on the US, the anti-narcotics movement, and the anti-immigrants movement, events that carry notions of race/ethnicity.

Former Texas Governor, George W. Bush, claimed that he limited his decisions on whether to intervene to two matters: (1) if there is any doubt about an individual's guilt or innocence, and (2) whether the courts had ample opportunity to review all legal issues in the case. Technically, Mr. Bush could only grant a death row inmate a 30-day reprieve from execution. However, as governor, Bush appointed the Texas Board of Pardons and Parole, giving its members the authority to grant clemency requests, like commutations. But, the Board never varied from Bush's position on the 113 executions and one act of clemency granted during his five-year tenure as governor. In fact, Bush approved more executions than any other governor in any state since the death penalty was reinstated in 1976.

Bush had the authority, though he never used it, to overrule an act of clemency by the Board. In Florida, former Republican Governor Robert Martinez was the first governor in the history of Florida who, given the opportunity, failed to use his clemency powers in any of the

90 capital cases he reviewed (Radelet and Pierce, 1991). Crucially, the Florida Pardons and Parole Board holds no public hearings, votes by phone, or fax, and does not explain its reasoning, making it difficult to fully capture the dynamics of capital punishment.

Notice that a commutation, while a more limited form of clemency, shares many attributes of its parent power; yet clemency and an acquittal is not the same thing. For instance, clemency in states like Ohio cannot be granted until after an individual has been convicted. Guilt must first be established. Again, this variation has created confusion among those vested in capital punishment.

Therefore, the question is whether an individual will be granted total forgiveness or a qualified degree of mercy by reducing the death sentence to a lesser charge. Being acquitted means that the suspect did not commit a crime. A grant of commutation is not a declaration that no crime took place, but only that the capital sentence will be reduced. In the case of a pardon, the results of conviction will no longer be in effect. As such, a guarantee of acquittal is not a prerequisite for granting clemency.

Finally, to obtain a more holistic view of capital punishment, three additional death sentence outcomes are noted below, which, in addition to executions, commutations (the most common form of executive clemency), will be included in the quantitative analyses of the current study to avoid gaps in the research methodology, or, worse, skewed results.

Capital Sentence Declared Unconstitutional by State or US Supreme Court

In addition to methodological concerns that could arise for not including these various death penalty outcomes, the central question, then, would be: why would a capital sentence be declared unconstitutional by a State or US Supreme Court and what would it mean for the inmate? A detailed response to this question (and to the next two questions) is beyond the scope of this chapter. There are too many procedural issues, and a few substantive ones, such as no death penalty for rape of an adult, no death penalty for offenders under 18 years of age. Suffice it to say that a death sentence could be declared unconstitutional for several reasons, but mostly for some type of error during the guilt/innocence or sentencing stages of the trial process. Acker (1999), for example, cites that a death sentence could be declared unconstitutional for issues dealing with evidentiary irregularities, inadequate jury instructions, prosecutorial misconduct, defense attorney errors, improper exclusion of jurors and many more.

Another condition under which this could take place is when the sentence or conviction (usually just the sentence) is overturned as a result of death penalty statutes being void. Though, the practice of removing individuals from a sentence of death because of statutes being struck down on appeal occurred mostly between *Furman* and *Gregg*. This, however, does not mean that the guilt/innocence of the individual will be affected, but it could be. Thus, when this occurs their death sentences will be vacated to life imprisonment with opportunity of parole.

Conviction Affirmed, Sentence Overturned by Appellate Court

The central questions in this case would be: why would a conviction be affirmed, but the sentence overturned by appellate court? And, what is the end result for the inmate? According to attorney Alan Clarke (1999), who has handled death penalty cases from beginning to end, this is partly due to the nature of capital sentencing; that is, bifurcated trials, which allow much room for error. As stated above, it is important to underscore the fact that trials in capital cases are split in two. There is a guilt phase and a penalty phase. The jury first determines the guilt or innocence of the accused; followed by another proceeding in which the same jury decides the sentence. Here, it is important to note that when federal judges, who are appointed, reverse death sentences (usually to life imprisonment) affirmed by a State Supreme Court Justice, it's usually because of ineffective assistance of counsel, a common practice in California (Elias and Fried, 1999). Therefore, appeals courts could vacate death sentences while upholding the convictions of the lower courts. Again, notice that the dynamics of final outcomes are crucial to understanding the significance of race and ethnicity in crime and punishment in its totality.

Conviction and Sentence overturned by Appellate Court

Why would a conviction and sentence be overturned by appellate court and what would that mean for the inmate? Along with error, this is partly due to the two-stage process of capital cases. For instance, insufficient evidence in the first stage (conviction) could create problems in the second stage (sentencing) and thus could lead to a new trial or re-sentencing (Clarke, 1999). Additionally, if either the conviction or the sentence is vacated (e.g., during review) by the State's highest appellate court, the case could be remanded to the trial court for additional proceedings or for retrial. However, as a result of retrial or re-sentencing, the death sentence could be re-imposed. As such, given the nature of death penalty cases, appeals courts could vacate sentences while overturning the convictions.

In short, these decisions take place for various reasons, but mostly for some type of error during the bifurcated trial. Errors could lead to a retrial or new sentencing, even an acquittal. Errors do not only happen in capital cases, like murder cases, they also happen in other felony cases, such as robbery. Further, while there are various possible outcomes for these decisions, the most common one is a death sentence overturned to life imprisonment, at times with the possibility for parole. Clearly, the dynamics of capital punishment in America are complex, elusive, slippery, and mysterious, creating confusion, possibly creating gaps in research methodology, or resulting in skewed findings. Let us now turn to the operationalization of the variables presented in this book, detailed as an illustration of the complexity of research methodology and the possible problems that could arise if the data are not properly managed.

RESEARCH VARIABLES FOR CURRENT STUDY

Dependent Variables

Again, following the coding of the data set, variable 31 (Q14C1: Reason for inmate's removal from under sentence of death), the dependent variable, was originally divided into 9 categories: (1) executed, (2) deceased by other causes, (3) capital sentence declared unconstitutional by State or US Supreme Court, (4) sentence commuted, (5) conviction affirmed, sentence overturned by appellate court, (6) conviction and sentence overturned by appellate court, (7) other [removals], (8) information not available at this office, and (9) unknown/NA. While the last category is coded as missing, the cases actually constitute individuals who are still under the sentence of death. As such, the last category is actually a possible death sentence outcome. Since no action has taken place, this is an indication, by default, of life imprisonment for those who still remain under the sentence of death.

Based on the previous section and an examination of the data for Texas, Florida, and California, the following five dichotomous dependent variables representing death sentence outcomes are the most appropriate for the analysis in the present study:

1. Those executed versus those still sentenced to death in 1995.
2. Sentence commuted versus those executed, plus those still sentenced to death in 1995.
3. Capital sentence declared unconstitutional by State or US Supreme Court versus those executed, plus those still sentenced to death in 1995.
4. Conviction affirmed, sentence overturned by appellate court versus those executed, plus those still sentenced to death in 1995.
5. Conviction overturned (and therefore also the sentence overturned) by appellate court versus those executed, plus those still sentenced to death in 1995.

For the first dichotomous dependent variable, the variable was renamed as CAPPUN. The first category was left in its original form, and coded as 1 under the label of executed, and the 9th category was recoded as 0 under the label of not executed. Since the circumstances in which the decisions for categories 3 through 8 take place are different from category 9, they were excluded from the model. Excluding such categories will allow for a valid sentencing outcome comparison between those executed and those still under the sentence of death in 1995. Also, since the second category contains individuals (52) who died of other causes [natural cause (22), suicide (19), murdered by another inmate (3), other (3), unknown/NA (5)], it was deleted from the analysis. This category, for instance, reveals nothing in terms of death sentence outcomes and the decision-making process.

The second dichotomous dependent variable was renamed COMMUT. The 4th category was recoded as 1 under the label of commuted, and the 1st and 9th categories were combined and recoded as 0 under the label of not commuted. The 3rd and 5th through 8th categories were excluded from the model. The third dichotomous dependent variable was named UNCONSTI. The 3rd category was recoded as 1 under the label of unconstitutional, and the 1st and 9th were combined and recoded as 0 under the label of not unconstitutional. The 4th through 8th categories were excluded from the model.

The fourth dichotomous dependent variable was named SENOVERT. The 5th category was recoded as 1 under the label of sentence overturned, and the 1st and 9th categories were combined and recoded as 0 under the label of sentence not overturned. The 3rd, 4th, and the 6th through 8th categories were excluded from the analysis. Finally, the 5th dichotomous dependent variable was renamed CONSENOT. The 6th category was recoded as 1 under the label of conviction sentence overturned, and the 1st and 9th categories were combined and recoded as 0 under the label of conviction sentence not overturned. The 3rd, 4th, 5th, 7th, and 8th categories were excluded from the model.

The dependent variables in these analyses, then, are death sentence outcomes: (1) execution (CAPPUN), (2) commutation (COMMUT), (3) sentence declared unconstitutional (UNCONSTI), (4) sentence overturned (SENOVERT), and (5) conviction and sentence overturned (CONSENOT). The coding will be 0/1. For instance, whether a defendant gets executed (yes=1) or not, and, whether a defendant receives a commutation (yes=1) or not. Evidently, the proper coding and recoding of dependent variables is essential to ensure that the statistical models are well fitted, generating reliable and valid results. The two types of independent variables (socio-demographic variables and criminal history variables) that will be included in logistic regression models will be discussed next.

Criminal History Data (Independent Variables)

Like the creation of dependent variables, the proper creation of independent variables is essential to avoid problems that might result in flawed or skewed statistical results. Further, in analyzing the role of race and ethnicity in crime and punishment, it is important to control for criminal history of the offender because conservatives often argue that race and ethnicity differences in outcomes are due to differences in the criminal history. Theoretically, a prior history record influences the perception of job opportunities and thus the risk of recidivism, regardless of the individuals' job history. Therefore, sentencing decisions may be guided by the belief that a prior criminal history is a clear indication of recidivism.

Given the fact that several prior studies have included the offender's criminal history information in their analyses (see Tables 1 and 2), and have found such variables to be statistically significant in this type of analysis, and the claim that the inmate's official prior criminal record is often a mandatory consideration in deciding whether the inmate should be granted a commutation (Ammons, 1994), a criminal history variable will be included in the current analyses.

Again, following the coding of the data set, variable 19 (Q10A: Prior felony convictions) was originally divided into four categories: (1) yes, (2) no, (3) unknown, and (4) unknown/NA. The variable was renamed as PRFELCON. It should be underscored that since this variable contains missing data, which could create problems, unreliable estimates, in the regression models if the proper precautions are not taken, a few modifications need to be made. One common and efficient option is to replace missing values with the mean value of the variable, and to use a dummy variable for each variable that has missing values, which describes the data as either missing or present. Dummy variables will allow us to test whether the cases with missing values on the presence of prior felonies differ significantly from the cases without missing data. If systematic differences do exist, dummy variables should control for them and the model can be interpreted appropriately. In short, a dummy variable will be created for "prior felony" missing data, coded 0 when the data are not missing and 1 when they are. In addition, missing data for "prior felony" will be coded with the mean value of the variable. Thus, the third category (156 cases) and the last category (65 cases), were recoded and given the mean value of the variable. Also, by recoding these two categories with the mean value of the variable, no cases will be lost; and therefore will not have an effect on the dependent variables. The first two categories were left in their original form, but recoded as 0/1.

Socio-Demographic (Independent) Variables

Like criminal history variables, socio-demographic variables must be properly operataionalized to capture their significance in crime and punishment, especially race and ethnicity. In effect, offender's race and ethnicity, which have been used as a proxy for racial and ethnic threat and have been linked to punitive measures by the US criminal justice system, will be the variables of principal interest in this research. A number of studies (see Tables 1 and 2) have shown that race and ethnicity play a significant and substantial role in the various stages of the capital punishment process. Thus, the following two variables are being used to create a new variable: RACE/ETHNIC.

To be more specific, variable 9 (Q4A: Race) was originally divided into five categories: (1) white, (2) black, (3) American Indian or Alaskan Native, (4) Asian or Pacific Islander, and (5) other. The third and fourth categories were recoded as missing because of the small number of cases (5 and 16 respectively) and the fact that the focus of the study is on African Americans, Caucasians, and Mexicans.[46]

Variable 10 (Q4B: Hispanic origin) was originally divided into four categories: (1) Hispanic, (2) non-Hispanic, (3) not known, and (4) unknown/NA. Given the fact that the third and fourth categories contain missing cases (127 and 55 cases, respectively), it will not be possible to include all of the cases. The RACE/ETHNIC variable, then, included Latinos [both black (1) and white (241)], African Americans (636), and Caucasians (873), the "reference" group/category, for a total of 1,751 cases. While the data indicate that the skin color of an individual is an influential factor in how one is treated, the data also indicate that country of origin, culture, and race are also influential factors in how one is treated. As such, given this and the fact that there are only seven black Latinos, it was decided to combine both white and black Latinos (242). Still, while the number of black Latinos is small, this could present a problem in the statistical models.

Since threat theory suggests that criminal male offenders are more likely to receive the worst sanctions, another variable to include would be sex, especially since there is widespread disagreement as to whether there is a clear pattern of sex discrimination in capital punishment. However, due to the small number of female defendants, sex was not included in the analysis. Nonetheless, recall that in Bedau's (1964) study of New Jersey, only one female received a death sentence in the 53 years covered by his study, and her sentence was commuted. Similarly, in the 51 years covered by Bedau (1965) in Oregon, only three females were sentenced to die, and all three sentences were

---

[46] Had the 3rd and 4th categories been retained in their original form, problems of zero cells would have plagued the analysis. And, since no cases fall under the 5th category, it is irrelevant.

commuted. Also, in the 68 years cover by Marquart et al. (1994) in Texas, the three women with death sentences were commuted, and in Maryland, only one female in 25 years was sentenced to death and her sentence was commuted (McCafferty, 1962). Lastly, Pridemore's (2000) study showed similar findings. As the number of females on death row increase, though, women must be included in the analysis.

Another critical variable to the current analysis is level of education. Given the limitations of the original data, this variable will serve as an indicator for "class," income, and employment, which have also been linked to punitive measures by political and economic elites. According to some estimates, approximately 90% of those charged with capital murder are indigent when arrested (Vick, 1995), and virtually all are indigent by the time their cases reach the appellate courts. Adequate resources are among the most significant factors influencing the outcome of death penalty cases, and education is one of them. As with prior felony convictions, education influences the perception of job opportunities and thus the risk of recidivism (Urbina, 2008).

Variable 17 (Q8: Education at first conviction of capital offense) was originally divided into 13 categories: (1) 7th grade or less, (2) 8th grade, (3) 9th grade, (4) 10th grade, (5) 11th grade, (6) 12th grade/GED, (7) 1st year of college, (8) 2nd year of college, (9) 3rd year of college (10) 4th year of college (11) more than 4 years of college, (12) not known, and (99) unknown/NA. The variable was renamed as EdLEVEL and recoded to reflect the number of years of completed school. The 1st category was recoded as 7, the 2nd as 8, the 3rd as 9, the 4th as 10, the 5th as 11, the 6th as 12, the 7th as 13, the 8th as 14, the 9th as 15, the 10th as 16, and the 11th as 17. The 12th category (295 cases) was combined with the last category (76 cases) and then coded with the mean value of the variable, representing missing data. Additionally, as with "prior felony," a dummy variable was created for missing data. However, without measures for income and employment, it's difficult to fully capture the significance of economics based solely on education.

Since prior research has indicated that marital status may play a role in the final disposition of a death sentence, a marital status variable is included in the current analysis. Theoretically, marital status is an indication of stability, and thus, viewed as a measure of future recidivism. Pridemore (2000), for instance, found that capital offenders who are married are less likely to be executed than those who are not.

Variable 16 (Q7: Marital status) was originally divided into six categories: (1) married, (2) divorced, (3) widowed, (4) never married, (5) not known, and (6) unknown/NA. The variable was renamed as MARRIED and recoded to separate the married from the unmarried. The first category was left in its original form, coded as 1. The second, third, and fourth categories were combined and recoded as 0. The last category was coded with the mean value of the variable, representing missing data, and, as with prior felony and education, a dummy variable was created for missing data. Of course, the problem here is that this does not capture individuals who are not formally married, but are living together as a couple.

Also, in view of the increase in the rate of executions as inmates' legal appeals are exhausted, a decrease in availability of federal appellate review due to recent habeas corpus modifications, and the concomitant decline in executives exercising their power to commute, the time under a death sentence is critical. The number of years under a death sentence was also included in the analysis as a control variable, since the longer the inmates are on death row, the more likely their execution, given that they were sentenced in different years. The "reason for inmate's removal from under sentence of death" (variable 31) and "year of inmate's removal from under of sentence of death" (variable 33) were utilized to calculate this new variable: IMPRISON. For those whose death sentence was removed (for whatever reason), years under a death sentence is equal to the year the sentence was removed minus the year they were sentenced to die. For those still under a death sentence in 1995, years under a death sentence is equal to 1995 minus the year sentenced to die.

Therefore, no modifications have been made to variable 33 (Q14C3: Year of inmate's removal from under sentence of death), which ranges from 1975 to 1995 (1975-1995 cases only for California, Florida, and Texas). Additionally, since this variable is only going to be used to create an additional variable, and it will not be included in the regression, the missing values (1,184 cases in the last category, 99: unknown/NA) will not affect the regression estimates. Notice that in this case, the "missing values" are not actually missing, but they are individuals who are still under the sentence of death.

Lastly, historically age when the offender committed the crime has been an influential factor in death penalty decisions. Recall that empirical studies have shown that age plays a role in the execution and commutation decision-making process (see Tables 1 and 2). This variable, then, serves as an indicator for youth, which, as the other variables herein, has been perceived as a threat not only to political and economic elites but to "mainstream America" and has been linked to punitive measures (Duran, 2009a, 2009b, 2009c; Rios, 2006; Urbina and Kreitzer, 2004). The next three variables were used to calculate the approximate age of offenders when they committed the capital offense, which is not in the data set, and thus could present a serious problem if the data are not properly recoded.

As for the previous variable, no modifications were made to variable 12 (Q5B: Date of birth–year), which ranges from 1917 to 1976 (1975-1995 cases only for California, Florida, and Texas), variable 22 (Q11B: Date of arrest for capital offense–year), which ranges from 1974 to 1995, and variable 24 (Q12B: Date of conviction for capital offense–year), which ranges from 1973 to 1995, since these variables were only used to create a new variable.

For cases with non-missing data on year of arrest, the age at time of offense was estimated by year of arrest minus the year of birth. Further, when year of arrest was missing (n=566), age at time of offense was estimated by year of conviction minus year of birth. There are several missing cases for year of arrest, which would be closer to the time when the offense was committed than the year of conviction, but since the calculated correlation between age arrested and age convicted is .978, this is a legitimate proxy for age at time of arrest. Again, notice the complexity of coding/recoding data, and the significance of using proper methodology, which if not, could result in serious statistical problems.

ANALYTICAL PROCEDURES

Like the coding/recoding of dependent and independent variables, the analytical procedure must be properly applied to avoid statistical problems, capture the role of included variables, and prevent flawed or skewed results, as detailed below. In this particular study, once the proper modifications were made, tabular analysis and logistic regression analysis, the principal analytic technique used, was performed on the three selected states separately (different models for each state) if it was determined that the interaction effect of state and race/ethnicity was statistically significant.

Logistic regression is in fact the method of choice when analyzing models with dichotomous dependent variables since performing multiple regression with a dichotomous dependent variable violates several OLS assumptions, which in turn leads to illogical predicted values and invalid hypothesis tests. Specifically, utilizing OLS regression with dichotomous dependent variables has four undesirable consequences: (1) illogical predicted probabilities, (2) heteroskedasticity, (3) non-normality, and (4) nonlinearity (Menard, 1995).

For instance, coding the dependent variable, Y, 0 when the event/outcome is absent and 1 when the event is present results in the mean of the variable being equal to the proportion of cases having a value of 1, and the predicted value Y (i.e., the conditional mean of Y given the value of the independent variables, X's, assuming linearity) can be interpreted as the predicted probability of a case falling into the event/outcome present category, given its value on the X's.

Further, in the case of illogical predicted probabilities, predicted values of Y may be greater than 1 or less than 0, values that fall beyond acceptable values for predicted probabilities because such probabilities cannot be greater than 1 or less than 0 in the "real world." With heteroskedasticity, the size of the residuals will depend on the value of the X's. These results in unbiased estimates, but standard errors will not be efficient, thus affecting significance tests. And, there will be a systematic pattern in the residuals. In the case of nonnormality, the residuals will not be normally distributed, thus sampling variances/standard errors will not be correctly estimated, resulting in invalid significance tests and confidence interval estimates. Lastly, with nonlinearity, there is inherent nonlinearity in the relationships involving a dichotomous dependent variable. Thus, violation of OLS assumptions leads to invalid hypothesis tests and unreliable results.

Therefore, logistic regression that models the log of the odds ratio (i.e., logit) is the appropriate method to use with a dichotomous dependent variable. A logistic regression model has a binary response variable as the dependent variable (i.e., a variable having only two outcomes, 0 and 1). It is common to use the generic terms failure and success for these two outcomes. The sum of the scores in the sample is then the number of successes. The mean of the 0 and 1 scores, which is the sum divided by the total sample size, equals the proportion of successes (Agresti and Finlay, 1997; Blalock, 1979). In other words, coding the dependent variable, Y, 0 when the event/outcome is absent and 1 when it is present results in the mean of the variable being equal to the proportion of cases having a value of 1, and the predicted value Y (i.e., the conditional mean of Y given the value of the independent variables, X's, assuming linearity) can be interpreted as the predicted probability of a case falling into the event/outcome present category, given its value on the X's.

The Statistical Package for the Social Sciences (SPSS) allows flexible and exhaustive ways to perform logistic regression. For example, it allows us to include both continuous and categorical variables, and it allows for automatic dummy and effect coding of categorical variables. It also computes several of the diagnostic statistics that are familiar from OLS linear regression.

The odds ratios, which are the building blocks of the logistic regression model equals the probability of an event divided by the probability of no event equals the probability of an event divided by one minus the probability of an event:

odds ratio = probability of event/probability of no event
            = probability of event/(1-probability of event).

Since probabilities (and odds ratios based on them) take an s-shaped nonlinear distribution, we take the natural log of the odds ratio to make the regression model linear in its parameters: log (probability of event/probability of nonevent)=log(odds ratio)=logit.

Additionally, since the logit (log-odds ratio) is the dependent variable in logistic regression, the following logistic regression equation is used to predict the log odds of an event happening and the odds ratio may be obtained by taking the antilog of the logit: $\log(\text{odds ratio})=B_0+B_1X_1+B_2X_2+\ldots+B_kX_k$.

The interpretation of parameter estimates (B's), which are derived using maximum likelihood estimation are as follows: (1) B_0 is the intercept and shows the value of log odds when all X's are equal to zero, (2) the B's show how much the log odds increase or decrease with a unit change in X, and (3) the antilog of the B's, Exp(B), shows how much the odds are multiplied for a unit change in X. For example, an Exp(B) equal to 1 shows equal odds (odds are 50/50), thus indicating no effect of X on the odds. And, values of Exp(B) over 1 show that the odds are increased for a unit change in X; values less than 1 show that the odds decrease. Notice that the probability, the odds, and the logit are three different ways of expressing exactly the same thing, something that can be confusing if not properly defined.

To reduce possible errors, measures of goodness of fit, significance test statistics, etc., logistic regression provides measures that are analogues to OLS regression. For instance, D_m = -2 Log Likelihood for the model $\approx$ Sum of Squares Error, and it shows how poorly the model fits the data; $G_m = D_o - D_m \approx$ F-test (note: H_o: β s=0); Cox and Snell R^2 $\approx$ Adjusted R^2; Nagelkerke $R^2 \approx R^2$; and Wald statistic $\approx$ t-test statistic for H_o: β =0.[47]

The log-likelihood is the criterion of selecting parameters in the logistic regression model. To be more specific, maximum likelihood techniques are used to maximize the value of the function, the log-likelihood function, which indicates how likely it is to obtain the observed values of Y, given the values of the independent variables and parameters, $\alpha, \beta_1, \ldots, \beta_k$.

As such, logistic regression is especially appropriate for the analysis of dichotomous and unordered nominal polytomous dependent variables. In logistic regression, the emphasis is on whether the classification of cases into one or the other of the categories of the dependent variable can be predicted by the independent variables. Instead of trying to predict the arbitrary value associated with a category, it may be helpful to reconceptualize the problem as trying to predict the probability that a case will be classified into one as opposed to the other of the two categories of the dependent variable. In logistic regression analysis, one may not only be interested in the frequency of correct as opposed to incorrect predictions of the exact value of the dependent variable, but one may also be interested in how well the model minimizes errors of predictions. With a finite number (usually only two) of the possible values of the dependent variable, one may sometimes be more concerned with whether the predictions are correct or incorrect than with how close the predicted values (predicted conditional means, which are equal to the predicted conditional probabilities) are to the observed (0 or 1) values of the dependent variable.

---

[47] For a detailed discussion of logistic regression, see Menard (1995).

Also, to further reduce the probability of statistical problems, it should be well understood that in logistic regression, if our principal concern is with how well the model fits the data, we use G_M and R^2_L, based on -2LL, to test for statistical and substantive significance. If our concern is less with the overall fit of the model and more with the accuracy with which the model predicts actual category membership on the dependent variable, the binomial d and one of the three indices of predictive efficiency (λ_p, τ_p, or Φ_p) are used to assess the statistical and substantive significance of the model. Above all, we need to emphasize that when the assumptions of logistic regression analysis are violated, calculations of a regression model may result in biased coefficients, inefficient estimates, or invalid statistical inference (Menard, 1995), creating serious problems with the obtained results.

In short, the dichotomous dependent variable (e.g., executed or not) makes logistic regression a more appropriate method than other estimating procedures available. This technique allows the conversation of logit coefficients into "odds ratios," the antilogs of logit coefficients, indicating how much more likely an outcome is for a specific predictor category. For dichotomous predictors, odds ratios indicate how much more likely an outcome is for one category as opposed to another. For continuous predictors, the odds ratio indicates how much more likely an outcome is when the predictor increases by one unit. Thus, logistic regression analysis is well suited for the analyses of the five selected dichotomous dependent variables. Also, while the principal focus of these analyses is the odds ratio for African American and Latino defendants, controlling for other relevant variables, the odds ratios for all independent variables will be discussed. Finally, as detailed herein, given the complexity of this type of research methodology, consequential problems are likely to arise if the data are not properly treated.

METHODOLOGICAL PROBLEMS

Clearly, no study is characterized by complete objectivity; that is, free of bias (Urbina, 2003c, 2007). For this particular study, there are three crucial problems to address. The first will be disaggregating the Latino category, a major challenge given that from government documents to newspapers and even academic literature, Latinos are seldom identified by their exact ethnicity.[48] However, by making use of the latest sophisticated technology and the various sources of information available we should be able to identify the specific ethnicity of the Latinos who were executed from 1975 to 2010, which will be used for descriptive purposes (see Chapter 6). Also, the latest figures show that the Latina and Latino population in Florida is predominately Cuban, while in California and Texas, the Latina and Latino population is predominately Mexican, indicating that states may be used as proxies for ethnicity. However, it's possible that the proxies might not capture the influence of ethnicity in its totality.

The second major problem is missing data. Though, since a number of "remedies" have been applied, as detailed above, it is expected that the estimates, if altered, will not be affected substantially or significantly. Further, the dummy variables included in the model for prior felony convictions, education, and marital status enable us to determine whether the data are missing at random or whether the cases with missing data somehow are systematically different from those for which data are provided. And, if there is a significant difference between sets of cases with data missing and those with available data, the inclusion in the model of each of these dummy variables control for this systemic component.

The third major problem, and perhaps the most critical, is the fact that multiple regression models, if not properly treated, may give conflicting results, depending on what variables are included in the analysis, how they are measured, and what period of observation is employed, as illustrated above (Urbina, 2007).[49] In this particular study, since the data have already been collected and coded, we must work with the selected variables, the selected time frame, and the given population. Of course, as detailed in this chapter, careful attention is being given to the research methodology, but still these problems could result in consequential findings.

---

[48] Recall that in certain points in time in the past Mexicans have been identified as "white."

[49] Another factor to consider as a control variable is the structural context of the death sentence and death sentence outcomes. As mentioned earlier, most of the studies discussed herein focused on offender and victim characteristics and not on the structural context of the death sentence or the death sentence outcome.

Further, aggravating and mitigating factors of an act may help to determine the seriousness of the offense in the mind of decision-makers, and thus may be influential factors in final disposition (Urbina, 2005; Urbina and Kreitzer, 2004; Urbina and White, 2009). And, although data on type of counsel, the relationship between victim and offender, and victim characteristics are widely available for executed inmates, such information is not collected in a central database for capital offenders whose death sentences have been commuted. Therefore, since such data are not readily available, one would need to examine the individual files of all individuals with commuted death sentences, a task that is beyond the scope of this study. Similarly, the lack of data on the victim's race in the current study adds an additional shortcoming, since, as mentioned earlier, strong evidence of racial and ethnic disparities in both the charging and sentencing stage have been shown in past studies (see Chapter 3).

Also, recall that past research has identified type of legal counsel, relationship to victim, victim's race, and whether the murder occurred together with a felony as important predictors of the decision to execute or commute the sentence (see Tables 1 and 2). As such, a failure to test for or control for a legitimate case characteristic could introduce a risk of errors in the analysis if, for instance, the omitted variable is correlated with the outcome of interest. One should be especially aware of the possibility that omitted variables may interact with variables in the system, producing nonadditive relationships. Still, while additional variables could be utilized, a more representative sample of the selected categories and perhaps a longer time frame could enhance the analysis, the existing data will suffice to conduct the study and, hopefully, with the precautions noted above, provide tentative conclusions.

Finally, while not directly related to this particular study, it is important to acknowledge that state-by-state comparisons are not likely to reveal much about the effect of capital punishment, because states differ in many ways, including their willingness to execute. Therefore, careful analysis will be performed in the hope of improving the study's validity and reliability. In effect, since the analysis is highly historical (see Chapter 2), quantitative (see Chapter 5), and qualitative (see Chapter 6), the data will be more inclusive in indicating the types of findings that support or refute the hypotheses, as we seek to better understand the role of race and ethnicity in capital punishment.

Having addressed these problems, the study presented in this book seeks to determine: (1) which ethnic Latino members are on death row; (2) which ethnic Latino members have been executed; and (3) how severe the death sentence outcome (execution, commutation, sentence or conviction being overturned by the courts as well as remaining under the sentence of death) disparities are among various ethnic groups. In short, from this analysis, we are able to obtain a more realistic picture of capital punishment in American over time. In the next chapter, quantitative research findings for the distribution of capital punishment in California, Florida, and Texas from 1975 to 1995 will be presented, which includes the capitol of capital punishment, Texas, followed by qualitative research findings for Latinos executed in the US from 1975 to 2010 in Chapter 6.

CHAPTER 5

Research Findings for California, Florida, and Texas: A Quantitative Analysis

"The truth is rarely pure and never simple."

--Oscar Wilde

This chapter presents the results of the tabular and logistic regression analyses that provide tests of the hypotheses derived from Urbina's (2003a) four-threat theory, noted in Chapter 2, to examine the role of race and ethnicity in crime and punishment.[50] The tabular results (Tables 3 to 7) are presented first followed by the logistic regression findings (Tables 8 to 16).

TABULAR ANALYSES

In Table 3 and the following tables, the chi-square (X^2) test statistic and its associated significance level (p) reveal whether derived cell

---

[50] Logistic regression models were computed for the five dichotomous dependent variables mentioned in Chapter 5. In addition, models were created for the third (capital sentence declared unconstitutional by State or US Supreme Court) and fourth (conviction affirmed, sentence overturned by appellate court) dependent variables combined. Due to the small number of cases, though, the results presented here are for the latter. While these two dispositions are not identical, they are very similar (e.g., both focus on the sentence and not the conviction).

frequencies differ significantly from the frequencies expected given the marginal distributions of the independent and dependent variables. Goodman and Kruskal tau (τ) and lambda (λ) are proportional reduction in error measures of association that give the strength of the relationship between the independent and dependent variables. The p-value reveals the level of statistical significance.

Table 3 presents the results of the cross-tabulation of death sentence disposition by state. Of all inmates removed from the sentence of death in California, 2.4% were executed, 10.6% had their sentences commuted, 62.4% had their sentences declared unconstitutional or overturned, and 24.7% had their convictions overturned. In Florida, 8.5% were executed, 1.5% had their sentences commuted, 64.4% had their sentences declared unconstitutional or overturned, and 25.7% had their convictions overturned. In Texas, 39.5% were executed, 14.8% had their sentences commuted, 6.3% had their sentences declared unconstitutional or overturned, and 39.5% had their convictions overturned.

Table 3: Cross-tabulation of Death Sentence Outcomes by State

Disposition	California	Florida	Texas	Total Percent
Executed	2.4	8.5	39.5	19.3
Commuted	10.6	1.5	14.8	7.6
Sentence unconstitutional or overturned	62.4	64.4	6.3	42.4
Conviction overturned	24.7	25.7	39.5	30.7
Total Percent	100.00	100.00	100.00	100.00
N	85	343	256	684

$X^2 = 259.504$ $\lambda = .216$ $\tau = .163$
$P = .000$ $P = .000$ $P = .000$

Table 3 shows marked differences in death sentence dispositions across states. Of all inmates removed from the sentence of death, 2.4% of those in California were executed compared with 8.5% of those in Florida, and 39.5% of those in Texas. Commutations also differed across states with 1.5% of cases in Florida receiving commutations, 10.6% in California compared with 14.8% in Texas. In Florida and

California, the majority of cases (64.4% and 62.4%, respectively) had their death sentences overturned or declared unconstitutional by the courts while only 6.3% of the cases in Texas had a similar outcome. On the other hand, a higher percentage of cases in Texas (39.5%) had their convictions overturned, while 24.7% of the cases in California and 25.7% of the cases in Florida had their convictions overturned. The X^2 test indicates that the relationship between state and death sentence disposition is statistically significant. The τ and λ statistics show that the strength of the association between state and disposition is weak to moderate and statistically significant.

These results show that California carried out the lowest percentage of executions and granted a low percentage of commutations while it overturned a high percentage of death sentences as well as convictions. Florida granted the lowest percentage of commutations, but had the highest percentage of sentences being declared unconstitutional or overturned by the courts. Texas carried out the highest percentage of executions, 20 times greater than California and five times greater than Florida, it also granted the highest percentage of commutations as well as convictions overturned, but a very low percentage of sentences declared unconstitutional or overturned. California and Florida had a similar pattern of dispositions.

Overall, these results provide partial support for Urbina's (2003a) predictions, noted in Chapter 2. Predictions were made that Texas, followed by Florida, and California, would be: (1) more likely to execute; (2) less likely to commute; (3) less likely to declare a death sentence unconstitutional; (4) less likely to overturn a death sentence; and (5) less likely overturn a conviction. The results provide support for hypotheses 1, 3, and 4. Also, in Chapter 2 alternative hypotheses suggested that Texas, followed by Florida, and California, would be: (1) more likely to declare a death sentence unconstitutional; (2) more likely to overturn a death sentence; and (3) more likely overturn a conviction. (Note: Hypotheses 3 and 4 were combined.) Thus, the results provide support for the third alternative hypothesis.

Table 4 presents the cross-tabulation of death sentence disposition by race/ethnicity for all three states in the study combined. Of all Latinos removed from the sentence of death, 23.1% were executed, 11.5% had their sentences commuted, 28.2% had their sentences declared unconstitutional or overturned, and 37.2% had their convictions overturned. Of all African Americans removed from the sentence of death, 18.8% were executed, 6.1% had their sentences commuted, 44.1% had their sentences declared unconstitutional or overturned, and 31.0% had their convictions overturned. Of all Caucasian inmates removed from the sentence of death, 18.8% were executed, 7.8% had their sentences commuted, 44.3% had their sentences declared unconstitutional or overturned, and 29.1% had their convictions overturned.

Table 4: Cross-tabulation of Death Sentence Outcomes by Race/Ethnicity

Disposition	Latino	African American	Caucasian	Total Percent
Executed	23.1	18.8	18.8	19.3
Commuted	11.5	6.1	7.8	7.6
Sentence unconstitutional or overturned	28.2	44.1	44.3	42.4
Conviction overturned	37.2	31.0	29.1	30.7
Total Percent	100.00	100.00	100.00	100.00
N	78	245	361	684

$X^2 = 8.524$ $\lambda = .018$ $\tau = .005$
$P = .202$ $P = .327$ $P = .090$

Table 4 shows some differences in death sentence dispositions by race/ethnicity. Of all inmates whose death sentences were removed, 23.1% of Latinos were executed compared with 18.8% of African Americans and 18.8% of Caucasians. Similarly, 11.5% of Latinos were granted commutations compared with 6.1% of African Americans and 7.8% of Caucasians. Turning to the death sentence being overturned or declared unconstitutional, 28.2% of Latinos received this disposition compared with 44.1% of African Americans and 44.3% of Caucasians. Finally, for convictions overturned, 37.2% of Latinos fell in this category compared with 31% of African Americans and 29.1% of Caucasians. Neither the X^2 test statistic nor the two measures of association were statistically significant; thus, there is no relationship between race/ethnicity and death sentence disposition.

Notice, however, that the distribution of dispositions for Caucasians and African Americans is nearly identical. Latinos, though, were most likely to be executed, have their sentences commuted, and have their convictions overturned, while they were much less likely to have their sentences overturned or declared unconstitutional by the courts. Thus, these results provide mixed support for the four-threat theory. Recall that in Chapter 2, the four-threat theory of death sentence outcomes suggested the following five points, that in California, Florida, and Texas (in ascending order): (1) African Americans would be more likely to be executed than Mexicans, definitely more likely than Cubans, and, certainly more likely than Caucasians; (2) African Americans would be less likely to receive a commutation than Mexicans, definitely less likely than Cubans, and certainly less likely than Caucasians; (3) African Americans would be less likely to have their sentence declared unconstitutional than Mexicans, definitely less likely than Cubans, and certainly less likely than Caucasians; (4) African Americans would be less likely to have their sentence overturned than Mexicans, definitely less likely than Cubans, and certainly less likely than Caucasians; and (5) African Americans would be less likely to have their conviction overturned than Mexicans, definitely less likely than Cubans, and certainly less likely than Caucasians.

It was also indicated that the four-threat theory of death sentence outcomes leads to competing hypotheses. Given the complex nature of the decision-making process, the opposite could also be possible for the last three hypotheses. As such, it was predicted that in California, Florida, and Texas (in ascending order): (1) African Americans would be more likely to have their sentence declared unconstitutional than Mexicans, definitely more likely than Cubans, and certainly more likely than Caucasians; (2) African Americans would be more likely to have their sentence overturned than Mexicans, definitely more likely than Cubans, and certainly more likely than Caucasians; and (3) African Americans would be more likely to have their conviction and sentence overturned than Mexicans, definitely more likely than Cubans, and certainly more likely than Caucasians. Thus, while the findings for African Americans and Caucasians, which are similar, are contrary to predictions in Chapters 2, the findings for Latinos provide partial support for the four-threat theory. The findings for Latinos do not support hypotheses 2 but partially support hypotheses 1, 3, and 4. Additionally, the findings for Latinos provide partial support for the third alternative hypothesis.

Table 5 presents the cross-tabulation of death sentence dispositions by race/ethnicity in California. Of all Latino inmates removed from the sentence of death, 7.1% had their sentences commuted, 64.3% had their sentences declared unconstitutional or overturned, and 28.6% had their convictions overturned. Of all African American inmates removed from the sentence of death, 7.1% had their sentences commuted, 64.3% had their sentences declared unconstitutional or overturned, and 28.6% had their convictions overturned. Of all Caucasian inmates removed from the sentence of death, 4.7% were executed, 14.0% had their sentences commuted, 60.5% had their sentences declared unconstitutional or overturned, and 20.9% had their convictions overturned.

Table 5: Cross-tabulation of Death Sentence Outcomes by Race/Ethnicity in California

Disposition	Latino	African American	Caucasian	Total Percent
Executed	---	---	4.7	2.4
Commuted	7.1	7.1	14.0	10.6
Sentence unconstitutional or overturned	64.3	64.3	60.5	62.4
Conviction overturned	28.6	28.6	20.9	24.7
Total Percent	100.00	100.00	100.00	100.00
N	14	28	43	85

X^2 = 3.436 λ = .000 τ = .007
P = .752   P = —a   P = .949

a. Cannot be computed because of the asymptotic standard error = 0.

Again, as in the previous table, Table 5 shows some differences in death sentence dispositions by race/ethnicity. Of all inmates whose death sentence was removed, 4.7% of Caucasians were executed, but no African American or Latino inmates were executed. For commutations, 7.1% of Latinos were granted commutations compared with 14.0% of African Americans and 14.0% of Caucasians. Also, for death sentences that were declared unconstitutional or overturned, 64.3% of Latinos and 64.3% of African Americans received this disposition compared with 60.5% of Caucasians. Finally, for convictions overturned, 28.6% of Latinos and 28.6% of African

Americans fell in this category compared with 20.9% of Caucasians. Neither the $\mathbf{X}^2$ test statistic nor the measures of association were statistically significant; thus, there is no relationship between race/ethnicity and death sentence disposition in California.

Overall, results provide mixed support for predictions in Chapter 2. Notice that the distribution of dispositions for African Americans and Latinos is identical. Caucasians were most likely to be executed, and have their sentences commuted, while they were slightly less likely to have their sentences overturned or declared unconstitutional as well as their convictions overturned by the courts. The distribution of commutations, then, provides partial support for the four-threat theory of death sentence outcomes. Findings do not support hypotheses 1 and 3, but partially support hypotheses 2 and 4. Additionally, the findings provide partial support for all three alternative hypotheses.

Table 6 presents the cross-tabulation of death sentence dispositions by race and ethnicity in Florida. Of all Latino inmates removed from the sentence of death, 5.3% were executed, 68.4% had their sentences declared unconstitutional or overturned, and 26.3% had their convictions overturned. Of all African American inmates removed from the sentence of death, 6.8% were executed, 2.3% had their sentences commuted, 63.2% had their sentences declared unconstitutional or overturned, and 27.8% had their convictions overturned. Of all Caucasian inmates removed from the sentence of death, 9.9% were executed, 1.0% had their sentences commuted, 64.9% had their sentences declared unconstitutional or overturned, and 24.1% had their convictions overturned.

Table 6, like the previous tables, reveals some small differences in death sentence dispositions by race and ethnicity. Of all inmates whose death sentences were removed, 5.3% of Latinos were executed compared with 6.8% of African American and 9.9% of Caucasians. For commutations, 2.3% of African Americans were granted commutations compared with 1.0% of Caucasians. No commutations were granted to Latinos. Also, for death sentences that were declared unconstitutional or overturned, 68.4% of Latinos received this disposition compared with 63.2% of African Americans and 64.9% of Caucasians. Lastly, for convictions overturned, 26.3% of Latinos fell in this category compared with 27.8% of African Americans and 24.1% of Caucasians. As in the previous table, neither the $\mathbf{X}^2$ test statistic nor one of the measures of association were statistically significant; thus, there is no relationship between race/ethnicity and death sentence disposition in the state of Florida during the time under analysis.

Table 6: Cross-tabulation of Death Sentence Outcomes by Race/Ethnicity in Florida

Disposition	Latino	African American	Caucasian	Total Percent
Executed	5.3	6.8	9.9	8.5
Commuted	---	2.3	1.0	1.5
Sentence unconstitutional or overturned	68.4	63.2	64.9	64.4
Conviction overturned	26.3	27.8	24.1	25.7
Total Percent	100.00	100.00	100.00	100.00
N	19	133	191	343

X^2 = 2.777 λ = .000 τ = .002
P = .836   P = —a   P = .949
a. Cannot be computed because of the asymptotic standard error = 0.

Again, overall, these findings provide mixed support for the noted predictions in Chapter 2. Notice that the distribution of dispositions for African Americans and Caucasians is very similar. Caucasians were most likely to be executed, while they were less likely to have their convictions overturned by the courts. African Americans were most likely to have their sentences commuted and have their convictions overturned, while they were less likely to have their sentences overturned or declared unconstitutional. Latinos were most likely to have their sentences overturned or declared unconstitutional, while they were less likely to be executed, and have their sentences commuted. The distribution of dispositions, especially for sentences overturned or declared unconstitutional and overturned convictions, in California and Florida is very similar, and provides partial support for the four-threat theory. Specifically, the findings do not support hypotheses 1, 3, 4, or 5 but partially support hypothesis 2, and provide partial support for all three alternative hypotheses.

Table 7 presents the cross-tabulation of death sentence dispositions by race and ethnicity in Texas. Of all Latino inmates removed from the sentence of death, 37.8% were executed, 17.8% had their sentences commuted, and 44.4% had their convictions overturned. Of all African American inmates removed from the sentence of death, 44.0% were executed, 11.9% had their sentences commuted, 7.1% had their sentences declared unconstitutional or overturned, and 36.9% had their convictions overturned. Of all Caucasian inmates removed from the sentence of death, 37.0% were executed, 15.7% had their sentences commuted, 7.9% had their sentences declared unconstitutional or overturned, and 39.4% had their convictions overturned.

Table 7: Cross-tabulation of Death Sentence Outcomes by Race/Ethnicity in Texas

Disposition	Latino	African American	Caucasian	Total Percent
Executed	37.8	44.00	37.0	39.5
Commuted	17.8	11.9	15.7	14.8
Sentence unconstitutional or overturned	---	7.1	7.9	6.3
Conviction overturned	44.4	36.9	39.4	39.5
Total Percent	100.00	100.00	100.00	100.00
N	45	84	127	256

$X^2 = 5.372$ $\lambda = .039$ $\tau = .005$
$P = .497$ $P = .604$ $P = .748$

Table 7, like the previous tables, shows some differences in death sentence dispositions by race and ethnicity. Specifically, of all inmates whose death sentences were removed, 37.8% of Latinos were executed compared with 44.0% of African Americans and 37.0% of Caucasians. For commutations, 17.8% of Latinos were granted commutations compared with 11.9% of African Americans and 15.7% of Caucasians. Also, for death sentences that were declared unconstitutional or overturned, 7.1% of African Americans received this disposition compared with 7.9% of Caucasians. Latinos had no death sentences declared unconstitutional or overturned. Lastly, for convictions overturned, 44.4% of Latinos fell in this category compared with 36.9% of African American and 39.4% of Caucasians. Neither the X^2 test statistic nor the two measures of association were statistically significant; thus, there is no relationship between race/ethnicity and death sentence disposition in the state of Texas.

Overall, these results provide partial support for the cited predictions in Chapter 2. As the table indicates, the distribution, especially for sentences overturned or declared unconstitutional, for African Americans and Caucasians is very similar. Caucasians were most likely to have their sentences overturned or declared unconstitutional, while they were less likely to be executed. African Americans were most likely to be executed, while they were less likely to have their sentences commuted and have their convictions overturned. Latinos were most likely to have their sentences commuted and have their convictions overturned, while less likely to have their sentences overturned or declared unconstitutional.

Finally, note that the distribution of dispositions for California and Florida, which is similar, differs in each category from Texas' disposition distribution. California is less likely to execute, and Florida is less likely to commute. Texas, though, is most likely to execute, grant commutations, and overturn a conviction, but less likely to overturn a sentence or declare a sentence unconstitutional. Also, these findings show that the experiences of Latinos differ from those of African Americans and Caucasians, whose experiences are similar.

These findings provide partial support for the four-threat theory of death sentence outcomes. Thus, while the findings are not statistically significant, the distribution of dispositions in California, Florida, and Texas from 1975 to1995 for African Americans, Caucasians, and Latinos suggests that the possibility of discrimination in death sentence outcomes remains. In the next section, the results of a more advanced analytical technique, logistic regression, are presented, to better understand capital punishment in American over time.

LOGISTIC REGRESSION ANALYSIS

The multivariate analysis in this chapter is used to investigate the apparent race/ethnicity and state effects suggested in the cross-tabulations. In contrast to these bivariate tabulations, multivariate analysis allows for the study of simultaneous effects for many different factors, and the unique, independent contribution of each factor also can be determined. This allows us to unravel the effects of the variables concerned, such as demographic characteristics and criminal history.

As indicated in Chapter 4, the main explanatory variables used in the analysis are state of disposition and offender's race/ethnicity. Additional control variables include offender's age, education, prior felonies, marital status, and years on death row.

Three of the variables, education, prior felonies, and marital status, contain missing data for a large number of cases. To prevent loss of these cases from the analysis, missing values were replaced with the mean of their corresponding variables. In addition, a dummy variable was included for each of those three variables, which indicates if each value is missing (dummy=1) or present (dummy=0). This method allows us to control for any significant differences between cases that did not have missing data and those where the mean value was used.

Four logistic models were run. All the models used the same set of nine explanatory variables described in Chapter 4, plus the three dummy variables for missing data.[51] The four models were run twice, first using Caucasians and then African Americans as the reference category, respectively.[52]

In addition, to check for possible multicollinearity, correlation matrices, tolerances, and variance inflation factors were computed. The results obtained do not indicate problematic relationships among the variables included in the models. For instance, tolerance statistics range from low (.729) to high (.960) and variance inflation factors range from low (1.041) to high (1.371), indicating low levels of multicollinearity among the independent variables. Given these results, we proceeded to test for interaction effects.

Logistic Regression Results

Table 8 presents the results of tests for interaction between state and race-ethnicity. In this table, X_1^2 is the X^2 obtained for the model containing the main effects of all independent variables mentioned

---

[51] Gender was excluded from the analysis because of the small number of cases.

[52] Logistic regressions models were also computed without the dummies for variables with missing values. And, as in the analysis presented herein, two sets of logistic regressions were computed: (1) Caucasians as the reference group, and (2) African Americans as the reference group. In both cases, Texas was used as reference.

above; X_2^2 is the X^2 obtained when the interaction effects between state and race/ethnicity are added to the model; diff is the difference between X_2^2 and X_1^2; and significance is the p-value associated with the differences between X_2^2 and X_1^2. A statistically significant difference between X_2^2 and X_1^2 indicates that the effect of race/ethnicity on the disposition of interest differs across states, necessitating estimation of separate models for each state.

Table 8: Tests for Interaction Effects: Race-Ethnicity × State

Disposition	X_1^2	X_2^2	Diff	Significance
Execution	185.5	189.5	4.0	0.403
Commutation	96.1	99.9	3.8	0.430
Sentence overturned	300.5	307.4	6.9	0.139
Conviction overturned	176.8	180.4	3.6	0.462

Contrary to our expectations, Table 8 reveals that none of the tests for interaction between state and race/ethnicity were statistically significant. These tests indicate that the effects of race-ethnicity on death sentence dispositions did not differ across states. Therefore, logistic regression models can be estimated pooled across states.

Logistic Regression Using Caucasians and Texas as the Reference Groups

Table 9 presents the results of the logistic regression that estimates the probability of a person under a death sentence being executed versus remaining under a death sentence. The first column in Table 9 gives the logit coefficients that show how much the log of the odds of execution increase for a unit increase in the independent variable; the second column shows the odds ratios, antilogs of the logit coefficients, that express how many times the odds or probability of execution is multiplied for a unit change in the independent variable; the third column displays the standard error estimates associated with the logit coefficients; the fourth column gives the Wald test statistics, the statistical significance of which are indicated by the asterisks in column six; column five contains the R coefficients which, like standardized coefficients in OLS regression, allow comparison of the relative importance of the independent variables in predicting the probability of execution; and the final column contains the probability difference coefficients which express the change in the probability of execution for each unit change in the independent variable as a percentage. Since the logit, odds ratio, and probability difference coefficients merely are different ways of expressing the same effect, the discussion of the logistic regression results will focus on the probability difference coefficients, which are the most interpretable, and the R coefficients that assess the relative strength of the predictors.

Contrary to expectations, African Americans and Latinos were not significantly more likely to be executed than Caucasians. Holding all other independent variables constant, African Americans were 4.17% less likely to be executed than Caucasians, while Latinos were 3.25% less likely to be executed than Caucasians, but these differences were not statistically significant at the P<.05 level. Instead, the R coefficients and Wald tests indicate that state was the most important statistically significant predictor of the probability of execution. The probability difference coefficients reveal that California was 48.35% less likely than Texas to execute inmates under a sentence of death, while Florida was 30.15% less likely to carry out the death penalty. The remaining statistically significant predictors of the probability of execution include time under the death sentence, prior felony convictions, and approximate age at the time of the capital offense. Consistent with normative theories, having a prior felony conviction increased the odds of execution by almost 20 percent (19.01%), while the probability increased nearly 3 percent (2.74%) for every year spent on death row. Finally, for every year increase in the age of the offender at the time of the capital offense, the odds of being executed increased by approximately one half of one percent (.54%).

The results in Table 9 are consistent with our earlier cross-tabular results. For example, in Table 3 there were marked differences in the propensity of states to actually carry out the death sentence by executing the offender, with Texas executing nearly 40 percent of inmates removed from under the sentence of death from 1975 to 1995. On the other hand, Table 4 showed no difference in the percentage of African Americans and Caucasians executed (18.8% in each category), while 23.1% of Latinos were executed.

Table 9: Multivariate Logistic Regression Model: Executed/Under Death Sentence

Variable	Logit (B)	Odds Ratio (Exp (B))	S.E.	Wald	R	Prob[a] Diff
Race-ethnicity:						
African Americans	-0.17	0.85	0.23	0.54	0.00	-4.17
Latinos	-0.13	0.88	0.31	0.17	0.00	-3.25
Time under death sentences	0.11	1.12	0.02	23.77	0.16	2.74**
Prior felony convictions	0.80	2.23	0.28	7.95	0.08	19.01**
Age at time of offense	0.02	1.02	0.01	2.79	0.03	0.56*
Marital status	-0.01	0.99	0.22	0.00	0.00	-0.36
Education	-0.02	0.98	0.05	0.18	0.00	-0.56
State:						
California	-4.08	0.02	0.72	32.25	-0.19	-48.35**
Florida	-1.40	0.25	0.24	34.36	-0.20	-30.16**
Dummies for missing data:						
Education	-0.16	0.85	0.38	0.17	0.00	-3.91
Martial status	-1.75	0.17	1.08	2.66	-0.03	-35.22
Prior felony conviction	0.50	1.65	0.43	1.37	0.00	12.31
Constant	-2.94	-	0.77	14.69	-	-**

N = 1,199   **p < .05
X^2 = 185.52**   *p < .01

a. Probability difference=((odds ratio/(1+odds ratio)) -.5)*100

In addition, the findings in Table 9 provide support for theories that suggest legal and criminal justice process variables are the primary determinants of execution, while extra-legal variables are irrelevant. Here, race/ethnicity variables failed to be significant, while years under the sentence of death, prior felony convictions, and age at time of the capital offense proved to be significant predictors of the probability of execution.

Finally, the significant X^2 statistic in Table 9 indicates that the model provides a good fit to the data. However, an examination of the classification table shows that the model correctly classifies non-executions more than executions. Only 2 of the 132 executed in the three states (i.e., 1.52%) were correctly classified as having been executed. Taken together, these findings indicate that, while the model fits the data reasonably well, there are other factors not in the model that influence the probability of being executed.

Table 10 presents the results of the logistic regression that estimates the probability of an individual under a death sentence receiving a commutation versus executed plus remaining under a death sentence. As in the previous table, contrary to expectations, African Americans and Latinos were not significantly more likely to receive a commutation than Caucasians. Holding all other independent variables constant, African Americans were 9.25% less likely to receive a commutation than Caucasians, while Latinos were 16.39% less likely to be commuted than Caucasians, but these differences were not statistically significant at the P<.05 level. Instead, the R coefficients and Wald tests indicate that the dummy variable for prior felony convictions was the most important statistically significant predictor of the probability of commutation. The remaining statistically significant predictors of the probability of commutation include time under the death sentence, education, dummy variable for missing education, and state. The probability difference coefficients reveal that California was 23.57% less likely than Texas to grant a commutation to inmates under a sentence of death, while Florida was 38.71% less likely to commute a death sentence. Also, for every year of additional education, the odds of commutation decreased by 6.23%. However, the dummy variable for education shows that the odds of commutations increased by 25.55% for inmates with missing data on education. For every year spent on death row, the odds of receiving a commutation decreased by 3.95%.

The results in Table 10 are consistent with earlier cross-tabular results. For example, Table 3 showed marked differences in the propensity of states to grant commutations, with Texas commuting nearly 15 percent of inmate's death sentences from 1975 to 1995, while California and Florida commuted a much lower percentage of death sentences, especially Florida, (10.6% and 1.5%, respectively). Table 4, however, showed no substantial difference, especially between African Americans and Caucasians having their sentences commuted.

The findings in Table 10 provide support for theories that suggest legal and criminal justice process variables are the primary determinants of commutations, while, as in the previous table, extra-legal variables are irrelevant. In this particular model, race/ethnicity variables failed to be significant, while years under the sentence of death, and education proved to be significant predictors of the probability of commutation.

Table 10: Multivariate Logistic Regression Model: Commuted/
Executed and Under Death Sentence

Variable	Logit (B)	Odds Ratio (Exp(B))	S.E.	Wald	R	Prob Diff
Race-ethnicity:						
African American	-0.37	0.69	0.37	1.05	0.00	-9.25
Latinos	-0.68	0.51	0.46	2.24	-0.02	-16.39
Time under death sentence	-0.16	0.85	0.04	13.13	-0.16	-3.95**
Prior felony convictions	0.05	1.05	0.40	0.01	0.00	1.22
Age at time of offense	-0.03	0.97	0.02	1.28	0.00	-0.65
Marital status	0.15	1.16	0.36	0.17	0.00	3.68
Education	-0.25	0.78	0.10	6.11	-0.10	-6.23**
State:						
California	-1.02	0.36	0.41	6.20	-0.10	-23.57**
Florida	-2.06	0.13	0.52	15.92	-0.18	-38.71**
Dummies for missing data:						
Education	1.13	3.09	0.42	7.31	0.11	25.55**
Martial status	-1.14	0.32	0.71	2.61	-0.04	-25.80
Prior felony conviction	2.02	7.57	0.37	30.54	0.26	38.33**
Constant	1.40	-	1.25	1.24	-	-

N =   1,199   **p < .05
X^2 =   96.11**   *p < .01

The significant X^2 statistic in Table 10 indicates that the model provides a good fit to the data. An examination of the classification table, however, shows that the model correctly classifies non-commutations more than commutations. Only 3 of the 52 commutation received in the three states (i.e., 5.77%) were correctly classified as having been commuted. Taken together, these findings indicate that, while the model fits the data reasonably well, there are other factors not in the model that influence the probability of receiving a commutation.

Table 11 presents the results of the logistic regression that estimates the probability of individuals having their death sentences overturned or declared unconstitutional by the courts versus those executed plus those remaining under a death sentence. Contrary to expectations, African Americans were not significantly more likely to have their sentences overturned or declared unconstitutional than Caucasians. However, Latino inmates were significantly less likely to have their sentences overturned. Holding all other independent variables constant, Latinos were 17.36% less likely to have their death sentences overturned than Caucasians, a statistically significant difference at the .05 level. African Americans were 2.03% less likely to have their death sentences overturned than Caucasians, but as mentioned above, this difference was not statistically significant at the P<.05 level. The R coefficients and Wald tests indicate that state was the most important statistically significant predictor of the probability of having a death sentence overturned or declared unconstitutional. The probability difference coefficients reveal that California was 27.87% more likely than Texas to overturn a sentence of death, while Florida was 43.79% more likely to overturn a death sentence. The remaining statistically significant predictors of the probability of having a death sentence declared unconstitutional or overturned include time under the death sentence, prior felony convictions, marital status, education, and the dummy variable for education. Consistent with normative theories, having a prior felony conviction decreased the odds of having a death sentence declared unconstitutional or overturned by almost 13 percent (-12.43%), while the probability decreased over 2 percent (-2.26%) for every year spent on death row. Being married increased the odds of having a death sentence declared unconstitutional or overturned by nearly 15 percent (14.63%), while the probability decreased over 3 percent (-3.25%) for every additional year of education. The dummy variable for education missing, however, indicates that missing data on education increased the odds of having a death sentence declared unconstitutional or overturned by the courts by over 18 percent (18.44%).

Table 11: Multivariate Logistic Regression Model: Sentence Overturned/ Executed and Under Death Sentence

Variable	Logit (B)	Odds Ratio (Exp(B))	S.E.	Wald	R	Prob Diff
Race-ethnicity:						
African Americans	-0.08	0.92	0.16	0.26	0.00	-2.03
Latinos	-0.72	0.48	0.27	7.23	-0.06	-17.36**
Time under death sentence	-0.09	0.91	0.02	27.65	-0.13	-2.26**
Prior felony convictions	-0.51	0.60	0.16	9.55	-0.07	-12.43**
Age at time of offense	-0.01	0.99	0.0.1	2.22	-0.01	-0.36
Marital status	0.60	1.83	0.17	12.26	0.08	14.63**
Education	-0.13	0.88	0.04	9.28	-0.07	-3.25**
State:						
California	1.26	3.52	0.30	17.40	0.10	27.87**
Florida	2.71	15.10	0.28	97.29	0.25	43.79**
Dummies for missing data:						
Education	0.77	2.17	0.19	16.64	0.10	18.44**
Martial status	-0.17	0.84	0.34	0.25	0.00	-4.25
Prior felony conviction	-0.02	0.98	0.32	0.00	0.00	-0.38
Constant	-0.79	-	0.59	1.82	-	-

N = 1,199   **$p < .05$
X^2 = 300.46**   *$p < .01$

The results in Table 11 are consistent with earlier cross-tabular results. Table 3 showed marked differences in the propensity of states to overturn a death sentence, with California and Florida overturning over 60 percent (62.4% and 64.4%, respectively) of the death sentences removed during the 1975-1995 period, while Texas overturned 6.3% of the death sentences removed. Table 4 showed only a slight difference in the percentage of African Americans and Caucasians having their sentences overturned or declared unconstitutional (44.1% and 44.3%, respectively), while 28.2% of Latinos had their death sentences declared unconstitutional or overturned by the courts.

The findings in Table 11 provide support for theories that suggest legal and criminal justice process factors are the primary determinants of having a death sentence declared unconstitutional or overturned, while extra-legal variables are important, but not the most important. In this case, the race/ethnicity variable for African American failed to be significant, while Latino, years under the sentence of death, prior felony convictions, marital status, and education proved to be significant predictors of the probability of having a death sentence declared unconstitutional or overturned by the courts.

The significant X^2 statistic in Table 11 indicates that the model provides a good fit to the data. An examination of the classification table, though, shows that the model correctly classifies sentences not overturned more than those overturned. Only 57 of the 290 death sentences declared unconstitutional or overturned in the three states (i.e., 19.66%) were correctly classified as having been overturned. Taken together, these findings indicate that, while the model fits the data reasonably well, there are other factors not in the model that influence the probability of having a death sentence declared unconstitutional or overturned by the courts.

Table 12 presents the results of the logistic regression that estimates the probability of a conviction being overturned in death penalty cases by US courts versus executed plus remaining under a death sentence. As in Tables 9 and 10, contrary to our expectations, African Americans and Latinos were not significantly more likely to have their convictions overturned than Caucasians. Holding all other independent variables constant, African Americans were 3.22% more likely to have their convictions overturned than Caucasians, while Latinos were 8.29% less likely to have their convictions overturned than Caucasians, but these differences were not statistically significant at the P<.05 level. Instead, the R coefficients and Wald tests indicate that the number of years under the sentence of death and dummy variable for prior felony convictions were the most important statistically significant predictors of the probability of the conviction being overturned. The remaining statistically significant predictors of the probability of the conviction being overturned include marital status, education, dummy variable for education missing, and the state of California. The probability difference coefficients reveal that California was 29.16% less likely than Texas to overturn a conviction of those under a sentence of death, while Florida was 1.06% more likely to overturn a conviction. Also, being married increased the odds of having a conviction overturned by over 16 percent (16.13%). For every year of additional education, the odds of having a conviction overturned decreased by 1.93%. However, for the dummy variable for education missing, the odds increased by 10.46% for those with missing data on education. Similarly, the dummy variable for prior felony conviction showed that having missing data on a prior felony conviction increased the odds of having a conviction overturned by 31.18%. For every year spent on death row, the odds of an overturned conviction decreased by 3.48%.

The results in Table 12 are also consistent with earlier cross-tabular results. For example, Table 3 showed marked differences in the propensity of states to overturn a conviction, with Texas overturning the convictions nearly 40 percent of the death sentences removed from 1975 to 1995, while California and Florida overturned a much lower percentage (24.7% and 25.7%, respectively) of convictions. Table 4, however, showed no substantial difference, especially between African Americans and Caucasians having their convictions overturned in death penalty cases by the courts.

As in the previous three tables, the findings in Table 12 provide support for theories that suggest legal and criminal justice process factors are the primary determinants of having a conviction overturned in death penalty cases, while, as in Tables 9 and 10, extra-legal variables appear to be irrelevant. As noted above, in this particular model, race/ethnicity variables failed to be significant, while years under the sentence of death, marital status, and education proved to be significant predictors of the probability of having a conviction overturned in death penalty cases.

The significant X^2 statistic in Table 12 indicates that the model provides a good fit to the data. An examination of the classification table, though, shows that the model correctly classifies convictions not overturned more than those that were overturned. Only 38 of the 210 overturned convictions in the three states (i.e., 18.10%) were correctly classified as having been overturned. Taken together, these findings indicate that, while the model fits the data reasonably well, there are other factors not in the model that influence the probability of having a conviction overturned in death penalty cases.

Table 12: Multivariate Logistic Regression Model: Conviction Overturned/ Executed and Under Death Sentence

Variable	Logit (B)	Odds Ratio (Exp(B))	S.E.	Wald	R	Prob Diff
Race-ethnicity: African Americans	0.13	1.14	0.18	0.51	0.00	3.22
Latinos	-0.33	0.72	0.25	1.76	0.00	-8.29
Time under death sentence	-0.14	0.87	0.02	40.54	-0.18	-3.48**
Prior felony convictions	-0.23	0.79	0.20	1.38	0.00	-5.74
Age at time of offense	0.01	1.01	0.01	1.29	0.00	0.28
Marital status	0.67	1.95	0.18	13.68	0.10	16.13**
Education	-0.08	0.93	0.04	3.00	-0.03	-1.93**
State: California	-1.33	0.26	0.26	25.54	-0.14	-29.16**
Florida	0.04	1.04	0.18	0.05	0.00	1.06
Dummies for missing data: Education	0.42	1.53	0.23	3.43	0.03	10.46**
Martial status	-0.34	0.71	0.38	0.80	0.00	-8.48
Prior felony conviction	1.46	4.31	0.23	40.45	0.18	31.18**
Constant	-0.52	-	0.59	0.78	-	-

N = 1,199   **p < .05
X^2 = 176.76**   *p < .01

<u>Logistic Regression using African Americans and Texas as the Reference Groups</u>

Tables 13-16 present the second set of results, which utilized African Americans and Texas as reference groups. Since the only major alterations as a result of switching the reference group are the coefficients for the race-ethnicity variables (and the constant), only the findings for African American, Latino, and Caucasian variables are discussed. As in Table 9, Table 13 presents the results of the logistic regression that estimates the probability of a person under a death sentence being executed versus remaining under a death sentence.

As in Table 9, the race-ethnicity variables are not statistically significant. Caucasians and Latinos were not significantly more likely to be executed than African Americans. Holding all other independent variables constant, Caucasians were 4.17%, as in Table 9, more likely to be executed than African Americas, while Latinos were 0.93% more likely to be executed than African Americans, but these differences were not statistically significant at the P<.05 level.

Table 13: Multivariate Logistic Regression Model: Executed/Under Death Sentence

Variable	Logit (B)	Odds Ratio (Exp(B))	S.E.	Wald	R	Prob Diff
Race-ethnicity:						
African American	0.17	1.18	0.23	0.54	0.00	4.17
Latinos	0.04	1.04	0.33	0.01	0..00	0.93
Time under death sentence	0.11	1.12	0.02	23.77	0.16	2.74**
Prior felony conviction	0.80	2.23	0.28	7.95	0.08	19.01**
Age at time of offense	0.02	1.02	0.01	2.79	0.03	0.56*
Marital status	-0.01	0.99	0.22	0.00	0.00	-0.36
Education	-0.02	0.98	0.05	0.18	0.00	-0.56
State:						
California	-4.08	0.02	0.72	32.25	-0.19	-48.35**
Florida	-1.40	0.25	0.24	34.36	-0.20	-30.16**
Dummies for missing data:						
Education	-0.16	0.85	0.38	0.17	0.00	-3.91
Martial status	-1.75	0.17	1.08	2.66	-0.03	-35.22
Prior felony conviction	0.50	1.65	0.43	1.37	0.00	12.31
Constant	-3.11	-	0.76	16.87	-	-**

N = 1,199   **p < .05
X^2 = 185.52**   *p < .01

Table 14: Multivariate Logistic Regression Model: Commuted/
Executed and Under Death Sentence

Variable	Logit (B)	Odds Ratio (Exp (B))	S.E.	Wald	R	Prob Diff
Race-ethnicity:						
Caucasians	0.37	1.45	0.37	1.05	0.00	9.25
Latinos	-0.31	0.74	0.49	0.40	0.00	-7.61
Time under death sentence	-0.16	0.85	0.04	13.13	-0.16	-3.95**
Prior felony convictions	0.05	1.05	0.40	0.01	0.00	1.22
Age at time of offense	-0.03	0.97	0.02	1.28	0.00	-0.65
Marital status	0.15	1.16	0.36	0.17	0.00	3.68
Education	-0.25	0.78	0.10	6.11	-0.10	-6.23**
State:						
California	-1.02	0.36	0.41	6..20	-0.10	-23.57**
Florida	-2.06	0.13	0.52	15.92	-0.18	-38.71**
Dummies for missing data:						
Education	1.13	3.09	0.42	7.31	0.11	25.55**
Martial status	-1.14	0.32	0.71	2.61	-0.04	-25.80
Prior felony conviction	2.02	7.57	0.37	30.54	0.26	38.33**
Constant	1.02	-	1.23	0.70	-	-

N = 1,199   **p < .05
X^2 = 96.11**   *p < .01

Table 14 presents the results of the logistic regression that estimates the probability of an individual under a death sentence receiving a commutation versus being executed plus remaining under a death sentence. As in Table 10, the race-ethnicity variables are not statistically significant. Caucasians and Latinos were not significantly more likely to have their death sentence commuted than African Americans. Holding all other independent variables constant, Caucasians were 9.25%, as in Table 10, more likely to have a death sentence commuted than African Americas, while Latinos were 7.61% less likely to be granted a commutation than African Americans, but these differences were not statistically significant at the P<.05 level. Thus, the results indicate that as far as commutations, African Americans, Caucasians, and Latinos were treated similarly in California, Florida, and Texas.

Table 15 presents the results of the logistic regression that estimates the probability of individuals having their death sentence overturned or declared unconstitutional by the courts versus those executed plus those remaining under a death sentence. As in Table 11, the race-ethnicity variable for Latinos is statistically significant, while the race variable for Caucasians is not statistically significant. Caucasians were not significantly more likely to have their death sentences declared unconstitutional or overturned than African Americans, while Latinos were significantly less likely to have their death sentences declared unconstitutional or overturned by the courts than African Americans. Holding all other independent variables constant, Caucasians were 2.03%, as in Table 9, more likely to have their death sentences declared unconstitutional or overturned by the US courts than African Americas, but again, this difference was not statistically significant at the P<.05 level. Latino inmates were 15.55% less likely to have their death sentences declared unconstitutional or overturned than African Americans, a statistically significant difference at the P<.01 level. It should be underscored that the difference is more substantial between Latinos and Caucasians (-17.36%) than Latinos and African Africans (-15.55%).

Table 16 presents the results of the logistic regression that estimates the probability of a conviction being overturned in death penalty cases by the courts versus executed plus remaining under a death sentence. The race-ethnicity variable for Latinos, which was not statistically significant in Table 12, is statistically significant, while the race variable for Caucasians is not statistically significant. Caucasians were not significantly more likely to have their convictions overturned than African Americans, while Latinos were significantly less likely to have their convictions overturned by the courts than African Americans. Holding all other independent variables constant, Caucasians were 3.22%, as in Table 12, less likely to have their convictions overturned than African Americas, but again, this difference was not statistically significant at the P<.05 level. Latinos were 11.39% less likely to have convictions overturned than African Americans, a statistically significant difference at the P<.01 level.

Table 15: Multivariate Logistic Regression Model: Sentence
Overturned/Executed and Under Death Sentence

Variable	Logit (B)	Odds Ratio (Exp(B))	S.E.	Wald	R	Prob Diff
Race-Ethnicity:						
Caucasians	0.08	1.08	0.16	0.26	0.00	2.03
Latinos	-0.64	0.53	0.28	5.36	-0.05	-15.55*
Time under death sentence	-0.09	0.91	0.02	27.65	-0.13	-2.26**
Prior felony convictions	-0.51	0.60	0.16	9.55	-0.07	-12.43**
Age at time of offense	-0.01	0.99	0.01	2.22	-0.01	0.36
Marital status	0.60	1.83	0.17	12.26	0.08	14.63**
Education	-0.13	0.88	0.04	9.28	-0.07	-3.25**
State:						
California	1.26	3.52	0.30	17.40	0.10	27.87**
Florida	2.71	15.10	0.28	97.29	0.25	43.79**
Dummies for missing data:						
Education	0.77	2.17	0.19	16.64	0.10	18.44**
Martial status	-0.17	0.84	0.34	0.25	0.00	-4.25
Prior felony conviction	-0.02	0.98	0.32	0.00	0.00	-0.38
Constant	-0.87	-	0.57	2.31	-	-

N = 1,199   **p < .05
X^2 = 300.46**   *p < .01

Table 16: Multivariate Logistic Regression Model: Conviction
Overturned/ Executed and Under Death Sentence

Variable	Logit (B)	Odds Ratio (Exp(B))	S.E.	Wald	R	Prob Diff
Race-ethnicity:						
Caucasians	-0.13	0.88	0.18	0.51	0.00	-3.22
Latinos	-0.46	0.63	0.26	3.17	-0.03	-11.39*
Time under death sentence	-0.14	0.87	0.02	40.54	-0.18	-3.48**
Prior felony convictions	-0.23	0.79	0.20	1.38	0.00	-5.74
Age time of offense	0.01	1.01	0.01	1.29	0.00	0.28
Marital status	0.67	1.95	0.18	13.68	0.10	16.13**
Education	-0.08	0.93	0.04	3.00	-0.03	-1.93*
State:						
California	-1.33	0.26	0.26	25.54	-0.14	-29.16**
Florida	0.04	1.04	0.18	0.05	0.00	1.06
Dummies for missing data:						
Education	0.42	1.53	0.23	3.43	0.03	10.46*
Martial status	-0.34	0.71	0.38	0.80	0.00	-8.48
Prior felony conviction	1.46	4.31	0.23	40.45	0.18	31.18**
Constant	-0.39	-	0.57	0.47	-	-

N = 1,199   **p < .05
X^2 = 176.76***   *p < .01

SUMMARY OF FINDINGS

While the death sentences disposition results for race (i.e., African Americans, Caucasians) are not statistically significant, some results for the ethnicity (i.e., Latino) variable are statistically significant. After controlling for time under the death sentence, prior felony convictions, age at time of the offense, marital status, education, and state (and the inclusion of three dummy variables for missing data), the results for the Latino variable are statistically significant for two dispositions: (1)

death sentence declared unconstitutional or overturned by the courts; and (2) death sentence conviction overturned by the courts.

In Tables 11 and 15, the results show that Latinos who were under the sentence of death in California, Florida, and Texas from 1975 to 1995 were less likely to have their death sentences declared unconstitutional by state or US Supreme Court or overturned by an appellate court than both African Americans and Caucasians. Table 16 shows that Latino inmates were less likely to have their convictions overturned by an appellate court during this 20-year period in the three states than African Americans and Caucasians. While the death sentence disposition results for African Americans are contrary to the first five hypotheses discussed in Chapter 2, which suggested that African Americans would be the group most disadvantaged, the findings for Latino inmates do not provide support for hypotheses 1 and 2 (on executions and commutations), but provide partial support for hypotheses 3, 4, and 5, which suggested that Latinos would be less likely to have a death sentence declared unconstitutional or overturned, and less likely to have a conviction overturned than Caucasians. Overall, the findings provide partial support for the four-threat theory of death sentence outcomes.

The logistic regression results presented in this chapter provide support for orthodox theories. Several legal factors (e.g., prior felony conviction, time under the sentence of death, and age at the time of offense) were statistically significant in several models. These findings indicate that while all the models fit the data reasonably well, there are other factors not in the models that influence the probability of execution, commutation of the death sentence, having a death sentence declared unconstitutional or overturned, and having a conviction overturned. In short, the findings indicate that differential treatment in death sentence dispositions is not completely a phenomenon of the past. While the death sentence disposition results for African Americans are contrary to our hypotheses, the results for Latino inmates provide partial support for Urbina's four-threat theory of death sentence outcomes. Finally, to gain further insight into the role of race and ethnicity in crime and punishment, the next chapter will explore the ethnic experience by not only investigating the exact ethnicity of Latinos executed in the United States from 1975 to 2010, but also by exploring various elements leading to death row, and, ultimately, execution.

## CHAPTER 6

Race, Ethnicity, and Gender from 1608 to 2010: A Qualitative Analysis

"Capital punishment turns the state into a murderer. But imprisonment turns the state into a gay dungeon-master."

--Jesse Jackson

In Chapter 2, a detailed discussion of the history of race (African American and Caucasian) and ethnic (Mexican) relations in the US was provided, exploring how historical forces, like conquest, colonialism, slavery, immigration, race, and criminal law have influenced the dynamics of crime and punishment in America over time, with the central of objective of better understanding the pragmatic implications and ramifications of historical forces, and, ultimately, setting the historical, legal, theoretical, and philosophical foundation for the study of capital punishment. A critical examination of the role of race and ethnicity in capital punishment literature was then detailed in Chapter 3, followed, in Chapter 4, by a discussion of the logistics for the empirical study presented in this book, paying particular attention to various problems that may arise when using limited data sets or the use of improper methodology. Chapter 5 presents the quantitative findings, which indicate that the historical influence of race and ethnicity in crime and punishment extends into the late 20th Century America. In this chapter, a qualitative examination of the historical legacy of executions in America within the context of race, ethnicity, and gender is provided, focusing primarily on the role of ethnicity, Latinos, on executions, an area that, as noted herein, has received limited academic search and publication. More globally, seeking to better understand the role of race and ethnicity in crime and punishment, in its totality, this chapter also makes note of executions during slavery, female executions, juvenile executions, and the execution of foreign nationals in the United States, dating back to 1608. Invariably, qualitative findings in this chapter indicate that the influence of race and ethnicity in the distribution of punishment extends into the 21st Century.

HOW MANY MEXICANS IS A HORSE WORTH?

To begin, while fictitious, the following story illustrates the role of race and ethnicity in the US by, strategically, asking a polemic question. That is, in his novel, *George Washington Gomez* (1990:178-179), Paredes shows the experience of living with conflicting and consequential historical legacies (like conquest, colonialism, slavery, and immigration), while trying to illustrate the influence of race and ethnicity in crime and punishment using a mathematical experiment, where the minor character of Orestes is an immigrant son of an exiled revolutionary intellectual living in a fictitious town called Jonesville in the Rio Grande Valley (Texas) during *la chia*, the Great Depression. Orestes poses the question to his best friend, the novel's protagonist George Washington Gomez, whom everyone calls Gualinto:

> [Orestes:] "By the way, you know how many Mexicans a horse is worth?"

> ["Gualinto:] "What kind of trick are you setting me up for?"

> "No trick. I was just reading the paper, and I figured it out . . . Two men were sentenced in court yesterday here in Jonesville. A Mexican for stealing old man Osuna's prize Arabian stud and a Negro for killing a Mexican in a fight over the price of a bottle of tequila . . . The Mexican got ten years, the Negro two . . . So you would think that before the law in this town a horse is worth five Mexicans."

> "It figures."

"But wait. The stolen horse was recovered safe and sound from the Mexican who stole him. Not a scratch on his hide even. While the Mexican the *parna* [black] killed is stone cold-dead. No way of getting him back to life. What if the Mexican who stole the horse had killed it? He would have got at least twenty years. So you can figure then that the horse is worth ten Mexicans."

"You always were good at arithmetic."

"But that's not all. You know that in murder cases Mexicans and Negros get double the sentence a white man would get. So what if the Mexican had been killed by a Gringo? The Gringo would have got off with a year. One divided into twenty: a Mexican then is worth one-twentieth the value of a horse. But that isn't all of it . . . Chances are that the Gringo's sentence would be suspended. Then how much would a Mexican be worth? What's one-twentieth of zero? Ask El Colorado [red-man, Indian]. He's studying book-keeping, he ought to know. And shake his hand for me."

THE COLOR OF JUSTICE

Invariably, the influence of race and ethnicity in crime and punishment continues to be a pressing issue in America, with the distribution of capital punishment being governed by the simultaneous interaction of historical legacies, conflictive race and ethnic relations as well as the influence of *color and economics*. In effect, as detailed in Chapters 2 to 5, the history of executions in the United States is a story shaped and re-shaped by race and ethnicity of the offender and victim, and further fused by various other factors at different points in time and space. As such, to further debunk historical myths about the effects of race and ethnicity in capital punishment in the United States, one needs to document the Mexican experience (and, of course, the experience of other ethnic and racial groups), which has been left out from the *pages of history*, due in part to the unavailability of data sets containing delineated information.

As noted in Chapter 1, a more holistic examination of capital punishment in America, particularly as we seek to provide a sound interpretation of executions, one needs to look beyond the traditional African American/Caucasian ("black/white") approach, which excludes not only Mexicans, but also the specifics of the various ethnic groups, like Cubans and Puerto Ricans, that constitute the Latina/o community. Consequently, as a result of adopting a dichotomous approach of theorizing, investigating, and publishing, little is actually known about executed Mexicans and Latinos in general in the US since states started executing under the 1976 *Gregg* decision (Urbina, 2004a, 2007). Of what ethnic group, for instance, were those Latinos who were executed from 1975 to 2010? What were the experiences and characteristics of the individuals executed during this time period, the most crucial death penalty era in modern times? Based on the studies cited herein (see Chapter 3) and the conflictive history of race and ethnic relations between Caucasians and Mexicans (see Chapter 2), we would expect that most, if not all, of the Latinos who were executed from 1975 to 2010 were of Mexican heritage. Further, considering the historical legacy of hate in Texas, the capitol of capital punishment, we would predict that most, if not all, of the post-*Gregg* executions took place in Texas. Therefore, the main objective of this chapter is to go beyond the African American/Caucasian traditional approach by disaggregating the group of Latinos who were executed from 1975 to 2010 in the United States, focusing primarily (but not exclusively) on Mexicans and the selected issues that tend to influence the dynamics of capital punishment over time.

The next section will begin by discussing the process and the various sources that were utilized to determine the exact ethnicity of Latinos executed in the United States during the last 35 years. After describing the techniques used to collect evidence of ethnic identity, an examination of the information on ethnic profiles will follow. Such investigation will provide insight into the existence of ethnic differences in executions, revealing a more realistic picture of the role of race and ethnicity in capital punishment. Further, if differential treatment exists, as predicted, the data will enhance our understanding of when, how, and why Mexicans are more likely to be executed. After an analysis of the *execution evidence*, the impact of race and ethnicity in commutations will be explored. Such examination will provide insight into the struggle that some individuals go through in the hope of being granted a commutation, and thus not ending up executed. A critical analysis of the *price of American justice* will be provided, followed by an argument that capital punishment in America is highly symbolic, and then a call is made for people to consider the underlying motive of executions, *underneath it all*! The chapter will then conclude by making predictions as to whether similar ethnic and racial trends would apply to other death sentence outcomes, like sentences or convictions being overturned.

IN SEARCH OF THE EVIDENCE: FROM UNDER THE SHADOWS

Along with the application of proper methodologies, as detailed in Chapter 4, the biggest challenge in this book has been delineating the exact ethnicity of all Latinos executed in the US from 1975 to 2010. To begin, not all states keep race and ethnicity information of inmates under a sentence of death (death row) other than "white" and "black," and the majority of states do not differentiate between the different Latino groups, with record keeping methods varying widely across states (Urbina, 2002b, 2008). As a result, information on Latinos, especially for specific Latino groups, is scant or unreliable (Urbina, 2007). In effect, as stated herein, even state and national data sets either include Latinos with whites or treat all Latinos as a unitary group; or, exclude them altogether. Given this set of circumstances, then, triangulated methods (multiple procedures) were used to gather evidence of ethnicity in order to reduce possible sources of error, as we aim to establish data sets that will be utilized in future investigations, using more advanced statistical procedures.

Specifically, with the objective of obtaining valid and reliable information, multiple published sources of information were utilized in determining the ethnicity of Latinos executed during the last 35 years.[53]

---

[53] Sources include: Amnesty International, 1999; *Atlanta Journal and Constitution*, 1991; Bentele, 1993; *Courier-Journal*, 1993; Crocker, 1999; Dieter, 1997; Halperin, 1997; Hayes, 1999b; *Houston Chronicle*, 1992a, 1993b; League of Latin American Citizens, 1999; *Los Angeles Times*, 1994; Marquart et al., 1994; *New York Times*, 1985; 1993b; Office of the Attorney General of Texas, 1999; Office of the Mexican Consulate, 1999; *Phoenix Gazette*, 1993; *Sacramento Bee*, 1994; *San Diego Union-Tribune*, 1985a; 1994; *San Francisco Chronicle*, 1993b; Snell, 1996; Texas Department of Corrections,1999; Texas Department of Criminal Justice,1999; *Washington Post*, 1994.

In addition to published sources, numerous e-mail messages were sent out, made multiple phone calls, and sent several letters via US mail to various government agencies (e.g., state offices of the attorney general, departments of corrections, departments of criminal justice, and police departments), political and professional organizations (e.g., League of Latin American Citizens or LULAC, National Association for the Advancement of Color People or NAACP, Amnesty International, Hispanic National Bar Association, American Civil Liberties Union, Mexican American Legal Defense and Educational Fund), individuals (e.g., attorneys, judges, authors), newspapers (both national and international), magazines (both Spanish and English), radio stations (Spanish), television stations (Spanish), among others, in the hope of not only obtaining the needed information, but also reliable information. In some cases, relevant information was obtained, but in most cases the information was not available, clearly showing the difficulty of conducting research on specific Latino groups.

The combination of several sources of information, though, served to confirm the identity of executed Latinos. In fact, overall, the use of triangulated methods proved to be an efficient research approach, as the findings of one method reinforced and validated the findings of another, which is essential as we try to develop reliable and valid qualitative data that can eventually be used in quantitative research. As such, when investigating the Mexican experience, or any other ethnic or racial group, it is particularly important to utilize multiple procedures in gathering evidence to reduce possible sources of error, while avoiding problems that might arise, and, more importantly, avoid generating flawed or skewed results.

CAPITAL PUNISHMENT OVER TIME: EXPLORING THE EVIDENCE

An Historical Reminder of Crime and Punishment in America

While sensitive and provoking, to better capture the essence of crime and punishment in modern America, one must obtain an appreciation for the transformations of the US, which have in one way or another influenced the nature of crime and punishment. After conquest in 1848, for example, violence and brutality against Mexicans eventually escalated into racial and ethnic oppression comparable to that of African Americans in the Jim Crow South (see Chapter 2). However, although widely known in the Mexican community and among some scholars, the history of mob violence and lynching, or so-called "illegal" executions, of Mexicans remains relatively unknown to the general public (Allen, Lewis, Litwack, and Als, 2000; Dray, 2002). In fact, despite the recent flourishing of academic investigation, publication, and dialogue on lynching, scholars continue to overlook anti-Mexican violence, with the majority of information focusing on lynching against African Americans. More globally, while people normally tend to hear or associate historical brutality with African Americans, the realities of Mexicans and Latinos in general have been twisted or omitted in both public dialogue and academic discourse, sometimes releasing outright lies (Noboa, 2005; Pizarro, 2005), eloquently explored by Mirande (2005), Moore (2007), and Zuberi and Bonilla-Silva (2008).

In effect, the influence of race and ethnicity in crime and punishment has been traced by some scholars. In one of the few early studies exploring the lynching of Mexicans, for example, Dunbar and Kravitz (1976) found that "For a Mexican living in America from 1882 to 1930, the chance of being a victim of mob violence was equal to those of an African American living in the South." More recently, in a provoking study, Carrigan and Webb (2003) document "that the danger of lynching for a Mexican resident in the United States was nearly as great, and in some stances greater, than the specter of mob violence for a black person in the American South," a revelation consistent with historical data presented in Chapter 2 and the quantitative findings presented in the previous chapter.

Exploring the impact of race and ethnicity in executions from the late 19th Century to the later part of the 20th Century (1890 to 1986), Aguirre and Baker (1989, 1997) found that 773 prisoners were executed in the Southwest, with 105 (14%) of the executed people being of Mexican heritage. Then, documenting the role of race and ethnicity in capital punishment for a large part of the 20th Century, reporter Don Reid (1973:109), who witnessed some 190 executions in Texas between 1923 and 1972, the year *Furman* was decided by the US Supreme and thus temporally stopping executions, until *Gregg* was decided in 1976, cited:

it took no study for me to accept that simple, ignorant men committed more crimes of violence than did sophisticated men of means. And, it took but little time to realize that when sophisticated men of means did commit crimes of violence, they seldom were executed for them. Those who were electrocuted were the blacks, Mexican-Americans, the poor whites and whites out of favor in their communities for one reason or another, having nothing to do with the criminal allegations for which they died.

This observation regarding the influence of race and ethnicity in crime and punishment is consistent with Giardini and Farrow (1952), who found that Mexicans constituted the third largest group of individuals under the sentence of death in Texas from 1924 to 1952. In effect, of the 506 men who were placed on death row in Texas between 1924 and 1964, 361 eventually died in the electric chair: 229 African Americans, 108 Caucasians, and 23 Mexicans (*San Antonio Express News*, 1999). Together, these investigations reveal the influence of race and ethnicity in capital punishment up until the *Furman* (1972) and *Gregg* (1976) decisions, which set a new era of capital punishment, quantitatively analyzed in Chapters 4 and 5, and executions, with Latino executions being examined in this chapter.

Latinos Ejecutados/Executed, 1975-2010

First, for comparative purpose, it should be noted that of the 313 executions between 1975 and 1995 in the United States (the timeframe employed in the quantitative analyses presented in Chapters 4 and 5), 17 were Latino inmates (NAACP Legal Defense Fund and Death Penalty Information Center, 1999). Other sources, however, report that there were 19 Latino executions (Snell, 1996). Further, not surprisingly, the data show that the 17 identified Latino executions took place in Texas, the capitol of capital punishment. The origin of the two remaining Latino executions (cited by Snell, 1996), is unclear, but based on the numerous sources mentioned above, including the fashion in which both cases were treated in the news media, it seems that one of the two executions took place in Florida and the other execution in Utah.

Second, recall that while the focus of this chapter is on executed Latinos from 1975 to 2010 in the US, no one was actually executed between 1973 and 1976 as a result of the *Furman* (1972) decision by the Supreme Court (see Chapter 4). In fact, the first post-*Gregg* (1976) execution took place on January 17, 1977, and the last on December 16, 2010.

Third, of the 1234 individuals who have been executed in the US since *Gregg* (1976), 13 were executed in California, 69 in Florida, and 466 in Texas, the three states included in our quantitative analysis (Chapters 4 and 5), constituting the majority of executions nationwide. Of the 1234 nationwide executions from *Gregg* to 2010, 92 were Latino executions, identified as "white" or "black" Latino men. As noted in Table 17, of the 92 Latino executions nationwide, the majority (78) of Latinos were executed in Texas, with 5 being executed in Florida.[54] As such, of the 92 executed Latinos in the US from 1975 to 2010 (or, more precisely, from 1977 to 2010), 83 were executed in the three states included in our quantitative analysis, and thus accounting for the majority of Latino executions nationwide. As for the exact ethnicity of Latinos executed from 1975 to 2010, the central focus and objective of this chapter, the great majority were of Mexican heritage, as predicted. Specifically, of the 92 Latinos executed during this era, 75 were Mexican, 3 Cuban, 2 Honduran, 2 Puerto Rican, 1 Dominican, and 1 Paraguayan, as reported in Table 17.[55] For a complete listing of all post-*Furman* executions; that is, all executed people in the United States from 1976 to 2010, see table in Appendix.

---

[54] The remaining executions by race and ethnicity in California, Florida, and Texas between 1975 and 1995 were identified as follows: 68 Caucasians, 46 African Americans, one "American Indian or Alaskan Native," one "Asian or Pacific Islander," and one "white" of unknown ethnicity and race (Snell, 1996).

[55] Like Cubans and Puerto Ricans, the nation's population of Dominican heritage is heavily concentrated in a single place, with the majority of Dominicans (53%) resided in New York City in 2000.

Table 17: Latinos Executed in the United States, 1975-2010

#	Name	Date of Execution	State of Execution	Defendant/Victim Race-Ethnicity	Method of Execution
1.	Jesse de la Rosa [a]	May 15, 1985	Texas	Mexican/Asian	Lethal Injection
2.	Henry Martinez Porter	Jul. 09, 1985	Texas	Mexican/White	Lethal Injection
3.	Rudy Esquivel	Jun. 09, 1986	Texas	Mexican/White	Lethal Injection
4.	Richard Andrade	Dec. 18, 1986	Texas	Mexican/Latino	Lethal Injection
5.	Ramon Hernandez	Jan. 30, 1987	Texas	Mexican/Latino	Lethal Injection
6.	Elisio Moreno	Mar. 04, 1987	Texas	Mexican/White	Lethal Injection
7.	Dale Pierre Selby*	Aug. 28, 1987	Utah	Unknown/3White	Lethal Injection
8.	Aubrey Adams*	May 04, 1989	Florida	Unknown/White	Electrocution
9.	Carlos de Luna	Dec. 07, 1989	Texas	Mexican/Latino	Lethal Injection
10.	Ignacio Cuevas [a]	May 23, 1991	Texas	Mexican/2White	Lethal Injection
11.	Joe Angel Cordova	Jan. 22, 1992	Texas	Mexican/White	Lethal Injection
12.	Jesus Romero [a]	May 20, 1992	Texas	Mexican/Latino	Lethal Injection
13.	Carlos Santana	Mar. 23, 1993	Texas	Dominican/Latino	Lethal Injection
14.	Ramon Montoya Facunda	Mar. 25, 1993	Texas	Mexican/White	Lethal Injection
15.	Leonel Torres Herrera [a]	May 12, 1993	Texas	Mexican/Latino	Lethal Injection
16.	Ruben Cantu	Aug. 24, 1993	Texas	Mexican/Latino	Lethal Injection
17.	Jessie Gutierrez [b]	Sep. 16, 1994	Texas	Mexican/White	Lethal Injection
18.	Mario S. Marquez	Jan. 17, 1995	Texas	Mexican/Latino	Lethal Injection
19.	Esequel Banda	Dec. 11, 1995	Texas	Mexican/White	Lethal Injection
20.	Luis Mata	Aug. 22, 1996	Arizona	Mexican /Latino	Lethal Injection

Table 17 (Continued): Latinos Executed in the United States, 1975-2010

#	Name	Date of Execution	State of Execution	Defendant/Victim Race-Ethnicity	Method of Execution
21.	Joe Gonzales [a]	Sep. 18, 1996	Texas	Mexican/White	Lethal Injection
22.	Pedro Medina	Mar. 25, 1997	Florida	Cuban/Black	Electrocution
23.	Davis Losada	Jun. 04, 1997	Texas	Mexican/Latino	Lethal Injection
24.	Irineo Tristan Montoya	Jun. 18, 1997	Texas	Mexican/White	Lethal Injection
25.	Mario Benjamin Murphy [a]	Sep. 17, 1997	Virginia	Mexican/White	Lethal Injection
26.	Jose Jesus Ceja*	Jan. 21, 1998	Arizona	Unknown/Latino, White	Lethal Injection
27.	Angel Francisco Breard	Apr. 14, 1998	Virginia	Paraguayan /White	Lethal Injection
28.	Jose Villafuerte	Apr. 22, 1998	Arizona	Honduran/Latino	Lethal Injection
29.	Pedro Cruz Muniz	May 19, 1998	Texas	Mexican/White	Lethal Injection
30.	Leopoldo Narvaiz	Jun. 26, 1998	Texas	Mexican/4White	Lethal Injection
31.	Genaro Ruiz Camacho	Aug. 26, 1998	Texas	Mexican/Black	Lethal Injection
32.	David Castillo	Sep. 23, 1998	Texas	Mexican/Latino	Lethal Injection
33.	Javier Cruz	Oct. 01, 1998	Texas	Mexican/2White	Lethal Injection
34.	Roderick Abeyta*	Oct. 05, 1998	Nevada	Unknown/White	Lethal Injection
35.	Martin Vega	Jan. 26, 1999	Texas	Mexican/Latino	Lethal Injection
36.	George Cordova	Feb. 10, 1999	Texas	Mexican /Latino	Lethal Injection
37.	Andrew Cantu	Feb. 16, 1999	Texas	Mexican/3White	Lethal Injection
38.	Jose De La Cruz [a]	May 04, 1999	Texas	Mexican/Latino	Lethal Injection
39.	Joseph Trevino	Aug. 18, 1999	Texas	Mexican/Latino	Lethal Injection
40.	Ignacio Ortiz	Oct. 27, 1999	Arizona	Mexican/Latino	Lethal Injection

Table 17 (Continued): Latinos Executed in the United States, 1975-2010

#	Name	Date of Execution	State of Execution	Defendant/Victim Race-Ethnicity	Method of Execution
41.	Jose Gutierrez	Nov. 18, 1999	Texas	Mexican/White	Lethal Injection
42.	Paul Nuncio*	Jun. 15, 2000	Texas	Unknown/White	Lethal Injection
43.	Jesse San Miguel	Jun. 29, 2000	Texas	Mexican/White	Lethal Injection
44.	Juan Soria	Jul. 26, 2000	Texas	Mexican/White	Lethal Injection
45.	Oliver Cruz	Aug. 09, 2000	Texas	Mexican/White	Lethal Injection
46.	Miguel Flores	Nov. 09, 2000	Texas	Mexican/White	Lethal Injection
47.	Edward Castro	Dec. 07, 2000	Florida	Mexican/White	Lethal Injection
48.	Adolph Hernandez	Feb. 08, 2001	Texas	Mexican/Latino	Lethal Injection
49.	Juan Raul Garza	Jun. 19, 2001	Federal	Mexican/3Latino	Lethal Injection
50.	Jose Santellan	Apr. 10, 2002	Texas	Mexican/Latino	Lethal Injection
51.	Rodolfo Hernandez	Apr. 30, 2002	Texas	Mexican/Latino	Lethal Injection
52.	Johnny Martinez	May 22, 2002	Texas	Mexican/White	Lethal Injection
53.	Javier Suarez Medina	Aug. 14, 2002	Texas	Mexican/Latino	Lethal Injection
54.	Rigoberto Sanchez –Velasco	Oct. 02, 2002	Florida	Cuban/Latino	Lethal Injection
55.	Leonard Rojas	Dec. 04, 2002	Texas	Mexican/1White, 1Latino	Lethal Injection
56.	John Baltazar	Jan. 15, 2003	Texas	Mexican/Latino	Lethal Injection
57.	John Elliott*	Feb. 04, 2003	Texas	Unknown/Latino	Lethal Injection
58.	Juan Chavez	Apr. 22, 2003	Texas	Mexican/Latino	Lethal Injection
59.	Andrew Flores	Sep. 21, 2004	Texas	Mexican/Latino	Lethal Injection

Table 17 (Continued): Latinos Executed in the United States, 1975-2010

#	Name	Date of Execution	State of Execution	Defendant/Victim Race-Ethnicity	Method of Execution
60.	Peter Miniel*	Oct. 06, 2004	Texas	Unknown/White	Lethal Injection
61.	Anthony Fuentes	Nov. 17, 2004	Texas	Mexican/White	Lethal Injection
62.	Alexander Martinez	Jun. 07, 2005	Texas	Mexican/Latino	Lethal Injection
63.	David Aaron Martinez	Jul. 28, 2005	Texas	Mexican/White	Lethal Injection
64.	Luis Ramirez	Oct. 20, 2005	Texas	Mexican/Latino	Lethal Injection
65.	Jaime Elizalde	Jan. 31, 2006	Texas	Mexican/2Latino	Lethal Injection
66.	Robert Salazar Jr.	Mar. 22, 2006	Texas	Mexican/Latino	Lethal Injection
67.	Jackie Wilson*	May 04, 2006	Texas	Unknown/White	Lethal Injection
68.	Jesus Aguilar	May 24, 2006	Texas	Mexican/2Latino	Lethal Injection
69.	Angel Maturino Resendiz	Jun. 27, 2006	Texas	Mexican/Latino	Lethal Injection
70.	Richard Hinojosa	Aug. 17, 2006	Texas	Mexican/White	Lethal Injection
71.	Angel Diaz	Dec. 13, 2006	Florida	Puerto Rican/White	Lethal Injection
72.	Carlos Granados	Jan. 10, 2007	Texas	Mexican/Latino	Lethal Injection
73.	Robert Perez	Mar 06, 2007	Texas	Mexican/2Latino	Lethal Injection
74.	Vincent Gutierrez	Mar. 28, 2007	Texas	Mexican/Latino	Lethal Injection
75.	Lionell Rodriguez	Jun. 20, 2007	Texas	Mexican/Asian	Lethal Injection
76.	Gilberto Reyes	Jun. 21, 2007	Texas	Mexican/White, Latino	Lethal Injection
77.	John Joe Amador	Aug. 29, 2007	Texas	Mexican/White	Lethal Injection
78.	Jose Ernesto Medellin	Aug. 05, 2008	Texas	Mexican/1White, 1Latino	Lethal Injection
79.	Heliberto Chi	Aug. 07, 2008	Texas	Honduran/White	Lethal Injection

Table 17 (Continued): Latinos Executed in the United States, 1975-2010

#	Name	Date of Execution	State of Execution	Defendant/Victim Race-Ethnicity	Method of Execution
80.	Michael Rodriguez	Aug. 14, 2008	Texas	Mexican/White	Lethal Injection
81.	Virgil Martinez	Jan. 28, 2009	Texas	Mexican/4Latino	Lethal Injection
82.	Ricardo Ortiz	Jun. 29, 2009	Texas	Mexican/Latino	Lethal Injection
83.	David Martinez	Feb. 04, 2009	Texas	Mexican/2Latino	Lethal Injection
84.	James Edgard Martinez	Mar. 10, 2009	Texas	Puerto Rican/2White	Lethal Injection
85.	Luis Cervantes Salazar	Mar. 11, 2009	Texas	Mexican/Latino	Lethal Injection
86.	Michael Rosales	Apr.15, 2009	Texas	Mexican/Black	Lethal Injection
87.	Yosvanis Valle	Nov. 10, 2009	Texas	Cuban/Latino	Lethal Injection
88.	Michael Sigala	Mar. 2, 2010	Texas	Mexican/2Latino	Lethal Injection
89.	Samuel Bustamente	Apr. 27, 2010	Texas	Mexican/Latino	Lethal Injection
90.	Rogelio Cannady	May 19, 2010	Texas	Mexican/Latino	Lethal Injection
91.	John Alba	May 25, 2010	Texas	Mexican/Latino	Lethal Injection
92.	Peter Cantu	Aug. 17, 2010	Texas	Mexican/2 White	Lethal Injection

Total executions by state: Texas (78), Florida (5), Arizona (4), Virginia (2), Nevada (1), Utah (1), and Federal (1).

Mexican:	75	Puerto Rican:	2	Unknown:	8
Cuban:	3	Dominican:	1		
Honduran:	2	Paraguayan:	1		

*Classified as unknown because it was not possible to trace them to Latino Heritage, or trace their exact ethnicity.

[a]Executed close to major Mexican holidays.

[b]Executed on Mexico's Independence Day (September 16).

Identity, Citizenship, and National Origin

Again, unlike African Americans and Caucasians, establishing ethnic identity, citizenship, or national origin is critically complicated largely because of how information is collected and compiled, combined with social changes, like diversity and multiculturalism, as documented by Urbina's forthcoming book, *Latinas y Latinos in the United States: 21st Century Dynamics of Multiculturalism*. Among the various issues, I will make note of some of the more pressing issues in the data gathering process, utilizing a few selected death penalty stories to illustrate the complexity of delineating ethnic information; that is, discovering the exact ethnicity of executed Latinos, as we seek to better understand the role of ethnicity in capital punishment.

As for ethnic identity, one of the Mexican defendants, for example, executed on December 11, 1995, was once identified by a Yaqui-Mexican (who was once the defendant's neighbor) as part Yaqui Indian and part Mexican (Hayes, 1999b), making it difficult to determine if indeed he was Mexican.[56] As for citizenship, some of the Mexican defendants could have been US citizens, but actually classified themselves as "Mexican" in formal documents or verbal dialogue (Crocker, 1999; *New York Times*, 1985; Office of the Attorney General of Texas, 1999; Texas Department of Criminal Justice, 1999), resulting in possible confusion as to whether they were US citizens or foreign nationals. In regards to national origin, some of the executed Mexicans were in fact Mexican nationals (Amnesty International, 1999; Bentele, 1993; *Courier-Journal*, 1993; Halperin, 1997; *Houston Chronicle*, 1993c; *Los Angeles Times*, 1994; *New York Times*, 1993a, 1993b; *Sacramento Bee*, 1994; *San Francisco Chronicle*, 1993b). Though, in some sources, their exact nationality was unclear.

As an illustration of the complexity of establishing ethnic identity, citizenship, or national origin, consider the story of two executed Latinos. For these two individuals, the evidence indicates that one person was executed (apparently under the identity of a "white" Latino) in Florida in 1989 and the other (apparently under the identity of a

---

[56] "The Yaquis are a famously fierce tribe, originally from northwestern Mexico, but now living partly in the U.S." (Shorris, 1992:420). Some of these individuals (or "Los Indios," as they call themselves) live in Arizona (Hayes, 1999b).

"black" Latino) in Utah in 1987. I, however, was unable to find evidence tying these individuals to a specific ethnic group or to Latino heritage (Kinder, 1982; *St. Petersburg Times*, 1989a, 1989b). These two individuals, though, are worth noting for several reasons, especially the fashion in which they were treated by the media and the criminal justice system.

According to one observer, who lived approximately 30 miles from where the Florida murder was committed, and who attended the trial for several days, the defendant was born in New Mexico but moved to Florida as a child (Hayes, 1999a). Hayes (1999a) found that the Florida School and State Employment records had "white-Hispanic" and "white-non-Hispanic" on the forms then, but everything in his records indicated strictly "white"; that is, Caucasian and not "white" Latino (or "white" Mexican), as Mexicans are "white," by law, an intriguing historical element, as documented by Lopez (2006). Hayes (1999a), who also followed the proceedings of this particular death row inmate in various newspapers (e.g., *Ocala Star* and *Orlando Sentinel*), found no evidence of Latino heritage for this Florida execution, revealing the difficulty of locating information containing explicit ethnicity, and thus the complexity of conducting research on Latinos.

The death row inmate executed in Utah in 1987 is also worth noting. Based on the inmate's data file (including appeals), the defendant was born in Trinidad, and there is some indication that "he MAY have been 'Indian [and] Black' but nothing to indicate that he was in any way Hispanic" (Hayes, 1999a). Kinder (1982:81) notes that the defendant was once identified by an air force official as a "young black airman, a twenty-year old Trinidadian named . . . ." In effect, Kinder (1982) found that the defendant was born in the isle of Tobago, which lies in the azure waters of the Caribbean east of Venezuela, and lived there until three. Twenty miles to the southwest of Tobago is Trinidad, where the defendant, who often received a "good licking" grew up (Kinder, 1982:238).[57] There are, however, three important caveats regarding this particular inmate. First, he spoke some Spanish and while in San Antonio, Texas he "managed to fall in love with a Mexican . . ." (Kinder, 1982:250). This could have led to the "Latino" identification. Second, the charge to the county by his attorneys was

---

[57] These southernmost islands in the West Indies, once under the British rule, now comprise a country named simply Trinidad and Tobago.

"perhaps the lowest fee in the state's history for a case of this magnitude" (Kinder, 1982:290), bringing into question the influence of money, or lack of. Third, suggesting the possible role of race/ethnicity in crime and punishment, while a note was passed to a juror that read "hang the niggers," the judge denied a mistrial and he was convicted by an all-white (Caucasian) jury (*Chicago Daily Law Bulletin*, 1992:1), bringing into question the "color of justice," and, more fundamentally, the legitimacy of American justice.

As such, since it was impossible to trace these two individuals to a specific ethnic group or to Latino heritage, these two inmates were classified, along with 6 other individuals whose exact ethnicity was not possible to identify, as not of known Latino origin. As for the two noted inmates executed in Florida and Utah, this conclusion is supported by Culver (1992:59) who claims that "Texas is the only state to have executed Hispanics" between 1977 and 1990. In all, while the task of locating the exact ethnicity of executed Latinos from 1975 to 2010 was tedious and laborious, only a few had to be classified as "unknown" because of the inability to locate their ethnicity. Again, as reported in Table 17, of the 92 executed Latinos, 75 were Mexican, 3 Cuban, 2 Honduran, 2 Puerto Rican, 1 Dominican, 1 Paraguayan, and 8 of unknown ethnicity.

Defining Characteristics of Executed Latinos

As documented in Chapter 2, the experience of African Americans, Caucasians, Mexicans, and other racial and ethnic groups tends to be shaped and re-shaped by various historical forces. In the area of crime and punishment, here are some of the more pressing characteristics of executed Latinos from 1975 to 2010, which are consistent with observations made by other investigators. Or, more precisely, the characteristics of Mexican death row inmates since the great majority of executed Latinos were of Mexican heritage. First, considering the often cited fear by white America, the majority of victims were actually Latino, with the rest being non-Latino, African American, Asian, or Caucasian, indicating that most homicides were Latino-on-Latino, as reported in Table 17. Second, most death row inmates had prior criminal records, which, of course, is part of the typical profile of people who get arrested, indicated, prosecuted, convicted, sentenced, sent to jail or prison, and, in capital punishment cases, executed. Third, while some defendants remained under the sentence of death for only a few months before the execution was carried out, most stayed on death row for several years before they were executed, which is also typical of the majority of all executions in America, putting the utility of executions in question.

Fourth, every single executed Latino, especially the Mexican defendants, had non-professional jobs, if they were employed prior to their arrest, with the majority of defendants being young at the time of the crime, uneducated, and sometimes their income was "just barely enough to get by" (*Atlanta Journal and Constitution*, 1991; *Courier-Journal*, 1993; Halperin, 1997; *Houston Chronicle*, 1992a, 1992b, 1993a, 1993b; *Los Angeles Times*, 1985b, 1994; *New York Times*, 1985, 1987, 1993b, 1995b; *Phoenix Gazette*, 1995; Office of the Attorney General of Texas, 1999; *Sacramento Bee*, 1994; *San Diego Union-Tribune*, 1985a, 1985b, 1986; Texas Department of Criminal Justice, 1999; *Washington Post*, 1994), revealing that if defendants were not indigent at the time of their arrest, they were soon indigent due to resource considerations. In effect, according to an attorney who witnessed one of the executions: "I think it [capital punishment] is at best extremely arbitrary, at worst extremely discriminatory against the poor" (*New York Times*, 1995a:24; Urbina, 2004a, 2008).

Fifth, in American jurisprudence, an essential legal element in judicial proceedings is the defendant's ability to be "competent" to stand trial. Yet, based on social history, where information was available, some of the defendants, most of them being of Mexican heritage, were "mildly mentally retarded" or suffered from "severe brain impairment" (*Baltimore Sun*, 1995; *Houston Chronicle*, 1992a, 1995; *Independent*, 1995; *New York Times*, 1995b; *Phoenix Gazette*, 1995; Office of the Attorney General of Texas, 1999), a common element found among the incarcerated population, as documented by Urbina in *A Comprehensive Study of Female Offenders: Life Before, During, and After Incarceration* (2008). For instance, Mario Marquez, Mexican executed in Texas for killing his 18-year-old wife and 14-year-old niece, had an IQ below 70, which is considered mentally retarded (*Baltimore Sun*, 1995; *Independent*, 1995; *Houston Chronicle*, 1995; *Phoenix Gazette*, 1995). In effect, Keyes, Edwards, and Perske (1999:3) found that Marquez "had an IQ estimated at 65, with adaptive skills of a 7 year old." Charged with rape and murder, Miguel Angel Flores, another Mexican, was represented by a court-appointed lawyer who was unable to speak Spanish, with the defense final argument at the sentencing phase taking less than ten minutes (when normally it can take up to three hours). The defense attorney actually argued against Miguel's only hope of avoiding a death sentence, and the jury never learned of Miguel's mental impairments. In fact, even the prosecution objected to the defense "speech" as a misstatement of the law.

Sixth, executed Latinos tend to have a lengthy history of chronic alcohol abuse and extensive drug use (*Houston Chronicle*, 1992b, 1993a, 1993b; *New York Times*, 1985, 1987; Office of the Attorney General of Texas, 1999; *San Diego Union-Tribune*, 1985a, 1985b, 1986, 1987), also a common trait among incarcerated people, situations that seem to worsen stress and depression, which in turn led to suicidal thoughts and even suicide (Urbina, 2008).

Seventh, some Latino defendants did not show signs of remorse, which in part contributed to the execution (*New York Times*, 1986; Urbina, 2003b, 2004a). Though, perhaps more than a sign of viciousness, lack of remorse could be due in part to the very nature of Latino criminality and punishment, as in the case of Henry Martinez Porter, Mexican executed in Texas for the slaying of Fort Worth police officer Henry Mailloux: ". . . I shot a man who shot me first" (*San Diego Union-Tribune*, 1985a:4). More globally, "acceptance of criminal responsibility," or remorse, varies by race and ethnicity. In effect, considering powerful historical forces, including American criminal law (see Chapters 2 and 3), combined with various other reasons, like cultural standards of appropriate behavior, quality of legal representation, and intercultural and legal miscommunication (Urbina, 2004b), African American and Latino defendants are thought to be less likely to express remorse than Caucasian defendants. For instance, in a state-wide study, "Language Barriers in the Wisconsin Court System: The Latino/a Experience," Urbina (2004b:91) reports that "equal access to the law is being denied to non-English speaking Latinos/as in our nation's courts due to poor (or lack of) interpretation."

Eighth, of the 92 Latinos executed from 1975 to 2010, several death row inmates claimed innocence. For example, the final words of Lionel Herrera, Mexican executed in Texas for killing a police officer, were: "I am innocent, innocent, innocent. Make no mistake about this. I owe society nothing. I am an innocent man and something very wrong is taking place tonight" (*Houston Chronicle*, 1993b:1), not an unrealistic claim in that a significant number of death row inmates have now been found innocent through the application of DNA and other investigative techniques (as in the case of Illinois during the last few years), not to mention the number of innocent people who have been executed. In this regard, several Mexican nationals currently on death row in Texas claim innocence (see Table 18). As such, Mexico and some other countries have not extradited fugitives on some occasions unless the death sentence was waived in the United States (*Phoenix Gazette*, 1993; Urbina, 2003b), as illustrated by the highly publicized Florida case involving Jose Luis del Toro, who fled to Mexico after committing a murder in Florida.[58]

Finally, some of the executed Mexicans were not only represented by inadequate counsel, but at times no Mexican American or other minority jurors served on the petitioner's trial jury (*Houston Chronicle*, 1992a; *New York Times*, 1986; Office of the Attorney General of Texas, 1999; *Sacramento Bee*, 1994; *Washington Post*, 1994), an historical situation significantly influencing the role of race and ethnicity in crime and punishment (Lopez, 2004). For instance, Rudy Esquivel was sentenced to death by an all-white jury and executed in Texas in 1986, and Roman Mata died on death row in Texas in 2000 after 15 years under a death sentence imposed by an all-white jury. Their frustration was summed up by Henry Porter of San Antonio, executed in 1985 after being on death row for nearly eight years: "They call it equal justice, but it's your justice . . . a Mexican life is worth nothing" (*New York Times*, 1985:11), in a sense, resonating the essence of the question in the beginning of this chapter, "How many Mexicans is a horse worth?" More globally, Pat Clark, executive director of Death Penalty Focus, made the following observation: "it's interesting that many folks consider the U.S. a more civilized country than Mexico and yet Mexico doesn't have such a barbaric penalty"

---

[58] After a 20-month international legal and political dance between Mexico and the United States, 23-year old Jose Luis del Toro was extradited to Florida for the November 7, 1997 murder of Sheila Bellush. Since the US extradition treaty with Mexico requires states to waive the death penalty before Mexico sends a homicide defendant back for prosecution, Del Toro did not face the death penalty. Instead, prosecutors seek a life sentence. Del Toro, who was arrested in Mexico in November 1997 and returned on July 12, 1999, was convicted for first degree murder and burglary and was sentenced to life in prison on July 6, 2000.

(*San Francisco Chronicle*, 1993b:15).[59] In all, even though it's difficult to mathematically quantify the role of race and ethnicity in crime and punishment based on this descriptive information, executed Mexicans (and the other executed Latinos) seem to have defining characteristics, distinguishing them from both African American and Caucasian death row inmates facing execution or receiving a commutations, as reported below.

THE SIGNIFICANCE OF COMMUTATIONS IN CAPITAL PUNISHMENT

As in executions, the possible influence of race and ethnicity in commutation decisions ought to be examined to control for possible race and ethnic effects. To begin, in a battle against time, and the government, to avoid execution, commutations have been viewed by some as "hope," as a last "possibility" of not losing an additional life, or as some would say, another murder in the hands of the state (see Chapter 4). However, while there was widespread pressure for the commutation of several Latino defendants, especially Mexican nationals, based largely on claims of ethnic discrimination, violation of civil rights, violation of international treaties, innocence, lack of adequate financial and legal representation, mental illness, youth at the time of the offense, irreversibility of mistakes, or a history of chronic drug abuse and neglect of the defendants, the executions were carried out, particularly in Texas.[60]

In exploring the significance of race and ethnicity from an international context, it seems that the majority of foreign nationals, most of them being Mexican (see Table 18), sentenced to death in the United States from 1975 to 2010 have been convicted in violation of their rights (Article 36) under the Vienna Convention of 1963 (*Amnesty International*, 1999; *National Law Journal*, 1998; Urbina, 2004a, Vandiver, 1999; Warren, 1999). Article 36, which requires authorities in the country where people are arrested to notify their country (e.g.,

---

[59] Except for military people, Mexico abolished the sentence of death in 1929. And, while on the books, it has not been used in the military.

[60] See Radelet and Zsembik (1993) and Vandiver (1999) for two qualitative analyses of commutations.

consulate, State Department) within 12 hours of the arrest, of the Vienna Convention on Consular Relations is an international treaty that became US law in 1969.

However, some legal experts claim that the US has followed a double-standard in the application of international law. For instance, Robert Brooks, a Virginia attorney who represented Mario Benjamin Murphy, Mexican national executed in Virginia for the murder-for-hire slaying of a US Navy cook, reports that "the State Department maintains a double standard when applying Article 36" (Halperin, 1997:6). According to Brooks, while the "State Department insists on being notified whenever Americans are jailed abroad and that while failure to comply with Article 36 within 12 hours of an arrest is grounds for diplomatic protest, it allows the law to go unheeded when foreign nationals are arrested in the United States" (Halperin, 1997:6), an issue that tends to bring out the passion, hatred, and hypocrisy of some people when the situation involves Mexico and the US (Urbina and Smith, 2007). In effect, critics report that "People are going to death in violation of every article . . . in every case, Mexican consulates were not notified until after their citizens had been convicted and given the death sentence" (Halperin, 1997:6). Contrast this with the 1994 caning of Michael Fay, an 18-year old male from Ohio who was lashed four times on his bare buttocks with a rattan cane in Singapore for vandalizing cars. Before the sentence was carried out, there was an enormous outcry from Americans expressed in the US media; again, a common reaction in the US when something happens to Americans in Mexico, while thousands of abuses are routinely taking place against Mexicans in the US, with many of such abuses by the very agents of the law (see Chapter 2).

Notably, during these last 35 years, 1975-2010, when Mexican nationals approached their execution date, particularly in Texas, the Mexican government (including the President and state governors), protestors on both sides of the border, organizations like the League of Latin American Citizens, religious groups, and international organizations called on the governor to commute the sentences (*Los Angeles Times*, 1994; *Sacramento Bee*, 1994; *Phoenix Gazette*, 1993; Urbina, 2004a), often citing the effect of race and ethnicity in capital punishment.

Consider, for instance, the story of three Mexican nationals on death row. Ramon Montoya Facunda, executed in Texas in 1993 for killing a Dallas police officer, was the first Mexican citizen executed in the US post-*Gregg* (1976). Montoya spent more than a decade on death row without any contact with the Mexican consulate. When Mexican authorizes finally learned of his case, Montoya's legal appeals were nearly over and the only remaining option was to appeal for clemency. Being the first Mexican national to be executed in Texas in 51 years, there were worldwide protestations, as cited by various news stories. On behalf of Montoya, the Mexican National Human Rights Commission, the Vatican, as well as the National Network of Civil Rights Organizations made up of more than 30 Mexican groups, called for a reprieve, not challenging his guilt, but only objecting to the death sentence, which was viewed as prejudiced, racist, repugnant, and barbarous (Bentele, 1993; *Courier-Journal*, 1993; *Houston Chronicle*, 1993c; *Sacramento Bee*, 1994; *San Diego Union-Tribune*, 1994; Tierney, 1992).

Irineo Tristan Montoya, executed in 1997 for apparently killing South Padre Island businessman John Kilheffer, was the second Mexican citizen executed in the US since Ramon Montoya was put to death in 1993. Notably, "after a lengthy police interrogation conducted without the benefit of counsel," Tristan, who was 18 at the time of the crime, "reportedly signed a four-page confession in English, a language he did not speak, read, or write." As such, a director of Comite Nacional de La Raza expressed his concerns about the mechanics of capital punishment in America:

> This is the global aspect–not only are we trying to save the life of an innocent man and how he was used as a scapegoat–but it's also a protest of the justice system that is discriminatorily used against people of color (Dieter, 1997; Edwards, 1993; *Los Angeles Times*, 1994; *New York Times*, 1993a; *Sacramento Bee*, 1994; Zuniga, 1993).

Reporting Tristan's execution, "Today, They Killed Him," reported a Mexico City newspaper, while the headline in *La Jornada*, a leading Mexico City daily newspaper, read: "Indignation!"

In the case of a third Mexican national, Jose Ernesto Medellin, executed in 2008 for the murder of Jennifer Ertman and Elizabeth Pena, Medellin gained international notoriety when Mexico sued the US in the International Court of Justice on behalf of 51 Mexican nationals indicating that the US had violated Article 36. Originally, the US government argued that Mexico's suit was "an unjustified, unwise and ultimately unacceptable intrusion in the United States criminal justice system," but reversed its position shortly. The US Supreme Court agreed to hear the case on May 1, 2007, but dismissed the case to allow Texas to comply with the US government directive. The Texas Court of Criminal Appeals refused to change its decision, with one judge accusing the White House of an "unprecedented, unnecessary and intrusive exercise of power over the Texas court system." In response, the Bush administration asked the US Supreme Court to overturn the Texas court's decision, with the US government telling the justices that the Texas court's decision, if not reversed, "will place the United States in breach of its international law obligation" to comply with the International Court of Justice's decision and that it would "frustrate the president's judgment that foreign policy interests are best served by giving effect to that decision." The Court rejected the Bush Administration's arguments, and on July 16, 2008, the International Court of Justice asked for a stay of execution on behalf of Medellin and four other Mexican nationals whom they claimed did not receive a fair trial. However, on July 17, 2008, a spokesperson for Texas Governor Rick Perry said that the state would continue with the execution and that "The world court has no standing in Texas and Texas is not bound by a ruling or edict from a foreign court. It is easy to get caught up in discussions of international law and justice and treaties. It's very important to remember that these individuals are on death row for killing our citizens." Again, these cases not only illustrate the complexity of executions and the global nature of capital punishment, but also defined elements and characteristics of Mexican inmates.

Of course, such characterizations are not only related to the situation of Mexican nationals, but also Mexican Americans and Latinos in general. For instance, the case of Leonel Herrera, Mexican American executed in 1993, also brought national and international protestations on the grounds of innocence (Dieter, 1997; Edwards, 1993; *Houston Chronicle*, 1993b; *New York Times*, 1993b), with elements paralleling cases involving Mexican nationals.

Together, independent of nationality and over the protestations of the Mexican government and national and international organizations, Mexican citizens and Mexican Americans have been executed, often under extremely questionable circumstances, with some cases receiving wide publicity, while in others, total silence (Dieter, 1997; Edwards,

1993; Halperin, 1997; *Houston Chronicle*, 1993a, 1993b, 1993c; *Los Angeles Times*, 1985a, 1985b, 1994; *New York Times*, 1993b; *Phoenix Gazette*, 1993; *Sacramento Bee*, 1994; *San Diego Union-Tribune*, 1985a, 1993, 1994; *San Francisco Chronicle*, 1993b; *Washington Post*, 1993, 1994). In the case of Roman Montoya, for example, outside the Texas' prison unit where the execution took place, protestors held candles and chanted in Spanish, "Justice! and "Life, not death!" The demonstration was the largest in several years for a Texas execution (*Houston Chronicle*, 1993c). At other times, though, "there were no conferences . . . no Hollywood stars speaking out for [death row inmates] . . . no international attention riveted on [their] case . . . no speeches . . . no rallies" (Urbina, 2004a; *Washington Post*, 1993:9).

At the end, for some death row inmates of Mexican heritage, the bold headline across the front page of *La Jornada* summarized the end result after the death sentence of Ramon Montoya, for instance, was carried out in one word: **"EXECUTED."** Other Mexico City newspapers, like *El Nacional*, made similar statements and criticized the execution on various grounds, but, primarily, the influence of race and ethnicity in crime and punishment. In the US, Ramon Montoya's lawyer made the following observation of the action by the Mexican government on behalf of Montoya and other Mexicans on death row: "they have done everything you could ask a Government to do . . . unfortunately, to use the vernacular of Texas, Mr. Montoya is a wetback who killed a white cop" (*Los Angeles Times*, 1994; *New York Times*, 1993b:19), resonating the role of race and ethnicity in capital punishment in America.

Foreign Nationals on Death Row in the United States

As reported in cross-national studies, in this new era of crime and punishment, capital punishment has truly become a legal sanction that transcends borders and justice systems, with race and ethnicity being central elements in the judicial process (Ruddell and Urbina, 2004, 2007). In effect, with the globalization of crime and punishment, the current trend of executing foreign nationals and the ethnic profile discussed above is likely to continue. As shown in Table 18, as of July 28, 2010, there are 131 foreign nationals currently under the sentence of death in the US. Notice that while there are people from 34 different countries, most (91) of those under the death sentence are from Latin countries, with the majority coming from Mexico (58), followed by Cuba (10), and El Salvador (8).

Table 18: Foreign Nationals Currently Under the Sentence of Death in the United States

#	Name	Country of Origin	State*
1.	Benito Albarran Ocampo	Mexico	Alabama
2.	Albert Carreon Martinez	Mexico	Arizona
3.	Carlos Avena Guillen	Mexico	California
4.	Omar Fuentes Martinez	Mexico	California
5.	Hector Juan Ayala Medrano	Mexico	California
6.	Vicente Benavides Figueroa	Mexico	California
7.	Constantino Carrera Montenegro	Mexico	California
8.	Jose Lupericio Casares	Mexico	California
9.	Abelino Martinez Jaquez	Mexico	California
10.	Sergio Ochoa Tamayo	Mexico	California
11.	Ramon Salcido	Mexico	California
12.	Alfredo Valdez Reyes	Mexico	California
13.	Jaime Armando Hoyos	Mexico	California

Table 18 (Continued): Foreign Nationals Currently Under the Sentence of Death in the United States

#	Name	Country of Origin	State*
14.	Tomas Verano Cruz	Mexico	California
15.	Luis Maciel Hernandez	Mexico	California
16.	Enrique Parra Duenas	Mexico	California
17.	Samuel Zamudio Jimenez	Mexico	California
18.	Martin Mendoza Garcia	Mexico	California
19.	Daniel Covarrubias Sanchez	Mexico	California
20.	Jorge Contreras Lopez	Mexico	California
21.	Juan Sanchez Ramirez	Mexico	California
22.	Ignacio Tafoya Arriola	Mexico	California
23.	Juan Manuel Lopez	Mexico	California
24.	Eduardo David Vargas	Mexico	California
25.	Arturo Juarez Suarez	Mexico	California
26.	Marcos Esquivel Barrera	Mexico	California
27.	Juan de Dios Ramirez Villa	Mexico	California
28.	Ruben Gomez Perez	Mexico	California
29.	Magdaleno Salazar Nava	Mexico	California
30.	Victor Miranda Guerrero	Mexico	California
31.	Alfredo Valencia Salazar	Mexico	California
32.	Huber Joel Mendoza Novoa	Mexico	California

Table 18 (Continued): Foreign Nationals Currently Under the Sentence of Death in the United States

#	Name	Country of Origin	State*
33	Adrian Camacho Gil	Mexico	California
34.	Jose Luis Leon Elias	Mexico	California
35.	Santiago Pineda Hernandez	Mexico	California
36.	Dora Gudino Zamudio	Mexico	California
37.	Jesus Penuelas Vazquez	Mexico	California
38.	Carlos Martinez	Mexico	California
39.	Santiago Martinez Alonso	Mexico	California
40.	Pedro Hernandez Alberto	Mexico	Florida
41.	Jorge Galindo Espriella	Mexico	Nebraska
42.	Carlos Perez Gutierrez	Mexico	Nebraska
43.	Jose Trinidad Loza	Mexico	Ohio
44.	Horacio Reyes Camarena	Mexico	Oregon
45.	Ricardo Serrano Pineda	Mexico	Oregon
46.	Miguel Padilla Lozano	Mexico	Pennsylvania
47.	Cesar Fierro Reyna	Mexico	Texas
48.	Hector Garcia Torres	Mexico	Texas
49.	Humberto Leal Garcia	Mexico	Texas
50.	Roberto Moreno Ramos	Mexico	Texas
51.	Edgar Tamayo Arias	Mexico	Texas
52.	Ruben Ramirez Cardenas	Mexico	Texas
53.	Ramiro Ibarra Rubi	Mexico	Texas
54.	Ignacio Gomez	Mexico	Texas

Table 18 (Continued): Foreign Nationals Currently Under the Sentence of Death in the United States

#	Name	Country of Origin	State*
55.	Virgilio Maldonado Rodriguez	Mexico	Texas
56.	Felix Rocha Diaz	Mexico	Texas
57.	Ramiro Hernanadez	Mexico	Texas
58.	Juan Carlos Alvarez Banda	Mexico	Texas
59.	Juan Lizcano Ruiz	Mexico	Texas
60.	Manuel Machado Alvarez	Cuba	California
61.	Manuel Valle	Cuba	Florida
62.	Omar Blanco	Cuba	Florida
63.	Manolo Rodriguez	Cuba	Florida
64.	Leonardo Franqui	Cuba	Florida
65.	Pablo San Martin	Cuba	Florida
66.	Marbel Mendoza	Cuba	Florida
67.	Jesus Delgado	Cuba	Florida
68.	Juan Carlos Chavez	Cuba	Florida
69.	Jose Echavarria	Cuba	Nebraska
70.	Irving Ramirez	El Salvador	California
71.	Julian Beltran	El Salvador	California
72.	Joaquin Arevano	El Salvador	Georgia
73.	Manuel Ortiz	El Salvador	Louisiana
74.	Walter Alexander Sorto	El Salvador	Texas
75.	Hector Medina Romero	El Salvador	Texas
76.	Gilmar Alexander Guevara	El Salvador	Texas
77.	Alfredo Prieto	El Salvador	Virginia
78.	Dung Anh Trinh	Vietnam	California
79.	Lam Nguyen	Vietnam	California
80.	Hung Mai	Vietnam	California
81.	Thao Tan Lam	Vietnam	Louisiana

Table 18 (Continued): Foreign Nationals Currently Under the Sentence of Death in the United States

#	Name	Country of Origin	State*
82.	Thong Lee	Vietnam	Mississippi
83.	Cam Ly	Vietnam	Pennsylvania
84.	Chuong Duong	Vietnam	Texas
85.	Johnny Morales	Honduras	California
86.	Edgardo Fuentes	Honduras	California
87.	Clemente Aguirre	Honduras	Florida
88.	Dennis Celaya	Honduras	Texas
89.	Edgardo Cubas	Honduras	Texas
90.	Samreth Sam Pan	Cambodia	California
91.	Run Peter	Cambodia	California
92.	Mao Hin	Cambodia	California
93.	Thavirak Sam	Cambodia	Pennsylvania
94.	Lim Kim	Cambodia	Texas
95.	Guillermo Arbelaez	Colombia	Florida
96.	Rory Conde	Colombia	Florida
97.	German Sinisterra	Colombia	Federal
98.	Arboleda Ortiz	Colombia	Federal
99.	Robert Gordon	Jamaica	Florida
100.	Paul Howell	Jamaica	Florida
101.	Lancelot Armstrong	Jamaica	Florida
102.	Albert Reid	Jamaica	Pennsylvania
103.	Sean Smith	Bahamas	Florida
104.	Ian Lightbourn	Bahamas	Florida
105.	Dolan Darling	Bahamas	Florida
106.	Mohammed Sharifi	Iran	Alabama
107.	Homman Ashkan	Iran	California
108.	Michael Apelt	Germany	Arizona
109.	Miguel Bacigalupo	Peru	California
110.	Tauro Waidla	Estonia	California
111.	Sonny Enraca	Philippines	California
112.	John Ghobrial	Egypt	California
113.	Jose Francisco Guerra	Guatemala	California
114.	Vaene Sivongxay	Laos	California

Table 18 (Continued): Foreign Nationals Currently Under the Sentence of Death in the United States

#	Name	Country of Origin	State*
115.	Charles Ng	China	California
116.	Noel Doorbal	Trinidad	Florida
117.	Terance Valentine	Costa Rica	Florida
118.	Pablo Ibar	Spain	Florida
119.	Michael LeGrand	France	Louisiana
120.	Ronald Smith	Canada	Montana
121.	Avram Vineto	Serbia	Nebraska
122.	Sioasi Vanisi	Tonga	Nebraska
123.	Abdul Awkal	Lebanon	Ohio
124.	Aham Fawzi	Jordan	Ohio
125.	Borgela Philistin	Haiti	Pennsylvania
126.	Syed Rabani	Bangladesh	Texas
127.	Victor Saldano	Argentina	Texas
128.	Bernanrdo Tercero	Nicaragua	Texas
129.	Linda Carty	St. Kitts/UK	Texas
130.	Jurijus Kadamovas	Lithuania	Federal
131.	Iouri Mikhel	Russia	Federal

* Totals by jurisdiction: California (56), Texas (24), Florida (21), Pennsylvania (5), Nevada (4), Federal (4), Louisiana (3), Ohio (3), Alabama (2), Arizona (2), Oregon (2), Georgia (1), Mississippi (1), Montana (1), Nebraska (1), Virginia (1).

THE MACHINERY OF CAPITAL PUNISHMENT: DEADLY MISTAKES?

As shown in the Appendix of this book, in the 34 years (1976-2010) since the US Supreme Court reinstated executions under *Gregg*, 1234 people have been executed and the number of death row inmates has drastically increased into the thousands. A focal question, then: How many death penalty cases end in false convictions? And, by extension, do race and ethnicity play a role in cases resulting in false convictions, or, worse, executions? In truth, nobody knows how many may be innocent, but research, through forensic science like DNA, strongly indicates that some death row inmates are innocent. Some critics claim that at least eight innocent people have been executed since *Gregg*, others estimate that about 1% of death row inmates who are executed are innocent, while still others cite that the figure is much higher because once a person is executed the case is normally closed, and the majority of cases are never reviewed for possible error once the person is convicted and given the sentence of death. In effect, one study found that from 1976 to 1998 at least 75 people were wrongly sentenced to die (McCormick, 1998). Invariably, contrary to the popular legal standard of guilty beyond a reasonable doubt, at least 39 people have been executed in the face of strong evidence of innocence or grave doubt about guilty, as in the case of some inmates of Mexican heritage.

The next question, then, would be: how do innocent people get wrongfully convicted and executed? The list of factors is long and complicated, but a possible factor is the influence of race and ethnicity, governed by police officers and court officials, like judges, prosecutors, juries, and even defense attorneys (see Chapters 2, 3, and 5). A second driving force of wrongful convictions is inexperienced, incompetent, or unprepared lawyers for the defendants, as judges tend to assign death penalty cases to inexperienced lawyers. As cited throughout this book, not only is capital punishment one of the most complicated legal sanctions, but also one of the most expensive. Yet, just a few years ago, Alabama was paying lawyers $20 an hour, up to a cap of $1,000, to prepare for a death penalty case, and $40 an hour to litigate in court. In Texas, one lawyer delivered a 26-word statement at the sentencing trial: "You are an extremely intelligent jury. You've got that man's life in your hands. You can take it or not. That's all I have to say," and Jesus Romero, Mexican, was executed in 1992 (McCormick, 1998).

More recently, an investigation by the *Chicago Tribune* found that of 131 death row inmates executed in Texas under George W. Bush, who claimed fair trials throughout his tenure as governor (1995-2000), 43 included defense attorneys publicly punished for misconduct, either before or after their work on the given death penalty cases; 40 involved trials where defense attorneys presented no evidence or had only one witness during the sentencing phase of the two-stage trial; 29 included a psychiatrist who gave testimony that the American Psychiatric Association condemned as unethical and untrustworthy; 23 included jailhouse informants, consider to be among the least credible witnesses; and 23 included visual hair analysis, which has been proven to be unreliable. Finally, suggesting the possible role of race and ethnicity in capital punishment judicial proceedings, "expert" witnesses for the state have actually told jurors in several trials that African Americans,

Mexicans, and Latinos, in general, are more likely to be dangerous in the future than Caucasians.

Justice at Last: The Story of *Clarence*, *Ricardo*, and *Christopher*

For the betterment of the criminal justice system, defendants, and society at large, the current capital punishment era is being redefined with modern technological advances. As for the possible influence of race, Clarence Brandley, an African American janitor, was accused of killing a white girl in Texas in 1980. A police officer, apparently, told Brandley and a fellow white janitor that one of them would be executed for the crime then looked at Brandley, saying: "Since you're the nigger, you're elected." Later, it was discovered that prosecutors suppressed evidence, and he was freed after 10 years in prison.

As for possible role of ethnicity, Ricardo Aldape Guerra, Mexican national wrongfully convicted and sentenced to death in 1982 for the murder of a Houston police officer, was released on April 15, 1997, after spending nearly 15 years on death row in Texas. Soon after his arrest, Mexican consular officers worked closely with volunteer lawyers representing Aldape, obtained affidavits from witnesses in Mexico in 1991-1992, and continued working closely with the defense counsel in state post-conviction proceedings. During this time, the Mexican government funded travel expenses for two of Aldape's lawyers, who traveled to Mexico to obtain previously undiscovered evidence. Then, in 1992, the Houston Consul General was instrumental in obtaining new counsel for Aldape from the prestigious law firm of Vinson & Elkins. After spending millions of dollars on Aldape's defense, lawyers convinced a federal judge that Aldape was innocent of all charges, with an appellate court judge upholding a federal court ruling that cited police and prosecutorial misconduct in the homicide investigation (Ampudia, 2010). After Aldape's release, the attorney who led the law firm's efforts stated that he would have never represented Aldape had it not been for the involvement of Mexican consular officers and the Mexican government.

At the turn of the century, Christopher Ochoa, Mexican American, was released from prison in 2001 after serving 12 years on death row in Texas for a rape/murder he did not commit. In his defense, Ochoa was assisted by the Wisconsin Innocence Project, housed at the University of Wisconsin Law School and run by law professors and students.

Headed by well-known criminal defense lawyers Barry Scheck and John Pray of the Wisconsin Innocence Project, the defense, using DNA testing, showed that Ochoa could not have murdered an Austin woman during a Pizza Hut robbery in 1988. In effect, in this new era of capital punishment, for innocent people on death row across the US, the Wisconsin Innocence Project has become one of the most sophisticated and leading *defenders* of those who are presumed innocent, a symbol of hope for those who may have been wrongfully convicted.

FEMALE EXECUTIONS IN THE UNITED STATES

Perhaps because, in comparison to men, few women have been executed in the US, their experiences have received minimal attention in academic investigations and public dialogue, making it difficult to explore the role race and ethnicity in capital punishment in its totality. To begin, since no records were kept and there was no media during the early days in America, with newspapers not becoming common until the mid-1800s, it's difficult to know the exact number of executed women in the US. Worse, in the case of minority women, little attention was given to the execution of slaves and Mexican women during the 17th and 18th Centuries, with some states keeping no records of executions, and thus making it difficult to examine the experience of the executed women. Still, it's estimated that about 505 women were executed in the US between 1608 and 1900, with 306 being verifiable cases. Among the executed women, at least seven girls were hanged. Native American Hannah Ocuish, aged 12, was probably the youngest female execution, publicly hanged in Connecticut on December 20, 1786. Rebecca Nurse, aged 71, was the oldest, hanged for witchcraft on July 19, 1692.

In all, it's estimated that about 567 women have been executed in the US since 1632, constituting about 2.8% of the estimated 20,000 executions, and, as of September 2010, 60 women are currently on death row. Finally, possibly more so than with African American and Caucasian women, the experiences of executed Mexican women and Latinas in general are difficult to investigate and thus seldom mentioned in academic discourse, due in part to the unavailability of data, a smaller number of Mexican women executed, and no Latinas being executed in over a century. The cases of two Mexican women, though, illustrate the experience of executed women in the early days in America.

The Story of *Juanita* and *Chipita*

The 4th of July in 1851 was being celebrated in Downieville, California when a drunken miner, Fredrick Cannon, went to the house of Josefa "Juanita" Loaiza-Segovia, a petite, beautiful, and young Mexican girl, kicking her cabin door open, harassing her, calling her a prostitute, and trying to rape her. She was pregnant at the time. Cannon was chased away, but the next day on July 5th 1851, he returned and Juanita fatally stabbed him. Quickly, a lynch mob formed. She was apprehended, dragged out, and a trial was held in the main town plaza with a hastily selected judge, a jury of 12, and lawyers for both sides. During the 4-hour trial, every statement for Juanita was ignored, and the person given the testimony her behalf was harassed and beaten by the angry mob. Juanita refused to speak on her own behalf; though, she did request to see a priest, but was denied. Juanita was declared guilty, taken to her home, and given two hours to get ready for death. As Juanita was about to be hung on the Jersey bridge, she adjusted the rope around her own neck, letting her long hair fall free, her arms and cloths tied down, and a cap over her face, with her final words: "Adios Senores." William Ballou who witnessed Juanita's hanging wrote, "I arrived in Downieville on July 5, 1851, the mob took her out and hung her. It was the first woman I ever saw hung, and it was the most degrading sight I had ever saw." Indeed, Juanita is often cited as the first "legally" executed female in California, occurring soon after the Treaty of Guadalupe Hidalgo which ended the Mexican-American War in 1848.

As another historical illustration: Josefa "Chipita" Rodriguez, Mexican American, was convicted for murder and hanged from a mesquite tree in San Patricio, Texas on November 13, 1863. Her last words were: "No soy culpable" (I am not guilty). A century later, the Texas Legislature passed a resolution noting that Chipita did not receive a fair trial, situations that have *possibly* influenced the dynamics of capital punishment in the context of race, ethnicity, and gender.

Notably, while multiple Latinas, mostly Mexicans were lynched, hanged, or "legally" executed before the 20th Century, no Latinas were executed in the United States during the 20th or early part of the 21st Century. In fact, as shown in Table 19, of the 51 women (17 African Americans and 34 Caucasians) executed in the last 110 years, no Latinas have been executed from 1900 to 2010.

Table 19: Women Executed in the United States, 1900-2010

#	Name	Age	State of Execution	Date of Execution	Race	Method of Execution
1.	Dora Wright	38	Oklahoma	Jul. 17, 1903	Black	Hanging
2.	Mary Rogers	29	Vermont	Dec. 08, 1905	White	Hanging
3.	Mary Farmer	21	New York	Mar. 29, 1909	White	Electrocution
4.	Virginia Christian	17	Virginia	Aug. 16, 1912	Black	Electrocution
5.	Pattie Perdue	-	Mississippi	Jan. 13, 1922	Black	Hanging
6.	Anna Knight	-	Mississippi	Oct. 13, 1922	Black	Hanging
7.	Ruth Snyder	34	New York	Jan. 12, 1928	White	Electrocution
8.	Ada LeBoeuf	38	Louisiana	Feb. 01, 1929	White	Hanging
9.	Selena Gilmore	-	Alabama	Jan. 24, 1930	Black	Electrocution
10.	Eva Douglas	52	Arizona	Feb. 21, 1930	White	Hanging
11.	Irene Schroeder	22	Pennsylvania	Feb. 23, 1931	White	Electrocution
12.	Anna Antonio	27	New York	Aug. 08, 1934	White	Electrocution
13.	Julia Moore	-	Louisiana	Feb. 08, 1935	Black	Hanging
14.	May Carey	55	Delaware	Jun. 07, 1935	White	Hanging
15.	Eva Coo	41	New York	Jun. 27, 1935	White	Electrocution

Table 19 (Continued): Women Executed in the United States, 1900-2010

#	Name	Age	State of Execution	Date of Execution	Race	Method of Execution
16.	Mary Francis Creighton	38	New York	Jul. 16, 1936	White	Electrocution
17.	Mary Holmes	35	Mississippi	Apr. 29, 1937	Black	Hanging
18.	Marie Porter	38	Illinois	Jan. 28, 1938	White	Electrocution
19.	Anna Marie Hahn	31	Ohio	Dec. 07, 1938	White	Electrocution
20.	Ethel Juanita Spinelli	58	California	Nov. 21, 1941	White	Lethal Gas (first)*
21.	Toni Jo Henry	26	Louisiana	Nov. 28, 1942	White	Electrocution
22.	Rosanna Phillips	25	N. Carolina	Jan. 01, 1943	Black	Lethal Gas
23.	Sue Logue	43	S. Carolina	Jan. 15, 1943	White	Electrocution
24.	Mildred Johnson	23	Mississippi	May 19, 1944	Black	Electrocution
25.	Helen Fowler	37	New York	Nov. 16, 1944	Black	Electrocution
26.	Bessie Mae Smith (Williams)	19	N. Carolina	Dec. 29, 1944	Black	Lethal Gas
27.	Lena Baker	44	Georgia	Mar. 05, 1945	Black	Electrocution
28.	Corinne Sykes	20	Pennsylvania	Oct. 14, 1946	Black	Electrocution
29.	Rosa Marie Stinette	49	S. Carolina	Jan. 17, 1947	Black	Electrocution

Table 19 (Continued): Women Executed in the United States, 1900-2010

#	Name	Age	State of Execution	Date of Execution	Race	Method of Execution
30.	Louise Peete	62	California	Apr. 11, 1947	White	Lethal Gas
31.	Martha Jule Beck	30	New York	Mar. 08, 1951	White	Electrocution
32.	Ethel Rosenberg	35	Federal	Jun. 19, 1953	White	Electrocution
33.	Earle Dennison	55	Alabama	Sep. 04, 1953	White	Electrocution
34.	Bonnie Brown Heady	41	Federal	Dec. 18, 1953	White	Lethal Gas
35.	Blanch "Dovie" Dean	55	Ohio	Jan. 15, 1954	White	Electrocution
36.	Betty Butler	26	Ohio	Jun. 12, 1954	Black	Electrocution
37.	Barbara Graham	32	California	Jun. 03, 1955	White	Lethal Gas
38.	Rhonda Belle Martin	50	Alabama	Oct. 11, 1957	White	Electrocution
39.	Elizabeth Duncan	58	California	Aug. 08, 1962	White	Lethal Gas
40.	Velma Barfield	52	N. Carolina	Nov. 02, 1984	White	Lethal injection
41.	Karla Faye Tucker	37	Texas	Feb. 24, 1998	White	Lethal Injection
42.	Judias Buenoano	54	Florida	Mar. 30, 1998	White	Electrocution
43.	Betty Lou Beets	62	Texas	Feb. 24, 2000	White	Lethal Injection
44.	Christian Riggs	28	Alabama	May 02, 2000	White	Lethal Injection

Table 19 (Continued): Women Executed in the United States, 1900-2010

#	Name	Age	State of Execution	Date of Execution	Race	Method of Execution
45.	Wanda Jean Allen	41	Oklahoma	Jan. 11, 2001	Black	Lethal Injection
46.	Marilyn Kay Plantz	40	Oklahoma	May 01, 2001	White	Lethal Injection
47.	Lois Nadean Smith	61	Oklahoma	Dec. 04, 2001	White	Lethal Injection
48.	Lynda Lyon Block	54	Alabama	May 10, 2002	White	Electrocution
49.	Aileen Wournoss	46	Florida	Oct. 09, 2002	White	Lethal Injection
50.	Frances Newton	40	Texas	Sep. 15, 2005	Black	Lethal Injection
51.	Teresa Lewis	41	Virginia	Sep. 23, 2010	White	Lethal Injection

*Martha Place was the first woman to be executed in the electric chair on March 20, 1899, and no woman has ever been executed by firing squad.

African American: 17   Caucasian: 34

SUMMARY OF COMMONALITIES AMONG EXECUTED LATINOS

- **Drug Usage:** Drug or alcohol abuse was common among prisoners, with indication that some inmates were able to access illicit drugs even while in prison.
- **Mental Illness:** Mental illness seems to be common among death row inmates from the time they enter prison.
- **Low IQ:** A common trend among executed Latinos, in addition to mental illness, seemed to be a low IQ.
- **Ineffective Counsel:** Inexperienced, incompetent, or unprepared counsel was common and detrimental, especially for foreign nationals.
- **Claim of Innocence:** Several defendants claimed innocence.

- **Religious Beliefs:** During their lengthy stay on death row, inmates seemed to find hope in God, especially as they waited for their execution date.
- **The Human Side of Death Row Inmates:** Some prisoners acknowledged their wrongs, became humble, and asked for forgiveness.
- **Final Words of Faith:** In some cases, as inmates were about to be executed, they accepted Jesus Christ as their Lord and Savior.

Consider, for instance, the final statement of Henry Martinez Porter, executed in Texas:

> I want to thank Father Walsh for his spiritual help. I want to thank Bob Ray (Sanders) and Steve Blow for their friendship. What I want people to know is that they call me a cold-blooded killer when I shot a man that shot me first. The only thing that convicted me was that I am a Mexican and that he was a police officer. People hollered for my life, and they are to have my life tonight. The people never hollered for the life of the policeman that killed a thirteen-year-old boy who was handcuffed in the back seat of a police car. The people never hollered for the life of a Houston police officer who beat up and drowned Jose Campo Torres and threw his body in the river. You call that equal justice. This is your equal justice. This is America's equal justice. A Mexican's life is worth nothing. When a policeman kills someone he gets a suspended sentence or probation. When a Mexican kills a police officer this is what you get. From there you call me a cold-blooded murderer. I didn't tie anyone to a stretcher. I didn't pump any poison into anybody's veins from behind a locked door. You call this justice. I call this and your society a bunch of cold-blooded murderers. I don't say this with any bitterness or anger. I just say this with truthfulness. I hope God forgives me for all my sins. I hope that God will be as merciful to society as he has been to me. I'm ready, Warden.

THE PRICE OF AMERICAN JUSTICE

Understanding the role of race and ethnicity in capital punishment in its totality also requires acknowledgement of the global nature of crime and punishment, and, while polemic, the price of American justice. To begin, some experts argue that while the presumed "dangerousness" of offenders has been a focal point of discourse, especially in anti-criminal movements, like the war on drugs, anti-terrorism, and anti-immigrants, the actual dangerousness has been far from the truth of the unspoken motives of social control policies (Lynch, 2007). As for the influence of race and ethnicity, according to some critics, from the advent of the war on drugs, Mexicans have been a prime target of politicians, government officials, law enforcement, and immigration hawks (Castaneda, 2009; Bender, 2005; Kong, 2010). In fact, at about the time that people were talking about the introduction of crack cocaine into the ghetto, and thus the criminalization of African American ghettos in the mid-1980s, Zatz (1984:165) found that prior record, suggesting dangerousness, was "used primarily against Chicanos, perhaps because they are seen as specializing in drug trafficking from Mexico," a trend that extends into 2010 (Kong, 2010), with *dangerousness simply serving as rationalization and legitimization for expansion and control* (Duran, 2009a, 2009b, 2009c; Romero, 2001, 2008).

Other critics report that beyond the presumed dangerousness that characterizes Mexicans, Mexicans, Latinos in general, and, of course, poor African Americans and Caucasians have limited financial resources to defend themselves in criminal proceedings (Reiman and Leighton, 2009), particularly in death penalty cases, which are extremely complicated, lengthy, and expensive. For instance, with limited resources, it is difficult for defendants to hire a private attorney, especially experienced and competent lawyers, and thus some defendants must depend on public defenders or court-appointed attorneys, who may not be highly skilled in death penalty cases. In reality, with the majority of public defenders trying their respected death penalty case for the first time, the great majority of defendants find themselves represented by attorneys that are learning the logistics of capital cases for the first time in their career, putting into question the very essence of American criminal law; that is, equality under the law. As such, there might be some truth to the saying, "if you do not have the capital you will get the capital punishment."

SYMBOLIC JUSTICE

In exploring the role of race and ethnicity in crime and punishment, including executions, other critics question whether the *expansion, power, and control thesis* is more symbolic than pragmatic. That is, arguably, executions serve as a symbol of insult not only toward executed Mexicans, but to all Mejicanos of the world, especially when Mexicans are executed close to major Mexican holidays, or, as in the case of Jessie Gutierrez, actually executed (or, perhaps, sacrificed) on Diez y Seis de Septiembre (Mexico's Independence Day, September 16). In fact, to some observers, the execution of a Mexican is not only an act against the individual, but the execution is carried out against Mexico, its people, its culture, and Mexico's governmental policy that forbids executions (Mexico abolished the death penalty in 1929). According to anthropologist Tony Zavaleta, for example, whichever way one puts it, the end result is clear: when executions take place, especially when race-ethnicity is influential, in violation of international law of possibly innocent people, the state is "shedding Mexican blood on American soil . . . [it is] like slitting the throat of a sacrificial lamb" (Halperin, 1997:4-5).

CAPITAL PUNISHMENT: UNDERNEATH IT ALL

Finally, probably more polemical than the influence of race, ethnicity, gender, or economics, lies what could possibly be *underneath it all*, the things we would rather not hear or write about. To begin, executioners no longer wear sheets and hoods to hide their identities, but hide behind a curtain, with three prison guards administering the lethal chemicals comprising Sodium Thiopental, Pavulon, and Potassium Chloride to stop the heart. Showing the brutal attitude of executioners, in a April 1998 Texas execution, Joseph Cannon, white, was strapped down to a gurney awaiting death with needles in his arm, but then the executioners pumped up the injection apparatus to a degree that the deathly chemicals were released with such a force that Cannon's vein blew and formed a hematoma, requiring 15 minutes before another vein could be found. Witnessing the savage spectacle, his mother reportedly collapsed. In another Texas execution, the parents of inmate Pedro Cruz Muniz, Mexican, were told that they would be allowed in the viewing room to see Muniz die by lethal injection. Upon noticing that Muniz's family was of mixed race and ethnicity, apparently Mexican, black, and a red haired white skinned person, the rules suddenly changed and Pedro's family members were told that they would have to wait out in the street while Pedro was being killed, indicating that the influence of race and ethnicity in Texas extends to family members of inmates. When Pedro's death was announced, Texas Department of Corrections guards who were congregating in the streets were reported to be laughing boisterously within sight of Pedro's family, in a sense, showing gross disrespect for human dignity.

At a more profound level, in *Capital Punishment and Latino Offenders* (2003a), Urbina argues that the historical demon of discrimination is not only deeply rooted in American history and culture, but that it's in the inner core of the American psyche. Once capital punishment in America is analyzed it its totality over time, Urbina (2008:179) bluntly states:

> Capital punishment in the United States persists mostly for historical, political, ideological, religious, economical, and social reasons—having little to do with safety or practicality. Fundamentally, capital punishment is one of the biggest demons that the world has ever invented. Now, what is the driving force behind this demon? The most powerful single driving force is *indifference*.

> Executions are brutal, vicious, expensive, irreversible, like an everlasting struggle against cancer that continues to get worse and worse. And, at the very bottom of its motive, there lies an historical mystery. As the harshest criminal sanction, capital punishment has been promoted by promising political language, which is designed to make lies sound truthful, government action logical and honorable, murder by the state legal (with a notion of legitimacy and justice), and to a fragile, feared, and mal-informed society, an appearance of global power and solidarity.

> The executioners are part of the legal system and its laws, which are assumed to be unalterable, like the word of God. The executioners are serving the state, which has the power to absolve them from this elusive demon. Yet, they do not even know why they are executing. But, of course, they are *not* supposed to. The

executioners accept the law almost as they accept the weather, which is, of course, unpredictable by nature. When questioned, the executioners are likely to reply with: "respect for constitutionalism and legality!" No one would support capital punishment if one were not psychologically and emotionally driven on by some powerful demon whom s/he can neither resist nor understand its truth and reality.

CONCLUSION

The evidence shows that 75 of the 92 Latinos executed from 1975 to 2010 were of Mexican heritage, with 78 of the 92 Latino executions taking place in Texas. Based on the results, it appears that while Mexicans have been classified as "white," through the give and take of treaty making in *In re Rodriguez* (1897), final outcomes are quite different, with race and ethnicity continuing to play a role in crime and punishment. In the case of capital punishment, it seems that Mexicans and Latinos in general have received the worst of both worlds: punishment without due process, putting in question the legitimacy of American criminal laws, with *equality under the law* becoming more pressing when Mexican nationals are executed. In effect, on numerous occasions, the Mexican government's call for "fair trials" and formal requests, like Mexico "would like the sentences of . . . Mexicans condemned to death in the United States to be commuted to life imprisonment," were to no avail (*Los Angeles Times*, 1994; *Phoenix Gazette*, 1993; *Sacramento Bee*, 1994; *San Diego Union-Tribune*, 1994; *San Francisco Chronicle*, 1993a:4).

Notably, for Mexicans on death row, protestations do not seem to be entirely the byproduct of the release of one Mexican on death row or the execution of another. According to Tony Garza, former Texas Secretary of State, ". . . from the sense of the left and right, Mexico was being scapegoated" (Halperin, 1997:3). Today, in 2011, we could possibly say that the war between Mexico and the United States ended 163 years ago, but the long legacy of hate and vindictiveness seems to remain. Internationally, with the globalization of crime and punishment and thus newly defined borders, "it is easier to rationalize the harsh treatment of persons who are essentially 'outsiders'" (Blalock, 1967:206). According to Nieling and Urbina (2008:233), in part because the United States considers itself a 'moral' and 'law-and-order' society, the U.S. has a phobia of the *outsider*, the *different*, and the *stranger*. As an institutionalized state of feeling and thinking, such phobia has manifested itself into ignorance, with in turn has resulted in viciousness and vindictiveness. Likewise, fear of those who threaten our interests or the status quo, has manifested itself into low levels of tolerance.

In sum, the data show that the experiences of Mexicans (and Latinos in general) on death row differ from the experiences of African Americans and Caucasians. Ultimately, then, the central objective of this chapter would be that this information will facilitate the development of data sets that will eventually enable us to quantitatively test the effects of race (African Americans, Caucasians, and other racial groups) and ethnicity (Mexicans and other ethnic groups) in capital punishment. More globally, Mexicans and the various ethnic groups within the Latina and Latino community constitute a separate group, distinct from African Americans and Caucasians, and thus must be treated accordingly in academic research, publication, and dialogue.

## CHAPTER 7

Conclusion: Transforming an Historical Culture of Executions

"When I was fourteen my father was so ignorant I could hardly stand to have the old man around. But when I got to be twenty-one, I was astonished at how much he had learned in seven years."

--Mark Twain

As noted in the previous chapters, among the many questions hotly debated by social scientists, two focal questions continue to be debated with great interest and passion: (1) does race and ethnicity continue to play a role in crime and punishment in the United States?; and (2) if race and ethnicity continue to be influential crime and punishment, what are the forces resulting race and ethnic variation? An examination of the literature reveals that the historical legacy of race and ethnic discrimination continues to be present not only in the American society, but also in the criminal justice system, to include law enforcement, the judicial system, and the penal system (see Chapters 2 and 3), to include capital punishment (see Chapters 3, 4, and 5). In effect, testing for race and ethnic effects in death sentence dispositions in California, Florida, and Texas from 1975 to 1995 (see Chapters 4 and 5), and by exploring the experience of Latinos executed in the US from 1975 to 2010 (see Chapter 6), it seems that issues of hate, prejudice, and discrimination in death penalty cases are not restricted to African Americans or poor Caucasians (see Chapters 3, 5, and 6), but also inflicted on Mexicans and Latinos in general. Together, according to Urbina (2008:176), punishment and injustice are governed by the historical legacy of hate,

233

and "Hate in the United States has not only been one of the biggest 'demons,' but one that refuses to die, like an immortal demon in a Hollywood horror movie . . . the 'demon' always manages to make a comeback."

RESEARCH FINDINGS IN THEORETICAL PERSPECTIVE

In seeking to further comprehend capital punishment in American over time, the quantitative research findings presented in this book (see Chapter 5) are now placed in theoretical perspective. To begin, the findings indicate that no statistical variation was found by race-ethnicity across states, which could be attributed to a number of factors. One possible explanation for not finding race or ethnic differences in death sentence dispositions across states could be that states do not differ significantly in terms of capital cases, or, at least, as sought by the prosecutor. Alternatively, the proxies used to represent Cubans (i.e., Latinos in Florida) and Mexicans (i.e., Latinos in California and Texas) were not sensitive enough to pick up statistical differences in the treatment of Mexicans and Cubans. Further, with a significant Mexican migrant population, there is a possibility that Florida has a larger Mexican population than expected, and some of the Latinos sentenced to death in Florida were Mexican rather than Cuban.

The quantitative results presented in Chapter 5 showing that there is no difference in death sentence dispositions between African Americans and Caucasians could also be attributed to several factors. One explanation could be that, as discussed in Chapter 2, Caucasians on death row are those identified as "white trash." They are "lower class whites" who do not have the resources to avoid death row, though not necessarily executed. These "whites," like African Americans, could possibly be socially and politically disadvantaged, with fewer resources with which to hire private attorneys and pay bail or fines than richer defendants (see Chapters 6), to secure an acquittal. Perhaps they were viewed as members of a segment of society who are not worth the high expense of an execution, but who society does not want out in the streets. Their experiences in terms of resources and how they are perceived are perhaps similar to those of African Americans. This may be a homogenous population that is viewed by the courts in a very similar fashion regardless of their race or ethnicity, much like the days of slavery, when landowners would much rather lose an "unworthy free white" in a dangerous job than a healthy black slave, who could make money for the white landowner, a practice that continued for years as America aimed to becoming the richest country in the world. In short, class differences between African American and Caucasian inmates on death row could be small; and thus, there is no statistical difference in death sentence dispositions between these groups in California, Florida, and Texas for the years under study.

The research finding that Mexicans (and Latinos in general) are the most disadvantaged group and not African Americans, as predicted, could be attributed to several historical and legal factors (see Chapters 2 and 6), including that where there is a high concentration of people of Mexican heritage or some other ethnic group, Mexicans replace African Americans as the most oppressed group in the community, consistent with other investigations (Carrigan and Webb, 2003; Dunbar and Kravitz, 1976; McWilliams, 1990).

Another question raised by the findings presented in Chapter 5 is why did a group that has been identified as "white" by law suffer the worst injustice in sentences and convictions being overturned by the courts, but not in executions and commutations? One explanation could be that legal discretion, which seems to be most critical in the sentencing stage, occurs in later stages for Mexican and other Latino inmates, as noted by Urbina's (2007) analysis of race and ethnic discrimination in multivariate studies. Possibly, the great majority of defendants were of Mexican heritage, who may be perceived as specializing in narcotics trafficking from Mexico, or even terrorists, and thus too dangerous to be out in the streets if they are to be released in the future. For instance, if paroled, there is the possibility that Latinos, especially Mexicans, will leave the country given the close proximity to Mexico. Further, international treaties make it difficult to bring offenders back to the United States, and countries, like Mexico, that do not have the death penalty tend to be reluctant to extradite prisoners who might face the death penalty (see Chapter 6). For Mexican offenders, differences in treatment could also be partly attributed to southern culture and beliefs (see Chapters 2 and 6), as reported by Almaguer (2008), Bender (2005), De Leon (1983), McWilliams (1990), and Mirande (1987). The fact that some acts took place in border states, like California and Texas, where the heritage of Mexican land grants and immigration patterns from Mexico are the strongest, could also have an impact on the decision to overturn a sentence or a conviction. Lastly, and perhaps most importantly, the fact that these two dispositions do not receive the kind of local, state, national, or international attention, especially from the offenders' country of origin, that executions and commutations attract (see Chapter 6), could have a detrimental impact on whether a death sentence is declared unconstitutional or overturned and whether a conviction is overturned by the courts, but not in execution or commutation cases.

Another possibly influential factor in the decision-making process is the law itself. Immigration laws, for instance, which are governed by federal statutes normally mean lengthy sentences for convicted immigrants, especially those who are illegally in the country, becoming a nightmare for immigrants who have no place to go when their country of origin refuses to take them back. Or, if defendants are illegally in the country, they either accept deportation or remain in prison for however long it takes to appeal their case (Kong, 2010; Motomura, 2010; Romero, 2001). At the end of the 20th Century, before 9/11, New York University Law Professor Arthur Helton noted that immigration law truly ". . . subjects individuals to arbitrary detention . . . " (Rodriguez, 1999:2), with Congress having very little sympathy for immigrants. After the September 11, 2001 terrorist attacks on the US, immigrants became the prime targets of the so-called national security movement, which in truth, is more symbolic than pragmatic (Bacon, 2009; Castaneda, 2009; Romero, 2008). In effect, among the most impacted by the "backlash of terror anxiety" have been Mexicans on both sides of the border (Corcoran, 2006).

While immigration law might not have a direct impact on some convicted offenders, the law has a detrimental influence on others, as there are a number of foreign nationals, mostly Mexicans, under the sentence of death in the United States (see Chapter 6). As such, there is a possibility that the legal decision-making process was partially influenced by immigration law and the anti-immigrant movement, as noted by the 2010 Arizona law (see Chapter 2). There is also the possibility that the decision to overturn a death sentence or conviction of a Mexican or other Latino inmate was influenced by the political nature of immigration law, and, by extension, the fear of possible voter reprisal.

The literature also suggests that Mexicans and other Latinos may have more difficulty filing appeals than African Americans and Caucasians due to limitations such as fluency in English, a situation that in some cases contributed to their death sentence. In fact, a study of executions from 1890 to 1986 in the Southwest by Aguirre and Baker (1989) showed that Mexicans were the least likely of any ethnic or racial group to file an appeal before their execution. As cited in Chapter 6, in some cases Mexican defendants signed homicide confessions written in English that they could not read, with language barriers being one of the most consequential issues facing Mexicans (and Latinos in general) in court, including death penalty cases (Urbina, 2004b, 2007).

Finally, racial and ethnic differential treatment in capital punishment could also be attributed to the fact that, with the exception of Cubans, Mexicans and other Latinos have historically been used as scapegoats (see Chapter 2), and, in the case of Mexican nationals, further governed by powerful historical factors (see Chapter 6). Together, for Mexicans on death row in the US, inequality in punishment could be largely attributed to the continuous imperial legacy of hate, prejudice, ignorance, and hypocrisy, deeply rooted in American history and culture and fused in the inner core of the American psyche.

THE GLOBAL NATURE OF CAPITAL PUNISHMENT

In the US, discrepancy in the distribution of punishment is largely due to the fact that when it comes to race and ethnicity, American criminal law is a double-edged sword: as it attempts to resolve a set of conflicts, it creates another. In the case of capital punishment, although some perceived *Furman* (1972) and *Gregg* (1976) as the end of the drastic sentencing disparities in death penalty in America, the decisions have resulted in questionable effects on death sentence dispositions, a trend that extends into 2011. In particular, the wide discretion that led to *Furman* (1972), which supposedly was reduced by *Gregg* (1976), has yet to be eliminated. If the findings presented in Chapter 5 hold truth, these decisions attempted to remedy the capricious element in processing capital cases at the sentencing stage, but not for later stages, such as sentences being overturn, or convictions being overturn by the courts.

While social change in America seems to be highly valued and widely propagated, the history of relationships between African

Americans, Caucasians, Mexicans, and people of other races and ethnicities indicate that legal reform sometimes boils down to *symbolic justice*. Politicians, legislators, law enforcement, and other government officials support capital punishment as a symbol of their toughness on crime, with a strong focus on order, law, and legality, with little regard for equality, legitimacy, or justice. In effect, support for the death penalty has become a litmus test, even among the general public, to determine how tough one is willing to be on crime. Opposition to what some see as the perfect criminal sanction invariably is interpreted as symbolic of softness on violent crime: anti-American! Or worse, as the saying goes: "reform consists in taking the bone away from a dog" (Newman, 1985:149).

In effect, in analyzing the application of capital punishment in America over time, empirical evidence supports the argument that race and ethnicity continue to play a role in crime and punishment (see Chapters 3, 5, and 6), so institutionalized that even in the 1987 *McCleskey* case, the US Supreme Court refused to accept statistical evidence to support a claim that the death penalty had been applied in a racially discriminatory fashion. Notably, according to Kramer (1994:32), "despite the many supposed safeguards, what matters most is who you are, who you kill, and who your lawyer is."

More globally, from whatever angle the situation is analyzed, the criminal justice system reserves its harshest sanctions for the lower classes. Contrary to the popular imagination, jails and prisons were built to punish poor criminals, with a strategic focus on power, control, and expansion, an historical movement masterfully documented by Foucault (1995), Reiman and Leighton (2009), and Lynch (2007). In the case of the death penalty, Kappeler, Blumberg, and Potter (1996:326) say, capital punishment "is disproportionately applied to the poor, illiterate, African-Americans and Hispanics," while Rentschler (1994:19) proclaims:

> The death penalty is so widely accepted largely because it provides a measure of seeming certainty to a society greatly frustrated by its inability to solve its most vexatious problems. But it is a simplistic answer, akin to the primitive law of the jungle. It is evidence of a society unwilling and incapable of coming to grips rationally with hard challenges. Capital punishment makes a mockery of such noble legal canons as equal justice under law. . . . The death penalty is reserved exclusively

for society's little people, its powerless, its rabble, its dregs. This alone makes capital punishment wrong in a just society.

The case of O.J. Simpson and the Menendez brothers, for instance, are illustrations of the power of wealth, supporting the Russian proverb: "No one is hanged who has money in his pocket." Or, "If you've got the capital, you don't get the punishment" (Page, 1995:15).

In sum, as cited by Bohm (1989:192), "capital punishment offers a simplistic and believable solution to a complex phenomenon of which the public is frightened and of which it is generally uninformed." Arguably, since efforts to change discriminatory patterns have failed, perhaps an appropriate solution would be to eliminate the death penalty, as most developed countries around the world have, with the US and Japan being the only fully developed countries that retain this savage practice. This proposition, however, is very unlikely, given the political climate surrounding crime and punishment. For instance, in 1986, in his last remaining days in office, New Mexico Governor Toney Anaya stirred major controversy by granting executive clemency to all five prisoners on New Mexico's death row (Anaya, 1993). Republican Governor George Ryan received harsh criticisms for commuting the death sentences of 167 inmates (including three Mexicans) to life in prison and pardoning four inmates after concluding that the capital punishment system in Illinois was "haunted by the demon of error" (Pierre and Lydersen, 2003:1A). Ryan told his staff, "I can't play God," and took action (January 11, 2003) just a few days before leaving office. To the disappointment of many, Ryan announced in a televised speech:

> Because our three-year study has found only more questions about the fairness of sentencing, because of the spectacular failure to reform the system, because we have seen justice delayed for countless death row inmates with potentially meritorious claims, because the Illinois death penalty system is arbitrary and capricious–and therefore immoral–I no longer shall tinker with the machinery of death.[61]

---

[61] Ryan's decision to empty the entire state's death row was the culmination of an exhaustive review of Illinois death row cases when Ryan ordered a moratorium on executions after discovering that 13 death row inmates had been

One of the leading authorities in the area of capital punishment, Professor Hugo Bedau, who has studied the matter extensively for over 50 years, called Governor Ryan's decision "the most remarkable political act against the death penalty by any governor in our history" (Pierre and Lydersen, 2003:14A). As expected, the resulting debate was partly fueled by the perception that a governor who commutes a death sentence verges on committing political suicide.

In short, the following statement by Groves (1991:111) demonstrates the continuous pattern of injustices within the US criminal justice system as a whole:

> People are inclined to personalize evil, to employ it, to stuff it into another human being. That way we can find the culprit, detect the enemy. This is psychologically tempting. It allows us to 'locate' evil, to see it, spit at it, hate it, blame it, perhaps even to kill it. This is one 'logic' behind the death penalty.

THE GLOBAL NATURE OF PUNISHMENT AND JUSTICE: REFLECTIONS

While people continue to be socialized to blindly believe in the "equality under the law" slogan, the historical record indicates that the notion of equality is more of an illusion than a reality. In the context of the criminal justice system, as Thrasymachus once remarked, "In every case the laws are made by the ruling party in its own interest. By making these laws they define as 'just' for their subjects whatever is for their own interest, and they call anyone who breaks them a 'wrongdoer' and punish him according." In the case of capital punishment, lynching and hangings have simply transformed into what is now defined as "legal" executions, with grave injustices continuing into 2011, in a sense, a new form of slavery in 21st Century America. Or, better said, in the words of Clarence Darrow, "From the beginning . . . a procession

---

wrongly convicted. Ryan then came to the realization that the entire system was simply too error prone (Urbina, 2002b). As a safety precaution, Ryan noted, "They will be confined in a cell that is 5 feet by 12 feet . . . in the summer months, the temperature gets as high as 100 degrees. It is a stark and dreary existence. Life without parole has even, at times, been described by prosecutors as a fate worse than death" (Pierre and Lydersen, 2003:14A).

of the poor, the weak, and the unfit have gone through our jails and prisons to their deaths. They have been the victims."

If homicides are considered in their totality, the committed murders are relatively few (though not justifiable), in comparison to the crimes, including homicides, strategically committed in operations like wars of economic acquisition and policies which result in massive starvation, environmental destruction, or genocide. While people who commit "street murder" are likely to face execution, members of the elite class commit crime with impunity, never risking the possibility of execution. Further, murder, for instance, killed about 16,000 people in 2004. Yet, here are a few examples of how much more deadly some "non-murders," or as sometimes cited, "elite crimes" are:

- Unsafe and defective merchandise kills about 20,000 people per year.
- Occupational diseases and hazards kill about 35,000 per year.
- *Hospital error* kills about 100,000 people per year.
- Poor diets and inactivity kill about 300,000 people per year.
- Tobacco use kills about 430,000 people per year (Robinson, 2008:203).

Economics, Crime, and Punishment

Understanding the role of race and ethnicity in crime and punishment, particularly homicide, as the only offense for which a person may be executed by the state, requires an exploration of the forces of economics. In the mid-1980s, at about the time crack cocaine was being introduced into the ghetto, Currie (1985:169) reported, "Around the world, at every level of economic development, increasing equality goes hand in hand with lower risks of homicide." Toward the end of the 20th Century, the authors of another study reported, "the results suggest that both inequality and poverty have significant and independent positive effects on rates of homicide in U.S. cities following the largest increase in the economic gap between rich and poor in our nation's history" (Kovandzic, Vieraitis, and Yeisley, 1998:569). Recently, Reiman and Leighton (2009) noted that the US criminal justice system requires a defined and effective ideology to fool enough people, enough of the time. Lynch (2007) illustrates not only the failure of America's prison system, but the devastating consequences of what is now the biggest prison system in the world. Yet, legislators, politicians, law enforcement, and other government officials continue to call for more jails and prisons, longer and harsher sentences, and the death penalty for more offenses, with some warriors of law-and-order arguing for the execution of children, as reported by Urbina (2005) and Urbina and White (2009).

TRANSFORMING AN HISTORICAL CULTURE OF VIOLENCE, INEQUALITY, AND INJUSTICE

If we are to truthfully develop and implement innovative and strategic mechanisms that will actually make a significant difference in achieving universal safety, equality, peace, and justice not only in the United States but throughout the world, it is time that the US be more inclusive and reach out to all segments of the American society, instead of continuing with the historical tradition of prejudice, discrimination, intimidation, exploitation, marginalization, and neglect.

American Criminal Law: Lo Pasado No Ha Pasado

"At the heart of the American paradigm is the perception that law and its agents (for example, police officers, correctional officers, attorneys and judges) are color-blind and thus justice is impartial, objective and seeks *la verdad* (the truth). But, *la realidad* (reality) differs" Urbina (2003c:124). As documented by Lopez (2006), the American legal system determines what our race-ethnicity is and how we live it in our everyday lives.   In 21st Century America, according to Urbina (2003c:122),

> often times so-called scientific paradigms mythicize history, truth and reality, and function as a cruel and brutal form of social control, consequently creating a glass ceiling that keeps the stranger, the outsider, and the foreigner, the 'other' and those who are perceived as different and/or threatening in their place.

Crucially, as indicated in the literature, law continues to be used to subvert, justify, and legitimize the existing order and thus inequality and injustice continue. In effect, research suggests that contemporary racial and ethnic prejudice and discrimination in punishment, including the death penalty, is rooted less in overt discrimination by individual actors in society than in more subtle and complex racial and ethnic politics and ideologies, such as the very structure and mechanism of American democracy and subconscious cognitive processes pre-dating legal documents, like the Constitution, and through compounding decisions of actors in law enforcement, the judicial system, and the court system that amplify inequality and injustice for nonwhites, especially the poor and immigrants.

Further, contrary to the notion of smooth linear social change for the betterment of the majority,

> Human experiences indicate that whatever passes as 'good' (or in the name of progress) or 'evil' has something to do directly or indirectly with the identification, classification, formation, and implementation of a governing mechanism vis-à-vis labels like conservatives, liberals, underdogs, over dogs, middle dogs and top dogs by way hierarchy, superiority, inferiority, domination, subornation and rule (Urbina, 2003c:124).

In the words of Friedman (1993:82), "laws and legal institutions are part of the system that keeps the structure [of inequality] in place, or allows it to change only in approved and patterned ways. . . . Law protects power and property; it safeguards wealth; and, by the same token, it perpetuates the subordinate status of the people on the bottom," revealing *que lo pasado no ha pasado* (the past has not passed).

Justice in 21st Century America: Dondé Esta La Justicia?

After five centuries, arguably, of being engaged in a crusade for justice in America, while telling the world that the US is a strong believer and advocate of equality, freedom, democracy, and justice, we would expect to find a system that is truly working with great efficiency, equality, and justice. In reality, the truth is far from the propagated principles of law, equality, and justice; reflecting, instead, a continued legacy of injustice.

For instance, as changes are being implemented, new forms of racial and ethnic discrimination are shifted to either earlier or later stages of the judicial process, while influencing law enforcement and correctional practices in the process. As such, implemented procedural mechanisms are unlikely to detect new forms of prejudice and discrimination, which have become quite complicated and subtle, throughout the lengthy legal process, from arrest to indictment, to sentencing, and to appeal, like the selection of jurors, judges' rulings, inequalities in the quality of defense counsel, and even media coverage. As such, for appeal courts "to require specific evidence of racial discrimination in capital cases turned out to be a hollow victory for the anti-death penalty cause, since few defendants who are actual victims of racism will be able to provide specific and decisive evidence of that racism" (Cholbi, 2006:258). In actuality, as noted by Cholbi (2006), death penalty trials rarely feature well defined racist "smoking guns," like the audio tapes presented in O.J. Simpson's murder trial in California of police officer Mark Fuhrman using blatant racist language. In fact, not only in death penalty cases, but in most felony trials, few defendants are able to provide specific evidence of discrimination within criminal trial proceedings, and even fewer defendants are able to mathematically prove discrimination of extra- or pre-judicial circumstances because of the very nature of its complexity, making it difficult to capture the role of race and ethnicity in crime and punishment in its totality.

Resonating the eras of lynching and hanging, Cholbi (2006:278) illustrates how, along with Mexicans and other Latinos, African Americans continue to

> face greater costs as murderers and those who murder them are given the equivalent of a discount on murder. The result is that the interests, indeed the very lives, of African-Americans are given less weight than the lives and interests of other Americans. This result along is morally troubling. Yet this implied inequality in the value of African-American lives and interests has far-reaching effects on liberty. Because the value of one's liberties can depend on their relation to other people's liberties, inequalities of liberty between individuals produce inequalities in expectations and opportunities. In the case of African-Americans and capital punishment, their liberties, while in a formal sense equal to the liberties of whites, are worth less, in a real sense, than the liberties of whites.

In short, the application capital punishment raises grave questions of equal justice before the law and, by extension, of the legitimacy of the American criminal justice system. Worse, once the government begins to strip away the constitutional, statutory, and international rights of the most vulnerable people, the "spillover" effect is extremely rapid and consequential for all minorities, poor whites, immigrants, and eventually US citizens, a situation that should propel people to infuse transformation in the American society.

Global Movements

While it appears that global movements are a new phenomenon, things of modernity, global movements date back to antiquity, with present-day globalization simply being a re-defined transformation of the world by the superpowers in an effort to maintain their economic, political, and military power and control, while reinventing slavery and reforming colonial mechanisms and practices. As such, as in the past, modern movements have a clandestine side, though, much more complicated and, in a sense, gravely consequential for the entire world. For instance, the so-called "war on terrorism" was not the beginning of the current transnational war on crime, but just another catalyst or justification for greater militarization in the United States, especially along the US-Mexico border, and throughout the world, with the US continuing to have an imperial presence and dominance.

Within a context of law-and-order, as noted by Sanchez (2007:176), the universal message seems to be that "the domestic subject of terror and the global subject of terror are one and the same: both are dark, both are outside the boundaries of society, and both are monstrous." In reality, the new transnational strategies of war, punishment, and confinement are the latest defense mechanism of the empire. The anti-terrorism movement is further complimented by the anti-drugs and anti-immigrants movements to reinforce the social control ideology of the state. Then, as in casualties of war, the ultimate punishment for those the government wishes to control and silence is execution.

With some states having no death penalty in their statutes, the federal death penalty can be seen as a *safety valve* for offenders (Mysliwiec, 2010), while conveying a message of power, control, and safety for a feared society and a free-market economy during difficult times. Though, as in the state level, the focal question of whether to have a death penalty statute is in actuality more historical, political, symbolic, and ideological than legal or pragmatic.

The Ideology of Punishment: Beyond Executions

Beyond the ideology of capital punishment and the savage nature of executions, according to Urbina (2008:209), "the modern logic of the U.S. correctional system can be summed in one word: *imprisonment*." Crucially, contrary to the argument of *national security*, "present social control laws are fueled as much by the expression of popular anger and the desire for revenge as by the honest attempt to develop and implement mechanisms of reducing crime and the fear it creates" (Urbina, 2008:220). Worse, the new logic of social control becomes a leading force in the very same problem we are arguably trying to solve: crime.

Together, criminal law and social policy function to sustain the power, control, and expansion ideology of the ruling class, masking inequality and injustice precisely because these formal missions appear to be effective, colorblind, objective, and legitimate, while propagating the illusion that the *playing field* is now even in society. In reality, "in a free-market economy where cut-throat competition and institutionalized greed are the norm, those who are the most vulnerable become scapegoats and easy targets of blame during periods of economic hardship, social instability, or political uncertainty" (Urbina, 2008:212), as seen worldwide during the aftermath of September 11, 2001 with Middle-Easterners and the anti-immigrant movement in Arizona in 2010. Clearly, not only is American criminal law a key force in perpetuating social inequality, but social policy continues to govern the everyday experience of people outside the criminal justice system.

Case in point: After years of advocating adversity and multiculturalism, it's embarrassing and humiliating that it was not until July 2010 that the University of Texas' governing board voted to rename a dormitory and a park named after former leaders of the Ku Klux Kan, historically the most notorious terrorist group in America. The dormitory, built in 1955 on the banks of Waller Creek at the University of Texas at Austin, was named for William Stewart Simkins, a leader of the KKK in Florida and who taught at the UT law school from 1899 to 1929. The park had been named for Simkins' brother, former University of Texas regent Judge Eldred Simkins, who was also involved with the Klan. From a humanistic standpoint, it's truly ironic that just 4.5% of students on the UT-Austin campus were African Americans in 2010. Obviously, like a ghost, the historical legacies of the past continue to brutalize African American in all domains of life, a continued ideology of manipulation, intimidation, power, and control.

Leveling the Field Among Those Who Operate the Machinery of Justice

Historically, all decision-makers in the criminal justice system, as in all domains of life, were white men. Then, eventually, a slight *window* was forced open in which women, African Americans, Mexicans, and other racial and ethnic minorities could participate. In essence, after centuries of presumed social change, we would expect a certain level of equality, a balance, in the representation of those who operate the machinery of justice. In plain 21st Century, though, reports show that "dominant [court] actors (judges, prosecutors) are white in contemporary United States" (Ulmer and Johnson, 2004:145; Urbina, 2005; Urbina and Kreitzer, 2004; Urbina and White, 2009). In effect, like African Americans, Mexicans, and other Latinas and Latinos have been excluded from the most powerful positions in the legal and political system, like governors, legislators, judges, prosecutors, and defense attorneys. As reported by Gomez (2000), there has been a glass ceiling on Mexicans' participation in the American legal system.

In effect, revealing just how *white* one side of the criminal justice system is and how *dark* the other side of the legal spectrum is, one judge was quoted as saying: "You are reluctant to send white offenders to prisons that are largely black. It seems the prisons are becoming more and more black, and judges are leery because they have heard horror stories about things that happened, violence and whatnot" (Ulmer and Kramer, 1996:400). Of course, extra-judicial discrimination takes place way before minority defendants even enter the judicial system. Barlow and Barlow (2002:338, 349) cite a police officer who admitted that he stops and questions African Americans "because it is precisely what his supervisors want him to do," and some African American police officers also admitted that they practice racial profiling and actually see it as a "necessary and legitimate tool for police officers." Other examples of discrimination before a trial begins include prosecutors who, aware of jurors' prejudice, conservative views, or conservative religious beliefs, are prone to prosecute African Americans or Mexicans in homicide cases. Once the trial begins, there are subtle, but deadly, ways prosecutors and judges may ultimately affect the defendants' right to a fair and impartial jury, and, ultimately, the outcome of the trial, by, for example, allowing attorneys to make religious references during legal proceedings, including death penalty trials (Chavez and Miller, 2009).

Consequently, since police and judicial practices are highly institutionalized in the American culture, it's possible that minority representation in the legal system might not significantly alter *normalized* judicial behavior. It's been suggested that having minority attorneys could even work against minority defendants, especially in jury trials, in that juries continue to be predominately white and conservative; or, more precisely, it could result in a "backlash" by those who have been the deciders of life and death. A situation recently expressed by Kaplan (2009a:75) that "courts talk like upper-class white men and subordinate those who do not." As a whole, African American and Mexican attorneys may be poorly situated to actually influence the decision-making process if they do not hold positions of power across the entire political and judicial system. In fact, to the extent that African Americans and Latinos disproportionately represent what some scholars have characterized as "the working class" of the legal profession, or the "tokens," their presence may have minimal impact on the distribution of justice (Hagan, Huxter, and Parker, 1988).

In our quest for equal representation in the political and legal system to maintain equilibrium in the judicial system, it's obvious that less is known about jurors' behavior, where juries' racial composition and unspoken beliefs have the potential to influence final decisions, as well as the process by which decisions are reached (Sommers, 2007). For instance, one study analyzed 340 trials and found that the higher the number of whites to blacks on juries, the more likely blacks were to be sentenced to death, especially if the victim was white (Bowers, Steiner, and Sandys, 2001), with similar findings were reported in a non-felony study analyzing 317 juries in Texas comprised of whites and Latinos (Daudistel, Hosch, Holmes, and Graves, 1999). Another study found that the more whites on juries, the more conviction-prone were the juries, a trend that became more pressing if the defendant was Latino (Perez, Hosch, Ponder, and Trejo, 1993). In effect, between 1983 and 2001, more than 50 African American men were convicted by all-white juries, with cases showing a pattern of black juror exclusion by prosecutors. Not surprisingly, all 50 African Americans were executed.

As documented by renowned constitutional scholar Richard Delgado, racism is really never eliminated, it simply transforms itself, always coming back in one way or another. In 21st Century America, as suggested by the findings presented in this book, some legal decision-makers might seem concerned about the appearance of prejudice when defendants are rich African Americans or Mexicans to avoid signs of racism, but such concerns may not be as consistent with other ethnic or racial minorities, especially if they are poor or negatively characterized by stereotypes, as in the case of Mexican immigrants and Middle-Easterners. For example, white government officials were not so concerned about hiding their prejudice against Asian Americans following the attacks on Pearl Harbor in 1941 or Arab defendants in the wake of the September 11, 2001 terrorist attacks on the US (Welch, 2006).

In sum, in a call for justice in the very essence of democracy, equal representation among those who operate the machinery of justice, scholars have reported the utility of a balanced judicial system in a number of recent studies. King, Johnson, and McGeever (2010:26-27) found that "more racial diversity in the bar results in less racial disparity in criminal sentencing," and conclude that "efforts to diversify the legal profession may have the ancillary benefit of minimizing unequal treatment across racial lines." More globally, the authors predict that states with more African Americans per capita in the legal profession would have less racial disparities in the prison system and in the application of the death penalty. In a non-death penalty study, Ward, Farrell, and Rousseau (2009:757) found that "increasing racial and ethnic group representation in justice-related occupations is considered a potential remedy to racial inequality in justice administration, including sentencing disparity." In fact, Phillips (2008:839) notes that positive results can already be found in some cases; that is, findings from his death sentencing study in Texas "suggest that Hispanics wield more political power and are a greater presence within criminal justice, such as on juries."

In all, *equal representation must be present to maintain equilibrium in the legal system.* In this context, in his writing on "democratic social control," Braithwaite (2002:166-167) advocates a more equitable distribution of authority in processes of social control, as a mechanism for "enhancing the effectiveness, legitimacy, and ultimately the social justice of systems of social control" (Ward, Farrell, and Rousseau, 2009:768). Universally, this "control balance" in the operation of the American judicial system is in reality an essential element of liberty and democracy, if we are to meet the promise of equal justice under the law.

Humanizing Difference

As noted throughout this book, the capital punishment debate has revolved around individual executions, leaving aside the many costs of discrimination to African Americans, Mexicans, and other racial and ethnic minorities, as a *class*; that is, the minority community as a whole. Dating back to the days of lynching and hangings, later transformed into "legal" executions, death penalty practices have been unjust and thus unconstitutional because even if African American or Mexican defendants deserve to die, the greater likelihood of their execution violates their equal status under the law. Implicitly, since the lives of African Americans and Mexicans are treated as less valuable than the lives of whites, current death penalty practices afford African Americans and Mexicans less than the full protection of supposed constitutional rights. In effect, the debate tends to neglect that capital punishment and constitutionality involve two sides of the same coin, in that by applying higher costs on African Americans and Mexicans for murder, the American legal system is arbitrarily imposing a market premium on them; yet, while the lesser likelihood that whites who murder African Americans or Mexicans will be executed violates African Americans' and Mexicans' rights to equal protection under the law. Resonating on the historical legacy of lynching and hangings, one scholar put it bluntly:

> African-Americans are treated unjustly because their lives and interests are being given less significance than the lives of other individuals, an injustice which is not confined to those murdered. The judicial system has effectively created a market for murder in which there exist comparatively greater incentives for killing African-Americans (Cholbi, 2006:269).

While not highly favored by warriors of law-and-order, like politicians, law enforcement, or even some scholars, like legal scholar Ernest van den Haag, who advocates capital punishment with obvious passion, though, backed only by sketchy and questionable argumentation, a moratorium is the most rational and humanistic solution to this historical demon. A moratorium on executions (of course, not on punishing murderers) will put an end to injustice, injustices that continue to accumulate as time goes by. Truthfully, in 21st Century America, it becomes a little more difficult to comprehend the creation of a legal system in which minorities, particularly African Americans and Mexicans, bear greater costs and have fewer benefits from the practice of capital punishment. Interestingly, as I am finalizing this book, with the divine help of Ilse Aglaé Peña, Governor Pat Quinn, a longtime supporter of capital punishment, signed legislation on March 9, 2011, abolishing the death penalty in Illinois, making Illinois the 16th state in the country without a death penalty, more than a decade after then Governor George Ryan imposed a moratorium on executions out of fear that the system was making deadly mistakes. (New York and New Jersey eliminated their death penalties in 2007, followed by New Mexico in 2009.) Citing his action as the most difficult decision he has made as governor, Quinn noted, "If the system can't be guaranteed, 100-percent error-free, then we shouldn't have the system . . . it cannot stand." In his decision to commute the sentences of all 15 men remaining on death row, Quinn referenced the 20 people sent to death row whose cases were overturned after evidence surfaced that they were innocent or convicted improperly. Governor Quinn also noted that capital punishment is too arbitrary in that a prosecutor might seek the death penalty in a case, while another in a similar crime might not, not to mention that death sentences might be imposed on minorities and poor people more often than on wealthy, white defendants.

In sum, by imposing lower costs on the murder of African Americans and Mexicans, the legal system unfairly disregards the value of their lives as human beings and liberties under the US Constitution. Evidently, "racial discrimination in capital sentencing is a form of social injustice, not merely a judicial wrong to particular defendants" (Cholbi, 2006:278). A moratorium, then, will function as a policy equivalent of a class action suit on behalf of the African American and

Mexican community (Cholbi, 2006), if we are to put an end to this historical trend of race and ethic discrimination. Or, how many more years will it take for us to realize that like slavery, lynching, or hangings, capital punishment, while it continues to be *legal* (like slavery was) is unconstitutional.

Thoughts for the Future

If the US is to be the country of the future and be on the forefront of globalization, including the globalization of knowledge, Americans should seriously consider making changes that will actually improve lives. In this context, the following are some recommendations that will be of utility in the process of transformation.

First, Americans need to come to the realization that the criminal justice system, to include law enforcement, the judicial system, and the penal system, and society as a whole cannot be significantly improved by simply passing more laws, as the US is the country with the most law in the world already. In fact, we need to be cautious of policies in all levels of government that promise an easy fix to complex situations. In truth, while some policies might sound logical, effective, and politically appealing, such policies or laws often led to severe ramifications, causing more uncertainty and chaos than they actually solve. Further, we need to be cautious about accepting the often cited "culture explanation" as a *last resort* approach to challenging problems within the American society.

Second, instead of neglecting, marginalizing, and silencing people, we should empower them with things like decent employment and a solid education that will enable them to become authors of their own lives. In the context of education, the world of academia needs to make an honest effort to include the voices that have traditionally been left out academic books, educational lectures, public discourse, this involves being inclusive in both research and publication by minority scholars, especially Latinas and Latinos, and more so, Mexican Americans, who constitute the majority of the Latina/o population in the US. To this end, not too long ago, Reyes and Halcon (1988:307) proclaimed, "what appears to be at the heart of the objection to brown-on-brown-research is not the credibility of our research, but an unspoken objection to a potential undermining of White expertise on minority issues."

Third, we need to make a sincere effort to see the others' world through their own eyes, as it is quite common for Americans to make quick judgments or generalizations about what they perceive to be the views, behaviors, or experiences of certain members of society. Worse, Americans tend to initiate aggressive movements against segments of society without truly understanding the situation in its totality.

Finally, we need to be cautious of the fact that injustices are often difficult to detect, to the point that most forms of discrimination are not even acknowledge by the courts, not to mention prejudice, as people try to be *politically correct*, with some modern racists wearing suits, not sheets. Crucially, as we claim to be excited about living in a democratic country, we tend to forget that cruelty has always had a human face, going back to the Declaration of Independence of 1776 (and even prior), a legal document allowing white men to dehumanize women, blacks, and other minorities. In essence, we must acknowledge that when people regularly experience inequality and injustice, democracy is in effect of little utility.

Hacia el Futuro: Towards the Future

More globally, with America experiencing unprecedented shifts, like international political and military crises, fragile national and international relations, and economic instability and uncertainty, how will mainstream America respond to certain minorities and poor people, who traditionally have been used as scapegoats during difficult times? Overall, the incarcerated population grew by 19% between 2000 and 2008. In effect, in mid-2008, one out of 131 (2.3 million) people were in jail or prison, with the majority being minorities. What will be the fate of *los de abajo* (the ones at the bottom)? As detailed in Chapter 2, the notion of *sal si puedes* (get out if you can) has been more of an illusion than a reality. Citing census data, a report released on September 16, 2010, showed that 1 in 7 Americans now live poverty, with the overall poverty rate climbing to 14.3% (43.6 million people). While poverty increased among all racial and ethnic groups, the levels are much higher for African Americans and Latinas/os. That is, the number of African Americans in poverty increased from 24.7% to 25.8%, for Latinas and Latinos it increased from 23.2% to 25.3%, for Caucasians the level increased from 8.6% to 9.4%, and, worse, child poverty rose from 19% to 20.7%. With a high concentration of African

Americans under the control of the criminal justice system, unemployed, or uneducated, what will become of the African American community? What will become of Latinas and Latinos, now not only the largest and fastest growing minority group, but the group with the longest life expectancy, accounting for about 15% of the population? According to a 2010 government report, Latinas and Latinos are expected to outlive Caucasians by two years and African Americans by more than seven years. A Latina or Latino born in 2006, for instance, could expect to live about 80 years and seven months, with life expectancy for a white being about 78 and almost 73 for a black. Most recently, according to a March 2011 Census Bureau release, Latinas and Latinos accounted, in the 2010 count, for more than half of the total US population increase since 2000, making Latinos the fastest growing group, on track to exceed 50 million, or roughly 1 in 6 Americans and, among US children, Latino children 1 in 4. What will be the fate of Mexican workers who live *sin techo* (without a roof over their heads), in the face of fear of deportation? What will be the fate of poor whites who are also the victims of social control movements? What will become of the thousands of women in prison, with the majority of them being mothers of young children, as the *criminal justice control web gets wider and wider*? From 2000 to 2008, the number of women inmates increased by 33%, with African American women being 3.5 times more likely to be incarcerated than Caucasian women and twice as likely as Latinas. Will the historical paradigm of prejudice, hate, vindictiveness, discrimination, hypocrisy, and ignorance disappear someday? *Por fin* (finally), it is our hope that this book inspires understanding, *coraje* (righteous anger), tolerance, equality, compassion, hope, justice, and peace. As Jovita Idar beautifully recommended in 1911, "Hay que trabajar juntos en virtud de los lazos de sangre que nos unen."

Afterword: The Future of Capital Punishment

"Science is meaningless because it gives no answer to the question, the only question of importance for us: 'What shall we do and how shall we live?'"

--Leo Tolstoy

As illustrated in this book, a close analysis of capital punishment over time reveals that the death penalty continues to be charged with notions of powerful historical forces, like conquest, colonialism, slavery, and immigration, the legacy of hate and stereotypes, and the governing dynamics of American criminal law. While arguments regarding the death penalty have ranged from biblical to genocide and from crimes of treason to the war on terror, two debates have remained highly fused over time in America: race and, to a lesser extent, economics.

Ultimately, then, if the US is truly vested in social change, there are two elements that must be equated: (1) a change in the American mentality regarding capital punishment, and (2) a restructuring of the political economy of capital punishment. In essence, these shifts are essential if we are to ever see a moratorium on the death penalty. In the process, of social conscious, we must wonder: How will what happens to *them* affect *us*?

ATTITUDES TOWARD CAPITAL PUNISHMENT

Some of the most consequential elements of racism, like equating biological inferiority to African Americans and Mexicans, has declined over the years, but new forms of racism have emerged, manifesting themselves in conservative social control policies, like the death penalty. While claiming to be fair, as the notion as always been since the signing of the Declaration of Independence, whites tend to believe that the reason blacks and Mexicans are punished is because they deserve it, and not because the criminal justice system is racially biased against minorities; quite simple, for some whites, discrimination no longer exists. In reality, with recent movements, like anti-terrorism, anti-narcotics, and anti-immigration, prejudiced whites seem to see the death penalty as a much-needed punishment to suppress the behavior of "dangerous" minorities, most notably, African Americans, Mexicans, and, more recently, Middle-Easterners. Illustrating the African American experience, Unnever and Cullen (2007:1284) report that "The resulting racial anger and the attribution that black crime is 'their fault' and not 'society's fault' may further justify the view that putting African American murderers to death is both richly deserved and needed for community protection." Worse, the popular belief among whites that African American and Latino crime is attributable to the failings of African Americans and Latinos, with no real weight given to biases in the criminal justice system, actually constitutes a more subtle form of racial prejudice. As such, according to Peffley and Hurwitz (2007), when these whites are confronted with an argument against the death penalty that is based on race or ethnicity, they passionately reject these arguments with such force that they end up expressing more anger and support for the death penalty than when no argument is presented. In fact, the authors conclude, "our most startling finding is that many whites actually become more supportive of the death penalty upon learning that it discriminates against blacks" (Peffley and Hurwitz, 2007:1006).

Conveniently and strategically, like during the slavery years, by denying the discrimination that African Americans, Mexicans, and other minorities face in the criminal justice system, whites are free to "blame the victim," or turn a blind eye on the brutality and injustices that African Americans and Mexicans suffer at the hands of the police, the judicial system, or the penal system. According to some scholars, "whites' resistance to racial arguments against the death penalty is likely motivated, at least in part, by racial animus, or at the very least, a mixture of racial insensitivity and ignorance about the reality of discrimination in the justice system" (Peffley and Hurwitz, 2007:1008). After centuries of *convenient ignorance* and hypocrisy, it's time that Americans recognize that when politicians, legislators, and other government officials justify their support for capital punishment because they are representing the "will of the people," these pronouncements ignore a discomforting reality; that is, that strong or high levels of support for the death penalty are deeply rooted in the views of the segment of society holding racist views toward African Americans or Mexicans (Unnever and Cullen, 2007).

It's also time that people realize, or acknowledge, that racism tends to be "rendered invisible" because it is deeply embedded in institutions and the consciousness of people, to the very fiber of Americans' psyche. Consequently, by inscribing African Americans and Mexicans as criminals, the false consciousness of the multi-billion dollar crime industry distracts us from the realities of crime, and, worse, our own victimization, manipulation, and subornation. Kaplan (2009a, 2009b) cites that the war on crime's ideological work of inscribing young minority men as criminals achieves neo-racism, in which "difference" is *now* identified through discourse of culture rather than biology, as it was characterized for centuries, precisely because race or ethnicity are never officially mentioned in movements of social control, as the officially relevant factor in the war on crime is not race or ethnicity, but criminality. In effect, as reported by Morin (2008), Latinos have not been shown to be more inclined to engage in drug activity than whites, and Latinos and African Americans are not necessarily more involved in narcotics distribution. As for the anti-immigrant movement, non-citizen Latin American immigrants are actually less likely to be involved in crime than citizens (Hagan and Palloni, 1999). Together, studies show that "Whites are actually three times more likely to be victimized by Whites than by minorities" (Dorfman and Schiraldi, 2001:4).

Finally, Hall (1980:117) reminds us that the media is a "major cultural and ideological force, standing in a dominant position with respect to the way in which social relations and political problems [are] defined and the production and transformation of popular ideologies in the audience addressed." According to Hall, media workers operate within a *professional code*, which works to legitimize hegemonic ideologies through its adherence to the value of objectivity, neutrality; similar to the operation of criminal justice agents. As such, the professional code is hegemonic in its reproduction of dominant ideology precisely because it purports to be progressive and unbiased, while allowing serious social issues to go unsolved. In retrospect, in the same way, then, that the American media has been used as a revolutionary force of social control, the media can effectively be utilized to educate the public about the reality of the role of race and ethnicity in crime, punishment, and justice, if we are truly vested in a crusade for social equality and justice.

In short, a majority of whites continue to support capital punishment; a majority of whites continue to believe that high levels of black or Mexican criminality are attributable mainly to dispositional characteristics, and a majority of whites continue to refuse to abandon support for the death penalty despite evidence that the governing mechanisms are gravely flawed (Peffley and Hurwitz, 2007). Within the Latina/o community, opposition to capital punishment has always been limited to a few activities, in that Latinos overall have failed to understand the politics of the death penalty. As a result, because most whites do not see widespread ethnic or racial discrimination in the criminal justice system, or in any other social domain, direct appeals or a moratorium based on claims of discrimination are unlikely to win their support in the future, unless, as noted in Chapter 7, Americans are indeed willing to acknowledge the continued historical brutality, realize that working together is not only vital during war time, but in all dimensions of social life, and, of course, truly vested in national social transformation.

THE CAPITALISM OF CAPITAL PUNISHMENT

"I'm beginning to believe that 'U.S.A.' stands for the underprivileged slaves of America" (Esposito and Wood, 1982:149), wrote a 20th Century prisoner reporting the violence and discrimination he witnessed behind prisons walls; though, it probably had not crossed his mind that during the time of his observation in the early 1980s the US was beginning to undertake the biggest shift in modern American corrections: a gradual and drastic increase in imprisonment, making America the number one incarcerator in the world, with an annual budget of 228 billion dollars as of 2007 (a multi-billion dollar budget bigger than the GDP of some countries).

At the turn of the century, Gilmore (2000:195) cautioned us that as the punishment industry was becoming a leading employer and producer for the US, and as "private prison and 'security' corporations bargain to control the profit of this traffic in human unfreedom, the analogies between slavery and prison abound," with the various anti-social control movements of the last several years expanding the power, control, and profit of the punishment industry. Of course, as detailed in Chapter 2, the punishment industry has its roots in the legacies of conquest, colonialism, slavery, immigration, and the very nature criminal law. For instance, the strategically racialized labor system rooted in the slave system cleared the path for the prison-industrial complex that flourished in the post-World War II era. In fact, just as new economic and social configurations provided fresh impetus to the acceleration of prison building during the post-World War II period, the aftermath of the 19th Century emancipation reproduced the racial hierarchies of slavery in the structures of the criminal justice system. Then, these transformations, combined with racism, imperialism, reindustrialization, and globalization, converged again in the 1960s, again in the 1970s, and again in the 21st Century, gaining momentum after the September 11, 2001 terrorist attacks on the US, a trend that continues into 2011. As documented by Foucault (1995), Fogel (1979), Churchill and Vander Wall (1992), and Urbina (2008), while failing to address the problems of violence, failing to rehabilitate, and failing to provide anything but a destructive response to issues of prejudice and racism, prisons have been the physical structures called upon to help respond to the chaos, fear, and uncertainty unleashed by the globalization of capital, and prisons, to include capital punishment, are also supposed to contain the array of conflict and struggle waged against those who presumably pose a threat to America. In essence, as noted by Mexican historian Rodolfo F. Acuna, sometimes "all it takes to change Americans is a little recession or another evil empire."

Driven by historical forces, racism, and globalization, the prison-industrial complex, with its corresponding mass incarceration, the rapid reinvigoration of the death penalty is part of a mechanism to institutionalize a new form of slavery, under the notion of social control and national security. While, in reality, the unspoken objective of the criminal justice system is to silence people, as it has for centuries, using the law as a mechanism. In effect, with the voting rights of millions of felons being restricted in the US, felony disenfranchisement is likely to drastically impact their social, educational, and economic position, and influence elections in all levels of government. Worse, the restrictions on voting rights are truly conveying a symbolic message of second-class citizenship (Martinez, 2004), and, in a sense, returning to the time when women, Mexicans, African Americans, and other racial and ethnic minorities could not vote, be educated, or own property, again, re-defining a new form of slavery.

More globally, punishment, to include capital punishment, is tied to the distribution of wealth in the world and consumption in society (Ruddell and Urbina, 2004, 2007). As such, as we look into the future, we must consider that by the end of the 20th Century the richest 1% of the population owned about 30% of the country's wealth, and the top 5% controlled 60% of the wealth. Interestingly, with 4% of the world's population, the US consumes 22% of its electricity, 25% of its oil, and 23% of its natural gas. How is this possible? Well, for one thing, national policies keep domestic inequality in place, while foreign policies continue to foster more, rather than less, global inequality, and thus a presumed need for boundaries, borders, and savage methods of social control. While in reality, "the only 'wall' that a genuine democracy must build, and one that guarantees it's true existence, is justice in all its dimensions and for all the people" (Oboler, 2008:9), if America is to be the country of the future.

Finally, as for the future of capital punishment, until the racial injustice in question is understood not as a judicial wrong done to African Americans, Mexicans, or other minorities, but as a political and moral wrong inflicted on African Americans or Mexicans as a class, we will realize that a moratorium on executions in the US is the most logical avenue in our quest for equality, justice, and peace in a democratic society. Of course,

> Since our lives are socialized so that we accept the status quo as *la verdad y la realidad*, revolutionizing alterations to the existing social order will require that we open up and make a serious and honest effort to the cause, if we are to actually move *hacia un major futuro en un mundo modero* (towards a better future in a modern world). However, as expected, any challenge to the existing order will be fought with great ferocity by those who wish to maintain the existing legacy of hypocrisy, hate, ignorance, dominance, and power (Urbina, 2003c:127).

Appendix

Table 20: People Executed in the United States, 1976-2010

#	Name	Date of Execution	State of Execution	Defendant/ Victim Race	Method of Execution
1*	Gary Gilmore	Jan. 17, 1977	Utah	W/W	Firing Squad
2	John Spenkelink	May 25, 1979	Florida	W/W	Electrocution
3*	Jesse Bishop	Oct. 22, 1979	Nevada	W/W	Gas Chamber
4*	Steven Judy	Mar. 09, 1981	Indiana	W/3W	Electrocution
5*	Frank Coppola	Aug. 10, 1982	Virginia	W/W	Electrocution
6	Charlie Brooks	Dec. 07, 1982	Texas	B/W	Lethal Injection
7	John Evans	Apr. 22, 1983	Alabama	W/W	Electrocution
8	Jimmy Lee Gray	Sep. 02, 1983	Mississippi	W/W	Gas Chamber
9	Robert Sullivan	Nov. 30, 1983	Florida	W/W	Electrocution
10	Robert Wayne Williams	Dec. 14, 1983	Louisiana	B/B	Electrocution
11	John Eldon Smith	Dec. 15, 1983	Georgia	W/2W	Electrocution
12	Anthony Antone	Jan. 26, 1984	Florida	W/W	Electrocution
13	John Taylor	Feb. 29, 1984	Louisiana	B/W	Electrocution
14	James Autry	Mar. 14, 1984	Texas	W/W	Lethal Injection
15	James Hutchins	Mar. 16, 1984	North Carolina	W/2W	Lethal Injection
16	Ronald O'Bryan	Mar. 31, 1984	Texas	W/W	Lethal Injection
17	Elmo Sonnier	Apr. 05, 1984	Louisiana	W/2W	Electrocution
18	Arthur Goode	Apr. 05, 1984	Florida	W/W	Electrocution

Table 20 (Continued): People Executed in the United States, 1976-2010

#	Name	Date of Execution	State of Execution	Defendant/ Victim Race	Method of Execution
19	James Adams	May 10, 1984	Florida	B/W	Electrocution
20	Carl Shriner	Jun. 20, 1984	Florida	W/W	Electrocution
21	Ivon Stanley	Jul. 12, 1984	Georgia	B/W	Electrocution
22	David Washington	Jul. 13, 1984	Florida	B/2W,B	Electrocution
23	Ernest Dobbert	Sep. 07, 1984	Florida	W/W	Electrocution
24	Timothy Baldwin	Sep. 10, 1984	Louisiana	W/W	Electrocution
25	James Dupree Henry	Sep. 20, 1984	Florida	B/B	Electrocution
26	Linwood Briley	Oct. 12, 1984	Virginia	B/W	Electrocution
27	Ernest Knighton	Oct. 30, 1984	Louisiana	B/W	Electrocution
28	Thomas Barefoot	Oct. 30, 1984	Texas	W/W	Lethal Injection
29f	Velma Barfield	Nov. 02, 1984	North Carolina	W/W	Lethal Injection
30	Timothy Palmes	Nov. 08, 1984	Florida	W/W	Electrocution
31	Alpha Otis Stephens	Dec. 12, 1984	Georgia	B/W	Electrocution
32	Robert Lee Willie	Dec. 28, 1984	Louisiana	W/W	Electrocution
33	David Martin	Jan. 04, 1985	Louisiana	W/4W	Electrocution
34	Roosevelt Green	Jan. 09, 1985	Georgia	B/W	Electrocution
35	Joseph Carl Shaw	Jan. 11, 1985	South Carolina	W/2W	Electrocution
36	Doyle Skillern	Jan. 16, 1985	Texas	W/W	Lethal Injection
37	James Raulerson	Jan. 30, 1985	Florida	W/W	Electrocution
38	Van Roosevelt Solomon	Feb. 20, 1985	Georgia	B/W	Electrocution
39	Johnny Paul Witt	Mar. 06, 1985	Florida	W/W	Electrocution
40*	Stephen Peter Morin	Mar. 13, 1985	Texas	W/W	Lethal Injection
41	John Young	Mar. 20, 1985	Georgia	B/3W	Electrocution
42	James Briley	Apr. 18, 1985	Virginia	B/2B	Electrocution

Table 20 (Continued): People Executed in the United States, 1976-2010

#	Name	Date of Execution	State of Execution	Defendant/ Victim Race	Method of Execution
43	Jesse de la Rosa	May 15, 1985	Texas	L/A	Lethal Injection
44	Marvin Francois	May 29, 1985	Florida	B/6B	Electrocution
45	Charles Milton	Jun. 25, 1985	Texas	B/B	Lethal Injection
46	Morris Mason	Jun. 25, 1985	Virginia	B/W	Electrocution
47	Henry Martinez Porter	Jul. 09, 1985	Texas	L/W	Lethal Injection
48# *	Charles Rumbaugh	Sep. 11, 1985	Texas	W/W	Lethal Injection
49*	William Vandiver	Oct. 16, 1985	Indiana	W/W	Electrocution
50*	Carroll Cole	Dec. 06, 1985	Nevada	W/W	Lethal Injection
51#	James Terry Roach	Jan. 10, 1986	South Carolina	W/ see #35	Electrocution
52	Charles William Bass	Mar. 12, 1986	Texas	W/W	Lethal Injection
53	Arthur Lee Jones	Mar. 21, 1986	Alabama	B/W	Electrocution
54	Daniel Thomas	Apr. 15, 1986	Florida	B/W	Electrocution
55*	Jeffrey Allen Barney	Apr. 16, 1986	Texas	W/W	Lethal Injection
56	David Funchess	Apr. 22, 1986	Florida	B/2W	Electrocution
57#	Jay Pinkerton	May 15, 1986	Texas	W/2W	Lethal Injection
58	Ronald Straight	May 20, 1986	Florida	W/W	Electrocution
59	Rudy Esquivel	Jun. 09, 1986	Texas	L/W	Lethal Injection
60	Kenneth Brock	Jun. 19, 1986	Texas	W/W	Lethal Injection
61	Jerome Bowden	Jun. 24, 1986	Georgia	B/W	Electrocution
62	Michael Smith	Jul. 31, 1986	Virginia	B/W	Electrocution
63	Randy Woolls	Aug. 20, 1986	Texas	W/W	Lethal Injection

Table 20 (Continued): People Executed in the United States, 1976-2010

#	Name	Date of Execution	State of Execution	Defendant/ Victim Race	Method of Execution
64	Larry Smith	Aug. 22, 1986	Texas	B/W	Lethal Injection
65	Chester Wicker	Aug. 26, 1986	Texas	W/W	Lethal Injection
66	John Rook	Sep. 19, 1986	North Carolina	W/W	Lethal Injection
67	Michael Wayne Evans	Dec. 04, 1986	Texas	B/L	Lethal Injection
68	Richard Andrade	Dec. 18, 1986	Texas	L/L	Lethal Injection
69*	Ramon Hernandez	Jan. 30, 1987	Texas	L/L	Lethal Injection
70*	Elisio Moreno	Mar. 04, 1987	Texas	L/W	Lethal Injection
71	Joseph Mulligan	May 15, 1987	Georgia	B/B	Electrocution
72	Edward Earl Johnson	May 20, 1987	Mississippi	B/W	Gas Chamber
73	Richard Tucker	May 22, 1987	Georgia	B/W	Electrocution
74	Anthony Williams	May 28, 1987	Texas	B/W	Lethal Injection
75	William Boyd Tucker	May 29, 1987	Georgia	W/W	Electrocution
76	Benjamin Berry	Jun. 07, 1987	Louisiana	W/W	Electrocution
77	Alvin Moore	Jun. 09, 1987	Louisiana	B/W	Electrocution
78	Jimmy Glass	Jun. 12, 1987	Louisiana	W/2W	Electrocution
79	Jimmy Wingo	Jun. 16, 1987	Louisiana	W/ see #78	Electrocution
80	Elliott Johnson	Jun. 24, 1987	Texas	B/W	Lethal Injection
81	Richard Whitley	Jul. 06, 1987	Virginia	W/W	Electrocution
82	John R.Thompson	Jul. 08, 1987	Texas	W/W	Lethal Injection
83	Connie Ray Evans	Jul. 08, 1987	Mississippi	B/A	Gas Chamber
84	Willie Celestine	Jul. 20, 1987	Louisiana	B/W	Electrocution
85	Willie Watson	Jul. 24, 1987	Louisiana	B/W	Electrocution
86	John Brogdon	Jul. 30, 1987	Louisiana	W/W	Electrocution

Table 20 (Continued): People Executed in the United States, 1976-2010

#	Name	Date of Execution	State of Execution	Defendant/ Victim Race	Method of Execution
87	Sterling Rault	Aug. 24, 1987	Louisiana	W/W	Electrocution
88	Beauford White	Aug. 28, 1987	Florida	B/ see #44	Electrocution
89	Wayne Ritter	Aug. 28, 1987	Alabama	W/ see # 7	Electrocution
90	Dale Pierre Selby	Aug. 28, 1987	Utah	B/3W	Lethal Injection
91	Billy Mitchell	Sep. 01, 1987	Georgia	B/W	Electrocution
92	Joseph Starvaggi	Sep. 10, 1987	Texas	W/W	Lethal Injection
93	Timothy McCorquodale	Sep. 21, 1987	Georgia	W/W	Electrocution
94	Robert Streetman	Jan. 07, 1988	Texas	W/W	Lethal Injection
95	Willie Darden	Mar. 15, 1988	Florida	B/W	Electrocution
96	Wayne Felde	Mar. 15, 1988	Louisiana	W/W	Electrocution
97	Leslie Lowenfield	Apr. 13, 1988	Louisiana	B/5B	Electrocution
98	Earl Clanton	Apr. 14, 1988	Virginia	B/B	Electrocution
99*	Arthur Bishop	Jun. 10, 1988	Utah	W/5W	Lethal Injection
100	Edward Byrne	Jun. 14, 1988	Louisiana	W/W	Electrocution
101	James Messer	Jul. 28, 1988	Georgia	W/W	Electrocution
102	Donald Gene Franklin	Nov. 03, 1988	Texas	B/W	Lethal Injection
103	Jeffrey Daugherty	Nov. 07, 1988	Florida	W/W	Electrocution
104	Raymond Landry	Dec. 13, 1988	Texas	B/B	Lethal Injection
105	George "Tiny" Mercer	Jan. 06, 1989	Missouri	W/W	Lethal Injection
106	Theodore Bundy	Jan. 24, 1989	Florida	W/W	Electrocution
107	Leon Rutherford King	Mar. 22, 1989	Texas	B/W	Lethal Injection
108	Aubrey Adams	May 04, 1989	Florida	W/W	Electrocution
109	Henry Willis	May 18, 1989	Georgia	B/W	Electrocution

Table 20 (Continued): People Executed in the United States, 1976-2010

#	Name	Date of Execution	State of Execution	Defendant/ Victim Race	Method of Execution
110	Stephen McCoy	May 24, 1989	Texas	W/W	Lethal Injection
111	Michael Lindsey	May 26, 1989	Alabama	B/W	Electrocution
112*	William Paul Thompson	Jun. 19, 1989	Nevada	W/W	Lethal Injection
113	Leo Edwards	Jun. 21, 1989	Mississippi	B/B	Gas Chamber
114*	Sean Patrick Flannagan	Jun. 23, 1989	Nevada	W/W	Lethal Injection
115	Horace F.Dunkins	Jul. 14, 1989	Alabama	B/W	Electrocution
116	Herbert Richardson	Aug. 18, 1989	Alabama	B/B	Electrocution
117	Alton Waye	Aug. 30, 1989	Virginia	B/W	Electrocution
118	James Paster	Sep. 20, 1989	Texas	W/W	Lethal Injection
119	Arthur Julius	Nov. 17, 1989	Alabama	B/B	Electrocution
120	Carlos de Luna	Dec. 07, 1989	Texas	L/L	Lethal Injection
121*	Gerald Smith	Jan. 18, 1990	Missouri	W/W	Lethal Injection
122*	Jerome Butler	Apr. 21, 1990	Texas	B/B	Lethal Injection
123	Ronald "Rusty" Woomer	Apr. 27, 1990	South Carolina	W/W	Electrocution
124	Jesse Tafero	May 04, 1990	Florida	W/2W	Electrocution
125	Winford Stokes	May 11, 1990	Missouri	B/W	Lethal Injection
126*	Leonard Marvin Laws	May 17, 1990	Missouri	W/2W	Lethal Injection
127	Johnny Ray Anderson	May 17, 1990	Texas	W/W	Lethal Injection
128 #	Dalton Prejean	May 18, 1990	Louisiana	B/W	Electrocution
129*	Thomas Baal	Jun. 03, 1990	Nevada	W/W	Lethal Injection
130	John Swindler	Jun. 18, 1990	Arizona	W/W	Electrocution

Table 20 (Continued): People Executed in the United States, 1976-2010

#	Name	Date of Execution	State of Execution	Defendant/ Victim Race	Method of Execution
131*	Ronald Gene Simmons	Jun. 25, 1990	Arizona	W/16W	Lethal Injection
132*	James Smith	Jun. 26, 1990	Texas	B/W	Lethal Injection
133	Wallace Norrell Thomas	Jul. 13, 1990	Alabama	B/W	Electrocution
134	Mikel Derrick	Jul. 18, 1990	Texas	W/W	Lethal Injection
135	Richard T. Boggs	Jul. 19, 1990	Virginia	W/W	Electrocution
136	Anthony Bertolotti	Jul. 27, 1990	Florida	B/W	Electrocution
137	George C. Gilmore	Aug. 31, 1990	Missouri	W/ see #126	Lethal Injection
138	Charles Coleman	Sep. 10, 1990	Oklahoma	W/W	Lethal Injection
139*	Charles Walker	Sep. 12, 1990	Illinois	W/2W	Lethal Injection
140	James Hamblen	Sep. 21, 1990	Florida	W/W	Electrocution
141	Wilbert L. Evans	Oct. 17, 1990	Virginia	B/B	Electrocution
142	Raymond R. Clark	Nov. 19, 1990	Florida	W/W	Electrocution
143	Buddy Earl Justus	Dec. 13, 1990	Virginia	W/W	Electrocution
144	Lawrence Lee Buxton	Feb. 26, 1991	Texas	B/W	Lethal Injection
145	Roy Allen Harich	Apr. 24, 1991	Florida	W/W	Electrocution
146	Ignacio Cuevas	May 23, 1991	Texas	L/2W	Lethal Injection
147	Jerry Bird	Jun. 17, 1991	Texas	W/W	Lethal Injection
148	Bobby Marion Francis	Jun. 25, 1991	Florida	B/B	Electrocution

Table 20 (Continued): People Executed in the United States, 1976-2010

#	Name	Date of Execution	State of Execution	Defendant/ Victim Race	Method of Execution
149	Andrew Lee Jones	Jul. 22, 1991	Louisiana	B/B	Electrocution
150	Albert Clozza	Jul. 24, 1991	Virginia	W/W	Electrocution
151	Derick Lynn Peterson	Aug. 22, 1991	Virginia	B/W	Electrocution
152	Maurice Byrd	Aug. 23, 1991	Missouri	B/4W	Lethal Injection
153¥	Donald Gaskins	Sep. 06, 1991	South Carolina	W/B	Electrocution
154	James Russell	Sep. 19, 1991	Texas	B/W	Lethal Injection
155	Warren McCleskey	Sep. 25, 1991	Georgia	B/W	Electrocution
156	Michael van McDougall	Oct. 18, 1991	North Carolina	W/W	Lethal Injection
157	G.W. Green	Nov. 12, 1991	Texas	W/see #92	Lethal Injection
158	Mark Hopkinson	Nov. 22, 1992	Wyoming	W/W	Lethal Injection
159	Joe Angel Cordova	Jan. 22, 1992	Texas	L/W	Lethal Injection
160	Ricky R. Rector	Jan. 24, 1992	Arkansas	B/W	Lethal Injection
161#	Johnny Frank Garrett	Feb. 11, 1992	Texas	W/W	Lethal Injection
162	David M. Clark	Feb. 28, 1992	Texas	W/2W	Lethal Injection
163	Edward Ellis	Mar. 03, 1992	Texas	W/W	Lethal Injection
164	Robyn L. Parks	Mar. 10, 1992	Oklahoma	B/A	Lethal Injection
165	Olan R. Robison	Mar. 13, 1992	Oklahoma	W/3W	Lethal Injection
166*	Steven B. Pennell	Mar. 14, 1992	Delaware	W/2W	Lethal Injection

Table 20 (Continued): People Executed in the United States, 1976-2010

#	Name	Date of Execution	State of Execution	Defendant/ Victim Race	Method of Execution
167	Larry Gene Heath	Mar. 20, 1992	Alabama	W/W	Electrocution
168	Donald Eugene Harding	Apr. 06, 1992	Arizona	W/2W	Gas Chamber
169	Robert Alton Harris	Apr. 21, 1992	California	W/2W	Gas Chamber
170	William Wayne White	Apr. 23, 1992	Texas	B/W	Lethal Injection
171	Justin Lee May	May 07, 1992	Texas	W/W	Lethal Injection
172	Stephen D. Hill	May 07, 1992	Arkansas	W/W	Lethal Injection
173	Nollie Martin	May 12, 1992	Florida	W/W	Electrocution
174	Jesus Romero	May 20, 1992	Texas	L/L	Lethal Injection
175	Roger Keith Coleman	May 20, 1992	Virginia	W/W	Electrocution
176	Robert Black	May 22, 1992	Texas	W/W	Lethal Injection
177	Edward D. Kennedy	Jul. 21, 1992	Florida	B/2W	Electrocution
178	Edward Fitzgerald	Jul. 23, 1992	Virginia	W/W	Electrocution
179	William Andrews	Jul. 30, 1992	Utah	B/see #90	Lethal Injection
180	Curtis Lee Johnson	Aug. 11, 1992	Texas	B/W	Lethal Injection
181	Willie LeRoy Jones	Sep. 15, 1992	Virginia	B/2B	Electrocution
182	James Demouchette	Sep. 22, 1992	Texas	B/2W	Lethal Injection
183	Ricky Lee Grubbs	Oct. 21, 1992	Missouri	W/W	Lethal Injection
184	John S. Gardner, Jr.	Oct. 23, 1992	North Carolina	W/2W	Lethal Injection

Table 20 (Continued): People Executed in the United States, 1976-2010

#	Name	Date of Execution	State of Execution	Defendant/ Victim Race	Method of Execution
185	Jeffrey Griffin	Nov. 19, 1992	Texas	B/B	Lethal Injection
186	Cornelius Singleton	Nov. 20, 1992	Alabama	B/W	Electrocution
187	Kavin Lincecum	Dec. 10, 1992	Texas	B/W	Lethal Injection
188	Timothy Bunch	Dec. 10, 1992	Virginia	W/A	Electrocution
189*	Westley Allan Dodd	Jan. 05, 1993	Washington	W/3W	Hanging
190	Charles Stamper	Jan. 19, 1993	Virginia	B/3W	Electrocution
191	Martsay Bolder	Jan. 27, 1993	Missouri	B/B	Lethal Injection
192*	John George Brewer	Mar. 03, 1993	Arizona	W/W	Lethal Injection
193*	James Allen Red Dog	Mar. 03, 1993	Delaware	N/W	Lethal Injection
194	Robert Sawyer	Mar. 05, 1993	Louisiana	W/W	Lethal Injection
195	Syvasky Poyner	Mar. 18, 1993	Virginia	B/2W, B	Electrocution
196	Carlos Santana	Mar. 23, 1993	Texas	L/L	Lethal Injection
197~	Ramon Montoya	Mar. 25, 1993	Texas	L/W	Lethal Injection
198	James Clark	Apr. 14, 1993	Arizona	W/4W	Lethal Injection
199	Robert Henderson	Apr. 21, 1993	Florida	W/3W	Electrocution
200	Darryl Stewart	May 04, 1993	Texas	B/W	Lethal Injection
201	Larry Joe Johnson	May 05, 1993	Florida	W/W	Electrocution
202	Leonel Herrera	May 12, 1993	Texas	L/L	Lethal Injection
203	John Sawyers	May 18, 1993	Texas	W/W	Lethal Injection
204*	Andrew Chabrol	Jun. 17, 1993	Virginia	W/W	Electrocution

Table 20 (Continued): People Executed in the United States, 1976-2010

#	Name	Date of Execution	State of Execution	Defendant/ Victim Race	Method of Execution
205	Thomas Dean Stevens	Jun. 28, 1993	Georgia	W/W	Electrocution
206	Markham Duff-Smith	Jun. 29, 1993	Texas	W/W	Lethal Injection
207#	Curtis Harris	Jul. 01, 1993	Texas	B/W	Lethal Injection
208	Walter Junior Blair	Jul. 21, 1993	Missouri	B/W	Lethal Injection
209#	Frederick Lashley	Jul. 28, 1993	Missouri	B/B	Lethal Injection
210	Danny Harris	Jul. 30, 1993	Texas	B/ see #207	Lethal Injection
211	Joseph Jernigan	Aug. 05, 1993	Texas	W/W	Lethal Injection
212	David Lee Holland	Aug. 12, 1993	Texas	W/W	Lethal Injection
213	Carl Kelly	Aug. 20, 1993	Texas	B/W	Lethal Injection
214#	Ruben Cantu	Aug. 24, 1993	Texas	L/L	Lethal Injection
215*	David Mason	Aug. 24, 1993	California	W/W	Gas Chamber
216*	Michael Durocher	Aug. 25, 1993	Florida	W/W	Electrocution
217	Richard Wilkerson	Aug. 31, 1993	Texas	B/W	Lethal Injection
218	Kenneth DeShields	Aug. 31, 1993	Delaware	B/W	Lethal Injection
219	Johnny James	Sep. 03, 1993	Texas	W/W	Lethal Injection
220	Joseph Wise	Sep. 14, 1993	Virginia	B/W	Electrocution
221	Antonio Bonham	Sep. 28, 1993	Texas	B/W	Lethal Injection
222	Frank Guinan	Oct. 06, 1993	Missouri	W/W	Lethal Injection

Table 20 (Continued): People Executed in the United States, 1976-2010

#	Name	Date of Execution	State of Execution	Defendant/ Victim Race	Method of Execution
223*	Anthony Cook	Nov. 10, 1993	Texas	W/W	Lethal Injection
224#	Christopher Burger	Dec. 07, 1993	Georgia	W/W	Electrocution
225	Clifford Phillips	Dec. 15, 1993	Texas	B/W	Lethal Injection
226	David Pruett	Dec. 16, 1993	Virginia	W/W	Electrocution
227*	Keith Wells	Jan. 06, 1994	Idaho	W/2W	Lethal Injection
228	Harold Barnard	Feb. 02, 1994	Texas	W/A	Lethal Injection
229	Johnny Watkins, Jr.	Mar. 03, 1994	Virginia	B/W	Electrocution
230	Feddie Lee Webb	Mar. 31, 1994	Texas	B/W	Lethal Injection
231	William Henry Hance	Mar. 31, 1994	Georgia	B/B	Electrocution
232*	Richard Lee Beavers	Apr. 04, 1994	Texas	W/W	Lethal Injection
233	Roy Allen Stewart	Apr. 22, 1994	Florida	W/W	Electrocution
234	Larry Anderson	Apr. 26, 1994	Texas	W/W	Lethal Injection
235	Timothy Spencer	Apr. 27, 1994	Virginia	B/W	Electrocution
236	Paul Rougeau	May 03, 1994	Texas	B/B	Lethal Injection
237	John Wayne Gacy	May 10, 1994	Illinois	W/12W	Lethal Injection
238	Edward Pickens	May 11, 1994	Arkansas	B/B	Lethal Injection
239	Jonas Whitmore	May 11, 1994	Arkansas	W/W	Lethal Injection
240*	John Thanos	May 17, 1994	Maryland	W/W	Lethal Injection
241	Stephen Nethery	May 27, 1994	Texas	W/W	Lethal Injection

Table 20 (Continued): People Executed in the United States, 1976-2010

#	Name	Date of Execution	State of Execution	Defendant/ Victim Race	Method of Execution
242	Charles Campbell	May 27, 1994	Washington	W/3W	Hanging
243	Denton Crank	Jun. 14, 1994	Texas	W/W	Lethal Injection
244	David Lawson	Jun. 15, 1994	North Carolina	W/W	Gas Chamber
245	Andre Deputy	Jun. 23, 1994	Delaware	B/2B	Lethal Injection
246	Robert Drew	Aug. 02, 1994	Texas	W/W	Lethal Injection
247	Hoyt Clines	Aug. 03, 1994	Arkansas	W/W	Lethal Injection
248	Darryl Richley	Aug. 03, 1994	Arkansas	W/ see #247	Lethal Injection
249	James Holmes	Aug. 03, 1994	Arkansas	W/ see #247	Lethal Injection
250	Harold Otey	Sep. 02, 1994	Nebraska	B/W	Electrocution
251	Jessie Gutierrez	Sep. 16, 1994	Texas	L/W	Lethal Injection
252*	George Lott	Sep. 20, 1994	Texas	W/2W	Lethal Injection
253	Walter Williams	Oct. 05, 1994	Texas	B/W	Lethal Injection
254	Warren Bridge	Nov. 22, 1994	Texas	W/W	Lethal Injection
255	Herman Clark	Dec. 06, 1994	Texas	B/W	Lethal Injection
256	Gregory Resnover	Dec. 08, 1994	Indiana	B/W	Electrocution
257	Raymond Kinnamon	Dec. 11, 1994	Texas	W/W	Lethal Injection
258	Jesse D. Jacobs	Jan. 04, 1995	Texas	W/W	Lethal Injection
259	Mario S. Marquez	Jan. 17, 1995	Texas	L/L	Lethal Injection

Table 20 (Continued): People Executed in the United States, 1976-2010

#	Name	Date of Execution	State of Execution	Defendant/ Victim Race	Method of Execution
260¥	Kermit Smith, Jr.	Jan. 24, 1995	North Carolina	W/B	Lethal Injection
261	Dana Ray Edmonds	Jan. 24, 1995	Virginia	B/W	Lethal Injection
262	Clifton Russell	Jan. 31, 1995	Texas	W/W	Lethal Injection
263	Willie Ray Williams	Jan. 31, 1995	Texas	B/W	Lethal Injection
264	Jeffrey D. Motley	Feb. 07, 1995	Texas	W/L	Lethal Injection
265	Billy Conn Gardner	Feb. 16, 1995	Texas	W/W	Lethal Injection
266	Samuel Hawkins	Feb. 21, 1995	Texas	B/W	Lethal Injection
267*	Nelson Shelton	Mar. 17, 1995	Delaware	W/W	Lethal Injection
268¥*	Thomas Grasso	Mar. 20, 1995	Oklahoma	W/B	Lethal Injection
269	Hernando Williams	Mar. 22, 1995	Illinois	B/W	Lethal Injection
270	James Free	Mar. 22, 1995	Illinois	W/W	Lethal Injection
271	Noble D. Mays	Apr. 06, 1995	Texas	W/W	Lethal Injection
272~	Nicholas Ingram	Apr. 07, 1995	Georgia	W/W	Electrocution
273	Richard Snell	Apr. 19, 1995	Arkansas	W/W	Lethal Injection
274	Willie Clisby	Apr. 28, 1995	Alabama	B/B	Electrocution
275*	Keith Zettlemoyer	May 02, 1995	Pennsylvania	W/W	Lethal Injection
276	Emmitt Foster	May 03, 1995	Missouri	B/B	Lethal Injection
277	Duncan McKenzie	May 10, 1995	Montana	W/W	Lethal Injection
278	Varnall Weeks	May 12, 1995	Alabama	B/B	Electrocution

Table 20 (Continued): People Executed in the United States, 1976-2010

#	Name	Date of Execution	State of Execution	Defendant/ Victim Race	Method of Execution
279	Thomas Lee Ward	May 16, 1995	Louisiana	B/B	Lethal Injection
280	Girvies Davis	May 17, 1995	Illinois	B/W	Lethal Injection
281	Darrell Gene Devier	May 17, 1995	Georgia	W/W	Electrocution
282	Willie Lloyd Turner	May 25, 1995	Virginia	B/W	Lethal Injection
283	Fletcher Thomas Mann	Jun. 01, 1995	Texas	W/W	Lethal Injection
284	Ronald K. Allridge	Jun. 08, 1995	Texas	B/W	Lethal Injection
285	John Fearance Jr.	Jun. 20, 1995	Texas	B/W	Lethal Injection
286	Karl Hammond	Jun. 21, 1995	Texas	B/W	Lethal Injection
287	Larry Griffin	Jun. 21, 1995	Missouri	B/B	Lethal Injection
288	Roger Dale Stafford	Jul. 01, 1995	Oklahoma	W/4W,1B,1L	Lethal Injection
289	Bernard Bolender	Jul. 18, 1995	Florida	W/3L/1W	Electrocution
290	Robert Murray	Jul. 26, 1995	Missouri	B/2B	Lethal Injection
291	Robert Brecheen	Aug. 11, 1995	Oklahoma	W/W	Lethal Injection
292	Vernon Sattiewhite	Aug. 15, 1995	Texas	B/W	Lethal Injection
293*	Leon Moser	Aug. 16, 1995	Pennsylvania	W/3W	Lethal Injection
294	Sylvester Adams	Aug. 18, 1995	South Carolina	B/B	Lethal Injection
295	Barry Lee Fairchild	Aug. 31, 1995	Arkansas	B/W	Lethal Injection

Table 20 (Continued): People Executed in the United States, 1976-2010

#	Name	Date of Execution	State of Execution	Defendant/ Victim Race	Method of Execution
296	Jimmie Jeffers	Sep. 13, 1995	Arizona	W/W	Lethal Injection
297	Carl Johnson	Sep. 19, 1995	Texas	B/B	Lethal Injection
298	Charles Albanese	Sep. 20, 1995	Illinois	W/W	Lethal Injection
299*	Phillip Lee Ingle	Sep. 22, 1995	North Carolina	W/4W	Lethal Injection
300	Dennis W. Stockton	Sep. 27, 1995	Virginia	W/W	Lethal Injection
301	Harold Joe Lane	Oct. 04, 1995	Texas	W/W	Lethal Injection
302*	Mickey Wayne Davidson	Oct. 19, 1995	Virginia	W/3W	Lethal Injection
303	Herman Charles Barnes	Nov. 13, 1995	Virginia	B/W	Lethal Injection
304	Robert Sidebottom	Nov. 15, 1995	Missouri	W/W	Lethal Injection
305	George Del Vecchio	Nov. 22, 1995	Illinois	W/W	Lethal Injection
306	Anthony Joe LaRette	Nov. 29, 1995	Missouri	W/W	Lethal Injection
307	Jerry White	Dec. 04, 1995	Florida	B/W	Electrocution
308	Philip Atkins	Dec. 05, 1995	Florida	W/L	Electrocution
309¥	Robert O'Neal	Dec. 06, 1995	Missouri	W/B	Lethal Injection
310	Bernard Amos	Dec. 06, 1995	Texas	B/W	Lethal Injection
311	Hai Hai Vuong	Dec. 07, 1995	Texas	A/2A	Lethal Injection
312*	Esequel Banda	Dec. 11, 1995	Texas	L/W	Lethal Injection
313	James Michael Briddle	Dec. 12, 1995	Texas	W/W	Lethal Injection

Table 20 (Continued): People Executed in the United States, 1976-2010

#	Name	Date of Execution	State of Execution	Defendant/ Victim Race	Method of Execution
314	Walter Correll	Jan. 4, 1996	Virginia	W/W	Lethal Injection
315	Richard Townes, Jr.	Jan. 23, 1996	Virginia	B/W	Lethal Injection
316	Billy Bailey	Jan. 25, 1996	Delaware	W/W	Hanging
317*	John Albert Taylor	Jan. 26, 1996	Utah	W/W	Firing Squad
318	William Flamer	Jan. 30, 1996	Delaware	B/2B	Lethal Injection
319*	Leo Jenkins	Feb. 09, 1996	Texas	W/W	Lethal Injection
320	Edward Dean Horsley	Feb. 16, 1996	Alabama	B/W	Electrocution
321	Jeffery Paul Sloan	Feb. 21, 1996	Missouri	W/W	Lethal Injection
322	William George Bonin	Feb. 23, 1996	California	W/4W	Lethal Injection
323	Kenneth Granviel	Feb. 27, 1996	Texas	B/B	Lethal Injection
324	Antonio James	Mar. 01, 1996	Louisiana	B/W	Lethal Injection
325	Richard Allen Moran	Mar. 30, 1996	Nevada	W/2W	Lethal Injection
326	Doyle Williams	Apr. 10, 1996	Missouri	W/W	Lethal Injection
327*	James Clark, Jr.	Apr. 19, 1996	Delaware	W/2W	Lethal Injection
328	Benjamin Brewer	Apr. 26, 1996	Oklahoma	W/W	Lethal Injection
329	Keith Daniel Williams	May 03, 1996	California	W/3L	Lethal Injection
330*	Robert South	May 31, 1996	South Carolina	W/W	Lethal Injection
331*	Daren Lee Bolton	Jun. 19, 1996	Arizona	W/W	Lethal Injection

Table 20 (Continued): People Executed in the United States, 1976-2010

#	Name	Date of Execution	State of Execution	Defendant/ Victim Race	Method of Execution
332	John Joubert	Jul. 17, 1996	Nebraska	W/2W	Electrocution
333	Joseph Savino	Jul. 17, 1996	Virginia	W/W	Lethal Injection
334	Tommie Smith	Jul. 18, 1996	Indiana	B/W, see #256	Lethal Injection
335	Fred Kornahrens	Jul. 19, 1996	South Carolina	W/3W	Lethal Injection
336	Emmet Nave	Jul. 31, 1996	Missouri	NA/W	Lethal Injection
337	Thomas Battle	Aug. 7, 1996	Missouri	B/B	Lethal Injection
338	William Frank Parker	Aug. 8, 1996	Arkansas	W/2W	Lethal Injection
339	Stephen Hatch	Aug. 9, 1996	Oklahoma	W/2W	Lethal Injection
340	Richard Oxford	Aug. 21, 1996	Missouri	W/2W	Lethal Injection
341	Luis Mata	Aug. 22, 1996	Arizona	L/L	Lethal Injection
342*	Michael Torrence	Sep. 6, 1996	South Carolina	W/3W	Lethal Injection
343*	Douglas Franklin Wright	Sep. 6, 1996	Oregon	W/3W	Lethal Injection
344	Raymond Lee Stewart	Sep. 18, 1996	Illinois	B/4W, 2B	Lethal Injection
345*	Joe Gonzales	Sep. 18, 1996	Texas	L/W	Lethal Injection
346	Larry Gene Bell	Oct. 4, 1996	South Carolina	W/2W	Electrocution
347	John Earl Bush	Oct. 21, 1996	Florida	B/W	Electrocution
348	Larry Lonchar	Nov. 14, 1996	Georgia	W/3W	Electrocution
349*	Doyle Cecil Lucas	Nov. 15, 1996	South Carolina	W/2W	Lethal Injection
350	Ellis Wayne Felker	Nov. 15, 1996	Georgia	W/W	Electrocution

Table 20 (Continued): People Executed in the United States, 1976-2010

#	Name	Date of Execution	State of Execution	Defendant/ Victim Race	Method of Execution
351	Ronald Bennett	Nov. 21, 1996	Virginia	B/W	Lethal Injection
352	Frank Middleton, Jr.	Nov. 22, 1996	South Carolina	B/B	Lethal Injection
353	Gregory Warren Beaver	Dec. 3, 1996	Virginia	W/W	Lethal Injection
354	John Mills, Jr.	Dec. 6, 1996	Florida	B/W	Electrocution
355	Larry Allen Stout	Dec. 10, 1996	Virginia	B/W	Lethal Injection
356	Richard Zeitvogel	Dec. 11, 1996	Missouri	W/W	Lethal Injection
357	Lem Tuggle	Dec. 12, 1996	Virginia	W/W	Lethal Injection
358	Ronald Lee Hoke	Dec. 16, 1996	Virginia	W/W	Lethal Injection
359	Earl Van Denton	Jan. 8, 1997	Arkansas	W/2W	Lethal Injection
360	Paul Ruiz	Jan. 8, 1997	Arkansas	L/see #359	Lethal Injection
361	Kirt Wainwright	Jan. 8, 1997	Arkansas	B/W	Lethal Injection
362	Billy Wayne Waldrop	Jan. 10, 1997	Alabama	W/W	Electrocution
363	Randy Greenawalt	Jan. 23, 1997	Arizona	W/4W	Lethal Injection
364	Eric Schneider	Jan. 29, 1997	Missouri	W/2W	Lethal Injection
365	Michael Carl George	Feb. 6, 1997	Virginia	W/W	Lethal Injection
366*	Richard Brimage, Jr.	Feb. 10, 1997	Texas	W/W	Lethal Injection
367	Coleman Gray	Feb. 26, 1997	Virginia	B/W	Lethal Injection
368	John Kennedy Barefield	Mar. 12, 1997	Texas	B/W	Lethal Injection

Table 20 (Continued): People Executed in the United States, 1976-2010

#	Name	Date of Execution	State of Execution	Defendant/ Victim Race	Method of Execution
369~	Pedro Medina	Mar. 25, 1997	Florida	L/B	Electrocution
370	David Lee Herman	Apr. 2, 1997	Texas	W/W	Lethal Injection
371	David Spence	Apr. 3, 1997	Texas	W/2W	Lethal Injection
372	Billy Joe Woods	Apr. 14, 1997	Texas	W/W	Lethal Injection
373	Kenneth Gentry	Apr. 16, 1997	Texas	W/W	Lethal Injection
374	Benjamin Boyle	Apr. 21, 1997	Texas	W/W	Lethal Injection
375	John Ashley Brown, Jr.	Apr. 24, 1997	Louisiana	W/W	Lethal Injection
376	Ernest Orville Baldree	Apr. 29, 1997	Texas	W/2W	Lethal Injection
377	Walter Hill	May 2, 1997	Alabama	B/3B	Electrocution
378	Terry Washington	May 6, 1997	Texas	B/W	Lethal Injection
379*	Scott Carpenter	May 8, 1997	Oklahoma	NA/W	Lethal Injection
380	Anthony Ray Westley	May 13, 1997	Texas	B/W	Lethal Injection
381*	Harry Charles Moore	May 16, 1997	Oregon	W/2W	Lethal Injection
382	Clifton Belyeu	May 16, 1997	Texas	W/W	Lethal Injection
383	Richard Drinkard	May 19, 1997	Texas	W/3W	Lethal Injection
384	Clarence Lackey	May 20, 1997	Texas	W/W	Lethal Injection
385	Bruce Callins	May 21, 1997	Texas	B/W	Lethal Injection
386	Larry Wayne White	May 22, 1997	Texas	W/W	Lethal Injection
387	Robert Madden	May 28, 1997	Texas	W/2W	Lethal Injection

Table 20 (Continued): People Executed in the United States, 1976-2010

#	Name	Date of Execution	State of Execution	Defendant/ Victim Race	Method of Execution
388	Patrick Rogers	Jun. 2, 1997	Texas	B/W	Lethal Injection
389	Kenneth Harris	Jun. 3, 1997	Texas	B/W	Lethal Injection
390	Dorsie Johnson	Jun. 4, 1997	Texas	B/W	Lethal Injection
391	Davis Losada	Jun. 4, 1997	Texas	L/L	Lethal Injection
392¥	Henry Francis Hays	Jun. 6, 1997	Alabama	W/B	Electrocution
393	Earl Behringer	Jun. 11, 1997	Texas	W/2W	Lethal Injection
394*	Michael Eugene Elkins	Jun. 13, 1997	South Carolina	W/W	Lethal Injection
395	David Stoker	Jun. 16, 1997	Texas	W/W	Lethal Injection
396	Eddie James Johnson	Jun. 17, 1997	Texas	B/2W,L	Lethal Injection
397~	Irineo Montoya	Jun. 18, 1997	Texas	L/W	Lethal Injection
398	William Lyle Woratzeck	Jun. 25, 1997	Arizona	W/W	Lethal Injection
399	Harold McQueen	Jul. 1, 1997	Kentucky	W/W	Electrocution
400	Flint Gregory Hunt	Jul. 2, 1997	Maryland	B/W	Lethal Injection
401	Roy Bruce Smith	Jul. 17, 1997	Virginia	W/W	Lethal Injection
402	Joseph Roger O'Dell, III	Jul. 23, 1997	Virginia	W/W	Lethal Injection
403	Robert West	Jul. 29, 1997	Texas	N/W	Lethal Injection
404	Ralph Cecil Feltrop	Aug. 6, 1997	Missouri	W/W	Lethal Injection
405	Eugene Wallace Perry	Aug. 6, 1997	Arkansas	W/2W	Lethal Injection

Table 20 (Continued): People Executed in the United States, 1976-2010

#	Name	Date of Execution	State of Execution	Defendant/ Victim Race	Method of Execution
406	Donald E. Reese	Aug. 13, 1997	Missouri	W/W	Lethal Injection
407	Carlton Jerome Pope	Aug. 19, 1997	Virginia	B/W	Lethal Injection
408	Andrew Six	Aug. 20, 1997	Missouri	W/W	Lethal Injection
409	James Carl Lee Davis	Sep. 9, 1997	Texas	B/B	Lethal Injection
410~	Mario Benjamin Murphy	Sep. 17, 1997	Virginia	L/W	Lethal Injection
411	Jessel Turner	Sep. 22, 1997	Texas	B/W	Lethal Injection
412	Samuel McDonald, Jr.	Sep. 24, 1997	Missouri	B/B	Lethal Injection
413*	Benjamin Stone	Sep. 25, 1997	Texas	W/2W	Lethal Injection
414	Johnny Cockrum	Sep. 30, 1997	Texas	W/W	Lethal Injection
415	Dwight Dwayne Adanandus	Oct. 1, 1997	Texas	B/W	Lethal Injection
416	Ricky Lee Green	Oct. 8, 1997	Texas	W/W	Lethal Injection
417	Gary Lee Davis	Oct. 13, 1997	Colorado	W/W	Lethal Injection
418	Alan Bannister	Oct. 22, 1997	Missouri	W/W	Lethal Injection
419	Kenneth Ray Ransom	Oct. 28, 1997	Texas	B/L	Lethal Injection
420	Aua Lauti	Nov. 4, 1997	Texas	A/A	Lethal Injection
421	Aaron Lee Fuller	Nov. 6, 1997	Texas	W/W	Lethal Injection
422	Earl Matthews	Nov. 7, 1997	South Carolina	B/W	Lethal Injection
423	Dawud Majid Mu'Min	Nov. 13, 1997	Virginia	B/W	Lethal Injection

Table 20 (Continued): People Executed in the United States, 1976-2010

#	Name	Date of Execution	State of Execution	Defendant/ Victim Race	Method of Execution
424	Walter Stewart	Nov. 19, 1997	Illinois	B/2W	Lethal Injection
425	Durlyn Eddmonds	Nov. 19, 1997	Illinois	B/B	Lethal Injection
426	Michael Eugene Sharp	Nov. 19, 1997	Texas	W/2W	Lethal Injection
427	Gary Burris	Nov. 20, 1997	Indiana	B/B	Lethal Injection
428	Charlie Livingston	Nov. 21, 1997	Texas	B/W	Lethal Injection
429	Robert E. Williams	Dec. 02, 1997	Nebraska	B/W	Electrocution
430	Michael Lockhart	Dec. 09, 1997	Texas	W/W	Lethal Injection
431	Michael Charles Satcher	Dec. 09, 1997	Virginia	B/W	Lethal Injection
432¥	Thomas Beavers	Dec. 11, 1997	Virginia	W/B	Lethal Injection
433*	Lloyd Wayne Hampton	Jan. 21, 1998	Illinois	W/W	Lethal Injection
434	Jose Jesus Ceja	Jan. 21, 1998	Arizona	H/LW	Lethal Injection
435*	Robert A. Smith	Jan. 29, 1998	Indiana	W/W	Lethal Injection
436*	Ricky Lee Sanderson	Jan. 30, 1998	North Carolina	W/W	Gas Chamber
437*f*	Karla Faye Tucker	Feb. 03, 1998	Texas	W/W	Lethal Injection
438*	Steven Renfro	Feb. 9, 1998	Texas	W/3W	Lethal Injection
439	Tony A. Mackall	Feb. 10, 1998	Virginia	B/W	Lethal Injection
440*	Michael Edward Long	Feb. 20, 1998	Oklahoma	W/2W	Lethal Injection

Table 20 (Continued): People Executed in the United States, 1976-2010

#	Name	Date of Execution	State of Execution	Defendant/ Victim Race	Method of Execution
441	Terry Allen Langford	Feb. 24, 1998	Montana	W/2W	Lethal Injection
442	Reginald Powell	Feb. 25, 1998	Missouri	B/2B	Lethal Injection
443¥	John Arnold	Mar. 6, 1998	South Carolina	W/B	Lethal Injection
444	Jerry Lee Hogue	Mar. 11, 1998	Texas	W/W	Lethal Injection
445	Douglas Buchanan	Mar. 18, 1998	Virginia	W/4W	Lethal Injection
446	Gerald Stano	Mar. 23, 1998	Florida	W/W	Electrocution
447	Leo Jones	Mar. 24, 1998	Florida	B/W	Electrocution
448	Milton Griffin-El	Mar. 25, 1998	Missouri	B/B	Lethal Injection
449	Ronald Watkins	Mar. 25, 1998	Virginia	B/W	Lethal Injection
450*f*	Judy Buenoano	Mar. 30, 1998	Florida	W/W	Electrocution
451	Daniel Remeta	Mar. 31, 1998	Florida	N/W	Electrocution
452~	Angel Francisco Breard	Apr. 14, 1998	Virginia	L/W	Lethal Injection
453	Glennon Sweet	Apr. 22, 1998	Missouri	W/W	Lethal Injection
454~	Jose Villafuerte	Apr. 22, 1998	Arizona	L/L	Lethal Injection
455#	Joseph Cannon	Apr. 22, 1998	Texas	W/W	Lethal Injection
456	Lesley Lee Gosch	Apr. 24, 1998	Texas	W/W	Lethal Injection
457*	Arthur Martin Ross	Apr. 29, 1998	Arizona	W/W	Lethal Injection
458	Frank Basil McFarland	Apr. 29, 1998	Texas	W/W	Lethal Injection
459	Steven Allen Thompson	May 8, 1998	Alabama	W/W	Electrocution
460#	Robert Anthony Carter	May 18, 1998	Texas	B/L	Lethal Injection

Table 20 (Continued): People Executed in the United States, 1976-2010

#	Name	Date of Execution	State of Execution	Defendant/ Victim Race	Method of Execution
461	Pedro Cruz Muniz	May 19, 1998	Texas	L/W	Lethal Injection
462	Douglas Edward Gretzler	Jun. 03, 1998	Arizona	W/2W	Lethal Injection
463	David Loomis Cargill	Jun. 10, 1998	Georgia	W/2W	Electrocution
464	Clifford Holt Boggess	Jun. 11, 1998	Texas	W/W	Lethal Injection
465	Johnny Pyles	Jun. 15, 1998	Texas	W/W	Lethal Injection
466	Dennis Wayne Eaton	Jun. 18, 1998	Virginia	W/W	Lethal Injection
467	Leopoldo Narvaiz	Jun. 26, 1998	Texas	L/4W	Lethal Injection
468	Wilburn A. Henderson	Jun. 08, 1998	Arkansas	W/W	Lethal Injection
469¥	John Plath	Jun. 10, 1998	South Carolina	W/B	Lethal Injection
470	Thomas Thompson	Jun. 14, 1998	California	W/W	Lethal Injection
471	Danny Lee King	Jun. 23, 1998	Virginia	W/W	Lethal Injection
472*	Stephen Wood	Aug. 05, 1998	Oklahoma	W/W	Lethal Injection
473	Zane Brown Hill	Aug. 14, 1998	North Carolina	W/W	Lethal Injection
474	Lance Chandler	Aug. 20, 1998	Virginia	B/W	Lethal Injection
475	Genaro Ruiz Camacho	Aug. 26, 1998	Texas	L/B	Lethal Injection
476	Johnile DuBois	Aug. 31, 1998	Virginia	B/W	Lethal Injection
477	Delbert Teague	Sep. 09, 1998	Texas	W/W	Lethal Injection

Table 20 (Continued): People Executed in the United States, 1976-2010

#	Name	Date of Execution	State of Execution	Defendant/ Victim Race	Method of Execution
478	David Castillo	Sep. 23, 1998	Texas	L/L	Lethal Injection
479	Kenneth Stewart	Sep. 23, 1998	Virginia	W/2W	Electrocution
480	Sammy Roberts	Sep. 25, 1998	South Carolina	W/2W+1B	Lethal Injection
481	Javier Cruz	Oct. 01, 1998	Texas	L/2W	Lethal Injection
482*	Roderick Abeyta	Oct. 05, 1998	Nevada	L/W	Lethal Injection
483	Jonathan Nobles	Oct. 07, 1998	Texas	W/2W	Lethal Injection
484*	Jeremy Sagastegui	Oct. 13, 1998	Washington	W/2W+1L	Lethal Injection
485#	Dwayne Allen Wright	Oct. 14, 1998	Virginia	B/B	Lethal Injection
486	Ronald Lee Fitzgerald	Oct. 21, 1998	Virginia	B/2B	Lethal Injection
487	Tyrone D. Gilliam	Nov. 16, 1998	Maryland	B/W	Lethal Injection
488	Kenneth McDuff	Nov. 17, 1998	Texas	W/2W	Lethal Injection
489	Kenneth Wilson	Nov. 17, 1998	Virginia	B/B	Lethal Injection
490	John Thomas Noland	Nov. 20, 1998	North Carolina	W/2W	Lethal Injection
491	Kevin Wayne Cardwell	Dec. 03, 1998	Virginia	B/B	Lethal Injection
492	Larry Gilbert	Dec. 04, 1998	South Carolina	B/W	Lethal Injection
493	J.D. Gleaton	Dec. 04, 1998	South Carolina	B/ see #492	Lethal Injection
494	Daniel Lee Corwin	Dec. 07, 1998	Texas	W/3W	Lethal Injection
495	Jeff Emery	Dec. 08, 1998	Texas	W/W	Lethal Injection

Table 20 (Continued): People Executed in the United States, 1976-2010

#	Name	Date of Execution	State of Execution	Defendant/ Victim Race	Method of Execution
496~	Tuan Nguyen	Dec. 10, 1998	Oklahoma	A/3W	Lethal Injection
497	Louis Truesdale	Dec. 11, 1998	South Carolina	B/W	Lethal Injection
498	James Ronald Meanes	Dec. 15, 1998	Texas	B/L	Lethal Injection
499	John Wayne Duvall	Dec. 17, 1998	Oklahoma	W/W	Lethal Injection
500	Andy Smith	Dec. 18, 1998	South Carolina	B/2B	Lethal Injection
501	John Glenn Moody	Jan. 05, 1999	Texas	W/W	Lethal Injection
502	John Walter Castro	Jan. 07, 1999	Oklahoma	N/W	Lethal Injection
503	Ronnie Howard	Jan. 08, 1999	South Carolina	B/A	Lethal Injection
504	Dobie Gillis Williams	Jan. 08, 1999	Louisiana	B/W	Lethal Injection
505	Kelvin Malone	Jan. 13, 1999	Missouri	B/2W	Lethal Injection
506	Jess James Gillies	Jan. 13, 1999	Arizona	W/W	Lethal Injection
507	Troy Farris	Jan. 13, 1999	Texas	W/W	Lethal Injection
508	Mark Arlo Sheppard	Jan. 20, 1999	Virginia	B/2W	Lethal Injection
509	Joseph Ernest Atkins	Jan. 22, 1999	South Carolina	W/1W1B	Lethal Injection
510	Martin Vega	Jan. 26, 1999	Texas	L/W	Lethal Injection
511	Darrick Gerlaugh	Feb. 03, 1999	Arizona	N/W	Lethal Injection
512#	Sean Sellers	Feb. 04, 1999	Oklahoma	W/3W	Lethal Injection

Table 20 (Continued): People Executed in the United States, 1976-2010

#	Name	Date of Execution	State of Execution	Defendant/ Victim Race	Method of Execution
513	Tony Leslie Fry	Feb. 04, 1999	Virginia	W/W	Lethal Injection
514~	Jaturun Siripongs	Feb. 09, 1999	California	A/2A	Lethal Injection
515	George Cordova	Feb. 10, 1999	Texas	L/L	Lethal Injection
516	Danny Lee Barber	Feb. 11, 1999	Texas	W/W	Lethal Injection
517	Andrew Cantu	Feb. 16, 1999	Texas	L/3W	Lethal Injection
518	Johnie Michael Cox	Feb. 16, 1999	Arkansas	W/3W	Lethal Injection
519*	Wilford Berry	Feb. 19, 1999	Ohio	W/W	Lethal Injection
520	James Rodden	Feb. 24, 1999	Missouri	W/W	Lethal Injection
521	Norman Green	Feb. 24, 1999	Texas	B/W	Lethal Injection
522~	Karl LaGrand	Feb. 24, 1999	Arizona	W/W	Lethal Injection
523~	Walter LaGrand	Mar. 03, 1999	Arizona	W/W	Gas Chamber
524	George A. Quesinberry Jr.	Mar. 09, 1999	Virginia	W/W	Lethal Injection
525	Roy Michael Roberts	Mar. 10, 1999	Missouri	W/W	Lethal Injection
526	Andrew Kokoraleis	Mar. 17, 1999	Illinois	W/W	Lethal Injection
527	David Lee Fisher	Mar. 25, 1999	Virginia	W/W	Lethal Injection
528	Charles Rector	Mar. 26, 1999	Texas	B/W	Lethal Injection
529*	James Rich	Mar. 26, 1999	North Carolina	W/W	Lethal Injection
530	Robert Excell White	Mar. 30, 1999	Texas	W/W	Lethal Injection

Table 20 (Continued): People Executed in the United States, 1976-2010

#	Name	Date of Execution	State of Execution	Defendant/ Victim Race	Method of Execution
531~	Alvaro Calambro	Apr. 5, 1999	Nevada	A/2W	Lethal Injection
532	Marion Albert Pruett	Apr. 12, 1999	Arkansas	W/W	Lethal Injection
533	Carl Hamilton Chichester	Apr. 13, 1999	Virginia	B/W	Lethal Injection
534	Roy Ramsey Jr.	Apr. 14, 1999	Missouri	B/2W	Lethal Injection
535	Arthur Ray Jenkins III	Apr. 20, 1999	Virginia	W/2W	Lethal Injection
536	David J. Lawrie	Apr. 23, 1999	Delaware	W/4W	Lethal Injection
537	Ralph E. Davis	Apr. 28, 1999	Missouri	B/W	Lethal Injection
538*	Aaron Foust	Apr. 28, 1999	Texas	W/W	Lethal Injection
539*	Eric Christopher Payne	Apr. 28, 1999	Virginia	W/1W1B	Lethal Injection
540	Ronald Dale Yeatts	Apr. 29, 1999	Virginia	W/W	Lethal Injection
541	Manuel Babbitt	May 04, 1999	California	B/W	Lethal Injection
542	Jose De La Cruz	May 04, 1999	Texas	L/L	Lethal Injection
543	Robert Wayne Vickers	May 05, 1999	Arizona	W/W	Lethal Injection
544	Clydell Coleman	May 05, 1999	Texas	B/B	Lethal Injection
545*	Edward Lee Harper	May 25, 1999	Kentucky	W/2W	Lethal Injection
546	Jessie Wise	May 26, 1999	Missouri	B/B	Lethal Injection
547	William Hamilton Little	Jun. 01, 1999	Texas	W/W	Lethal Injection

Table 20 (Continued): People Executed in the United States, 1976-2010

#	Name	Date of Execution	State of Execution	Defendant/ Victim Race	Method of Execution
548	Scotty Lee Moore	Jun. 03, 1999	Oklahoma	W/L	Lethal Injection
549	Bruce Kilgore	Jun. 16, 1999	Missouri	B/W	Lethal Injection
550	Michael Poland	Jun. 16, 1999	Arizona	W/2W	Lethal Injection
551~	Stanley Faulder	Jun. 17, 1999	Texas	W/W	Lethal Injection
552	Brian Baldwin	Jun. 18, 1999	Alabama	B/W	Electrocution
553	Robert Walls	Jun. 30, 1999	Missouri	W/W	Lethal Injection
554*	Charles Tuttle	Jul. 01, 1999	Texas	W/W	Lethal Injection
555*¥	Gary Heidnick	Jul. 06, 1999	Pennsylvania	W/2B	Lethal Injection
556	Tyrone Fuller	Jul. 07, 1999	Texas	B/W	Lethal Injection
557¥	Norman Lee Newsted	Jul. 08, 1999	Oklahoma	W/B	Lethal Injection
558	Allen Lee Davis	Jul. 08, 1999	Florida	W/3W	Electrocution
559¥	Thomas Strickler	Jul. 21, 1999	Virginia	W/B	Lethal Injection
560	Ricky Blackmon	Aug. 04, 1999	Texas	W/W	Lethal Injection
561	Charles Boyd	Aug. 05, 1999	Texas	B/W	Lethal Injection
562	Victor Kennedy	Aug. 06, 1999	Alabama	B/W	Electrocution
563	Kenneth Dwayne Dunn	Aug. 10, 1999	Texas	B/W	Lethal Injection
564	James Otto Earhart	Aug. 11, 1999	Texas	W/W	Lethal Injection
565	Marlon Williams	Aug. 17, 1999	Virginia	B/W	Lethal Injection
566	Joseph Trevino	Aug. 18, 1999	Texas	L/W	Lethal Injection

Table 20 (Continued): People Executed in the United States, 1976-2010

#	Name	Date of Execution	State of Execution	Defendant/ Victim Race	Method of Execution
567	David Leisure	Sep. 01, 1999	Missouri	W/W	Lethal Injection
568	Raymond Jones	Sep. 01, 1999	Texas	B/A	Lethal Injection
569	Mark Gardner	Sep. 08, 1999	Arkansas	W/3W	Lethal Injection
570*	Alan Willett	Sep. 08, 1999	Arkansas	W/2W	Lethal Injection
571	Willis Barnes	Sep. 10, 1999	Texas	B/B	Lethal Injection
572	William Davis	Sep. 14, 1999	Texas	B/B	Lethal Injection
573	Everett Lee Mueller	Sep. 16, 1999	Virginia	W/W	Lethal Injection
574*	Richard Wayne Smith	Sep. 21, 1999	Texas	W/W	Lethal Injection
575	Willie Sullivan	Sep. 24, 1999	Delaware	B/W	Lethal Injection
576	Harvey Lee Green	Sep. 24, 1999	North Carolina	B/W	Lethal Injection
577	Alvin Crane	Oct. 12, 1999	Texas	W/W	Lethal Injection
578	Jerry McFadden	Oct. 14, 1999	Texas	W/W	Lethal Injection
579*	Joseph Parsons	Oct. 15, 1999	Utah	W/W	Lethal Injection
580	Jason Joseph	Oct. 19, 1999	Virginia	B/B	Lethal Injection
581	Arthur Boyd	Oct. 21, 1999	North Carolina	W/W	Lethal Injection
582	Ignacio Ortiz	Oct. 27, 1999	Arizona	L/L	Lethal Injection
583	Domingo Cantu	Oct. 28, 1999	Texas	N/W	Lethal Injection

Table 20 (Continued): People Executed in the United States, 1976-2010

#	Name	Date of Execution	State of Execution	Defendant/ Victim Race	Method of Execution
584	Thomas Lee Royal, Jr.	Nov. 9, 1999	Virginia	B/B	Lethal Injection
585	Leroy Joseph Drayton	Nov. 12, 1999	South Carolina	B/W	Lethal Injection
586	Desmond Jennings	Nov. 16, 1999	Texas	B/2B	Lethal Injection
587	John Michael Lamb	Nov. 17, 1999	Texas	W/W	Lethal Injection
588	Jose Gutierrez	Nov. 18, 1999	Texas	L/W	Lethal Injection
589	David Junior Brown	Nov. 19, 1999	North Carolina	B/2W	Lethal Injection
590	Cornel Cooks	Dec. 02, 1999	Oklahoma	B/W	Lethal Injection
591	David Rocheville	Dec. 03, 1999	South Carolina	W/W	Lethal Injection
592	David Martin Long	Dec. 08, 1999	Texas	W/3W	Lethal Injection
593	Bobby Lynn Ross	Dec. 09, 1999	Oklahoma	B/W	Lethal Injection
594	D.H. Fleenor	Dec. 09, 1999	Indiana	W/2W	Lethal Injection
595	James Beathard	Dec. 09, 1999	Texas	W/W	Lethal Injection
596	Andre Graham	Dec. 09, 1999	Virginia	B/B	Lethal Injection
597*	Robert Atworth	Dec. 14, 1999	Texas	W/W	Lethal Injection
598	Sammie Felder	Dec. 15, 1999	Texas	B/W	Lethal Injection
599	Malcolm Johnson	Jan. 06, 2000	Oklahoma	B/W	Lethal Injection
600	David Duren	Jan. 07, 2000	Alabama	W/W	Electrocution
601#	Douglas Christopher Thomas	Jan. 10, 2000	Virginia	W/2W	Lethal Injection

Table 20 (Continued): People Executed in the United States, 1976-2010

#	Name	Date of Execution	State of Execution	Defendant/ Victim Race	Method of Execution
602	Earl Carl Heiselbetz, Jr.	Jan. 12, 2000	Texas	W/2W	Lethal Injection
603	Gary Alan Walker	Jan. 13, 2000	Oklahoma	W/W	Lethal Injection
604#	Steven Roach	Jan. 13, 2000	Virginia	W/W	Lethal Injection
605	Spencer Goodman	Jan. 18, 2000	Texas	W/W	Lethal Injection
606	David Hicks	Jan. 20, 2000	Texas	B/B	Lethal Injection
607	Larry Robison	Jan. 21, 2000	Texas	W/5W	Lethal Injection
608	Billy Hughes	Jan. 24, 2000	Texas	W/W	Lethal Injection
609#	Glen McGinnis	Jan. 25, 2000	Texas	B/W	Lethal Injection
610	James Moreland	Jan. 27, 2000	Texas	W/W	Lethal Injection
611	Michael Roberts	Feb. 10, 2000	Oklahoma	B/B	Lethal Injection
612	Anthony Lee Chaney	Feb. 16, 2000	Arizona	W/W	Lethal Injection
613	Terry Sims	Feb. 23, 2000	Florida	W/W	Lethal Injection
614	Cornelius Goss	Feb. 23, 2000	Texas	B/W	Lethal Injection
615	Anthony Bryan	Feb. 24, 2000	Florida	W/W	Lethal Injection
616*f*	Betty Lou Beets	Feb. 24, 2000	Texas	W/W	Lethal Injection
617	Odell Barnes	Mar. 01, 2000	Texas	B/B	Lethal Injection
618	Freddie Lee Wright	Mar. 03, 2000	Alabama	B/2W	Electrocution

Table 20 (Continued): People Executed in the United States, 1976-2010

#	Name	Date of Execution	State of Execution	Defendant/ Victim Race	Method of Execution
619	Ponchai Wilkerson	Mar. 14, 2000	Texas	B/A	Lethal Injection
620	Darrell "Young Elk" Rich	Mar. 15, 2000	California	N/W	Lethal Injection
621	Patrick Poland	Mar. 15, 2000	Arizona	W/2W	Lethal Injection
622	Timothy Gribble	Mar. 15, 2000	Texas	W/W	Lethal Injection
623	Lonnie Weeks, Jr.	Mar. 16, 2000	Virginia	B/H	Lethal Injection
624*	James Hampton	Mar. 22, 2000	Missouri	W/W	Lethal Injection
625	Kelly Lamont Rogers	Mar. 23, 2000	Oklahoma	B/W	Lethal Injection
626	Robert Tarver	Apr. 14, 2000	Alabama	B/W	Electrocution
627	Robert Glen Coe	Apr. 19, 2000	Tennessee	W/W	Lethal Injection
628	Ronald Keith Boyd	Apr. 27, 2000	Oklahoma	B/W	Lethal Injection
629*f	Christina Riggs	May 2, 2000	Arkansas	W/2W	Lethal Injection
630	Tommy Jackson	May 4, 2000	Texas	B/W	Lethal Injection
631	William Kitchens	May 09, 2000	Texas	W/W	Lethal Injection
632	Michael McBride	May 11, 2000	Texas	W/2W	Lethal Injection
633	James Richardson	May 23, 2000	Texas	B/W	Lethal Injection
634	Richard Foster	May 24, 2000	Texas	W/W	Lethal Injection
635	Charles Foster	May 25, 2000	Oklahoma	B/B	Lethal Injection
636	James Clayton	May 25, 2000	Texas	B/W	Lethal Injection

Table 20 (Continued): People Executed in the United States, 1976-2010

#	Name	Date of Execution	State of Execution	Defendant/ Victim Race	Method of Execution
637	Robert Carter	May 31, 2000	Texas	B/6B	Lethal Injection
638	James Robedeaux	Jun. 01, 2000	Oklahoma	N/W	Lethal Injection
639*	Pernell Ford	Jun. 02, 2000	Alabama	B/2W	Electrocution
640	Feltus Taylor	Jun. 06, 2000	Louisiana	B/W	Lethal Injection
641	Bennie Demps	Jun. 07, 2000	Florida	B/B	Lethal Injection
642	Roger Berget	Jun. 08, 2000	Oklahoma	W/W	Lethal Injection
643	Wayne Mason	Jun. 12, 2000	Texas	W/2W	Lethal Injection
644	John Burks	Jun. 14, 2000	Texas	B/L	Lethal Injection
645	William Bryson	Jun. 15, 2000	Oklahoma	B/W	Lethal Injection
646	Paul Nuncio	Jun. 15, 2000	Texas	L/W	Lethal Injection
647	Thomas Provenzano	Jun. 21, 2000	Florida	W/W	Lethal Injection
648#	Shaka Sankofa (Gary Graham)	Jun. 22, 2000	Texas	B/W	Lethal Injection
649	Bert Hunter	Jun. 28, 2000	Missouri	W/2W	Lethal Injection
650	Jessy San Miguel	Jun. 29, 2000	Texas	L/W	Lethal Injection
651	Michael Clagett	Jul. 06, 2000	Virginia	W/A, 2W, Other	Electrocution
652	Orien Joiner	Jul. 12, 2000	Texas	W/2W	Lethal Injection
653	Gregg Braun	Jul. 20, 2000	Oklahoma	W/W	Lethal Injection
654	Juan Soria	Jul. 26, 2000	Texas	L/W	Lethal Injection

Table 20 (Continued): People Executed in the United States, 1976-2010

#	Name	Date of Execution	State of Execution	Defendant/ Victim Race	Method of Execution
655	Brian Roberson	Aug. 09, 2000	Texas	B/W	Lethal Injection
656	Oliver Cruz	Aug. 09, 2000	Texas	L/W	Lethal Injection
657	George Wallace	Aug. 10, 2000	Oklahoma	W/2W	Lethal Injection
658	John Satterwhite	Aug. 16, 2000	Texas	B/W	Lethal Injection
659	Richard Wayne Jones	Aug. 22, 2000	Texas	W/W	Lethal Injection
660	David Earl Gibbs	Aug. 23, 2000	Texas	W/W	Lethal Injection
66*	Dan Hauser	Aug. 25, 2000	Florida	W/W	Lethal Injection
662	Gary Lee Roll	Aug. 30, 2000	Missouri	W/3W	Lethal Injection
663	Jeffrey Caldwell	Aug. 30, 2000	Texas	B/3B	Lethal Injection
664	Russel Burkett	Aug. 30, 2000	Virginia	W/2W	Lethal Injection
665	George Harris	Sep. 13, 2000	Missouri	B/B	Lethal Injection
666	Derek Barnabei	Sep. 14, 2000	Virginia	W/W	Lethal Injection
667	Ricky McGinn	Sep. 27, 2000	Texas	W/W	Lethal Injection
668	Bobby Lee Ramdass	Oct. 10, 2000	Virginia	B/O (Pakistani)	Lethal Injection
669	Jeffrey Dillingham	Nov. 01, 2000	Texas	W/W	Lethal Injection
670	Kevin Young	Nov. 03, 2000	South Carolina	B/W	Lethal Injection
671*	Donald Miller	Nov. 08, 2000	Arizona	W/W	Lethal Injection
672	Michael Sexton	Nov. 09, 2000	North Carolina	B/B	Lethal Injection

Table 20 (Continued): People Executed in the United States, 1976-2010

#	Name	Date of Execution	State of Execution	Defendant/ Victim Race	Method of Execution
673~	Miguel Flores	Nov. 09, 2000	Texas	L/W	Lethal Injection
674	Stacey Lawton	Nov. 14, 2000	Texas	B/W	Lethal Injection
675	James Chambers	Nov. 15, 2000	Missouri	W/W	Lethal Injection
676	Tony Chambers	Nov. 15, 2000	Texas	B/B	Lethal Injection
677	Dwayne L. Weeks	Nov. 17, 2000	Delaware	B/2B	Lethal Injection
678	Garry Miller	Dec. 05, 2000	Texas	W/W	Lethal Injection
679	Daniel Hittle	Dec. 06, 2000	Texas	W/W	Lethal Injection
680	Christopher Goins	Dec. 06, 2000	Virginia	B/B	Lethal Injection
681*	Edward Castro	Dec. 07, 2000	Florida	L/W	Lethal Injection
682	Claude Jones	Dec. 07, 2000	Texas	W/W	Lethal Injection
683	David Johnson	Dec. 19, 2000	Arkansas	B/B	Lethal Injection
684	Jack Clark	Jan. 09, 2001	Texas	W/L	Lethal Injection
685	Eddie Trice	Jan. 09, 2001	Oklahoma	B/B	Lethal Injection
686	Robert Glock	Jan. 11, 2001	Florida	W/W	Lethal Injection
687f	Wanda Jean Allen	Jan. 11, 2001	Oklahoma	B/B	Lethal Injection
688*	Floyd Medlock	Jan. 16, 2001	Oklahoma	W/W	Lethal Injection
689	Alvin Goodwin	Jan. 18, 2001	Texas	W/W	Lethal Injection

Table 20 (Continued): People Executed in the United States, 1976-2010

#	Name	Date of Execution	State of Execution	Defendant/ Victim Race	Method of Execution
690	Dion Smallwood	Jan. 18, 2001	Oklahoma	N/W	Lethal Injection
691	Mark Fowler	Jan. 23, 2001	Oklahoma	W/2W, A	Lethal Injection
692	Billy Ray Fox	Jan. 25, 2001	Oklahoma	W/2W, A, see #691	Lethal Injection
693	Caruthers Alexander	Jan. 29, 2001	Texas	B/W	Lethal Injection
694	Loyd Lafevers	Jan. 30, 2001	Oklahoma	W/W	Lethal Injection
695	D.L. Jones, Jr.	Feb. 01, 2001	Oklahoma	W/W	Lethal Injection
696	Stanley Lingar	Feb. 07, 2001	Missouri	W/W	Lethal Injection
697	Adolpho Hernandez	Feb. 08, 2001	Texas	L/L	Lethal Injection
698*	Thomas Akers	Mar. 01, 2001	Virginia	W/W	Lethal Injection
699	Robert Clayton	Mar.01, 2001	Oklahoma	W/W	Lethal Injection
700	Dennis Dowthitt	Mar. 07, 2001	Texas	W/W	Lethal Injection
701	Willie Ervin Fisher	Mar. 09, 2001	North Carolina	B/B	Lethal Injection
702*	Gerald Bivins	Mar. 14, 2001	Indiana	W/W	Lethal Injection
703*	Robert LeeMassie	Mar. 27, 2001	California	W/W	Lethal Injection
704*	Ronald Dunaway Fluke	Mar. 27, 2001	Oklahoma	W/3W	Lethal Injection
705	Thomas Ervin	Mar. 28, 2001	Missouri	W/2W, see#649	Lethal Injection
706	Jason Massey	Apr. 03, 2001	Texas	W/2W	Lethal Injection

Table 20 (Continued): People Executed in the United States, 1976-2010

#	Name	Date of Execution	State of Execution	Defendant/ Victim Race	Method of Execution
707*~	Sebastian Bridges	Apr. 21, 2001	Nevada	W/W	Lethal Injection
708	Mose Young	Apr. 25, 2001	Missouri	B/3W	Lethal Injection
709	David Goff	Apr. 25, 2001	Texas	B/W	Lethal Injection
710	David Dawson	Apr. 26, 2001	Delaware	W/W	Lethal Injection
711*f*	Marilyn Plantz	May 01, 2001	Oklahoma	W/W	Lethal Injection
712*	Clay King Smith	May 08, 2001	Arkansas	W/5W	Lethal Injection
713	Terrance James	May 22, 2001	Oklahoma	N/W	Lethal Injection
714	Sam Smith	May 23, 2001	Missouri	B/B	Lethal Injection
715	Abdullah T. Hameen	May 25, 2001	Delaware	B/B	Lethal Injection
716	Vincent Johnson	May 29, 2001	Oklahoma	B/B	Lethal Injection
717*	Timothy McVeigh	Jun . 11, 2001	Federal	W/129W, 32B, 5L, 2N	Lethal Injection
718	John Wheat	Jun. 13, 2001	Texas	W/W	Lethal Injection
719	Jay D. Scott	Jun. 14, 2001	Ohio	B/B	Lethal Injection
720	Juan Raul Garza	Jun. 19, 2001	Federal	L/3L	Lethal Injection
721	Miguel Richardson	Jun. 26, 2001	Texas	B/W	Lethal Injection
722	Jim Lowery	Jun. 27, 2001	Indiana	W/2W	Lethal Injection
723	Jerome Mallett	Jul. 11, 2001	Missouri	B/W	Lethal Injection

Table 20 (Continued): People Executed in the United States, 1976-2010

#	Name	Date of Execution	State of Execution	Defendant/ Victim Race	Method of Execution
724	James Wilkens, Jr.	Jul. 11, 2001	Texas	W/W	Lethal Injection
725	Jerald Wayne Harjo	Jul. 17, 2001	Oklahoma	N/W	Lethal Injection
726	Mack Hill	Aug. 08, 2001	Texas	W/W	Lethal Injection
727	Jeffrey Doughtie	Aug. 16, 2001	Texas	W/2W	Lethal Injection
728	Clifton White	Aug. 24, 2001	North Carolina	W/W	Lethal Injection
729*	James Elledge	Aug. 28, 2001	Washington	W/W	Lethal Injection
730	Jack Walker	Aug. 28, 2001	Oklahoma	W/2W	Lethal Injection
731	Ronald Frye	Aug. 31, 2001	North Carolina	W/W	Lethal Injection
732	James Knox	Sep. 18, 2001	Texas	W/L	Lethal Injection
733	Michael Roberts	Oct. 03, 2001	Missouri	W/W	Lethal Injection
734	David Junior Ward	Oct. 12, 2001	North Carolina	B/B	Lethal Injection
735	Christopher Beck	Oct. 18, 2001	Virginia	W/3W	Lethal Injection
736	Alvie James Hale	Oct. 18, 2001	Oklahoma	W/W	Lethal Injection
737#	Gerald Mitchell	Oct. 22, 2001	Texas	B/W	Lethal Injection
738	Stephen Johns	Oct. 24, 2001	Missouri	W/W	Lethal Injection
739	Terry Mincey	Oct. 25, 2001	Georgia	W/W	Lethal Injection
740	Jose Martinez High	Nov. 06, 2001	Georgia	B/W	Lethal Injection

Table 20 (Continued): People Executed in the United States, 1976-2010

#	Name	Date of Execution	State of Execution	Defendant/ Victim Race	Method of Execution
741*	Terry Clark	Nov. 06, 2001	New Mexico	W/W	Lethal Injection
742	Jeffrey Tucker	Nov. 14, 2001	Texas	W/W	Lethal Injection
743	Fred Gilreath	Nov. 15, 2001	Georgia	W/2W	Lethal Injection
744	Emerson Rudd	Nov. 15, 2001	Texas	B/B	Lethal Injection
745	John Hardy Rose	Nov. 30, 2001	North Carolina	W/W	Lethal Injection
746*f*	Lois Nadean Smith	Dec. 04, 2001	Oklahoma	W/W	Lethal Injection
747 ~	Sahib Al-Mosawi	Dec. 06, 2001	Oklahoma	O/2O (all Iraqi)	Lethal Injection
748	Byron Parker	Dec. 11, 2001	Georgia	W/W	Lethal Injection
749	Vincent Cooks	Dec. 12, 2001	Texas	B/W	Lethal Injection
750	James Johnson	Jan. 09, 2002	Missouri	W/4W	Lethal Injection
751	Michael Moore	Jan. 09, 2002	Texas	W/W	Lethal Injection
752	Jermarr Arnold	Jan. 16, 2002	Texas	B/L	Lethal Injection
753	Ronald Spivey	Jan. 24, 2002	Georgia	W/W	Lethal Injection
754	Stephen Wayne Anderson	Jan. 29, 2002	California	W/W	Lethal Injection
755	John Romano	Jan. 29, 2002	Oklahoma	W/W	Lethal Injection
756	Windell Broussard	Jan. 30, 2002	Texas	B/2B	Lethal Injection
757	Randall Hafdahl	Jan. 31, 2002	Texas	W/W	Lethal Injection

Table 20 (Continued): People Executed in the United States, 1976-2010

#	Name	Date of Execution	State of Execution	Defendant/ Victim Race	Method of Execution
758	David Woodruff	Jan. 31, 2002	Oklahoma	W/W, see #755	Lethal Injection
759	Michael Owsley	Feb. 06, 2002	Missouri	B/B	Lethal Injection
760	John Byrd, Jr.	Feb. 19, 2002	Ohio	W/W	Lethal Injection
761	Monty Delk	Feb. 28, 2002	Texas	W/W	Lethal Injection
762	Jeffrey Tokar	Mar. 06, 2002	Missouri	W/W	Lethal Injection
763	Gerald Tigner	Mar. 07, 2002	Texas	B/2B	Lethal Injection
764	Tracy Housel (dual citizenship)	Mar. 12, 2002	Georgia	W/W	Lethal Injection
765*	James Earl Patterson	Mar. 14, 2002	Virginia	W/W	Lethal Injection
766*	Daniel Zirkle	Apr. 02, 2002	Virginia	W/2W	Lethal Injection
767	Paul Kreutzer	Apr. 10, 2002	Missouri	W/W	Lethal Injection
768	Jose Santellan	Apr. 10, 2002	Texas	L/L	Lethal Injection
769	William Burns	Apr. 11, 2002	Texas	B/W	Lethal Injection
770	Gerald Casey	Apr. 18, 2002	Texas	W/W	Lethal Injection
771	Alton Coleman	Apr. 26, 2002	Ohio	B/W	Lethal Injection
772	Rodolfo Hernandez	Apr. 30, 2002	Texas	L/L	Lethal Injection
773¥	Richard Charles Johnson	May 03, 2002	South Carolina	W/B	Lethal Injection
774	Reginald Reeves	May 09, 2002	Texas	B/W	Lethal Injection
775ƒ*	Lynda Lyon Block	May 10, 2002	Alabama	W/W	Electrocution

Table 20 (Continued): People Executed in the United States, 1976-2010

#	Name	Date of Execution	State of Execution	Defendant/ Victim Race	Method of Execution
776	Leslie Martin	May 10, 2002	Louisiana	W/W	Lethal Injection
777	Ronford Styron	May 16, 2002	Texas	W/W	Lethal Injection
778	Johnny Martinez	May 22, 2002	Texas	L/W	Lethal Injection
779#	Napoleon Beazley	May 28, 2002	Texas	B/W	Lethal Injection
780	Stanley Baker	May 30, 2002	Texas	W/W	Lethal Injection
781	Walter Mickens	Jun. 12, 2002	Virginia	B/W	Lethal Injection
782	Daniel Reneau	Jun. 13, 2002	Texas	W/W	Lethal Injection
783	Robert Coulson	Jun. 25, 2002	Texas	W/2W	Lethal Injection
784	Jeffrey Williams	Jun. 26, 2002	Texas	B/B	Lethal Injection
785	Tracy Hansen	Jul. 17, 2002	Mississippi	W/W	Lethal Injection
786	Randall Eugene Cannon	Jul. 23, 2002	Oklahoma	W/W, see #694	Lethal Injection
787*	Earl Alexander Frederick	Jul. 30, 2002	Oklahoma	W/W	Lethal Injection
788	Richard Kutzner	Aug. 07, 2002	Texas	W/W	Lethal Injection
789#	T.J. Jones	Aug. 08, 2002	Texas	B/W	Lethal Injection
790~	Javier Suarez Medina	Aug. 14, 2002	Texas	L/L	Lethal Injection
791	Daniel Basile	Aug. 14, 2002	Missouri	W/W	Lethal Injection
792	Wallace Fugate	Aug. 16, 2002	Georgia	W/W	Lethal Injection

Table 20 (Continued): People Executed in the United States, 1976-2010

#	Name	Date of Execution	State of Execution	Defendant/ Victim Race	Method of Execution
793	Gary Etheridge	Aug. 20, 2002	Texas	W/W	Lethal Injection
794	Anthony Green	Aug. 23, 2002	South Carolina	B/W	Lethal Injection
795#	Toronto Patterson	Aug. 28, 2002	Texas	B/3B	Lethal Injection
796	Tony Walker	Sep. 10, 2002	Texas	B/B	Lethal Injection
797*	Michael Passaro	Sep. 13, 2002	South Carolina	W/W	Lethal Injection
798	Jessie Patrick	Sep. 17, 2002	Texas	W/W	Lethal Injection
799	Ronald Shamburger	Sep. 18, 2002	Texas	W/W	Lethal Injection
800	Rex Mays	Sep. 24, 2002	Texas	W/2W	Lethal Injection
801	Robert A. Buell	Sep. 25, 2002	Ohio	W/W	Lethal Injection
802	Calvin King	Sep. 25, 2002	Texas	B/B	Lethal Injection
803	James Powell	Oct. 01, 2002	Texas	W/W	Lethal Injection
804*~	Rigoberto Sanchez-Velasco	Oct. 02, 2002	Florida	L/L	Lethal Injection
805*f	Aileen Wournos	Oct. 09, 2002	Florida	W/W	Lethal Injection
806	William Putman	Nov. 13, 2002	Georgia	W/2W	Lethal Injection
807 ~	Mir Aimal Kasi	Nov. 14, 2002	Virginia	O(Pakistani) /W	Lethal Injection
808	Craig Ogan	Nov. 19, 2002	Texas	W/W	Lethal Injection
809	William Jones	Nov. 20, 2002	Missouri	W/W	Lethal Injection
810	William Chappell	Nov. 20, 2002	Texas	W/2W	Lethal Injection

Table 20 (Continued): People Executed in the United States, 1976-2010

#	Name	Date of Execution	State of Execution	Defendant/ Victim Race	Method of Execution
811	Leonard Rojas	Dec. 04, 2002	Texas	L/W, L	Lethal Injection
812	Ernest Basden	Dec. 06, 2002	North Carolina	W/W	Lethal Injection
813	Linroy Bottoson	Dec. 09, 2002	Florida	B/B	Lethal Injection
814	Desmond Carter	Dec. 10, 2002	North Carolina	B/W	Lethal Injection
815	Jerry Lynn McCracken	Dec. 10, 2002	Oklahoma	W/4W	Lethal Injection
816	James Collier	Dec. 11, 2002	Texas	W/2W	Lethal Injection
817	Jessie Williams	Dec. 11, 2002	Mississippi	W/W	Lethal Injection
818	Anthony Johnson	Dec. 12, 2002	Alabama	W/4W	Lethal Injection
819	Jay Neill	Dec. 12, 2002	Oklahoma	W/W	Lethal Injection
820	Earnest Carter	Dec. 17, 2002	Oklahoma	B/W?	Lethal Injection
821	Samuel Gallamore	Jan. 14, 2003	Texas	W/3W	Lethal Injection
822	John Baltazar	Jan. 15, 2003	Texas	L/L	Lethal Injection
823	Daniel Revilla	Jan. 16, 2003	Oklahoma	W/L	Lethal Injection
824	Robert Lookingbill	Jan. 22, 2003	Texas	W/W	Lethal Injection
825	Alva Curry	Jan. 28, 2003	Texas	B/L	Lethal Injection
826	Richard Dinkins	Jan. 29, 2003	Texas	W/2W	Lethal Injection
827	Granville Riddle	Jan. 30, 2003	Texas	W/W	Lethal Injection

Table 20 (Continued): People Executed in the United States, 1976-2010

#	Name	Date of Execution	State of Execution	Defendant/ Victim Race	Method of Execution
828~	John Elliott	Feb. 04, 2003	Texas	L/L	Lethal Injection
829	Kenneth Kenley	Feb. 05, 2003	Missouri	W/W	Lethal Injection
830	Henry Dunn, Jr.	Feb. 06, 2003	Texas	B/L	Lethal Injection
831	Richard Fox	Feb. 12, 2003	Ohio	W/W	Lethal Injection
832	Bobby Joe Fields	Feb. 13, 2003	Oklahoma	B/W	Lethal Injection
833	Richard Williams	Feb. 25, 2003	Texas	B/B	Lethal Injection
834	Amos King	Feb. 26, 2003	Florida	B/W	Lethal Injection
835	Bobby Cook	Mar. 11, 2003	Texas	W/W	Lethal Injection
836	Michael Thompson	Mar. 13, 2003	Alabama	W/W	Lethal Injection
837	Louis Jones, Jr.	Mar. 18, 2003	Federal	B/W	Lethal Injection
838	Walanzo Robinson	Mar. 18, 2003	Oklahoma	B/B	Lethal Injection
839	Keith Clay	Mar. 20, 2003	Texas	B/O (Indian)	Lethal Injection
840	John Michael Hooker	Mar. 25, 2003	Oklahoma	B/2B	Lethal Injection
841	Larry Moon	Mar. 25, 2003	Georgia	W/W	Lethal Injection
842	James Colburn	Mar. 26, 2003	Texas	W/W	Lethal Injection
843#	Scott Allen Hain	Apr. 03, 2003	Oklahoma	W/W	Lethal Injection
844	Don Wilson Hawkins	Apr. 08, 2003	Oklahoma	W/W	Lethal Injection
845	Earl C. Bramblett	Apr. 09, 2003	Virginia	W/W	Electrocution

Table 20 (Continued): People Executed in the United States, 1976-2010

#	Name	Date of Execution	State of Execution	Defendant/ Victim Race	Method of Execution
846	Larry Kenneth Jackson	Apr. 17, 2003	Oklahoma	B/B	Lethal Injection
847	Juan Chavez	Apr. 22, 2003	Texas	L/L	Lethal Injection
848	Gary Brown	Apr. 24, 2003	Alabama	W/W	Lethal Injection
849	David Brewer	Apr. 29, 2003	Ohio	W/W	Lethal Injection
850	Kevin Hough	May 02, 2003	Indiana	W/2W	Lethal Injection
851	Roger Vaughn	May 06, 2003	Texas	W/W	Lethal Injection
852	Carl Isaacs	May 06, 2003	Georgia	W/6W	Lethal Injection
853	Bruce Jacobs	May 15, 2003	Texas	W/W	Lethal Injection
854*	Newton Slawson	May 16, 2003	Florida	W/4W	Lethal Injection
855	Robert Knighton	May 27, 2003	Oklahoma	W/2W	Lethal Injection
856	Kenneth Charm	Jun. 05, 2003	Oklahoma	B/B	Lethal Injection
857	Kia Levoy Johnson	Jun. 11, 2003	Texas	B/W	Lethal Injection
858	Joseph Trueblood	Jun. 13, 2003	Indiana	W/3W	Lethal Injection
859	Ernest Martin	Jun. 18, 2003	Ohio	B/B	Lethal Injection
860	Lewis Eugene Gilbert	Jul. 01, 2003	Oklahoma	W/W	Lethal Injection
861	Hilton Crawford	Jul. 02, 2003	Texas	W/W	Lethal Injection
862	Robert Don Duckett	Jul. 08, 2003	Oklahoma	W/W	Lethal Injection

Table 20 (Continued): People Executed in the United States, 1976-2010

#	Name	Date of Execution	State of Execution	Defendant/ Victim Race	Method of Execution
863	Christopher Black	Jul. 09, 2003	Texas	B/B	Lethal Injection
864	Riley Dobi Noel	Jul. 09, 2003	Arkansas	B/3B	Lethal Injection
865	Bryan Toles	Jul. 22, 2003	Oklahoma	B/2B	Lethal Injection
866	Bobby Wayne Swisher	Jul. 22, 2003	Virginia	W/W	Lethal Injection
867	Cedric Ransom	Jul. 23, 2003	Texas	B/W	Lethal Injection
868	Jackie Lee Willingham	Jul. 24, 2003	Oklahoma	W/W	Lethal Injection
869	Allen Wayne Janecka	Jul. 24, 2003	Texas	W/W	Lethal Injection
870*	Harold McElmurry	Jul. 29, 2003	Oklahoma	W/2W	Lethal Injection
871	Tommy Fortenberry	Aug. 07, 2003	Alabama	W/4W	Lethal Injection
872	William Quentin Jones	Aug. 22, 2003	North Carolina	B/B	Lethal Injection
873*	Paul Hill	Sep. 03, 2003	Florida	W/2W	Lethal Injection
874*	Larry Hayes	Sep. 10, 2003	Texas	W/BW	Lethal Injection
875	Henry Lee Hunt	Sep. 12, 2003	North Carolina	N/W	Lethal Injection
876	Joseph Earl Bates	Sep. 26, 2003	North Carolina	W/W	Lethal Injection
877	Eddie Hartman	Oct. 03, 2003	North Carolina	W/W	Lethal Injection
878*	John Clayton Smith	Oct. 29, 2003	Missouri	W/2W	Lethal Injection
879	James Willlie Brown	Nov. 04, 2003	Georgia	W/W	Lethal Injection
880	Joseph Timothy Keel	Nov. 07, 2003	North Carolina	W/W	Lethal Injection

Table 20 (Continued): People Executed in the United States, 1976-2010

#	Name	Date of Execution	State of Execution	Defendant/ Victim Race	Method of Execution
881	John Dennis Daniels	Nov. 14, 2003	North Carolina	B/B	Lethal Injection
882	Robert Henry	Nov. 20, 2003	Texas	W/2W	Lethal Injection
883	Richard Duncan	Dec. 03, 2003	Texas	W/2W	Lethal Injection
884	Ivan Murphy, Jr.	Dec. 04, 2003	Texas	W/W	Lethal Injection
885	Robbie James Lyons	Dec. 05, 2003	North Carolina	B/W	Lethal Injection
886*	Ynobe Matthews	Jan. 06, 2004	Texas	B /W	Lethal Injection
887	Charles Singleton	Jan. 06, 2004	Arkansas	B/W	Lethal Injection
888	Raymond Dayle Rowsey	Jan. 09, 2004	North Carolina	W/W	Lethal Injection
889	Tyrone Peter Darks	Jan. 13, 2004	Oklahoma	B/B	Lethal Injection
890	Lewis Williams	Jan. 14, 2004	Ohio	B/W	Lethal Injection
891	Kenneth Eugene Bruce	Jan. 14, 2004	Texas	B/W	Lethal Injection
892	Kevin Zimmerman	Jan. 21, 2004	Texas	W/W	Lethal Injection
893	Billy Vickers	Jan. 28, 2004	Texas	W/W	Lethal Injection
894	John Glenn Roe	Feb. 03, 2004	Ohio	W/W	Lethal Injection
895	Johnny L. Robinson	Feb. 04, 2004	Florida	B/W	Lethal Injection
896	Edward Lagrone	Feb. 11, 2004	Texas	B/3B	Lethal Injection
897	Bobby Ray Hopkins	Feb. 12, 2004	Texas	B/2W	Lethal Injection

Table 20 (Continued): People Executed in the United States, 1976-2010

#	Name	Date of Execution	State of Execution	Defendant/ Victim Race	Method of Execution
898	Norman R. Cleary	Feb. 17, 2004	Oklahoma	W/W	Lethal Injection
899	Cameron Willingham	Feb. 17, 2004	Texas	W/3W	Lethal Injection
900	Marcus Cotton	Mar. 03, 2004	Texas	B/W	Lethal Injection
901	David Jay Brown	Mar. 09, 2004	Oklahoma	W/W	Lethal Injection
902	Brian Lee Cherrix	Mar. 18, 2004	Virginia	W/W	Lethal Injection
903	David Clayton Hill	Mar. 19, 2004	South Carolina	W/W	Lethal Injection
904~	Hung Thanh Le	Mar. 23, 2004	Oklahoma	A/A	Lethal Injection
905*	Lawrence Colwell, Jr.	Mar. 26, 2004	Nevada	W/W	Lethal Injection
906	William Wickline	Mar. 30, 2004	Ohio	W/2W	Lethal Injection
907	Dennis Orbe	Mar. 31, 2004	Virginia	W/W	Lethal Injection
908	Jerry McWee	Apr. 16, 2004	South Carolina	W/W	Lethal Injection
909	Jason Byram	Apr. 23, 2004	South Carolina	W/W	Lethal Injection
910	Kelsey Patterson	May 18, 2004	Texas	B/2B	Lethal Injection
911*	John Blackwelder	May 26, 2004	Florida	W/W	Lethal Injection
912	James Neil Tucker	May 28, 2004	South Carolina	W/2W	Electrocution
913	William Zuern	Jun. 08, 2004	Ohio	W/W	Lethal Injection
914	Robert Bryan	Jun. 08, 2004	Oklahoma	W/W	Lethal Injection
915	Steven Oken	Jun. 17, 2004	Maryland	W/W	Lethal Injection

Table 20 (Continued): People Executed in the United States, 1976-2010

#	Name	Date of Execution	State of Execution	Defendant/ Victim Race	Method of Execution
916	David Ray Harris	Jun. 30, 2004	Texas	W/W	Lethal Injection
917	Robert Karl Hicks	Jul. 01, 2004	Georgia	W/W	Lethal Injection
918*	Stephen Vrabel	Jul. 14, 2004	Ohio	W/2W	Lethal Injection
919	Eddie Albert Crawford	Jul. 19, 2004	Georgia	W/W	Lethal Injection
920*	Scott Mink	Jul. 20, 2004	Ohio	W/2W	Lethal Injection
921	Mark Bailey	Jul. 22, 2004	Virginia	W/2W	Lethal Injection
922	James Hubbard	Aug. 05, 2004	Alabama	W/W	Lethal Injection
923*	Terry Jess Dennis	Aug. 12, 2004	Nevada	W/W	Lethal Injection
924*	James Hudson	Aug. 18, 2004	Virginia	W/3W	Lethal Injection
925	Jasen Shane Busby	Aug. 25, 2004	Texas	W/2W	Lethal Injection
926	Windel Ray Workman	Aug. 26, 2004	Oklahoma	W/W	Lethal Injection
927	James Allridge	Aug. 26, 2004	Texas	B/W	Lethal Injection
928	James Reid	Sep. 09, 2004	Virginia	B/B	Lethal Injection
929	Andrew Flores	Sep. 21, 2004	Texas	L/L	Lethal Injection
930*	David Kevin Hocker	Sep. 30, 2004	Alabama	W/W	Lethal Injection
931	Edward Green III	Oct. 05, 2004	Texas	B/2B	Lethal Injection
932*	Peter Miniel	Oct. 06, 2004	Texas	L/W	Lethal Injection

Table 20 (Continued): People Executed in the United States, 1976-2010

#	Name	Date of Execution	State of Execution	Defendant/ Victim Race	Method of Execution
933	Sammy Perkins	Oct. 08, 2004	North Carolina	B/B	Lethal Injection
934	Donald Aldrich	Oct. 12, 2004	Texas	W/L	Lethal Injection
935	Adremy Dennis	Oct. 13, 2004	Ohio	B/W	Lethal Injection
936	Ricky Morrow	Oct. 20, 2004	Texas	W/W	Lethal Injection
937*	Charles Roache	Oct. 22, 2004	North Carolina	W/2W	Lethal Injection
938	Dominique Green	Oct. 26, 2004	Texas	B/B	Lethal Injection
939	Lorenzo Morris	Nov. 02, 2004	Texas	B/B	Lethal Injection
940	Robert Morrow	Nov. 04, 2004	Texas	W/W	Lethal Injection
941	Demarco McCullum	Nov. 09, 2004	Texas	B/W	Lethal Injection
942	Frederick McWilliams	Nov. 10, 2004	Texas	B/L	Lethal Injection
943	Frank Chandler	Nov. 12, 2004	North Carolina	W/W	Lethal Injection
944	Anthony Fuentes	Nov. 17, 2004	Texas	L/W	Lethal Injection
945*	James Porter	Jan. 04, 2005	Texas	W/L	Lethal Injection
946	Donald Beardslee	Jan. 19, 2005	California	W/2W	Lethal Injection
947	Troy Kunkle	Jan. 25, 2005	Texas	W/W	Lethal Injection
948	Timothy Carr	Jan. 25, 2005	Georgia	W/W	Lethal Injection
949	Dennis Bagwell	Feb. 17, 2005	Texas	W/4W	Lethal Injection
950	Stephen Mobley	Mar. 01, 2005	Georgia	W/W	Lethal Injection

Table 20 (Continued): People Executed in the United States, 1976-2010

#	Name	Date of Execution	State of Execution	Defendant/ Victim Race	Method of Execution
951	William H. Smith	Mar. 08, 2005	Ohio	B/B	Lethal Injection
952	George Hopper	Mar. 08, 2005	Texas	W/W	Lethal Injection
953	Donald Wallace	Mar. 10, 2005	Indiana	W4W	Lethal Injection
954	William Powell	Mar. 11, 2005	North Carolina	W/W	Lethal Injection
955	Jimmy Ray Slaughter	Mar. 15, 2005	Oklahoma	W/2W	Lethal Injection
956	Stanley Hall	Mar. 16, 2005	Missouri	B/W	Lethal Injection
957*	Glen Ocha	Apr. 05, 2005	Florida	W/W	Lethal Injection
958	Richard Longworth	Apr. 15, 2005	South Carolina	W/2W	Lethal Injection
959	Douglas Roberts	Apr. 20, 2005	Texas	W/L	Lethal Injection
960	Bill J. Benefiel, Jr.	Apr. 21, 2005	Indiana	W/W	Lethal Injection
961	Donald Jones	Apr. 27, 2005	Missouri	B/B	Lethal Injection
962*	Mario Centobie	Apr. 28, 2005	Alabama	W/W	Lethal Injection
963	Lonnie Wayne Pursley	May 03, 2005	Texas	W/W	Lethal Injection
964	Earl J. Richmond, Jr.	May 06, 2005	North Carolina	B/4B	Lethal Injection
965	George James Miller, Jr.	May 12, 2005	Oklahoma	W/W	Lethal Injection
966*	Michael Ross	May 13, 2005	Connecticut	W/4W	Lethal Injection
967	Vernon Brown	May 17, 2005	Missouri	B/2B	Lethal Injection

Table 20 (Continued): People Executed in the United States, 1976-2010

#	Name	Date of Execution	State of Execution	Defendant/ Victim Race	Method of Execution
968	Bryan Wolfe	May 18, 2005	Texas	B/B	Lethal Injection
969	Richard Cartwright	May 19, 2005	Texas	W/L	Lethal Injection
970	Gregory Scott Johnson	May 25, 2005	Indiana	W/W	Lethal Injection
971	Jerry Paul Henderson	Jun. 02, 2005	Alabama	W/W	Lethal Injection
972*	Alexander Martinez	Jun. 07, 2005	Texas	L/L	Lethal Injection
973	Robert Dale Conklin	Jul. 12, 2005	Georgia	W/W	Lethal Injection
974	Michael L. Pennington	Jul. 19, 2005	Oklahoma	B/W	Lethal Injection
975	Kevin Conner	Jul. 27, 2005	Indiana	W/3W	Lethal Injection
976	David Martinez	Jul. 28, 2005	Texas	L/W	Lethal Injection
977	George Sibley	Aug. 04, 2005	Alabama	W/W	Lethal Injection
978	Gary Sterling	Aug. 10, 2005	Texas	B/W	Lethal Injection
979	Kenneth Eugene Turrentine	Aug. 11, 2005	Oklahoma	B/B	Lethal Injection
980	Robert Alan Shields	Aug. 23, 2005	Texas	W/W	Lethal Injection
981	Timothy Johnston	Aug. 31, 2005	Missouri	W/W	Lethal Injection
982*f*	Frances Newton	Sep. 14, 2005	Texas	B/3B	Lethal Injection
983	John W. Peoples Jr.	Sep. 22, 2005	Alabama	W/3W	Lethal Injection
984*	Herman Dale Ashworth	Sep. 27, 2005	Ohio	W/W	Lethal Injection

Table 20 (Continued): People Executed in the United States, 1976-2010

#	Name	Date of Execution	State of Execution	Defendant/ Victim Race	Method of Execution
985	Alan Matheney	Sep. 28, 2005	Indiana	W/W	Lethal Injection
986	Ronald Ray Howard	Oct. 06, 2005	Texas	B/W	Lethal Injection
987	Luis Ramirez	Oct. 20, 2005	Texas	L/L	Lethal Injection
988	William Williams, Jr.	Oct. 25, 2005	Ohio	B/4B	Lethal Injection
989	Marlin Gray	Oct. 26, 2005	Missouri	B/2W	Lethal Injection
990	Melvin White	Nov. 03, 2005	Texas	W/W	Lethal Injection
991	Brian Steckel	Nov. 4, 2005	Delaware	W/W	Lethal Injection
992*	Arthur Hastings Wise	Nov. 04, 2005	South Carolina	B/4W	Lethal Injection
993	Charles Thacker	Nov. 09, 2005	Texas	W/W	Lethal Injection
994	Steven Van McHone	Nov. 11, 2005	North Carolina	W/2W	Lethal Injection
995	Robert Rowell	Nov. 15, 2005	Texas	W/W,L	Lethal Injection
996	Shannon Thomas	Nov. 16, 2005	Texas	B/3L	Lethal Injection
997	Elias Hanna Syriani	Nov. 18, 2005	North Carolina	A/A	Lethal Injection
998	Eric Randall Nance	Nov. 28, 2005	Arkansas	W/W	Lethal Injection
999	John R. Hicks	Nov. 29, 2005	Ohio	B/2B	Lethal Injection
1000	Kenneth Lee Boyd	Dec. 02, 2005	North Carolina	W/2W	Lethal Injection
1001	Shawn Humphries	Dec. 02, 2005	South Carolina	W/W	Lethal Injection

Table 20 (Continued): People Executed in the United States, 1976-2010

#	Name	Date of Execution	State of Execution	Defendant/ Victim Race	Method of Execution
1002	Wesley E. Baker	Dec. 05, 2005	Maryland	B/W	Lethal Injection
1003	Stanley Williams	Dec. 13, 2005	California	B/3A,W	Lethal Injection
1004	John Nixon	Dec. 14, 2005	Mississippi	W/W	Lethal Injection
1005	Clarence Ray Allen	Jan. 17, 2006	California	NA/4W	Lethal Injection
1006	Perrie Dyon Simpson	Jan. 20, 2006	North Carolina	B/W	Lethal Injection
1007	Marion Dudley	Jan. 25, 2006	Texas	B/3L	Lethal Injection
1008	Marvin Bieghler	Jan. 27, 2006	Indiana	W/2W	Lethal Injection
1009	Jaime Elizalde	Jan. 31, 2006	Texas	L/2L	Lethal Injection
1010	Glenn Benner	Feb. 07, 2006	Ohio	W/2W	Lethal Injection
1011	Robert Neville, Jr.	Feb. 08, 2006	Texas	W/NA	Lethal Injection
1012	Clyde Smith, Jr.	Feb. 15, 2006	Texas	B/W	Lethal Injection
1013	Tommie Hughes	Mar. 15, 2006	Texas	B/B	Lethal Injection
1014	Patrick Moody	Mar. 17, 2006	North Carolina	W/W	Lethal Injection
1015	Robert Salazar, Jr.	Mar. 02, 2006	Texas	L/L	Lethal Injection
1016	Kevin Kincy	Mar. 29, 2006	Texas	B/B	Lethal Injection
1017	Richard Alford Thornburg	Apr. 18, 2006	Oklahoma	W/3W	Lethal Injection
1018	Willie Brown	Apr. 20, 2006	North Carolina	B/B	Lethal Injection
1019*	Daryl Mack	Apr. 26, 2006	Nevada	B/W	Lethal Injection

Table 20 (Continued): People Executed in the United States, 1976-2010

#	Name	Date of Execution	State of Execution	Defendant/ Victim Race	Method of Execution
1020	Dexter Vinson	Apr. 27, 2006	Virginia	B/W	Lethal Injection
1021	Joseph Clark	May 02, 2006	Ohio	B/W	Lethal Injection
1022	Jackie Wilson	May 04, 2006	Texas	L/W	Lethal Injection
1023	Jermaine Herron	May 17, 2006	Texas	B/2W	Lethal Injection
1024	Jesus Aguilar	May 24, 2006	Texas	L/2L	Lethal Injection
1025	John Boltz	Jun. 01, 2006	Oklahoma	W/W	Lethal Injection
1026	Timothy Titsworth	Jun. 06, 2006	Texas	W/W	Lethal Injection
1027	Lamont Reese	Jun. 20, 2006	Texas	B/3B	Lethal Injection
1028~	Angel Maturino Resendiz	Jun. 27, 2006	Texas	L/L	Lethal Injection
1029	Sedley Alley	Jun. 28, 2006	Texas	W/W	Lethal Injection
1030	Derrick O'Brien	Jul. 11, 2006	Texas	B/L,W	Lethal Injection
1031*	Rocky Barton	Jul. 12, 2006	Ohio	W/W	Lethal Injection
1032* ¥	William Downs	Jul. 14, 2006	South Carolina	W/B	Lethal Injection
1033	Mauriceo Brown	Jul. 19, 2006	Texas	B/B	Lethal Injection
1034	Robert Anderson	Jul. 20, 2006	Texas	W/W	Lethal Injection
1035¥	Brandon Hedrick	Jul. 20, 2006	Virginia	W/B	Electrocution
1036	Michael Lenz	Jul. 27, 2006	Virginia	W/W	Lethal Injection
1037	William Wyatt, Jr.	Aug. 3, 2006	Texas	B/B	Lethal Injection

Table 20 (Continued): People Executed in the United States, 1976-2010

#	Name	Date of Execution	State of Execution	Defendant/ Victim Race	Method of Execution
1038*	Darrell Ferguson	Aug. 8, 2006	Ohio	W/3W	Lethal Injection
1039*	David Dawson	Aug. 11, 2006	Montana	W/3W	Lethal Injection
1040	Richard Hinojosa	Aug. 17, 2006	Texas	L/W	Lethal Injection
1041	Samuel Flippen	Aug. 18, 2006	North Carolina	W/W	Lethal Injection
1042	Justin Chaz Fuller	Aug. 24, 2006	Texas	B/W	Lethal Injection
1043	Eric Allen Patton	Aug. 29, 2006	Oklahoma	B/W	Lethal Injection
1044	James Malicoat	Aug. 31, 2006	Oklahoma	W/W	Lethal Injection
1045	Derrick Frazier	Aug. 31, 2006	Texas	B/2W	Lethal Injection
1046	Farley Matchett	Sep. 12, 2006	Texas	B/B	Lethal Injection
1047	Clarence Hill	Sep. 20, 2006	Florida	B/W	Lethal Injection
1048	Arthur Rutherford	Oct. 18, 2006	Florida	W/W	Lethal Injection
1049	Bobby Glen Wilcher	Oct. 18, 2006	Mississippi	W/2W	Lethal Injection
1050	Jeffrey Lundgren	Oct. 24, 2006	Ohio	W/5W	Lethal Injection
1051	Danny Rolling	Oct. 25, 2006	Florida	W,4W,1L	Lethal Injection
1052	Gregory Summers	Oct. 25, 2006	Texas	W/3W	Lethal Injection
1053	Larry Hutcherson	Oct. 26, 2006	Alabama	W/W	Lethal Injection
1054	Donell Jackson	Nov. 01, 2006	Texas	B/B	Lethal Injection

Table 20 (Continued): People Executed in the United States, 1976-2010

#	Name	Date of Execution	State of Execution	Defendant/ Victim Race	Method of Execution
1055	Willie Shannon	Nov. 08, 2006	Texas	B/L	Lethal Injection
1056¥	John Schmitt	Nov. 09, 2006	Virginia	W/B	Lethal Injection
1057~	Angel Diaz	Dec. 13, 2006	Florida	L/W	Lethal Injection
1058	Corey Hamilton	Jan. 09, 2007	Oklahoma	B/4W	Lethal Injection
1059	Carlos Granados	Jan. 10, 2007	Texas	L/L	Lethal Injection
1060	Jonathan Moore	Jan. 17, 2007	Texas	W/L	Lethal Injection
1061*	Christopher Swift	Jan. 30, 2007	Texas	W/2W	Lethal Injection
1062	James Jackson	Feb. 07, 200 7	Texas	B/3B	Lethal Injection
1063	Newton Burton Anderson	Feb. 22, 2007	Texas	W/3W	Lethal Injection
1064	Donald Miller	Feb. 27, 2007	Texas	W/2W	Lethal Injection
1065	Robert Perez	Mar. 06, 2007	Texas	L/2L	Lethal Injection
1066	Joseph Nichols	Mar. 07, 2007	Texas	B/W	Lethal Injection
1067	Charles Nealy	Mar. 20, 2007	Texas	B/A	Lethal Injection
1068	Vincent Gutierrez	Mar. 28, 2007	Texas	L/L	Lethal Injection
1069	Roy Lee Pippin	Mar. 29, 2007	Texas	W/2L	Lethal Injection
1070	James Lee Clark	Apr. 11, 2007	Texas	W/W	Lethal Injection
1071	James Filiaggi	Apr. 24, 2007	Ohio	W/W	Lethal Injection

Table 20 (Continued): People Executed in the United States, 1976-2010

#	Name	Date of Execution	State of Execution	Defendant/ Victim Race	Method of Execution
1072	Ryan Dickson	Apr. 26, 2007	Texas	W/2W	Lethal Injection
1073	Aaron Lee Jones	May 03, 2007	Alabama	B/2W	Lethal Injection
1074	David Woods	May 04, 2007	Indiana	W/L	Lethal Injection
1075	Philip Workman	May 09, 2007	Tennessee	W/W	Lethal Injection
1076	Charles Edward Smith	May 16, 2007	Texas	W/W	Lethal Injection
1077*	Robert Charles Comer	May 22, 2007	Arizona	W/W	Lethal Injection
1078*	Christopher Newton	May 24, 2007	Ohio	W/W	Lethal Injection
1079	Michael Griffith	Jun. 06, 2007	Texas	W/W	Lethal Injection
1080	Michael Lambert	Jun. 15, 2007	Indiana	W/W	Lethal Injection
1081	Lionell Rodriguez	Jun. 20, 2007	Texas	L/A	Lethal Injection
1082	Gilberto Reyes	Jun. 21, 2007	Texas	L/L	Lethal Injection
1083	Calvin Shuler	Jun. 22, 2007	South Carolina	B/W	Lethal Injection
1084	Jimmy Dale Bland	Jun. 26, 2007	Oklahoma	W/W	Lethal Injection
1085	Patrick Knight	Jun. 26, 2007	Texas	W/2W	Lethal Injection
1086	John Hightower	Jun. 26, 2007	Georgia	B/3B	Lethal Injection
1087*	Elijah Page	Jul. 11, 2007	South Dakota	W/W	Lethal Injection
1088	Lonnie Earl Johnson	Jul. 24, 2007	Texas	B/2W	Lethal Injection
1089	Darrell Grayson	Jul. 26, 2007	Alabama	B/W	Lethal Injection

Table 20 (Continued): People Executed in the United States, 1976-2010

#	Name	Date of Execution	State of Execution	Defendant/ Victim Race	Method of Execution
1090	Kenneth Parr	Aug. 15, 2007	Texas	B/W	Lethal Injection
1091	Frank Welch	Aug. 21, 2007	Oklahoma	W/W	Lethal Injection
1092	Johnny Ray Conner	Aug. 22, 2007	Texas	B/A	Lethal Injection
1093	Luther Williams	Aug. 23, 2007	Alabama	B/W	Lethal Injection
1094	DaRoyce Mosley	Aug. 28, 2007	Texas	B/W	Lethal Injection
1095	John Joe Amador	Aug. 29, 2007	Texas	L/W	Lethal Injection
1096	Tony Roach	Sep. 05, 2007	Texas	W/W	Lethal Injection
1097*	Daryl Holton	Sep. 12, 2007	Tennessee	W/3W,1 Other	Electrocution
1098	Clifford Kimmel	Sep. 20, 2007	Texas	W/3W	Lethal Injection
1099	Michael Richard	Sep. 25, 2007	Texas	B/W	Lethal Injection
1100	William Earl Lynd	May 06, 2008	Georgia	W/W	Lethal Injection
1101	Earl Wesley Berry	May 21, 2008	Mississippi	W/W	Lethal Injection
1102	Kevin Green	May 27, 2008	Virginia	B/W	Lethal Injection
1103	Curtis Osborne	Jun. 04, 2008	Georgia	B/2B	Lethal Injection
1104*	David Mark Hill	Jun. 06, 2008	South Carolina	W/2W,B	Lethal Injection
1105	Karl Chamberlain	Jun. 11, 2008	Texas	W/W	Lethal Injection
1106	Terry Lyn Short	Jun. 17, 2008	Oklahoma	W/A	Lethal Injection

Table 20 (Continued): People Executed in the United States, 1976-2010

#	Name	Date of Execution	State of Execution	Defendant/ Victim Race	Method of Execution
1107	James Earl Reed	Jun. 20, 2008	South Carolina	B/2B	Electrocution
1108	Robert Yarbrough	Jun. 25, 2008	Virginia	B/W	Lethal Injection
1109	Mark Dean Schwab	Jul. 01, 2008	Florida	W/L	Lethal Injection
1110	Carlton Akee Turner	Jul. 10, 2008	Texas	B/2B	Lethal Injection
1111	Kent Jermaine Jackson	Jul. 10, 2008	Virginia	B/W	Lethal Injection
1112	Dale Leo Bishop	Jul. 23, 2008	Mississippi	W/W	Lethal Injection
1113	Derrick Sonnier	Jul. 23, 2008	Texas	B/2B	Lethal Injection
1114	Christopher Scott Emmett	Jul. 24, 2008	Virginia	W/W	Lethal Injection
1115	Larry Davis	Jul. 31, 2008	Texas	B/W	Lethal Injection
1116~	Jose Medellin	Aug. 05, 2008	Texas	L/L,W	Lethal Injection
1117~	Heliberto Chi	Aug. 07, 2008	Texas	L/W	Lethal Injection
1118	Leon Dorsey	Aug. 12, 2008	Texas	B/2W	Lethal Injection
1119	Michael Rodrigeuz	Aug. 14, 2008	Texas	L/W	Lethal Injection
1120	Jack Alderman	Sep. 16, 2008	Georgia	W/W	Lethal Injection
1121	William Murray	Sep. 17, 2008	Texas	W/W	Lethal Injection
1122	Richard Henyard	Sep. 23, 2008	Florida	B/2B	Lethal Injection
1123	Jessie Cummings	Sep. 25, 2008	Oklahoma	W/W	Lethal Injection

Table 20 (Continued): People Executed in the United States, 1976-2010

#	Name	Date of Execution	State of Execution	Defendant/ Victim Race	Method of Execution
1124	Richard Cooey	Oct. 14, 2008	Ohio	W/2W	Lethal Injection
1125	Alvin Kelly	Oct. 14, 2008	Texas	W/W	Lethal Injection
1126	Kevin Michael Watts	Oct. 16, 2008	Texas	B/3A	Lethal Injection
1127	Joseph Ray Ries	Oct. 21, 2008	Texas	W/W	Lethal Injection
1128	Eric Nenno	Oct. 28, 2008	Texas	W/W	Lethal Injection
1129	Gregory Wright	Oct. 30, 2008	Texas	W/W	Lethal Injection
1130	Elkie Taylor	Nov. 6, 2008	Texas	B/B	Lethal Injection
1131	George Whitaker	Nov. 12, 2008	Texas	B/B	Lethal Injection
1132	Denard Manns	Nov. 13, 2008	Texas	B/W	Lethal Injection
1133	Gregory Bryant-Bey	Nov. 19, 2008	Ohio	B/W	Lethal Injection
1134	Robert Hudson	Nov. 20, 2008	Texas	B/B	Lethal Injection
1135*	Marco Allen Chapman	Nov. 21, 2008	Kentucky	W/2W	Lethal Injection
1136	Joseph Gardner	Dec. 05, 2008	South Carolina	B/W	Lethal Injection
1137	Curtis Moore	Jan. 14, 2009	Texas	B/3B	Lethal Injection
1138	James Callahan	Jan. 15, 2009	Alabama	W/W	Lethal Injection
1139	Frank Moore	Jan. 21, 2009	Texas	B/2B	Lethal Injection
1140	Reginald Perkins	Jan. 22, 2009	Texas	B/B	Lethal Injection

Table 20 (Continued): People Executed in the United States, 1976-2010

#	Name	Date of Execution	State of Execution	Defendant/ Victim Race	Method of Execution
1141	Darwin Brown	Jan. 22, 2009	Oklahoma	B/B	Lethal Injection
1142	Virgil Euristi Martinez	Jan. 28, 2009	Texas	L/4L	Lethal Injection
1143	Ricardo Ortiz	Jan. 29, 2009	Texas	L/L	Lethal Injection
1144	Steve Henley	Feb. 04, 2009	Tennessee	W/2W	Lethal Injection
1145	David Martinez	Feb. 04, 2009	Texas	L/2L	Lethal Injection
1146	Dale Devon Scheanette	Feb. 10, 2009	Texas	B/B	Lethal Injection
1147	Wayne Tompkins	Feb. 11, 2009	Florida	W/W	Lethal Injection
1148	Danny Bradley	Feb. 12, 2009	Alabama	W/W	Lethal Injection
1149	Johnny Ray Johnson	Feb. 12, 2009	Texas	B/B	Lethal Injection
1150	Edward Bell	Feb. 19, 2009	Virginia	B/W	Lethal Injection
1151	Luke Williams	Feb. 20, 2009	South Carolina	W/1L,1W	Lethal Injection
1152	Willie Earl Pondexter, Jr.	Mar. 03, 2009	Texas	B/W	Lethal Injection
1153	Kenneth Wayne Morris	Mar. 04, 2009	Texas	B/W	Lethal Injection
1154	James Edward Martinez	Mar. 10, 2009	Texas	L/2W	Lethal Injection
1155	Robert Newland	Mar. 10, 2009	Georgia	W/W	Lethal Injection
1156	Luis Cervantes Salazar	Mar. 11, 2009	Texas	L/L	Lethal Injection
1157	Michael Rosales	Apr. 15, 2009	Texas	L/B	Lethal Injection
1158	Jimmy Lee	Apr. 16, 2009	Alabama	B/B	Lethal Injection

Table 20 (Continued): People Executed in the United States, 1976-2010

#	Name	Date of Execution	State of Execution	Defendant/ Victim Race	Method of Execution
1159	William Mize	Apr. 29, 2009	Georgia	W/W	Lethal Injection
1160	Derrick Lamone Johnson	Apr. 30, 2009	Texas	B/B	Lethal Injection
1161	Thomas Ivey	May 08, 2009	South Carolina	B/2W	Lethal Injection
1162	Willie McNair	May 14, 2009	Alabama	B/W	Lethal Injection
1163	Donald Gibson	May 14, 2009	Oklahoma	W/W	Lethal Injection
1164	Michael Lynn Riley	May 19, 2009	Texas	B/W	Lethal Injection
1165	Dennis Skillicorn	May 20, 2009	Missouri	W/W	Lethal Injection
1166	Terry Lee Hankins	Jun. 02, 2009	Texas	W/2W	Lethal Injection
1167	Daniel Wilson	Jun. 03, 2009	Ohio	W/W	Lethal Injection
1168	Jack Trawick	Jun. 11, 2009	Alabama	W/W	Lethal Injection
1169	Michael DeLozier	Jul. 09, 2009	Oklahoma	W/2W	Lethal Injection
1170	John Fautenberry	Jul. 14, 2009	Ohio	W/W	Lethal Injection
1171	Marvallous Keene	Jul. 21, 2009	Ohio	B/2W,2B,1Other	Lethal Injection
1172	Jason Getsy	Aug. 18, 2009	Ohio	W/W	Lethal Injection
1173	John Marek	Aug. 19, 2009	Florida	W/W	Lethal Injection
1174	Stephen Lindsey Moody	Sep. 16, 2009	Texas	W/W	Lethal Injection
1175	Christopher Coleman	Sep. 22, 2009	Texas	B/3L	Lethal Injection

Table 20 (Continued): People Executed in the United States, 1976-2010

#	Name	Date of Execution	State of Execution	Defendant/ Victim Race	Method of Execution
1176	Max Payne	Oct. 08, 2009	Alabama	W/W	Lethal Injection
1177	Mark McClain	Oct. 20, 2009	Georgia	W/W	Lethal Injection
1178	Reginald W. Blanton	Oct. 27, 2009	Texas	B/L	Lethal Injection
1179	Khristian Oliver	Nov. 05, 2009	Texas	B/W	Lethal Injection
1180	Yosvanis Valle	Nov. 10, 2009	Texas	L/L	Lethal Injection
1181	John Muhammad	Nov. 10, 2009	Virginia	B/W	Lethal Injection
1182	Larry Elliot	Nov. 17, 2009	Virginia	W/W	Electric Chair
1183	Danielle Simpson	Nov. 18, 2009	Texas	B/W	Lethal Injection
1184	Robert Lee Thompson	Nov. 19, 2009	Texas	B/O	Lethal Injection
1185	Cecil Johnson	Dec. 02, 2009	Tennessee	B/3B	Lethal Injection
1186	Bobby Wayne Woods	Dec. 03, 2009	Texas	W/W	Lethal Injection
1187	Kenenth Biros	Dec. 08, 2009	Ohio	W/W	Lethal Injection
1188	Mathew E. Wrinkles	Dec. 11, 2009	Indiana	W/3W	Lethal Injection
1189	Vernon Smith	Jan. 07, 2010	Ohio	B/O	Lethal Injection
1190	Kenneth Mosley	Jan. 07, 2010	Texas	B/W	Lethal Injection
1191*	Gerald Bordelon	Jan. 07, 2010	Louisiana	W/W	Lethal Injection
1192	Gary Johnson	Jan. 12, 2010	Texas	W2W	Lethal Injection
1193	Julius Ricardo Young	Jan. 14, 2010	Oklahoma	B/2B	Lethal Injection

Table 20 (Continued): People Executed in the United States, 1976-2010

#	Name	Date of Execution	State of Execution	Defendant/ Victim Race	Method of Execution
1194	Mark Brown	Feb. 04, 2010	Ohio	B/O	Lethal Injection
1195	Martin Grossman	Feb. 06, 2010	Florida	W/W	Lethal Injection
1996	Michael Sigala	Mar. 02, 2010	Texas	L/L	Lethal Injection
1197	Joshua Maxwell	Mar. 02, 2010	Texas	W/L	Lethal Injection
1198	Lawrence Reynolds	Mar. 02, 2010	Ohio	W/W	Lethal Injection
1199	Paul Powell	Mar. 18, 2010	Virginia	W/W	Electric Chair
1200	Franklin Alix	Mar. 30, 2010	Texas	B/B	Lethal Injection
1201	Darryl Durr	Apr. 20, 2010	Ohio	B/W	Lethal Injection
1202	William Berkley	Apr. 22, 2010	Texas	W/L	Lethal Injection
1203	Samuel Bustamente	Apr. 27, 2010	Texas	L/L	Lethal Injection
1204	Kevin Varga	May 12, 2010	Texas	W/W	Lethal Injection
1205	Michael Beuke	May 13, 2010	Ohio	W/W	Lethal Injection
1206	Billy Galloway	May 13, 2010	Texas	W/W	Lethal Injection
1207	Rogelio Cannady	May 19, 2010	Texas	H/L	Lethal Injection
1208	Paul Woodward	May 19, 2010	Mississippi	W/W	Lethal Injection
1209	Gerald Holland	May 20, 2010	Mississippi	W/W	Lethal Injection
1210	Darick Walker	May 20, 2010	Virginia	B/2B	Lethal Injection

Table 20 (Continued): People Executed in the United States, 1976-2010

#	Name	Date of Execution	State of Execution	Defendant/ Victim Race	Method of Execution
1211	John Alba	May 25, 2010	Texas	L/L	Lethal Injection
1212	Thomas Whisenhant	May 27, 2010	Alabama	W/W	Lethal Injection
1213	George Jones	Jun. 02, 2010	Texas	B/B	Lethal Injection
1214	Melbert Ford	Jun. 09, 2010	Georgia	W/2W	Lethal Injection
1215	John Forrest Parker	Jun. 10, 2010	Alabama	W/W	Lethal Injection
1216	David Powell	Jun. 15, 2010	Texas	W/L	Lethal Injection
1217	Ronnie Gardner	Jun. 18, 2010	Utah	W/W	Firing Squad
1218	Michael Perry	Jul. 01, 2010	Texas	W/W	Lethal Injection
1219	William Garner	Jul. 13, 2010	Ohio	B/5B	Lethal Injection
1220	Derrick Jackson	Jul. 20, 2010	Texas	B/2W	Lethal Injection
1221	Joseph Burns	Jul. 21, 2010	Mississippi	W/W	Lethal Injection
1222	Roderick Davie	Aug. 10, 2010	Ohio	B/W,B	Lethal Injection
1223	Michael Land	Aug. 12, 2010	Alabama	W/W	Lethal Injection
1224	Peter Cantu	Aug. 17, 2010	Texas	L/2W	Lethal Injection
1225	Holly Wood	Sep. 09, 2010	Alabama	B/B	Lethal Injection
1226	Cal Brown	Sep. 10, 2010	Washington	W/W	Lethal Injection
1227	Teresa Lewis	Sep. 23, 2010	Virginia	W/2W	Lethal Injection
1228	Brandon Rhode	Sep. 27, 2010	Georgia	W/3W	Lethal Injection

Table 20 (Continued): People Executed in the United States, 1976-2010

#	Name	Date of Execution	State of Execution	Defendant/ Victim Race	Method of Execution
1229	Michael Benge	Oct. 06, 2010	Ohio	W/W	Lethal Injection
1230	Donald Wackerly	Oct. 14, 2010	Oklahoma	W/A	Lethal Injection
1231	Larry Wooten	Oct. 21, 2010	Texas	B/2B	Lethal Injection
1232	Jeffrey Landrigan	Oct. 26, 2010	Arizona	NA/1W	Lethal Injection
1233	Phillip Hallford	Nov. 04, 2010	Alabama	W/W	Lethal Injection
1234	John David Duty	Dec. 16, 2010	Oklahoma	W/W	Lethal Injection

* Volunteer: an inmate who has given up his/her appeals and requested the earliest execution date.

\# Juvenile at time of the crime.

~ Foreign national.

¥ White defendant executed for black victim.

ƒ Female.

Caucasian	694	Asian:	7
African American	424	N/A:	4
Latino[62]	91	Iraqi:	1
Native American:	12	Pakistani:	1

---

[62] For the ethnic distribution of executed Latinos, see Table 17. Note: In Table 17 one particular inmate is classified as Latino, and in the table above as white. As such, the count of 91 executed Latinos does not correspond with the count of 92 in Table 17 in that 1 inmate is classified as Latino in some sources and white in others.

Web, Newspaper Articles, and Other Information Cited

Acker, J. (1999). Personal communication with author via e-mail. December 20, 1999.

Acuna, R. (1990). California commentary: Life behind bars is no way to build character. *Los Angeles Times*, February 12:B7.

Aguirre, F. (2005). *Mendez v. Westminster School District*: How it affected *Brown v. Board of Education*. *Orange County Lawyer*, 47:4.

Amnesty International (1999). Execution of foreign nationals. Available at: http://www.amnesty-usa.org/abolish/fnnat.html.

Atlanta Journal and Constitution (1991). Man executed for role in prison siege. May 23:A13.

Baltimore Sun (1995). Man with 65 IQ executed of Texas rape, killing. January 18:A9.

Barrios, G. (2001). Missing in action; Mexican-Americans are virtually absent from Tom Brokaw's books on World War II. Where are our stories? A Latino war veteran asks. *San Antonio Press-News*, May 20.

Becklund, L. (1985). Immigrants may slow Latino achievements, study says. *Los Angeles Times*, December 10, 1985.

Bohm, R. (1999). Personal communication with author via e-mail. December 19, 1999.

Cardenas, J. (2002). History of WWII gets the Latino perspective. Available at: http://www.pbs.org/now/society/scrapbook2.html.

Chicago Daily Law Bulletin (1992). Drano killer' executed in Utah. July 30:1.

Clarke, A. (1999). Personal communication with author via telephone. December 14, 1999.

Corcoran, K. (2006). Mexican immigrants caught in backlash of terror anxiety. *San Jose Mercury News*, September 10:4S.

Courier-Journal (1993). Mexican executed for Texas slaying. March 26:A4.

Crocker, P.L. (1999). Personal communication with author via e-mail. May 3, 1999.

Dieter, R. (1997). Innocence and the death penalty: The increasing danger of executing the innocent. Death penalty information center, available at: http://www.essential.org/dpic/inn.html.

Edwards, D. (1993). Innocence and the death penalty: Assessing the danger of mistaken execution. Available at: http://www.essential.org/dpic/dpic.r06.html.

Elias, P. & Fried, R. (1999). A failure to execute. Available at: http://www.law/newsnetwork.com/ stories/death/.

Goldberg, D. (1996). City found liable in attack on MOVE. *The Washington Post*, June 25:A03.

Grogger, J. & Trejo, S. (2002). Falling behind or moving up? The intergenerational progress of Mexican Americans. Available at: http://www.ppic.org/publications/PPIC160/ppic160.abstract.html.

Halperin, R. (1997). Death penalty news. Available at: http://venus.soci.niu.edu/~archives/ABOLISH/ sep97/0226.html.

Hayes, K.W. (1999a). Personal communication with author via e-mail. May 27, 1999.

Hayes, K.W. (1999b). Personal communication with author via e-mail. May 7, 1999.

Houston Chronicle (1995). Execution cleared; no stay given retarded child-killer. January 17:A13.

Houston Chronicle (1993a). No stars for Ruben Cantu. September 4:A37.

Houston Chronicle (1993b). I am innocent, innocent. May 12:A1.

Houston Chronicle (1993c). Mexican national's execution draws angry remarks, protests. March 26:A34.

Houston Chronicle (1992a). Ex-migrant worker executed in teen's rape-murder. May 20:A18.

Houston Chronicle (1992b). Three-time loser is put to death. January 22:A13.

Independent, London (1995). Man with IQ of 65 is executed. January 18:13.

Keyes, D., Edwards, W. & Perske, R. (1999). Defendants with mental retardation executed in the United States since the death penalty was reinstated in 1976. Available at: http://www.essential.org/dpic/dpicmr.html.

Kramer, M. (1994). Frying them isn't the answer. *Time*, March 14:32.

La Voz de Aztlan (2000). Mexican migrant workers savagely attacked by racists in San Diego, California. Available at: http://aztlan.net/lynched.html.

League of Latin American Citizens (1999). Personal communication with author via telephone, Washington, DC office. May 20, 1999.

Levine, A. (2003). American education: Still separate, still unequal. *Los Angeles Times*, February 2.

Los Angeles Times (1994). Unexpected friend on death row. January 2:A1.

Los Angeles Times (1985a). Texan executed after assailing society as 'a bunch of cold-blooded murderers.' July 10:11.

Los Angeles Times (1985b). Texas executes man who killed policeman. July 9:A19.

McCormick, J. (1998). The wrongly condemned. *Newsweek*, 132.

NAACP Legal Defense Fund and Death Penalty Information Center (1999). Available at: http://www.essential.org/dpic/exec76-90 [and 91-95].gif.

National Law Journal (1998). Are 65 illegally on death row in U.S.? April 27:A16.

New York Times (1995a). Ghoulish murderer is executed in Texas. December 12:A24.

New York Times (1995b). Texan who killed ex-wife and her niece is executed. January 18:A16.

New York Times (1993a). Texas executes a Mexican killer, raising a furor across the border. March 26:A15.

New York Times (1993b). Mexico fights to stop U.S. execution. January 26:A19.

New York Times (1987). Texan who killed 6 in 1983 is executed by lethal injection. March 5:A9.

New York Times (1986). Texan executed by injection for killing of a drug agent. June 9:A19.

New York Times (1985). Killer put to death in Texas. July 10:A11.

Office of the Attorney General of Texas (1999). Defendants' information was provided to the author by Douglas Danzeiser, Assistant Attorney General. May 2, 1999.

Office of the Mexican Consulate (1999). Personal communication with author via telephone, Houston, Texas office. May 17, 1999.

Ortego, F. (2007). On war and remembrance: Hispanics and World War II. *La Prensa de San Antonio*, October 7.

Page, C. (1995). The murky line between who gets life or death. *Chicago Tribune*, August 2:Section 1:15.

Phoenix Gazette (1995). Inmate with low IQ is executed in Texas. January 17:A9.

Phoenix Gazette (1993). Execution of Mexican in Texas spurs protests. March 26:B5.

Pierre, R. & Lydersen, K. (2003). Illinois' Ryan empties state's death row. *Milwaukee Journal Sentinel*, January 12:1A, 14A.

Rentschler, W. (1994). The death penalty–a pivotal issue. *Chicago Tribune*, November 29:19.

Rodriguez, C. (1999). INS law means lengthy sentences for convicted immigrants. Available at: http://www.latino.com/news/news99/0414nlaw.htm.

Rohrlich, T. & Tulsky, F.N. (1996). Not all L.A. murder cases are equal. *Los Angeles Times*, A1: December 3, 1996.

Sacramento Bee (1994). Foes of death penalty have a friend: Mexico. June 26:A1.

San Antonio Express News (1999). Death row: Death row history. Available at: http://express-news.com/news/deathrow/history.shtml.

San Diego Union-Tribune (1994). A binational dance with death Mexicans on U.S. death row stir a growing furor. August 18:B11,13,15.

San Diego Union-Tribune (1993). Mexico's influence growing in U.S. political, fiscal clout now felt. August 22:A1.

San Diego Union-Tribune (1987). Texas executes murderer called jail-house lawyer. January 30:A20.

San Diego Union-Tribune (1986). Killer-rapist is executed by injection; 10th put to death in Texas this year. December 18:A14.

San Diego Union-Tribune (1985a). Texas man put to death for slaying. July 9:A4, 8.

San Diego Union-Tribune (1985b). Texas executes man for 1979 six-pack' murder. May 15:A3.

San Francisco Chronicle (1993a). Mexican officials visit San Quentin death row. August 7:B4.

San Francisco Chronicle (1993b). Mexico to fight California executions. August 5:A15.

St. Petersburg Times (1989a). Santeria dust fails defendants. May 2:B2.

St. Petersburg Times (1989b). Three executions scheduled. April 19:B2.

Streib, V. (1999). Personal communication with author via e-mail. December 20, 1999.

Texas Department of Corrections (1999). Personal communication with author via e-mail. June 20, 1999.

Texas Department of Criminal Justice (1999). Defendant's information was provided to the author by Christina Wooderson, administrative assistant for public information. June 10, 1999.

Tierney, C. (1992). Mexicans view U.S. death penalty as barbaric. Reuters, September 23: available in LEXIS.

Time (1970). J. Edgar Hoover speaks out with vigor. December 14:16-17.

Warren, M. (1999). Foreign nationals and the death penalty in the United States. Available at: http://www.essential.org/dpic/foreignnatl.html.

Washington Post (1994). For the road. July 8:A22.

Washington Post (1993). Texas, California executions. August 25:A9.

Weekly Arizonian. June 30, 1859.

Weekly Alta Californian. May 28, 1859.

Zuniga, J.A. (1993). The Wrong Man? *Houston Chronicle*, January 10:A1.

References

Acuna, R. (2010). *Occupied America: A history of Chicanos* (seventh edition). Upper Saddle River, NJ: Prentice Hall.

Acuna, R. (1998). *Sometimes there is no other side: Chicanos and the myth of equality*. Notre Dame: University of Notre Dame Press.

Acuna, R. (1988). *Occupied America* (third edition). New York: Harper Collins.

Agresti, A. & Finlay, B. (1997). *Statistical methods for the social sciences* (third edition). New Jersey: Prentice Hall.

Aguirre, A. & Baker, D. (2007). *Structured inequality in the United States: Discussions on the continuing significance of race, ethnicity, and gender* (second edition). Upper Saddle River, NJ: Prentice Hall.

Aguirre, A. & Baker, D. (1999). Slave executions in the United States: A descriptive analysis of social and historical factors. *The Social Science Journal*, 36:1-31.

Aguirre, A. & Baker, D. (1997). A descriptive profile of Mexican American executions in the Southwest. *The Social Science Journal*, 34(3):389-402.

Aguirre, A. & Baker, D. (1990). Empirical research on racial discrimination in the imposition of the death penalty. *Criminal Justice Abstracts*, 22:135-153.

Aguirre, A. & Baker, D. (1989). The execution of Mexican American prisoners in the Southwest. *Social Justice*, 16(4):150-161.

Aguirre, A. & Baker, D. (1988). A descriptive profile of the Hispanic penal population: Conceptual and reliability limitations in public use data. *The Justice Professional*, 3:189-200.

Aguirre, A., Davin, R., Baker, D. & Lee, K. (1999). Sentencing outcomes, race, and victim impact evidence in California: A pre-

and post-*Payne* comparison. *The Justice Professional*, 11:297-310.

Aguirre, A. & Turner, J. (2006). *American ethnicity: The dynamics and consequences of discrimination* (fifth edition). New York: McGraw-Hill.

Allen, J., Lewis, J., Litwack, L. & Als, H. (2000). *Without sanctuary: Lynching photography in America*. Santa Fe, NM: Twin Palms Publishers.

Almaguer, T. (2008). *Racial fault lines: The historical origins of White supremacy in California*. Berkeley: University of California Press.

Almaguer, T. (1994). *Racial fault lines: The historical origins of White supremacy in California*. Berkeley: University of California Press.

Ammons, L. (1994). Discretionary justice: A legal and policy analysis of a governor's use of the clemency power in the cases of incarcerated battered women. *Journal of Law and Policy*, 3:1-79.

Ampudia, R. (2010). *Mexicans on death row*. Houston: Arte Publico Press.

Anaya, T. (1993). Statement by Toney Anaya on capital punishment. *University of Richmond Law Review*, 27(2):177-183.

Anderson, J. & Hevenor, H. (1987). *Burning down the house*. New York: W.W. Norton and Company.

Arkin, S.D. (1980). Discrimination and arbitrariness in capital punishment: An analysis of post-*Furman* murder cases in Dade County, Florida, 1973-1976. *Stanford Law Review*, 33:75-101.

Bacon, D. (2009). *Illegal people: How globalization creates migration and criminalizes immigrants*. Boston, MA: Beacon Press.

Baldus, D., Pulaski, C. & Woodworth, G. (1983). Comparative review of death sentences: An empirical study of the Georgia experience. *Journal of Criminal Law and Criminology*, 74(3):661-770.

Baldus, D., Pulaski, C., Woodworth, G. & Kyle, F. (1980). Identifying comparatively excessive sentences of death: A quantitative approach. *Stanford Law Review*, 33:1-74.

Baldus, D., Woodworth, G., Grosso, C. & Christ, A. (2002). Arbitrariness and discrimination in the administration of the death penalty: A legal and empirical analysis of the Nebraska experience (1973-1999). *Nebraska Law Review*, 81:486-756.

Baldus, D., Woodworth, G. & Pulaski, C. (1990). *Equal justice and the death penalty*. Boston: Northeastern University Press.

Baldus, D., Woodworth, G. & Pulaski, C. (1985). Monitoring and evaluating contemporary death sentencing systems: Lessons from Georgia. *University of California, Davis Law Review*, 18(4):1375-1407.

Baldus, D., Woodworth, G., Zucherman, D., Weiner, N.A. & Broffitt, B. (1998). Symposium: Racial discrimination and the death penalty in the post-*Furman* era: An empirical and legal overview, with recent findings from Philadelphia. *Cornell Law Review*, 83(6):1638-1770.

Barlow, D. & Barlow, M. (2002). Racial profiling: A survey of African American police officers. *Police Quarterly*, 5:334-358.

Barnett, A. (1985). Some distribution patterns for the Georgia death sentence. *University of California, Davis Law Review*, 18:1327-74.

Bedau, H.A. (1965). Capital punishment in Oregon, 1903-1964. *Oregon Law Review*, 45(1):1-39.

Bedau, H.A. (1964). Death sentences in New Jersey, 1907-1960. *Rutgers Law Review*, 19(1):1-55.

Bell, D. (1992). *Faces at the bottom of the well: The permanence of racism.* New York: Basic Books.

Bell, D. (1980). *Brown v. Board of Education* and the interest-convergence dilemma. *Harvard Law Review*, 518:93.

Bensing, R.C. & Schroeder, O.J. (1960). *Homicide in an urban community.* Springfield, Illinois: Charles Thomas.

Bender, S. (2005). *Greasers and gringos: Latinos, law, and the American imagination.* New York: New York University Press.

Bentele, U. (1993). Race and capital punishment in the United States and South Africa. *Brooklyn Journal of Internal Law*, 19(2):235-271.

Bentele, U. (1985). The death penalty in Georgia: Still arbitrary. *Washington University Law Quarterly*, 62(4):573-646.

Berk, R., Li, A. & Hickman, L. (2005). Statistical difficulties in determining the role of race in capital cases: A re-analysis of data from the state of Maryland. *Journal of Quantitative Criminology*, 21:365-390.

Blalock, H. (1979). *Social statistics* (second edition). New York: McGraw-Hill.

Blalock, H. (1967). *Toward a theory of minority group relations.* New York: John Wiley & Sons.

Bohm, R. (1989). Humanism and the death penalty, with special emphasis on the post-*Furman* experience. *Justice Quarterly*, 6:173-195.

Bohm, R.M. & Haley, K.N. (1997). *Introduction to criminal justice.* New York: Glencoe.

Bok, D. & Bowen, W. (1998). *The shape of the river: Long-term consequences of considering race in college and university admissions.* Princeton: Princeton University Press.

Bonczar, T. (2003). *Prevalence of imprisonment in the U.S. Population, 1974-2001.* Bureau of Justice Statistics. Washington, DC: US Department of Justice.

Bonilla-Silva, E. (2006). *Racism without racists: Color-blind racism and the persistence of racial inequality in the United States* (second edition). Lanham, MD: Rowman & Littlefield Publishers.

Boris, S.B. (1979). Stereotypes and dispositions for criminal homicide. *Criminology*, 17(2):139-158.

Bosworth, M. & Flavin, J., eds. (2007). *Race, gender, and punishment: From colonialism to the war on terror.* Piscataway, NJ: Rutgers University Press.

Bowers, W. (1984). *Legal homicide.* Boston: Northeastern University Press.

Bowers, W. (1983). The pervasiveness of arbitrariness and discrimination under post-*Furman* capital statutes. *Journal of Criminal Law and Criminology*, 74(3):1067-1100.

Bowers, W. (1974). *Executions in America.* Lexington: D.C. Heath.

Bowers, W. & Pierce, G. (1980). Arbitrariness and discrimination under post-*Furman* capital statutes. *Crime and Delinquency*, 74:563-635.

Bowers, W., Steiner, B. & Sandys, M. (2001). Death sentencing in Black and White: An empirical analysis of jurors' race and jury racial composition. *University of Pennsylvania Journal of Constitutional Law*, 3:171-275.

Braithwaite, J. (2002). Charles Title's control balance and criminological theory. In S. Cote (ed.), *Criminological Theories: Bridging the Past to the Future.* Thousand Oaks, CA: Sage.

Braun, D. (1991). *The rich get richer: The rise of income inequality in the United States and the world.* Chicago: Nelson-Hall Publishers.

Brearley, H.C. (1930). The Negro and homicide. *Social Forces*, 9(2):247-253.

Bridge, F.M. & Mosure, J. (1961). *Capital punishment*. Columbus: Ohio Legislative Service Commission.

Brigham, W. (1996). Whatup in the hood?: The rage of African American film makers. In R.Curry & T. Allison (eds.), *States of rage: Emotional eruption, violence, and social change*. New York: New York University Press.

Brock, D., Cohen, N. & Sorensen, J. (2000). Arbitrariness in the imposition of death sentences in Texas: An analysis of four counties by offense seriousness, race of victim, and race of offender. *American Journal of Criminal Law*, 28:43-71.

Brokaw, T. (1998). *The greatest generation*. New York: Random House.

Camarillo, A. (1984). Chicanos in the American city. In E. Garcia, F. Lomeli & I. Ortiz (eds.), *Chicano studies: A multidisciplinary approach*. New York: Teachers College Press.

Carrigan, W. & Webb, C. (2003). The lynching of persons of Mexican origin or descent in the US, 1848-1929. *Journal of Social History*, 37:411-438.

Carter, R. & Smith, L. (1969). The death penalty in California: A statistical composite portrait. *Crime and Delinquency*, 15(1):63-76.

Castaneda, J. (2009). *Ex Mex: From migrants to immigrants*. New York: The New Press.

Chacon, J. & Davis, M. (2006). *No one is illegal: Fighting racism and state violence on the U.S.-Mexico border*. Chicago: Haymarket Books.

Chavez, L. (2008). *The Latino threat: Constructing immigration, citizens, and the nation*. Palo Alto, CA: Stanford University Press.

Chavez, H. & Miller, M. (2009). Religious reference in death sentence phases of trials: Two psychological theories that suggest judicial rulings and assumptions may affect jurors. *Lewis & Clark Law Review*, 13:1037-1084.

Cholbi, M. (2006). Race, capital punishment, and the cost of murder. *Philosophical Studies*, 127:255-282.

Chomsky, A. (2007). *"They take our jobs!" And 20 other myths about immigration*. Boston, MA: Beacon Press.

Churchill, W. & Vander Wall, J., eds. (1992). *Cages of steel: The politics of imprisonment in the United States*. Washington, DC: Maisonneuve Press.

Cobas, J., Duany, J. & Feagin, J. (2009). *How the United States racializes Latinos: White hegemony and its consequences*. Boulder, CO: Paradigm Publishers.

Cockcroft, J. (1982). Mexican migration, economic crisis, and the international labor struggle. In M. Dixon & S. Jonas (eds.), *The new nomads: From immigrant labor to transnational working class*. San Francisco: Synthesis Publications.

Cole, S. & Barber, E. (2003). *Increasing faculty diversity: The occupational choices of high-achieving minority students*. Cambridge: Harvard University Press.

Cooper, A.J. (1988). *A voice from the South*. New York: Oxford University Press.

Culver, J.H. (1992). Capital punishment, 1977-1990: Characteristics of the 143 executed. *Sociology and Social Research*, 76(2):59-61.

Currie, E. (1993). *Reckoning: Drugs, the cities, and the American future*. New York: Hill & Wang.

Currie, E. (1985). *Confronting crime: An American challenge*. New York: Pantheon.

Daudistel, H., Hosch, H., Holmes, M. & Graves, J. (1999). Effects of defendant ethnicity on juries' dispositions of felony cases. *Journal of Applied Social Psychology*, 29:317-336.

De Genova, N. (2004). The legal production of Mexican/migrant "illegality." *Latino Studies*, 2:160-185.

De Genova, N. & Ramos-Zayas, A.Y. (2003). *Latino crossings: Mexicans, Puerto Ricans, and the politics of race* and citizenship. New York: Routledge.

De Leon, A. (1983). *They called them greasers*. Austin: University of Texas Press.

Delgado, R., ed. (1995). *Critical race theory: The cutting edge*. Philadelphia: Temple University Press.

Diaz-Cotto, J. (2006). *Chicana lives and criminal justice: Voices from el barrio*. Austin: University of Texas Press.

Dike, S. (1982). *Capital punishment in the United States*. Hackensack: National Council on Crime and Delinquency.

Dorfman, L. & Schiraldi, V. (2001). *Off balance: Youth, race and crime in the news*. Washington, DC: Building Blocks for Youth.

Dray, P. (2002). *At the hands of persons unknown: The lynching of black America*. New York: Modern Library.

Dunbar, T. & Kravitz, L. (1976). *Hard traveling*. Pensacola: Ballinger Publishers.

Duran, R. (2009a). Legitimated oppression: Inner-city Mexican American experiences with police gang enforcement. *Journal of Contemporary Ethnography*, 38:143-168.

Duran, R. (2009b). Over-inclusive gang enforcement and urban resistance: A comparison between two cities. *Social Justice*, 36:82-101.

Duran, R. (2009c). The core ideals of the Mexican American gang. *Aztlan: A Journal of Chicano Studies*, 34:99-134.

Ehrmann, H. (1952). The death penalty and the administration of justice. *Annals of the American Academy of Political and Social Research*, 284:73-84.

Ekland-Olson, S. (1988). Structured discretion, racial bias, and the death penalty: The first decade after *Furman* in Texas. *Social Science Quarterly*, 69:853-873.

Esposito, B. & Wood, J., eds. (1982). *Prison slavery*. Washington, DC: Committee to Abolish Prison Slavery.

Ezekiel, R.S. (1995). *The racist mind: Portraits of American neo-Nazis and Klansmen*. New York: Viking.

Feagin, J.R. & Vera, H. (1995). *White racism: The basics*. New York: Routledge.

Florida Civil Liberties Union (1964). *Rape: Selective electrocution based on race*. Miami, FL: Florida Civil Liberties Union.

Fogel, D. (1979). *". . . we are the living proof": The justice model of corrections*. Cincinnati: Anderson.

Foley, L. (1987). Florida after the *Furman* decision: The effect of extralegal factors on the processing of capital cases. *Behavioral Sciences & the Law*, 5(4):457-465.

Foley, L. & Powell, R. (1982). The discretion of prosecution, judges, and juries in capital cases. *Criminal Justice Review*, 7:16-22.

Foner, E. (1998). Who is an American? In P.S. Rothenberg (ed.), *Race, class, and gender in the United States: An integrated study* (fourth edition). New York: St. Martin's Press.

Foucault, M. (1995). *Discipline and punish: The birth of the prison.* New York: Vintage Books.

Fox, J. & Rivera-Salgado, G., eds., (2004). *Indigenous Mexican migrants in the United States.* Boulder, CO: Lynne Rienner Publishers.

Franklin, J.H. & Moss, A.A. (1988). *From slavery to freedom: A history of Negro Americans* (sixth edition). New York: Alfred A. Knopf.

Fredrickson, G.M. (1981). *White supremacy: A comparative study in American and South African history.* Oxford: Oxford University Press.

Gans, H. (1995). *The war against the poor.* New York: Basic Books.

Garcia y Griego, M. (1997). The importation of Mexican contract laborers to the United States, 1942-1964. In D. Gutierrez (ed.), *Between two worlds: Mexican immigrants in the United States.* Wilmington, DE: Jaguar Books.

Garfinkel, H. (1949). Research note on inter- and intra-racial homicides. *Social Forces*, 27:369-381.

Garland, D. (1990). *Punishment and modern society.* Chicago: University of Chicago Press.

Gates, H. & West, C. (1997). *The future of the race.* New York: Vintage Books.

Giardini, G.I. & Farrow, R.G. (1952). The paroling of capital offenders. *The Annals of the American Academy of Political and Social sciences*, 284:85-94.

Gillespie, L.K. (2000). *Dancehall ladies.* Lanham: University of America.

Gilmore, K. (2000). Slavery and prison: Understanding the connections. *Social Justice*, 27:195-206.

Gilroy, P. (1993). *The Black Atlantic: Modernity and double consciousness.* Cambridge, MA: Harvard University Press.

Gomez, L. (2007). *Manifest destinies: The making of the Mexican American race.* New York: New York University Press.

Gomez, L. (2000). Race, colonialism, and criminal law: Mexicans and the American criminal justice system in territorial New Mexico. *Law & Society Review*, 34:1129-1202.

Gonzalez, G.G. & Fernandez, R. (1998). Chicano history: Transcending cultural models. In A. Darder & R. Torres (eds.), *The Latino studies reader: Culture, economy, and society.* Malden, MA: Blackwell Publishers.

Gordon, M. (1964). *Assimilation in American life: The role of race, religion, and national origins.* New York: Oxford University Press.

Gross, S. & Mauro, R. (1989). *Death and discrimination: Racial disparities in capital sentencing.* Boston: Northeastern University Press.

Gross, S. & Mauro, R. (1984). Patterns of death: An analysis of racial disparities in capital sentencing and homicide victimization. *Sanford Law Review,* 37:27-153.

Groves, C. (1991). Us and them: Reflections on the dialectics of moral hate. In B.D. MacLean & D. Milovanovic, *New directions in critical criminology.* Vancouver: Collective Press.

Gutierrez, D., ed. (1997). *Between two worlds: Mexican immigrants in the United States.* Wilmington, DE: Jaguar Books.

Hacker, A. (2003). *Two nations: Black & white, separate, hostile, unequal.* New York: Scribner.

Hagan, J., Huxter, M. & Parker, P. (1988). Class structure and legal practice: Inequality and mobility among Toronto lawyers. *Law & Society Review,* 22:9-55.

Hagan, J. (1974). Extra-legal attributes and criminal sentencing: An assessment of a sociological viewpoint. *Law and Society Review,* 8:357-383.

Hagan, J. & Palloni, A. (1999). Sociological criminology and the mythology of Hispanic immigration and crime. *Social Problems,* 46:617-632.

Hall, S. (1980). Introduction to media studies at the Centre. *Culture, media, language: Working papers in cultural studies, 1972-1979.* London: Hutchison.

Harrington, M. (1971). *The other America: Poverty in the United States.* Baltimore: Penguin Books.

Harrison, P.M. & Beck, A.J. (2006). *Prisoners in 2005.* Washington, DC: U.S. Department of Justice.

Hawkins, D. (1994). Ethnicity: The forgotten dimension of American social control. In G. Bridges & M. Myers (eds.), *Inequality, crime, and social control.* Boulder: Westview Press.

Heilburn, A., Foster, A. & Golden, J. (1989). The death penalty sentence in Georgia, 1974-1987. Criminal justice or racial injustice? *Criminal Justice and Behavior,* 16(2):139-154.

Herrnstein, R. & Murray, C. (1994). *The bell curve: Intelligence and class structure in American life.* New York: Free Press.

Hess, B.B., Markson, E.W. & Stein, P.J. (1998). Racial and ethnic minorities: An overview. In P.S. Rothenberg (ed.), *Race, class, and gender in the United States: An integrated study* (fourth edition). New York: St. Martin's Press.

Holmes, M. & Daudistel, H. (1984). Ethnicity and justice in the Southwest: The sentencing of Anglo, black, and Mexican American defendants. *Social Justice Quarterly*, 65:265-277.

hooks, b. (1995). *Killing rage: Ending racism.* New York: H. Holt & Company.

Huntington, S. (2004). The Hispanic challenge. *Foreign Policy*, March/April:30-45.

Irwin, J. & Austin, J. (2000). *It's about time: America's imprisonment binge* (third edition). Belmont: Wadsworth Publishing Company.

Jacoby, J. & Paternoster, R. (1982). Sentencing disparity and jury packing: Further challenges to the death penalty. *Journal of Criminal Law and Criminology*, 73(1):379-387.

Jensen, A. (1998). *G factor: The science of mental ability.* West Port: Praeger.

Johnson, E.H. (1957). Selective factors in capital punishment. *Social Forces*, 36:165-169.

Johnson, G.B. (1941). The Negro and crime. *The Annals*, 217:93-104.

Johnson, O.C. (1970). Is the punishment of rape equally administered to Negroes and whites in the state of Louisiana? In W.L. Patterson (ed.), *We charge genocide.* New York: International Publishers Company.

Johnson, R. (1990). *Death work: A study of the modern execution process.* Pacific Grove: Brooks/Cole Publishing Company.

Judson, C.J., Pandell, J.J., Owens, J.B., McIntosh, J.L. & Matschullat, D.L. (1969). A study of the California penalty jury in first degree murder cases. *Stanford Law Review*, 21:1297-1497.

Kalven, H. (1969). A study of the California penalty jury in first-degree murder cases. *Stanford Law Review*, 21:1297-1301.

Kaplan, P. (2009a). Looking through the gaps: A critical approach to the LAPD's Rampart Scandal. *Social Justice*, 36:61-81.

Kaplan, P. (2009b). Nihilism and mistaken identity: (Self)hate crime in *The Believer*. *Journal of Criminal Justice and Popular Culture*, 16:63-80.

Kappeler, V., Blumberg, M. & Potter, G. (1996). *The mythology of crime and criminal justice* (second edition). Prospect Heights, Illinois: Waveland.

Kappeler, V. & Potter, G. (2004). *The mythology of crime and criminal justice* (fourth edition). Prospect Heights: Waveland Press.

Karns, J. & Weinberg, L. (1991). The death sentence in Pennsylvania–1978-1990: A preliminary analysis of statutory and non-statutory factors. *Dickinson Law Review*, 95:691-738.

Keil, T. & Vito, G. (1995). Race and the death penalty in Kentucky murder trials: 1976-1991. *American Journal of Criminal Justice*, 10:17-36.

Keil, T. & Vito, G. (1990). Race and the death penalty in Kentucky murder trials: An analysis of post-*Gregg* outcomes. *Justice Quarterly*, 7:189-207.

Keil, T. & Vito, G. (1989). Race, homicide severity, and application of the death penalty: A consideration of the Barnett scale. *Criminology*, 27:511-531.

Kelly, H.E. (1976). Comparison of defense strategy and race as influences in differential sentencing. *Criminology*, 14:241-249.

Kinder, K. (1982). *Victim: The other side of murder*. New York: Delacorte Press.

King, J. (1981). *The biology of race*. Berkeley: University of California Press.

King, R., Johnson, K. & McGeever, K. (2010). Demography of the legal profession and racial disparities in sentencing. *Law & Society Review*, 44:1-32.

Kleck, G. (1981). Racial discrimination in criminal sentencing: A critical evaluation of the evidence with additional evidence on the death penalty: *American Sociological Review*, 46:783-805.

Klein, S.P. & Rolph, J.E. (1991). Relationship of offender and victim race to death penalty sentences in California. *Jurimetrics*, 32:33-48.

Klein, S.P. & colleagues (1987). Racial equity in prosecutor requests for the death penalty. Cited in D. Baldus, G. Woodworth, D. Zucherman, N. Weiner & B. Broffitt (1998), Symposium: Racial discrimination and the death penalty in the post-*Furman* era: An empirical and legal overview, with recent findings from Philadelphia. *Cornell Law Review*, 83(6):1638-1755.

Klepper, S., Nagin, D. & Tierney, L. (1983). Discrimination in the criminal justice system: A critical appraisal of the literature. In A. Blumstein, J. Cohen, S. Martin & M. Tonry (eds.), *Research on sentencing: The search for reform*, Volume 2. Washington, DC: National Academy Press.

Koeninger, R. (1969). Capital punishment in Texas, 1924-1968. *Crime and Delinquency*, 15(1):132-141.

Kong, L. (2010). Immigration, racial profiling, and white privilege: Community-based challenges and practices for adult educators. *New Directions for Adult and Continuing Education*, 125:65-77.

Kovandzic, T., Vieraitis, L. & Yeisley, M. (1998). The structural covariates of urban homicide: Reassessing the impact of income inequality and poverty in the post-Reagan era. *Criminology*, 36:569-599.

Levin, B. (2002). From slavery to hate crime laws: The emergence of race and status-based protection in American criminal law. *Journal of Social Issues*, 58:227-245.

Levin, J. & McDevitt, J. (1993). *Hate crimes: The rising tide of bigotry and bloodshed*. New York: Plenum Press.

Levin, M. (1997). *Why race matters: Race differences and what they mean*. Westport: Praeger.

Lewis, P. & Peoples, K. (1978). Life on death row: A post-*Furman* profile of Florida's condemned. In P.W. Lewis & K.D. Peoples (eds.), *The Supreme Court and the criminal process–cases and comments*. Philadelphia: Saunders.

Liebman, E. (1985). Appellate review of death sentences: A critique of proportionality review. *University of California, Davis Law Review*, 18:1433-1480.

Lopez, I.F.H. (2006). *White by law: The legal construction of race*. New York: New York University Press.

Lopez, I.F.H. (2004). *Racism on trial: The Chicano fight for justice*. Cambridge: Belknap Press of Harvard University Press.

Lynch, M. (2007). *Big prison, big dreams: Crime and the failure of America's penal system*. New Brunswick, NJ: Rutgers University Press.

Mangum, C.S. (1940). *The legal status of the Negro*. Chapel Hill: University of North Carolina Press.

Martinez, D.J. (2004). Felony disenfranchisement and voting participants: Considerations in Latino ex-prisoner reentry. *Columbia Human Rights Law Review*, 36:217-240.

Marquart, J., Ekland-Olson, S. & Sorensen, J. (1994). *The rope, the chair, and the needle: Capital punishment in Texas, 1923-1990.* Austin: University of Texas Press.

Massey, D. (1990). American apartheid: Segregation and the making of the underclass. *American Journal of Sociology,* 96:329-359.

McCafferty, J.A. (1962). Prisoners sentenced to death in Maryland, 1936-1961. In Report of the Legislative Council Committee on Capital Punishment, October 3, 1962. Baltimore, Maryland.

McCleskey v. Kemp, 481 U.S. 279 (1987).

McGehee, E.G. & Hildebrand, W.H., eds. (1964). *The death penalty: A literary and historical approach.* Boston: D.C. Heath.

McWilliams, C. (1990). *North from Mexico: The Spanish-speaking people of the United States* (second edition). Westport, CT: Praeger Publishers.

Meeks, E. (2007). *Border citizens: The making of Indians, Mexicans, and Anglos in Arizona.* Austin: University of Texas Press.

Menard, S. (1995). *Applied logistic regression analysis.* Thousand Oaks: Sage Publications.

Meyer, M. & Sherman, W. (1995). *The course of Mexican history* (fifth edition). New York: Oxford University Press.

Mirande, A. (2005). *The Stanford law chronicles: Doin' time on the farm.* Notre Dame: University of Notre Dame Press.

Mirande, A. (1989). *The Chicano experience: An alternative perspective.* Notre Dame: University of Notre Dame Press.

Mirande, A. (1987). *Gringo justice.* South Bend: Notre Dame Press.

Moore, W.L. (2007). *Reproducing racism: White space, elite law schools, and racial inequality.* Lanham, MD: Rowman & Littlefield Publishers.

Morin, J.L. (2008). Latinas/os and US prisons: Trends and challenges. *Latino Studies,* 6:11-34.

Morin, R. (1966). *Among the valiant.* Alhambra: Borden.

Motomura, H. (2010). The rights of others: Legal claims and immigration outside the law. *Duke Law Journal,* 59:1723-1786.

Myrdal, G. (1944). *An American dilemma.* New York: Harper & Row.

Mysliwiec, P. (2010). The federal death penalty as a safety value. *Virginia Journal of Social Policy & the Law,* 17:257-280.

Nelson, J. & Maddox, G.K. (1996). A rhetorical study of the MOVE diatribe in contemporary America. *The Pennsylvania Speech Communication Annual*, 1-3.

Newman, G. (1985). *The punishment response*. Albany: Harrow & Heston.

Ngai, M. (2005). *Impossible subjects: Illegal aliens and the making of modern America*. Princeton, NJ: Princeton University Press.

Nieling, S. & Urbina, M. (2008). Epilogue: Thoughts for the future. In M. Urbina, *A comprehensive study of female offenders: Life before, during, and after incarceration*. Springfield, IL: Charles C Thomas, Publisher, Ltd.

Noboa, J. (2005). *Leaving Latinos out of history: Teaching U.S. history in Texas*. New York: Routledge.

Oboler, S., ed. (2009). *Behind bars: Latino/as and prison in the United States*. New York: Palgrave Macmillan.

Oboler, S. (2008). Viviendo en el olvido: Behind bars, Latinos and prison. *Latino Studies*, 6:1-10.

Oboler, S., ed. (2006). *Latinos and citizenship: The dilemma of belonging*. New York: Palgrave Macmillan.

Palacios, V. (1996). Faith in fantasy: The Supreme Court's reliance on commutation to ensure justice in death penalty cases. *Vanderbilt University*, 49:311-372.

Paredes, A. (1990). *George Washington Gomez: A mexicotexan novel*. Houston: Arte Publico Press.

Partington, D. (1965). The incidence of the death penalty for rape in Virginia. *Washington and Lee Law Review*, 22:43-75.

Paternoster, R. (1984). Prosecutorial discretion in requesting the death penalty: A case of victim-based racial discrimination. *Law & Society Review*, 18:437-78.

Paternoster, R. (1983). Race of victim and location of crime: The decision to seek the death penalty in South Carolina. *Journal of Criminal Law and Criminology*, 74(3):754-785.

Paternoster, R. & Brame, R. (2008). Reassessing race disparities in Maryland capital cases. *Criminology*, 46:971-1007.

Paternoster, R. & Kazyaka, A. (1988). Racial considerations in capital punishment. In K.C. Haas & J.A. Inciardi (eds.), *Challenging capital punishment: Legal and social sciences approaches*. Newbury Park: Sage.

Peffley, M. & Hurwitz, J. (2007). Persuasion and resistance: Race and the death penalty in America. *American Journal of Political Science*, 51:996-1012.

Peña, I. & Urbina, M. (forthcoming). The dynamics of education and globalization in the new millennium: The unspoken realities. In M. Urbina (ed.), *Hispanics in the US criminal justice system: The new American demography*. Springfield, IL: Charles C Thomas, Publisher, Ltd.

Perales, A. (1974). *Are we good neighbors?* New York: Arno Press.

Perea, J. (1997). The black/white binary paradigm of race: The 'normal science' of American racial thought. *California Law Review*, 85:1213-1258.

Perez, D., Hosch, H., Ponder, B. & Trejo, G. (1993). Ethnicity of defendants and jurors as influences on jury decisions. *Journal of Applied Social Psychology*, 23:1249-1262.

Phillips, S. (2008). Racial disparities in the capital of capital punishment. *Houston Law Review*, 45:807-840.

Pizarro, M. (2005). *Chicanas and Chicanos in school: Racial profiling, identity battles, and empowerment*. Austin: University of Texas Press.

Pridemore, W. (2000). An empirical examination of commutations and executions in post-*Furman* capital cases. *Justice Quarterly*, 17(1):159-183.

Radelet, M. (1981). Racial characteristics and the imposition of the death penalty. *American Sociological Review*, 46:918-927.

Radelet, M., Lofquist, W.S. & Bedau, H.A. (1996). Death penalty symposium: Prisoners released from death row since 1970 because of doubts about their guilt. *Thomas and Cooley Law Review*, 13:907-966.

Radelet, M. & Pierce, G. (1991). Choosing those who will die: Race and the death penalty in Florida. *Florida Law Review*, 43(1):1-34.

Radelet, M. & Pierce, G. (1985). Race and prosecutorial discretion in homicide cases. *Law & Society Review*, 19:587-621.

Radelet, M. & Vandiver, M. (1983). The Florida Supreme Court and death penalty appeals. *Journal of Criminal Law and Criminology*, 73:913-926.

Radalet, M.L. & Zsembik, B.A. (1993). Executive clemency in post-*Furman* capital cases. *University of Richmond Law Review*, 27:289-314.

Reid, D. (1973). *Eyewitness: I saw 189 men die in the electric chair.* Houston: Cordovan Press.

Reggio, M.H. (1997). History of the death penalty. In L.E. Randa (ed.), *Society's final solution: A history and discussion of the death penalty*. Lanham: University Press of America.

Reiman, J. & Leighton, P. (2009). *The rich get richer and the poor get prison* (ninth edition). Upper Saddle River: Prentice Hall.

Reisler, M. (1997). Always the laborer, never the citizen: Anglo perceptions of the Mexican immigrant during the 1920s. In G. Gutierrez (ed.), *Between two worlds: Mexican immigrants in the United States*. Wilmington, DE: Jaguar Books.

Rex, J. (1983). *Race relations in sociological theory* (second edition). Boston: Routledge & Kegan Paul.

Reyes, M. & Halcon, J. (1988). Racism in academia: The old wolf revisited. *Harvard Educational Review*, 58:299-314.

Riedel, M. (1976). Discrimination in the imposition of the death penalty: A comparison of the characteristics of offenders sentenced pre-*Furman* and post-*Furman*. *Temple Law Quarterly*, 49:261-287.

Rios, V. (2006). The hyper-criminalization of black and Latino male youth in the era of mass incarceration. *Souls*, 8:40-54.

Robinson, M. (2008). *Death nation: The experts explain American capital punishment*. Upper Saddle River: Prentice Hall.

Romero, L. & Stelzner, L. (1985). Hispanics and the criminal justice system. In P. Cafferty & W. McCready (eds.), *Hispanics in the United States*. New Brunswick: Transaction Books.

Romero, M. (2008). Crossing the immigration and race border: A critical race theory approach to immigration studies. *Contemporary Justice Review*, 11:23-37.

Romero, M. (2006). Racial profiling and immigration law enforcement: Rounding up of usual suspects in the Latino community. *Critical Sociology*, 32:449-475.

Romero, M. (2001). State violence, and the social and legal construction of Latino criminality: From el bandido to gang member. *Denver University Law Review*, 78:1081-1118.

Romero, M. (1997). Class-based, gendered and racialized institution of higher education: Everyday life of academia from the view of

Chicana faculty. *Race, Gender & Class: Latina/o American Voices*, 4:151-173.

Romero, M. & Margolis, E. (2000). Integrating sociology: Observations on race and gender relations in sociology graduate programs. *Race and Society*, 2:1-24.

Romero, M. & Margolis, E. (1998). The department is very male, very white, very old, and very conservative: The functioning of the hidden curriculum in graduate sociology departments. *Harvard Educational Review*, 68:1-21.

Romero, M. & Serag, M. (2005). Violations of Latino civil rights resulting from INS and local police's use of race, culture and class profiling: The case of the Chandler Roundup in Arizona. *Cleveland Law Review*, 52:75-96.

Rowan, C. (1993). *Dream makers, dream breakers, the world of Justice Thurgood Marshall*. Boston: Little, Brown & Company.

Ruddell, R. & Urbina, M. (2007). Weak nations, political repression, and punishment. *International Criminal Justice Review*, 17:84-107.

Ruddell, R. & Urbina, M. (2004). Minority threat and punishment: A cross-national analysis. *Justice Quarterly*, 21:903-931.

Ruiz, V. (1997). Star struck: Acculturation, adolescence, and the Mexican-American woman, 1920-1950. In D. Gutierrez (ed.), *Between two worlds: Mexican immigrants in the United States*. Wilmington, DE: Jaguar Books.

Rushton, J.P. (1999). *Race, evolution and behavior*. New Brunswick: Transaction Publishers.

Sampson, R. & Lauritsen, J. (1997). Racial and ethnic disparities in crime and criminal justice in the United States. In M. Tonry (ed.), *Ethnicity, crime, and immigration: Comparative and cross-national perspectives*. Chicago: University of Chicago Press.

Sanchez, L. (2007). *The carceral contract: From domestic to global governance*. In M. Bosworth & J. Flavin (eds.), *Race, gender, and punishment: From colonialism to the war on terror*. Piscataway, NJ: Rutgers University Press.

Sanchez, R. (1998). Mapping the Spanish language along a multiethnic and multilingual border. In A. Darder & R. Torres (eds.), *The Latino studies reader: Culture, economy, and society*. Massachusetts: Blackwell Publishers.

Savitz, L. (1973). Black crime. In K. Miller & R. Dreger (eds.), *Comparative studies of blacks and whites in the United States.* New York: Seminar Press.

Sellin, T. (1980). *The penalty of death.* Beverly Hills: Sage Publications.

Sellin, T. (1959). *The death penalty.* Philadelphia: American Law Institute.

Shorris, E. (1992). *Latinos: A biography of the people.* New York: W W Norton & Company.

Smith, M. (1987). Patterns of discrimination in assessment of the death penalty: The case of Louisiana. *Journal of Criminal Justice,* 15:179-286.

Snell, T.L. (1996). *Capital punishment 1995.* U.S. Department of Justice, Bureau of Justice Statistics.

Sommers, S. (2007). Race and the decision making of juries. *Legal and Criminological Psychology,* 12:171-187.

Sorensen, J.R. & Wallace, D. H. (1995). Capital punishment in Missouri: Examining the issue of racial disparity. *Behavioral Sciences and the Law,* 13:61-80.

Steffensmeier, D. & Demuth, S. (2001). Ethnicity and judges' sentencing decisions: Hispanic-black-white comparisons. *Criminology,* 39:145-178.

Stein, N. (1995). Questions and answers about affirmative action. *Social Justice: A Journal of Crime, Conflict, and World Order,* 22(3):45-52.

Tabb, W. (1970). *The political economy of the black ghetto.* New York: W W Norton & Company.

Terman, L. (1906). Genius and stupidity: A study of some of the intellectual processes of seven 'bright' and seven 'stupid' boys. *Pedagogical Seminary,* 13:307-373.

Thomson, E. (1997). Discrimination and the death penalty in Arizona. *Criminal Justice Review,* 22(1):65-76.

Thomson, R. & Zimgraff, M. (1981). Detecting sentencing disparity: Some problems and evidence. *American Journal of Sociology,* 86:869-880.

Tonry, M., ed. (2006). *The future of imprisonment.* New York: Oxford University Press.

Trujillo, L. (1974). La evolucion del bandido 'Al Pachuco': A critical examination of criminological literature on Chicanos. *Issues in Criminology,* 9:43-67.

Ulmer, J. & Johnson, B. (2004). Sentencing in context: A multilevel analysis. *Criminology*, 42:137-177.

Ulmer, J. & Kramer, J. (1996). Court communities under sentencing guidelines: Dilemmas of formal rationality and sentencing disparity. *Criminology*, 34:383-408.

Unnever, J. & Cullen, F. (2007). The racial divide in support for the death penalty: Does white racism matter? *Social Forces*, 85:1281-1301.

Urbina, M., ed. (forthcoming). *Latinas y Latinos in the United States: 21ˢᵗ Century dynamics of multiculturalism.* Springfield, IL: Charles C Thomas, Publisher, Ltd.

Urbina, M., ed. (forthcoming). *Hispanics in the US criminal justice system: The new American demography.* Springfield, IL: Charles C Thomas, Publisher, Ltd.

Urbina, M. (2008). *A comprehensive study of female offenders: Life before, during, and after incarceration.* Springfield, IL: Charles C Thomas, Publisher, Ltd.

Urbina, M. (2007). Latinas/os in the criminal and juvenile justice systems. *Critical Criminology: An International Journal*, 15:41-99.

Urbina, M. (2005). Transferring juveniles to adult court in Wisconsin: Practitioners voice their views. *Criminal Justice Studies: A Critical Journal of Crime, Law and Society*, 18:147-172.

Urbina, M. (2004a). A qualitative analysis of Latinos executed in the United States between 1975 and 1995: Who were they? *Social Justice*, 31:242-267.

Urbina, M. (2004b). Language barriers in the Wisconsin court system: The Latino/a experience. *Journal of Ethnicity in Criminal Justice*, 2:91-118.

Urbina, M. (2003a). *Capital punishment and Latino offenders: Racial and ethnic differences in death sentences.* New York: LFB Scholarly Publishing.

Urbina, M. (2003b). Race and ethnic differences in punishment and death sentence outcomes: Empirical analysis of data on California, Florida and Texas, 1975-1995. *Journal of Ethnicity in Criminal Justice*, 1:5-35.

Urbina, M. (2003c). The quest and application of historical knowledge in modern times: A critical view. *Criminal Justice Studies: A Critical Journal of Crime, Law and Society*, 16:113-129.

Urbina, M. (2003d). Good Teachers Never Die. *Hispanic Outlook*, 13:31-32.

Urbina, M. (2002a). Death sentence outcomes. In D. Levinson (ed.), *Encyclopedia of Crime and Punishment*, 2:482-485. Thousand Oaks: Sage.

Urbina, M. (2002b). Furman and Gregg exit death row?: Un-weaving an old controversy. *The Justice Professional*, 15(2):105-125.

Urbina, M. & Kreitzer, S. (2004). The practical utility and ramifications of RICO: Thirty-two years after its implementation. *Criminal Justice Policy Review*, 15:294-323.

Urbina, M. & Smith, L. (2007). Colonialism and its impact on Mexicans' experience of punishment in the United States. In M. Bosworth & J. Flavin (eds.), *Race, gender, and punishment: From colonialism to the war on terror*. Piscataway, NJ: Rutgers University Press.

Urbina, M. & White, W. (2009). Waiving juveniles to criminal court: Court officials express their thoughts. *Social Justice*, 36:122-139.

U.S. Department of Justice, Bureau of Justice Statistics (1997). Capital punishment in the United States, 1973-1995 [computer file]. Compiled by the U.S. Department of Commerce, Bureau of the Census. ICPSR (ed.), Ann Arbor, Michigan: Inter-university Consortium for Political and Social Research [producer and distributor].

Vandiver, M. (1999). An apology does not assist the accused: Foreign nationals and the death penalty in the United States. *The Justice Professional*, 12:223-245.

Vandiver, M. (1993). The quality of mercy: Race and clemency in Florida death penalty cases, 1924-1966. *University of Richmond Law Review*, 27(2):315-343.

Vick, D. (1995). Poorhouse justice: Underfunded indigent defense services and arbitrary death sentences. *Buffalo Law Review*, 43(2):329-460.

Vito, G. & Keil, T. (1988). Capital sentencing in Kentucky: An analysis of the factors influencing decision making in the post-*Gregg* period. *Journal of Criminal Law and Criminology*, 79(2):483-503.

Wagner-Pacifici, R. (1994). *Discourse and destruction*. Chicago: The University of Chicago Press.

Walker, S. (2010). *Sense and nonsense about crime and drugs: A policy guide* (seventh edition). Belmont: Wadsworth Publishing Company.

Ward, G., Farrell, A. & Rousseau, D. (2009). Does racial balance in workforce representation yield equal justice? Race relations of sentencing in federal court organizations. *Law & Society Review*, 43:757-806

Welch, M. (2006). *Scapegoats of September 11th: Hate crimes and state crimes in the war on terror*. New Brunswick, NJ: Rutgers University Press.

Williams, P. (1997). *Seeing a color-blind future: The paradox of race*. New York: The Noonday Press.

Wolf, E.D. (1964). Abstract analysis of jury sentencing in capital cases: New Jersey: 1937-1961. *Rutgers Law Review*, 19:56-64.

Wolfgang, M. (1978). The death penalty: Social philosophy and social science research. *Criminal Law Bulletin*, 14(1):18-33.

Wolfgang, M. (1974). Racial discrimination in the death sentence for rape. In W. Bowers (ed.), *Executions in America*. Lexington: D.C. Heath and Company.

Wolfgang, M., Kelly, A. & Nodle, H. (1962). Comparison of the executed and the commuted among admissions to death row. *Journal of Criminal Law, Criminology and Police Science*, 53(3):301-311.

Wolfgang, M. & Riedel, M. (1976). Rape, racial discrimination, and the death penalty. In H. Bedau & C. Pierce, *Capital Punishment in the United States*. New York: AMS Press.

Wolfgang, M. & Riedel, M. (1975). Rape, race, and the death penalty in Georgia. *American Journal of Orthopsychiatry*, 45:658-668.

Wolfgang, M. & Riedel, M. (1973). Race, judicial discretion, and the death penalty. *The Annals*, 407:119-133.

Zatz, M. (1984). Race, ethnicity, and determinate sentencing: A new dimension to an old controversy. *Criminology*, 22(2):147-171.

Zeisel, H. (1981). Race bias in the administration of the death penalty: The Florida experience. *Harvard Law Review*, 95:456-468.

Zimring, F., Eigen, J. & O'Malley, S. (1976). Punishing homicide in Philadelphia: Perspectives on the death penalty. *University of Chicago Law Review*, 43:227-252.

Zuberi, T. & Bonilla-Silva, E., eds. (2008). *White logic, white methods: Racism and methodology.* Lanham, MD: Rowman & Littlefield Publishers.

Index